Juvenile Delinquency 00/01

First Edition

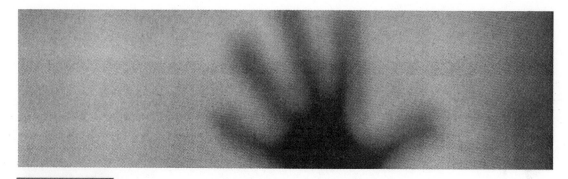

EDITOR

David R. Struckhoff
Loyola University, Chicago

David R. Struckhoff is the Executive Director of Justice Research Institute and an associate professor of criminal justice at Loyola University–Chicago. His field experience was as a diagnostic specialist in the Illinois Department of Corrections. Dr. Struckhoff received his doctorate in sociology from Southern Illinois University, Carbondale, where he participated in the Center for the Study of Crime, Delinquency, and Corrections. He sits on several boards in the academic and public and private sectors, and through Justice Research he regularly presents, publishes, and serves as a consultant to various agencies and governments.

Dushkin/McGraw-Hill
Sluice Dock, Guilford, Connecticut 06437

Visit us on the Internet
http://www.dushkin.com/annualeditions/

Credits

1. Juvenile Population: Definitions and Perceptions
Unit photo—© 1999 by Cleo Freelance Photography.
2. Causes and Correlates of Juvenile Delinquency
Unit photo—© 1999 by Cleo Freelance Photography.
3. Drugs, Sex, Law, Policy, and Other Compounding Issues
Unit photo—United Nations photo by Jane Schreibman.
4. Police, Juveniles, and the Law
Unit photo—AP photo by Michael Caulfield.
5. Juvenile Courts
Unit photo—© 1999 by PhotoDisc, Inc.
6. Juvenile Corrections
Unit photo—© 1999 by PhotoDisc, Inc.
7. The Positive View: What Can Be Done?
Unit photo—© 1999 by Cleo Freelance Photography.

Copyright

Cataloging in Publication Data
Main entry under title: Annual Editions: Juvenile delinquency 2000/2001
    1. Juvenile delinquency. 2. Juvenile corrections. I Struckhoff, David R., *comp.* II. Title: Juvenile delinquency.
ISBN 0–07–233371–5   364.36'   ISSN 1525-3619

First Edition

Cover image © 1999 PhotoDisc, Inc.

Printed in the United States of America   1234567890BAHBAH543210   Printed on Recycled Paper

Members of the Advisory Board are instrumental in the final selection of articles for each edition of ANNUAL EDITIONS. Their review of articles for content, level, currentness, and appropriateness provides critical direction to the editor and staff. We think that you will find their careful consideration well reflected in this volume.

EDITOR

David R. Struckhoff
Loyola University, Chicago

ADVISORY BOARD

Alyce Bunting
Texarkana College

John K. Burchill
Kansas Wesleyan University

Raymond A. Calluori
Montclair State University

Dick DeLung
Wayland Baptist University

Richard A. Dodder
Oklahoma State University

Robert M. Freeman
Shippensburg University

Angel D. Ilarraza Fuentes
Texas Christian University

John E. Holman
University of North Texas

Raymond G. Kessler
Sul Ross State University

John H. Lombardi
Southern University A&M College

Lynn Newhart
Rockford College

Michael Norman
Weber State College

James Oddo
Triton College

Robert M. Regoli
University of Colorado–Boulder

Cynthia Robbins
University of Delaware

P. S. Ruckman Jr.
Rock Valley College

Eberly L. Smith
Roanoke College

J. William Spencer
Purdue University

Steve Turner
East Central University

EDITORIAL STAFF

Ian A. Nielsen, Publisher
Roberta Monaco, Senior Developmental Editor
Dorothy Fink, Associate Developmental Editor
Addie Raucci, Senior Administrative Editor
Cheryl Greenleaf, Permissions Editor
Joseph Offredi, Permissions/Editorial Assistant
Diane Barker, Proofreader
Lisa Holmes-Doebrick, Program Coordinator

PRODUCTION STAFF

Brenda S. Filley, Production Manager
Charles Vitelli, Designer
Lara M. Johnson, Design/ Advertising Coordinator
Laura Levine, Graphics
Mike Campbell, Graphics
Tom Goddard, Graphics
Eldis Lima, Graphics
Juliana Arbo, Typesetting Supervisor
Jane Jaegersen, Typesetter
Marie Lazauskas, Typesetter
Kathleen D'Amico, Typesetter
Larry Killian, Copier Coordinator

Editors/Advisory Board Staff

To the Reader

In publishing ANNUAL EDITIONS we recognize the enormous role played by the magazines, newspapers, and journals of the public press in providing current, first-rate educational information in a broad spectrum of interest areas. Many of these articles are appropriate for students, researchers, and professionals seeking accurate, current material to help bridge the gap between principles and theories and the real world. These articles, however, become more useful for study when those of lasting value are carefully collected, organized, indexed, and reproduced in a low-cost format, which provides easy and permanent access when the material is needed. That is the role played by ANNUAL EDITIONS.

New to ANNUAL EDITIONS is the inclusion of related World Wide Web sites. These sites have been selected by our editorial staff to represent some of the best resources found on the World Wide Web today. Through our carefully developed topic guide, we have linked these Web resources to the articles covered in this ANNUAL EDITIONS reader. We think that you will find this volume useful, and we hope that you will take a moment to visit us on the Web at *http://www.dushkin.com* to tell us what you think.

One of the problems for students of behavior in our fast-paced society is the compression of information into "sound bites." We sacrifice depth of analysis for quick impressions. Unfortunately, sound bites do not contribute to understanding the complexity of human issues, or almost any issue, for that matter. We are beset by the scourge of oversimplification. This first edition of *Annual Editions: Juvenile Delinquency* seeks to offer both cutting-edge information and some of the classic thinking on the subject. These classics are often forgotten—leading us to repeat the omissions of the past, to reinvent the wheel, and to suffer from lack of necessary perspective.

Annual Editions: Juvenile Delinquency 00/01 reflects the concerns of educators and the general public with the issues of juvenile delinquency today and in the future. It is intended to stimulate discussion and sharpen critical reading ability. We ask you, our students, to look closely at who is writing the texts and the articles that you are reading. This gives you an edge in understanding the content. You are encouraged, likewise, to "consider the source." It is our conviction that poor theory and knowledge produce poor policy. We encourage the law enforcement efforts at sanitizing the community so that socializers, parents, teachers, clergy, and community activists can work with children in a safe and secure place that allows children to grow and blossom into fulfilled human beings.

I am deeply indebted to the Dushkin/McGraw-Hill team members for their professionalism and encouragement in this project. Our advisory editors and board are sterling and have opened our eyes to new viewpoints and issues. This group holds a considerable store of knowledge and experience in this field that is evident in the critiques they make and the suggestions for new articles that they have provided.

Special mention must be made of the staff at Justice Research, especially Patricia Riley, supportive colleagues, and my graduate assistant, Cody Stephens, at Loyola University, Chicago. Finally, special thanks to Tyler and Christopher Rinchiuso for giving cause to hope for the future.

Over its history, the *Annual Editions* series has become a forum as well as a source of information. You help shape the editions by your knowledge and views of the current events that influence our selections. We value and encourage your feedback and opinions. Our inclusion of relevant Web sites adds to the utility and depth of this edition's coverage. On the last pages is a prepaid article rating form. Please complete it and return it to us. Your opinions and suggestions are very important to us.

David R. Struckhoff
Editor

Contents

UNIT 1

Juvenile Population: Definitions and Perceptions

Seven selections in this section review the dynamics of the current state of juveniles and delinquency in the United States.

The concepts in bold italics are developed in the article. For further expansion please refer to the Topic Guide and the Index.

v

UNIT 2

Causes and Correlates of Juvenile Delinquency

In this section, seven articles discuss some of the unanswered questions of why juveniles commit crime. Increased violence at some schools is considered.

The concepts in bold italics are developed in the article. For further expansion please refer to the Topic Guide and the Index.

UNIT 3

Drugs, Sex, Law, Policy, and Other Compounding Issues

Five selections in this section
look at today's youth culture
and the effects it has on society.

UNIT 4

Police, Juveniles, and the Law

Interaction between the young
who are in gangs or in trouble
and law enforcement are addressed in this section's six articles.

UNIT 5

Juvenile Courts

In this section, six selections examine how juveniles, once apprehended, are processed through the court system.

The concepts in bold italics are developed in the article. For further expansion please refer to the Topic Guide and the Index.

UNIT 6

Juvenile Corrections

Six articles in this section discuss what juveniles can expect when they are incarcerated in jail or other type of correction facility.

The concepts in bold italics are developed in the article. For further expansion please refer to the Topic Guide and the Index.

ix

UNIT 7

The Positive View: What Can Be Done?

Eight articles in this section consider what steps can be taken to break the cycle of juvenile violence.

The concepts in bold italics are developed in the article. For further expansion please refer to the Topic Guide and the Index.

Topic Guide

This topic guide suggests how the selections and World Wide Web sites found in the next section of this book relate to topics of traditional concern to juvenile delinquency students and professionals. It is useful for locating interrelated articles and Web sites for reading and research. The guide is arranged alphabetically according to topic.

The relevant Web sites, which are numbered and annotated on pages 4 and 5, are easily identified by the Web icon (◎) under the topic articles. By linking the articles and the Web sites by topic, this ANNUAL EDITIONS reader becomes a powerful learning and research tool.

TOPIC AREA	TREATED IN	TOPIC AREA	TREATED IN
Biology	10. Of Arms and the Boy 11. Early Violence Leaves Its Mark on the Brain 18. Boys Will Be Boys ◎ *11, 12*	**Court, Juvenile**	26. Juvenile Felony Defendants in Criminal Courts 28. With Juvenile Court in Chaos, Critics Propose Their Demise 29. Children on Trial 31. Rolling the Dice in Juvenile Court 33. When Should Kids Go to Jail? 45. Crime and Punishment, Juvenile Division ◎ *1, 5, 24, 25, 26, 27, 28*
Childhood	1. Juvenile Population Characteristics 9. Why the Young Kill 12. Real Root Causes of Violent Crime 13. When Our Children Commit Violence 18. Boys Will Be Boys 29. Children on Trial 41. Breaking the Cycle of Juvenile Violence 44. Children's Crusade ◎ *6, 7, 11, 12, 14, 15, 36*	**Delinquency, Definitions and Parameters**	2. Juvenile Arrests 1996 3. Coming Crime Wave Is Washed Up 5. Part 1. Nature and Severity of Juvenile Crime 7. Juvenile Offenders: Should They Be Tried in Adult Courts? 8. Frustrated Officials Find Standard Answers Don't Suffice 14. From Adolescent Angst to Shooting Up Schools ◎ *1, 2, 5, 8, 10, 14*
Community and Delinquency	15. Culture of Youth 38. What Can We Do? 40. Saving the Nation's Most Precious Resources 43. Juvenile Justice Comes of Age ◎ *2, 4, 5, 8, 27, 31, 33, 36*	**Drugs**	16. Preventing Crime, Saving Children 17. Great Idea for Ruining Kids ◎ *1, 6, 15, 16, 18*
Corrections, Juvenile	32. Bastard Stepchild of *Parens Patriae* 33. When Should Kids Go to Jail? 34. Quick Fix: Pushing a Medical Cure for Youth Violence 35. Profits at a Juvenile Prison Come with a Chilling Cost 36. Juvenile Boot Camps 37. Wayward Boys' 'Shock Incarceration' Camp ◎ *1, 2, 5, 29, 30*	**Families**	12. Real Root Cause of Violent Crime 13. When Our Children Commit Violence 40. Saving the Nation's Most Precious Resources: Our Children 41. Breaking the Cycle of Juvenile Violence 44. Children's Crusade ◎ *4, 9, 31, 36*
Correlates of Delinquent Behavior	10. Of Arms and the Boy 15. Culture of Youth 23. Kids and Guns: From Playgrounds to Battlegrounds 40. Saving the Nation's Most Precious Resources: Our Children ◎ *11, 12, 21, 33, 34, 36*	**Gangs**	15. Culture of Youth 20. Tokyo's Teen Tribes 24. Sad Fact of Life: Gangs and Their Activities 25. Criminal Behavior of Gang Members ◎ *1, 5, 8, 31*

2

3

AE: Juvenile Delinquency

The following World Wide Web sites have been carefully researched and selected to support the articles found in this reader. If you are interested in learning more about specific topics found in this book, these Web sites are a good place to start. The sites are cross-referenced by number and appear in the topic guide on the previous two pages. Also, you can link to these Web sites through our DUSHKIN ONLINE support site at http://www.dushkin.com/online/.

The following sites were available at the time of publication. Visit our Web site—we update DUSHKIN ONLINE regularly to reflect any changes.

General Sources

1. Cecil Greek's Criminal Justice Links
http://www.fsu.edu/~crimdo/jd.html
Cecil Greek's links include at-risk youth, school crime, gangs, prevention programs, federal and state resources, juvenile court, and correctional and treatment programs.

2. Center on Juvenile and Criminal Justice
http://www.cjcj.org
The Center provides technical assistance to state and local governments interested in alternatives to incarceration.

3. Census Bureau (U.S.)
http://www.census.gov/population/www/socdemo/children.html
1990 Census information on children is available on this U.S. Census site.

4. Children's Advocacy Institute
http://www.acf.dhhs.gov/programs/cb
This site's goal is to address issues affecting children's well-being, health, and safety.

5. Juvenile Justice Sites
http://talkjustice.com/files/page15.htm
Juvenile Justice links include Youth Crime, School Crime, Delinquency Prevention Programs, Juvenile Justice Resources, Juvenile Court, and Correctional and Treatment Programs.

6. National Clearinghouse on Child Abuse and Neglect Information
http://www.calib.com/nccanch/
A national resource for professionals seeking information on the prevention, identification, and treatment of child abuse.

Juvenile Population: Definitions and Perceptions

7. Information Clearinghouse on Children
http://www.acusd.edu/childrensissues/comm.shtml
Among the commentaries on this site is "High School Shoot 'em Ups and Government by Anecdote," which discusses the media's negative role in reporting on juvenile crime.

8. OJJDP: Office of Juvenile Justice and Delinquency Prevention
http://www.ojjdp.ncjrs.org
Click on Facts & Figures for the latest on juvenile justice, delinquency prevention, and violence and victimization.

9. Statistics
http://www.ncjfcj.unr.edu/homepage/g2.html
Here are complete statistics on the juvenile population in the United States in narrative, not graphic, form.

10. Varieties of Media Crime
http://www.fsu.edu/~crimdo/lecture5.html
This lecture details cases of drugs, alcohol, and juvenile delinquency, pointing out media abuses.

Causes and Correlates of Juvenile Delinquency

11. Birth and the Origins of Violence
http://www.birthpsychology.com/violence/index.html
Among the perspectives on violence at this Web site are papers on the prenatal/perinatal roots of personal and social violence. Be sure to visit this fascinating site.

12. Brain Development and Learning
http://www.tyc.state.tx.us/prevention/braindev.htm
Judy Briscoe's points are that a child's first 3 years are critical to brain development and the influence of early environment on brain development is long lasting.

13. Partnerships against Violence Network
http://www.pavnet.org
A virtual library of information about violence and youth-at-risk is available on this PAVNET site. It includes data from seven federal agencies.

14. A Student's Perspective on Childhood Maltreatment and Juvenile Delinquency
http://www.concentric.net/~dfillmer/Delinquency.htm
This paper reports on the relationship between childhood maltreatment and a child's becoming delinquent.

Drugs, Sex, Law, Policy, and Other Compounding Issues

15. America's Children: Key National Indicators of Child Well-Being 1998
http://www.childstats.gov/ac1998/ac98.htm
This in-depth annual report includes sections on Child Poverty, Adolescent Mortality, Alcohol Use and Drug Use, and Youth Victims and Perpetrators of Serious Violent Crime.

16. Center for Substance Abuse Research (CESAR)
http://www.bsos.umd.edu/cesar/cesar.html
This CESAR site provides information regarding drugs, AIDS, and prevention and treatment of substance abuse and criminal justice data.

17. Juvenile Female Offenders
http://www.ojjdp.ncjrs.org/pubs/gender/
The Juvenile Female Offenders: A Status of the States Report, 1998 contains a history of female offenders, a profile of current adolescent female offenders, treatment options, and national efforts to address the problems.

18. Legalization of Drugs: The Myths and the Facts
http://www.frc.org/insight/is95c2dr.html
Robert L. Maginnis of the Family Research Council explores the issue of drug legalization in this 16-page article on the Web.

19. Tattooing and Body Piercing amongst Contemporary Youth and Youth Culture
http://www.urbanprimitive.com/academia/simon/1.html
Simon Leung offers this 13-page essay, which describes the youth subculture, using tattooing and body piercing as his focus for the discussion.

Police, Juveniles, and the Law

20. Community Policing Consortium
http://www.communitypolicing.org
This is the Web site of the Community Policing Consortium, a partnership of five of the leading police organizations in the United States, each committed to advancing policing philosophy through development of research and training.

21. Juvenile Violence and Gun Markets in Boston
http://www.ncjrs.org/txtfiles/fs000160.txt
This summary of a research presentation explains the importance of the availability of guns to juvenile violence.

22. Perspectives on Crime and Justice: 1997–1998
http://www.ncjrs.org/txtfiles/172851.txt
This lecture series includes crime patterns and future trends, drug abuse, gun violence, intermediate sanctions, and law enforcement issues, many related to juveniles.

23. Police-Corrections Partnerships
http://www.ncjrs.org/txtfiles1/175047.txt
Issues and practices discussed in this series include community policing, police patrol, crime patterns, and future trends.

Juvenile Courts

24. Children's Defense Fund
http://www.childrensdefense.org
Numerous articles, action alerts, and publications on children's issues are provided here.

25. Delinquents or Criminals: Policy Options for Young Offenders
http://www.urban.org/crime/delinq.html
Published on the Web by the nonpartisan Urban Institute, this paper, by Jeffrey Butts and Adele Harrell, covers the workings of America's juvenile courts and describes the current battle.

26. Juvenile Delinquents in the Federal Criminal System
http://www.ojp.usdoj.gov/bjs
This special report is printed in full on the Internet. It discusses the nature of the 468 juvenile delinquents who were referred to federal prosecutors for investigation in 1995.

27. National Center for Juvenile Justice (NCJJ)
http://www.ncjfcj.unr.edu/homepage/ncjj/homepage–revised/overview.htm
The NCJJ is dedicated to improving the quality of justice for children and their families. A brief overview of its mission, background, expertise, databases, audience, and staff is available at this Web site.

28. Oregon Peer (Teen) Courts Pages
http://www.ncn.com/~snews/peerct/open.htm
This Web site explains the workings of teen courts, in which peers deal with first-time offenders, setting the terms of their sentences. In turn, these offenders eventually must serve on the peer court.

Juvenile Corrections

29. An Examination of Three Model Interventions and Intensive Aftercare Initiatives
http://www.ncjrs.org/txtfiles/effectiv.txt
Included in this teleconference material from the OJJDP program is a description of how the Florida Environmental Institute operates, the Capital Offender Program, the Multi-Systemic Treatment Approach, and the Importance of Intensive Aftercare.

30. Juvenile Justice: Correction
http://www.ncjrs.org/jjcorr.htm
This extensive group of Web resources leads to articles on boot camp, good juvenile detention practices, evaluation of minority confinement, probation, and shock incarceration, among many others.

The Positive View— What Can Be Done?

31. Combatting Violence and Delinquency: The National Juvenile Justice Action Plan
http://www.ncjrs.org/txtfiles/jjplanfr.txt
The 128-page plan available here presents effective and innovative strategies designed to reduce violence and victimization.

32. Girl Power!
http://www.health.org/gpower/
This is a Department of Health and Human Services site to help encourage and empower 9- to 14-year-old girls to make the most of their lives.

33. Implementing the Balanced and Restorative Justice Model
http://www.ojjdp.ncjrs.org/pubs/implementing/contents.html
This site from the OPJJDP contains a complete description of the philosophy and workings of the Balanced and Restorative Justice Project.

34. The Juvenile Crime Challenge: Making Prevention a Priority
http://www.bsa.ca.gov/lhcdir/127rp.html
The entire Little Hoover Report from the State of California, which discusses prevention as a priority in the juvenile crime challenge, is available on this site.

35. A Legislator's Guide to Comprehensive Juvenile Justice
http://www.ncsl.org/programs/cyf/jjguide.htm
This report is offered by the National Conference of State Legislatures and is a thorough discussion of the reinvention of juvenile justice at the state level.

36. Long-Term Effects of Early Childhood Programs on Social Outcomes and Delinquency
http://www.futureofchildren.org/lto/03_lto.htm
Hirokazu Yoshikawa's report focuses on programs that have demonstrated long-term effects on antisocial behavior or delinquency. These programs have in common a combination of intensive family support and early education services. They also promise to be cost-effective.

We highly recommend that you review our Web site for expanded information and our other product lines. We are continually updating and adding links to our Web site in order to offer you the most usable and useful information that will support and expand the value of your Annual Editions. You can reach us at: http://www.dushkin.com/annualeditions/.

www.dushkin.com/online/

Unit Selections

1. **Juvenile Population Characteristics,** Howard N. Snyder and Eileen Poe
2. **Juvenile Arrests 1996,** Howard N. Snyder
3. **The Coming Crime Wave Is Washed Up,** Jacques Steinberg
4. **The Crackdown on Kids: The New Mood of Meanness toward Children—To Be Young Is to Be Suspect,** Annette Fuentes
5. **Part I: The Nature and Severity of Juvenile Crime** and **Part II: Juvenile Justice System History and Development,** *Privacy and Juvenile Justice Records*
6. **The Extent of Female Delinquency,** Meda Chesney-Lind and Randall G. Shelden
7. **Juvenile Offenders: Should They Be Tried in Adult Courts?** Michael P. Brown

Key Points to Consider

❖ What is delinquency? What is it in your state or nation?

❖ Why was "delinquency" created as a justice mechanism?

❖ Do you agree with the parameters on age of delinquency? Why or why not?

❖ What does the issue of public perception versus factual reality have to do with delinquency? How does it affect the treatment of youth in your community?

 **Links** **www.dushkin.com/online/**

7. **Information Clearinghouse on Children**
   http://www.acusd.edu/childrensissues/comm.shtml

8. **OJJDP: Office of Juvenile Justice and Delinquency Prevention**
   http://www.ojjdp.ncjrs.org

9. **Statistics** *http://www.ncjfcj.unr.edu/homepage/g2.html*

10. **Varieties of Media Crime** *http://www.fsu.edu/~crimdo/lecture5.html*

These sites are annotated on pages 4 and 5.

Juvenile delinquency is a construct. It didn't exist as a formal concept prior to the late 1800s. When they lamented—and they did—about the misconduct of the youngsters in their societies, the ancient Babylonians, Egyptians, Greeks, and Romans, or the ancient Chinese, may have had a term for it. But they didn't call it "juvenile delinquency" nor did they, as far as we know from hieroglyphics, records of the Oriental dynasties, and other sources, create much law about it. But since the coining of the term and the establishment of the first juvenile court in Cook County (Chicago), "juvenile delinquency" has certainly been evolving. Today, different states and nations use different criteria for defining delinquency—it is relative. Given the bad years we've recently had in the United States with juvenile violence, culminating in the shooting at Columbine High School in Littleton, Colorado, on April 20, 1999, it is hard to get an accurate sense either of the extent or the nature of the contemporary problem.

In regard to extent or prevalence, lost in our rhetoric these days is the fact that most, indeed the vast majority of juveniles, emerge generally unscathed from their teenage years. The percentage of youth we define as delinquent is modest. Yet worse than the misperceptions of the extent are the misperceptions of the resiliency of human nature. Many of us seem ready to give up on today's youth. In a recent *Chicago Tribune* editorial celebrating the 100th Anniversary of the Juvenile Court, Bernadine Dohrn of Northwestern University School of Law's Family and Justice Center noted that Babe Ruth, Robert Leroy (Satchel) Paige, and Ella Fitzgerald were all subjected to the juvenile court process. It worked for them; why will it not work today?

Samuel Walker has done us a great service by posing his "wedding cake" model of the crime and delinquency problem. At the bottom are the plethora, the masses, the hoard of "revolving door" crimes and misbehaviors—the drunks, the drunk drivers, the drug users, the disorderly, the petty thieves, the abusers, the general ne'er-do-wells who overpopulate the justice system. In the smaller, middle level are the serious criminals and delinquents that the system routinely deals with—muggers, killers, robbers, major thieves, bigger drug dealers and merchants, and the "dangerous" ones who worry us so much. But we don't see in the public view how well the system deals with them. We do see, and our attention is focused on, the celebrity cases—the statues and shining candles on the top of the cake that in reality are a small fraction of all the disorder. This year it is children killing classmates, last year it was O. J. Simpson; who knows what will capture the hearts of the media and the public tomorrow?

In this section we try to present a balanced view of the nature and extent of the problem. We deal with numbers, with history, with some of the more celebrated issues, but also with the sizable group of juveniles whose behavior has come to be so worrisome to so many of us. We hope that we as teachers, and our students who read this unit, can keep our perspective, which may help to bring some sanity to the discussions about delinquency.

Reference
Walker, Samuel, *Sense and Nonsense about Crime and Drugs: A Policy Guide*, Belmont, CA: Wadsworth, 1997.

Juvenile population characteristics

Juveniles in the United States today live in a world much different from that of their parents or grandparents. A greater proportion of juveniles live in poverty today than 20 years ago. More and more children are born to unmarried mothers. For many children, their parents are still children. Fewer children are being raised in two-parent families. Juveniles today live in a Nation with greater racial and ethnic diversity.

While high school dropout rates have fallen for most juveniles, the rates are still too high, especially in an employment market where unskilled labor is needed less and less.

This chapter presents a brief overview of some of the more commonly requested demographic, economic, and sociological statistics on juveniles. The sections summarize demographic and poverty data developed by the U.S. Bureau of the Census,

educational data from the National Center for Education Statistics, and birth statistics from the National Center for Health Statistics.

Acknowledgments

This chapter was prepared by Howard Snyder. Eileen Poe contributed significantly to sections in this chapter.

69 million Americans—more than 1 in 4—are under age 18

The juvenile population is growing

In 1995, 69 million persons in the United States were below age 18, the group commonly referred to as juveniles. The juvenile population declined during the late 1970's and early 1980's. Since 1984, however, it has been increasing. The juvenile population is projected to reach 74 million by the year 2010. Alone, this population growth will lead to an increased number of juvenile victims of abuse and neglect, more juvenile offenders, and increased case flow into the juvenile justice system.

The juvenile population in 2010 will also include a greater proportion of older juveniles and a greater proportion of racial and ethnic minorities. These changing demographic characteristics are correlated with social factors which, if current patterns hold, will produce added and differential demands on the various components of the juvenile justice system.

Between 1990 and 2010, the juvenile population in the U.S. will increase and become more racially and ethnically diverse

	Population		Increase	
	1990	2010	Number	Percent
All juveniles	64,185,000	73,617,000	9,432,000	15%
Ages 0–4	18,874,000	20,017,000	1,143,000	6
Ages 5–9	18,064,000	19,722,000	1,658,000	9
Ages 10–14	17,191,000	20,724,000	3,533,000	21
Ages 15–17	10,056,000	13,154,000	3,098,000	31
White	51,336,000	55,280,000	3,944,000	8%
Black	9,896,000	12,475,000	2,579,000	26
Native American	745,000	886,000	141,000	19
Asian/Pacific Islander	2,208,000	4,976,000	2,768,000	125
Hispanic origin	7,886,000	13,543,000	5,657,000	71%

■ Between 1990 and 2010, not only will the size of the juvenile population increase, but so will the average age.

■ The growth in the white juvenile population between 1990 and 2010 will be the result of an increase in white-Hispanics; the number of non-Hispanic white juveniles is expected to decline over the period.

Note: Race categories include persons of Hispanic origin. Persons of Hispanic origin can be of any race.

Sources: Bureau of the Census. (1993). *Current population reports, U.S. population estimates by age, sex, race and Hispanic origin: 1980 to 1991*. Bureau of the Census. (1993). *Current population reports, population projections of the U.S., by age, sex, race and Hispanic origin: 1993 to 2050*.

From *Juvenile Offenders and Victims, A National Report,* 1995, pp. 1-17. Reprinted by permission of the National Institute of Justice, National Criminal Justice Reference Service.

One in 8 juveniles is of Hispanic origin

In 1990, 12% of the juvenile population in the U.S. was of Hispanic origin. Persons of Hispanic origin can be of any race. Racially, 91% of Hispanic juveniles in 1990 were white, 5% were black, 1% were Native American, and 2% were Asian/Pacific Islander.

In 1992, 3 in 10 juveniles lived in urban areas

A metropolitan statistical area (MSA) contains a large central population along with adjacent communities that are integrated both economically and socially into the central population. The metropolitan area is the territory outside the central city but within the MSA. A non-metropolitan area refers to an area outside an MSA.

In 1992, 30% of juveniles lived in central cities, 47% lived in the metropolitan areas outside a central city, and 23% lived outside an MSA. Most

black juveniles and juveniles of Hispanic origin lived in central cities, while most white juveniles lived outside of central cities.

Where do juveniles live?	Central city	Metro-politan	Non-metro-politan	Total
All races	30%	47%	23%	100%
White	24	51	25	100
Black	56	28	16	100
Other	38	46	16	100
His-panic	52	39	8	100

Note: Race proportions include persons of Hispanic origin. Persons of Hispanic origin can be of any race.

Source: Bureau of the Census. (1993). Poverty in the United States: 1992. *Current Population Reports: Consumer Income.*

In 1992, 3 in 10 juveniles living in central cities were black, and 2 in 10 were Hispanic

More than 3 in 4 juveniles living outside of central cities in 1992 were non-Hispanic whites. In central cities, non-Hispanic whites were only 43% of the juvenile population.

What are the racial and ethnic profiles of juveniles living in different geographical areas?	All areas	Central city	Metro-politan	Non-metro-politan
White	80%	64%	86%	86%
Black	15	30	9	11
Other	5	6	5	3
Total	100%	100%	100%	100%
His-panic	12%	21%	10%	4

Note: Race proportions include persons of Hispanic origin. Persons of Hispanic origin can be of any race.

Source: Bureau of the Census. (1993). Poverty in the United States: 1992. *Current Population Reports: Consumer Income.*

In 1992, 14.6 million juveniles lived below the poverty level, which was 42% more juveniles living in poverty than in 1976

In 1992, 22% of all juveniles in the U.S. lived in poverty

In 1992 the poverty threshold for a family of four was $14,300. Juveniles under age 18 were 26% of the U.S. population, but were 40% of all persons living below the poverty level in 1992. Young juveniles were more likely to be poor than were older juveniles; 25% of children under age 6 lived in poverty compared with 19% of children ages 7–17.

Minority juveniles were more likely to live in poverty than were

nonminority juveniles. In 1992 the poverty rates for black juveniles (47%) and juveniles of Hispanic origin (40%) were far greater than the rate for white juveniles (17%).

Juveniles in the early 1990's were more likely to live in poverty than were juveniles in the 1970's. Between 1972 and 1992 poverty rates for juveniles increased from 16% to 22%, while they decreased from 15% to 13% for those over age 65.

In 1992 families with children were 3 times more likely to live in poverty than those without children. While poverty rates among families

without children remained stable between 1977 and 1992, the poverty rate among families with children increased from 13% to 18% during this time. The poverty rate among white families with children was 14% in 1992 compared with 39% among black families, 18% among families of other races, and 32% among Hispanic families.

Between 1976 and 1992 the number of juveniles living in poverty grew 42%. The number of black juveniles in poverty increased 30%, compared with a 45% increase for white juveniles. The larger increase in the number of white juveniles in poverty was influenced substantially by the 116% increase in the number of juveniles in poverty who were of Hispanic origin (who are predominately white).

Poor minority children are concentrated in central cities

Thirty percent of the juvenile population in the U.S. lived in central cities in 1992, but central cities housed 44% of all juveniles living in poverty. Metropolitan areas housed 47% of all juveniles and only 31% of juveniles living in poverty.

Even though a greater *proportion* of black than white juveniles in central cities were poor, there were nearly the same *number* of white and black juveniles living in poverty in central cities, since 64%

of all juveniles in central cities in 1992 were white.

Where do poor children live?	Central City	Metropolitan	Non-metropolitan	Total
All races	44%	31%	25%	100%
White	34	37	29	100
Black	60	22	18	100
Other	49	30	21	100
Hispanic	60	30	10	100

Note: Race proportions include persons of Hispanic origin. Persons of Hispanic origin can be of any race.

Poverty rates were lowest in metropolitan areas

Across all types of communities, black juveniles and juveniles of

Hispanic origin were more likely than were white juveniles and juveniles of other races to be poor in 1992.

For all groups, poverty rates were lower in metropolitan areas than in urban centers or rural areas.

What proportion of juveniles live in poverty in various geographical areas?	All areas	Central City	Metropolitan	Non-metropolitan
All races	22%	32%	14%	24%
White	17	24	12	20
Black	47	50	36	52
Other	23	30	15	30
Hispanic	40	46	31	48

Note: Race proportions include persons of Hispanic origin. Persons of Hispanic origin can be of any race.

Fewer children lived with both parents in 1990 than in the past

A growing proportion of children are born to unmarried mothers

In 1960, 1 birth in 20 was to an unmarried woman; by 1990 it was 1 birth in 4. Over the same time period, the number of divorces in the U.S. nearly tripled. As a result of both trends, more children are living in single-parent households.

Three in 4 juveniles in 1990 lived in two-parent families

Between 1970 and 1990 the proportion of children living in two-parent families declined from 85% to 73%. This decline was paralleled by a similar increase in the proportion of children living in families where only the mother was present.

The proportion of children living with a *never-married* single parent also increased, from less than 1% in 1970 to 8% in 1990.

Percent of children	1970	1980	1985	1990
Both parents	85%	77%	74%	73%
Single-headed	15	23	26	27
Mother	11	18	21	22
Father	1	2	3	3
Other	3	4	3	3

Note: Detail may not total 100% due to rounding.

Source: U.S. congress. (1992). *1992 green book.*

There were declines in the proportions of both white and black two-parent families

There were substantial declines between 1970 and 1990 in the proportions of two-parent families for both white and black families. Black fami-

lies, however, had the greatest decrease in the proportion of two-parent families. In 1970, 90% of white families with children under age 18 had both parents living at home. By 1990 this proportion had decreased to 77%. For black families, the decline was from 64% in 1970 to 39% in 1990. These declines in two-parent families resulted in far more mothers than fa-

Percent of families	White		Black	
	1970	1990	1970	1990
2-parent family	90%	77%	64%	39%
Mother only	9	18	33	56
Father only	1	4	3	4

Note: Detail may not total 100% because of rounding.

Source: U.S. Congress. (1992). *1992 green book.*

thers taking over the responsibility of the household.

Even though white households contained a smaller proportion of single-parent families, because of their greater numbers, the majority of single-parent families in 1990 were white.

Half of all children will spend some time in a single-parent home

Though a child may live in a particular type of family at a particular time, living arrangements for that child may change over time. While 25% of children lived in a single-parent home at one point in 1990, half of all children born during the 1970's and 1980's will spend at least some time in a single-parent home. More specifically, 36% of all white children, 43% of all children of Hispanic origin, and 80% of all black

children born between 1970 and 1980 will live in a single-parent household for some period of time.

The fact that a child lives with an unmarried mother does not necessarily

	Percent of all children in poverty who live in mother-only families			
	1976	**1970**	**1980**	**1990**
All races	24%	46%	53%	58%
White	21	37	41	47
Black	*	61	75	80
Hispanic	*	*	47	48

* Data not available

Note: Race proportions include persons ot Hispanic origin. Persons ot Hispanic origin can be of any race.

Source: National Center tor Education Statistics. (1993). *Youth indicators 1993: Trends in the well-being of American youth.*

mean that he or she lives in a single-parent home. In 1987, for example, more than 40% of unmarried, cohabitating adults had children in the home.

Children in single-parent families are more likely to be in poverty than those in two-parent families

In 1989, 46% of children in single-parent families were living in poverty. Those in families where only the mother was present were more likely to be in poverty (50%) than those in families where only the father was present (24%). In comparison, only 9% of children in two-parent families were living in poverty. Thus, most children in poverty are living with only their mothers.

200,000 babies were born to mothers below age 18 in 1991—4 in 5 of these mothers were unmarried

5% of all babies born in 1991 were born to juvenile mothers

In 1991, more than 200,000 babies were born to mothers under age 18. These births were 5% of the total number of births in the U.S. in 1991. Ninety-four percent of these births were to mothers ages 15–17, and 6% (12,000 births) were to mothers younger than age 15. Teen childbirth creates disadvantages for both the mother and infant. For example, infants born to teens are at more risk of low birth weight than any other group.

Births to unmarried teens have risen considerably

In 1991, 30% of all births were to unmarried women. The 1.2 million births to unmarried women in 1991 is 82%

more than in 1980. The 1991 figure translates into 45 births per 1,000 unmarried women ages 15–44.

In 1991 there were 159,000 births to unmarried women under age 18, 11,000 of which were to girls younger than 15. Births to mothers below age 18 accounted for 13% of all births to unmarried women. Between 1980 and 1991, the birth rate for unmarried women ages 15–17 increased by 50%.

Most teenage mothers are unwed mothers

In 1991 the mother was unmarried in 79% of all births to women under age 18. The proportion of births to unwed juveniles varied by age and race. The proportion of births to unwed mothers decreased with age—87% for 15-year-olds compared with 75% for 17-year-

olds. The proportion of births to unwed mothers was greater for blacks than for whites—70% for white mothers below age 18 and 96% for black mothers below age 18.

	Percent of births to unmarried women in 1991		
Age	**All races**	**White**	**Black**
All Ages	**30%**	**22%**	**68%**
Under 18	79	70	96
Under 15	91	84	98
15	87	80	97
16	81	73	96
17	75	66	95
18	68	58	92
19	59	49	88
20–24	39	30	75
25–29	19	14	55

Source: National Center for Health Statistics. (1993). *Monthly Vital Statistics Report 42(3).*

Who are the fathers?

- In 33% of the births to mothers age 19 or younger, the father was also a teenager. In 52% the fathers were ages 20–24.

- In 1991 there were 25 births in which the fathers were ages 15–19 for every 1,000 males in this age group. This represents a 6% increase over the 1990 rate and a 36% increase over the 1987 rate.

Infants born to teens have the greatest risk of low birth weight

Overall, in 1991 low birth weights occurred in 10% of births to mothers age 17 or younger. In contrast, 7% of births to those over age 17 were low birth weight births. In 1991 black teen mothers were more likely than white teen mothers to have a low birth weight baby.

Recent studies find sexual activity related to substance abuse

Two recent longitudinal studies of youth in high crime areas in Denver, Colorado, and Rochester, New York, found that juveniles reported a high prevalence of sexual activity and pregnancy. In subjects between ages 13 and 17, more than half of the boys and almost half of the girls reported that they had engaged in sexual intercourse and were currently sexually active. In addition, about 1 in 3 girls in the Denver and Rochester studies reported they had been pregnant at least once by age 17.

Girls who had been pregnant also reported substantially higher rates of substance abuse. This is a major public health concern because such behavior poses a significant threat to the well-being of not only the girls, but also to the children of these young mothers.

School dropout rates declined between 1978 and 1992

More than 383,000 students in grades 10 through 12 withdrew from school in 1992

Four percent of all high school students dropped out of school in 1992. Male and female students withdrew at about the same rate during 1992. Fifty-nine percent of students who dropped out of high school in 1992 were white, although dropout rates did not differ significantly by race or ethnicity.

The proportion of high school students dropping out declined from 7% in 1978 to 4% in 1992. The dropout rates for both white and black students declined, while there has been no clear trend for Hispanics.

Older high school students were more likely than younger students to drop out in 1992

More than half of the students who withdrew from school in 1992 were 17 or 18 years old. Correspondingly, the likelihood that a student in

Age of high school student	Percent who dropped out in 1992
15–16	2.5%
17	3.2
18	4.4
19	8.9

grade 12 would drop out of school in 1992 (7%) was more than double that of students in grades 10 and 11 (3%).

Dropout rates vary by family income level, not by type of community

The majority of students who dropped out of school in 1992 lived in middle income families. However, the likelihood of dropping out during the year was highest among high school students from low income families.

The proportion of students in central cities who dropped out in 1992 was not significantly greater than in other communities.

In 1992, 3.4 million persons ages 16–24 were high school dropouts

The cumulative result of these annual dropout rates reveals the extent of the dropout problem in the U.S. In 1992, 11% of all 16–24-year-olds had dropped out of school before receiving a high school degree. This rate was much higher for Hispanics (29%) than for blacks (14%) or whites (8%).

Thirty-nine percent of all dropouts withdrew from school before completing 10th grade. Nearly three-fifths of all Hispanic dropouts had less than a 10th grade education, compared with one-third of white dropouts and approximately one-fourth of black dropouts. Within income groups, the white and black dropout rates did not differ significantly. However, Hispanics in middle and low income groups dropped out at a higher rate than whites or blacks.

Cumulative dropout rates increased as income declined

Percent of 16–24-year-olds who were high school drop outs in 1992:			
	Race/ethnicity		
Family income	**White**	**Black**	**Hispanic**
All	8%	14%	29%
Low	19	24	45
Middle	8	10	25
High	2	1	10

Although the largest number of dropouts resided in suburban communities (46%), central cities had the greatest proportion of dropouts in the 16–24-year-old age group (13%).

On-time graduation is an indicator of how well students are progressing in the educational system

In 1991, 69% of young people who should have graduated from high school that year did so. On-time graduation rates varied by school system. Wealthier, suburban school systems had higher percentages of students completing high school on time than did schools in impoverished communities.

However, a student's decision to withdraw from school is not necessarily a permanent decision. Substantial numbers of persons who drop out of school early ultimately earn a high school diploma or obtain an alternative credential. Such actions lessen the consequences of dropping out of school.

For instance, a study of the sophomore class of 1980 revealed that 83% completed high school on time. By 1986 (3 years past their on-time graduation date), the completion rate had increased to 91%. Similarly, another study of students scheduled for graduation in 1992 found that 88%

were working towards high school completion or had already completed high school or passed an equivalency test by the spring of 1992. Among the dropouts from this group, more than half reported plans to pursue a general education diploma or to complete regular high school.

Why do juveniles drop out of school?

Four in 10 dropouts said they left high school because they did not like school or because they were failing. Just as many males as females reported they were leaving school because they could not get along with their teachers. More males than females dropped out because of school suspension or expulsion.

While most dropouts reported school-related reasons for leaving school, most female dropouts reported family-related reasons. Twenty-one percent of females and 8% of males dropped out because they became a parent. About 27% of females said they left school because they became pregnant. Twenty-six percent of white female dropouts reported pregnancy as a motive for dropping out, compared with 31% of Hispanic and 34% of black female dropouts. Blacks were far less likely to report getting married as a reason for leaving school (2%) than white (15%) or Hispanic (13%) dropouts.

More than a quarter of those dropping out of grades 10 through 12 reported job-related reasons for withdrawing. Male dropouts were more likely than female dropouts to report finding a job as the motive for leaving school (36% versus 22%).

Among 16–24-year-old Hispanics who spoke English at home, 14% were dropouts in 1992. Rates were substantially higher among those who spoke Spanish at home. Among this group of Hispanics, 30% of those who spoke English well dropped out, compared with 62% of those who spoke English poorly and 83% of those who did not speak English at all.

The dropout rate among 16–24-year-olds who had repeated more than one grade was 41%, compared with 17% of those who repeated only one grade and 9% of those who did not repeat any grades. Dropout rates were highest among those who repeated grades 7, 8, or 9 (34%) rather than those who repeated any grades between kindergarten and 6 (17%) or grades 10, 11, or 12 (19%).

What are the costs of dropping out?

A measure of the Nation's success in education is the proportion of youth completing high school. Possession of a high school diploma (or its equivalent) signifies that an individual should have sufficient knowledge and skills to function productively in society. Dropping out of school indicates that an individual is likely to lack these prerequisites and is at a relative disadvantage.

Advanced skills and technical knowledge will become increasingly important among job seekers during the 21st century. Consequently, the job outlook for high school dropouts is dismal. In 1992 the unemployment rate among those dropping out of school was 11%, compared with 7% for those who graduated from high school but did not attend college. Among dropouts who were employed full time, the median income was only half that of high school graduates. While the real income (income adjusted for inflation) of college graduates increased over the past 20 years, the real income of dropouts declined dramatically.

Youth who are not in school and not in the labor force are at high risk of delinquency, crime, and diminished success. The percentage of 16–19-year-olds not working or in school declined slightly between 1985 and 1990, from 5.3% to 5.0%. Still, in 1990 more than 680,000 youth were idle during this critical period of their development.

Sources

Annie E. Casey Foundation. (1994). *Kids count data book: State profiles of child well-being, 1994.* Baltimore, MD: Annie B. Casey Foundation.

Bucy, J., and Nichols, N. (1991). Homeless youth: Statement of the problem and suggested policies. *Journal of Health and Social Policy,* 2(4):66. Binghamton, NY: The Haworth Press, Inc.

Bureau of the Census. (1992). *1980–1989 revised estimates of the population of counties by age, sex, and race* [machine-readable data file]. Washington, DC: Bureau of the Census.

Bureau of the Census. (1992). *1990 census of population and housing: Modified age/race, sex, and Hispanic origin (MARS) State and county file* [machine-readable data file]. Washington, DC: Bureau of the Census.

Bureau of the Census. (1993). *1990 census of population and housing summary tape file 3C* [machine-readable data file]. Washington, DC: Bureau of the Census.

Bureau of the Census. (1993). *Current population reports, U.S. population estimates by age, sex, race, and Hispanic origin: 1980 to 1991,* Series P25-1095. Washington, DC: Bureau of the Census.

Bureau of the Census. (1993). *Current population reports, population projections of the U.S., by age, sex, race, and Hispanic origin: 1993 to 2050,* Series P25-1104. Washington, DC: Bureau of the Census.

Bureau of the Census. (1993). Poverty in the United States, 1992. *Current Population Reports: Consumer Income,* Series P60-185. Washington, DC: Bureau of the Census.

Centers for Disease Control and Prevention. (1993). Teenage pregnancy and birth rates—United States, 1990. *Morbidity and Mortality Weekly Report 42*(38). Waltham, MA: Massachusetts Medical Society.

Collins, J., McCalla, M., and Powers, L. (1990). *National study of law enforcement policies and practices regarding missing children and homeless youth: Executive summary.* Research Triangle Park, NC: Research Triangle Institute.

National Center for Education Statistics. (1993). *Dropout rates in the United States: 1992.* Washington, DC: U.S. Department of Education.

National Center for Education Statistics. (1993). *Youth indicators 1993: Trends in the well-being of American youth.* Washington, DC: U.S. Department of Education.

National Center for Education Statistics. (1994). *Education statistics on disk* [machine-readable data file]. Washington, DC: U.S. Department of Education.

National Center for Health Statistics. (1993). Advance report on final natality statistics, 1991. *Monthly Vital Statistics Report, 42*(3). Washington, DC: U.S. Department of Health and Human Services.

Office of Juvenile Justice and Delinquency Prevention. (1993). *Urban delinquency and substance abuse: Technical report.* Washington, DC: OJJDP.

U.S. Congress. (1992). *Overview of entitlement programs, 1992 green book: Background material and data on programs within the jurisdiction of the Committee on Ways and Means.* Washington, DC: U.S. Government Printing Office.

Juvenile Arrests 1996

Howard N. Snyder

In 1996, law enforcement agencies in the United States made an estimated 2.9 million arrests of persons under age 18.* According to the Federal Bureau of Investigation (FBI), juveniles accounted for 19% of all arrests and 19% of all violent crime arrests in 1996. The substantial growth in juvenile violent crime arrests that began in the late 1980's peaked in 1994. In 1996, for the second year in a row, the total number of juvenile arrests for Violent Crime Index offenses—murder, forcible rape, robbery, and aggravated assault—declined. Even with these declines (3% in 1995 and 6% in 1996), the number of juvenile Violent Crime Index arrests in 1996 was 60% above the 1987 level. In comparison, the number of adult arrests for a Violent Crime Index offense in 1996 was 24% greater than in 1987.

These findings are derived from data reported annually by local law enforcement agencies across the country to the FBI's Uniform Crime Reporting (UCR) Program. Based on these data, the FBI prepares its annual *Crime in the United States* report, which summarizes crimes known to the police and arrests made during the reporting calendar year. This information is used to characterize the extent and nature of juvenile crime that comes to the attention of the justice system. Other recent findings from the UCR Program are:

- Juveniles were involved in 37% of all burglary arrests, 32% of robbery arrests, 24% of weapon arrests, and 15% of murder and aggravated assault arrests in 1996.

*Throughout this Bulletin, persons under age 18 are referred to as juveniles. See Notes.

- About 1 in every 220 persons ages 10 through 17 in the United States was arrested for a Violent Crime Index offense in 1996.
- Juvenile murder arrests declined 3% between 1993 and 1994, 14% between 1994 and 1995, and another 14% between 1995 and 1996. Juvenile arrests for murder in 1996 were at their lowest level in the 1990's, but still 50% above the number of arrests in 1987.
- Between 1992 and 1996, juvenile arrests for burglary declined 7% and juvenile arrests for motor vehicle theft declined 20%.
- Juveniles were involved in 14% of all drug arrests in 1996. Between 1992 and 1996, juvenile arrests for drug abuse violations increased 120%.
- Juvenile arrests for curfew violations increased 21% between 1995 and 1996 and 116% between 1992 and 1996. In 1996, 28% of curfew arrests involved juveniles under age 15 and 29% involved females.
- In 1996, 57% of arrests for running away from home involved females and 41% involved juveniles under age 15.
- Arrests of juveniles accounted for 13% of all violent crimes cleared by arrest in 1996—more specifically, 8% of murders, 12% of forcible rapes, 18% of robberies, and 12% of aggravated assaults.

Violent crime arrests peaked at age 18

In general, arrests for most offenses increase with age, reaching a peak in the later teenage years, then decline. However, this decline is

sharp for some offenses and more gradual for others.

In 1996, 30% of juvenile arrests for Violent Crime Index offenses involved juveniles under age 15, with 1% under age 10. The number of violent crime arrests increased with each age group between 10 and 17 and peaked with 18-year-olds, although the numbers of arrests of 17- and 18-year-olds were nearly equal in 1996. Overall, violent crime arrests declined gradually with age; for example, in 1996, the number of violent crime arrests of persons age 24 was still 64% of the number for the peak age group.

Most Serious Offense	Peak Age of Arrest	Percent of Peak at Age 24
Violent Crime Index	18	64%
Murder	19	54
Forcible rape	18	43
Robbery	17	31
Aggravated assault	18	84
Property Crime Index	16	31
Burglary	16	29
Larceny-theft	16	32
Motor vehicle theft	16	22
Simple assault	16–17	93
Weapons	18	48
Drug abuse violations	18	55

Data source: Analysis of data from *Crime in the United States 1996*, table 38.

However, arrests for some violent crimes declined less with age than did others. For example, the number of arrests for aggravated assault changed relatively little between ages 18 and 24, while the number of robbery arrests declined substantially across these young adult years. Arrests for murder and forcible rape also showed far more decline with

From *Juvenile Justice Bulletin*, November 1997, pp. 4-12. Reprinted by permission of the U.S. Department of Justice, Office of Justice Programs, Office of Juvenile Justice and Delinquency Prevention.

For the second year in a row, arrests of juveniles for violent crimes declined in 1996, with murder arrests down 14% and robbery down 8%

Most Serious Offense	1996 Estimated Number of Juvenile Arrests	Percent of Total Juvenile Arrests Female	Under Age 15	Percent Change 1987–96	1992–96	1995–96
Total	**2,851,700**	**25%**	**32%**	**35%**	**21%**	**3%**
Crime Index total	855,400	25	38	14	2	−1
Violent Crime Index	135,100	15	30	60	3	−6
Murder and nonnegligent manslaughter	2,900	7	12	50	−18	−14
Forcible rape	5,600	2	34	−3	−7	0
Robbery	50,100	10	27	57	7	−8
Aggravated assault	76,600	20	32	70	2	−4
Property Crime Index	720,300	27	40	8	2	0
Burglary	135,100	10	38	−12	−7	3
Larceny-theft	502,400	34	42	14	9	0
Motor vehicle theft	72,800	15	26	9	−20	−10
Arson	10,100	11	67	36	7	−6
Nonindex						
Other assaults	234,100	28	41	100	29	3
Forgery and counterfeiting	8,600	37	12	3	8	−3
Fraud	27,000	25	29	6	62	6
Embezzlement	1,300	45	7	16	82	6
Stolen property (buying, receiving, possessing)	41,100	13	27	8	−5	−6
Vandalism	141,600	11	45	26	−2	−4
Weapons (carrying, possessing, etc.)	52,800	8	30	69	−10	−9
Prostitution and commercialized vice	1,300	52	13	−41	10	5
Sex offense (except forcible rape and prostitution)	17,200	8	50	8	−15	6
Drug abuse violations	211,500	13	17	133	120	6
Gambling	2,800	3	13	213	49	10
Offenses against the family and children	8,400	37	32	113	67	29
Driving under the influence	18,500	16	3	−28	22	20
Liquor law violations	155,200	30	11	−5	29	21
Drunkenness	23,500	17	14	−11	27	11
Disorderly conduct	215,000	24	34	93	44	9
Vagrancy	3,700	15	22	18	−14	−7
All other offenses (except traffic)	450,200	23	28	35	26	1
Suspicion	1,600	23	27	−33	−71	1
Curfew and loitering	185,100	29	28	113	116	21
Runaways	195,700	57	41	20	7	−5

◆ With the second year of decline, juvenile arrests for violent crimes in 1996 were below the 1993 level. However, the number of violent crime arrests in 1996 was still 60% above the 1987 level. If each Violent Crime Index arrest in 1996 involved a different juvenile, it would mean that 1 of every 220 persons ages 10 through 17 in 1996 was arrested for one of these crimes.

◆ The decline in murder arrests in 1996 follows declines in both 1995 and 1994. Even so, the number of arrests in 1996 was still 50% greater than in 1987.

◆ In 1996, females were involved in 15% of Violent Crime Index arrests, 34% of larceny-theft arrests, 30% of liquor law arrests, 29% of curfew arrests, and 57% of arrests for running away from home.

Data source: *Crime in the United States 1996* (Washington, DC: U.S. Government Printing Office, 1997), tables 29, 32, 34, 36, and 38. Arrest estimates were developed by the National Center for Juvenile Justice.

age than did arrests for aggravated assault.

In 1996, 40% of juvenile arrests for Property Crime Index offenses involved juveniles under age 15, with 2% under age 10. The peak age of arrest for property crimes was lower than for violent crimes. Like robbery arrests (and unlike arrests for aggravated and simple assault) property crime arrests declined sharply with age—the number of arrests of 24-year-olds was less than one-third that of the peak age.

One in four juvenile arrests in 1996 was an arrest of a female

Law enforcement agencies made 723,000 arrests of females below the age of 18 in 1996. Increases in arrests between 1992 and 1996 were greater for juvenile females than juvenile males in most offense categories.

Most Serious Offense	Percent Change in Juvenile Arrests 1992–1996 Female	Male
Violent Crime Index	25%	0%
Murder	−8	−19
Forcible rape	NA	−7
Robbery	20	6
Aggravated assault	28	−3
Property Crime Index	21	−4
Burglary	3	−8
Larceny-theft	25	2
Motor vehicle theft	−4	−23
Arson	10	6
Simple assault	45	24
Weapons	8	−11
Drug abuse violations	164	114
Curfew violations	139	108
Runaways	8	5

Data source: *Crime in the United States 1996*, table 35.

Juvenile arrests disproportionately involved minorities

The racial composition of the juvenile population in 1996 was approximately 80% white, 15% black, and 5% other races, with juveniles of Hispanic ethnicity being classified as white. In 1996, roughly equal numbers of arrests for violent crimes involved white and black youth. This was in contrast to the proportion of each group in the general population.

Most Serious Offense	White Proportion of Juvenile Arrests in 1996
Murder	39%
Forcible rape	55
Robbery	40
Aggravated assault	58
Burglary	74
Larceny-theft	71
Motor vehicle theft	58
Weapons	63
Drug abuse violations	62
Runaways	78

Data source: *Crime in the United States 1996,* table 43.

The Violent Crime Index monitors violence trends

The FBI assesses trends in the volume of violent crimes by monitoring four offenses that are consistently reported by law enforcement agencies nationwide and are pervasive in all geographical areas of the country. These four crimes are murder and nonnegligent manslaughter, forcible rape, robbery, and aggravated assault. Other crimes may be considered violent by their nature or effect (e.g., kidnaping, weapons possession, extortion, drug selling), but the four crimes that together form the Violent Crime Index have traditionally been used as the Nation's barometer of violent crime.

The juvenile violent crime arrest rate declined 12% from 1994 to 1996

The juvenile violent crime arrest rate in 1988 was nearly identical to the rate in 1980; in fact, this rate had changed little since the early 1970's. However, between 1988 and 1994, the rate increased 64%. This steady increase after years of stability focused national attention on the juvenile violent crime problem.

The most recent arrest and population data show that in 1996, the juve-

nile violent crime arrest rate declined 9% from the 1995 level, returning to the 1991 level. While the 1996 rate was still 42% above the 1988 level, 1996 is the second year in a row the juvenile violent crime arrest rate has declined, following a consistent pattern of increases dating back to the late 1980's.

Few juveniles are arrested for violent crimes

The juvenile Violent Crime Index arrest rate tells us that in 1996, there were 465 arrests for these violent crimes for every 100,000 youth in the United States between 10 and 17 years of age. If each of these arrests

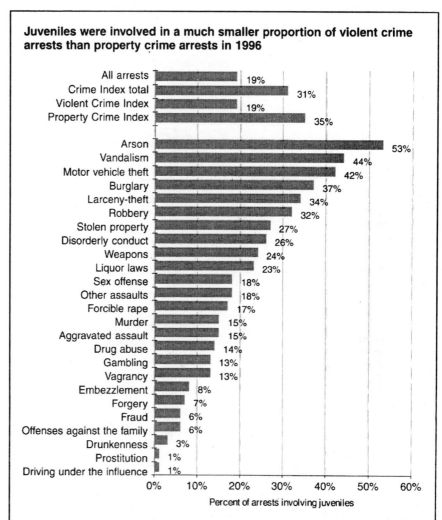

Juveniles were involved in a much smaller proportion of violent crime arrests than property crime arrests in 1996

- Nearly one-third (32%) of all persons arrested for robbery in 1996 were under age 18, substantially above the juvenile proportion of arrests for other violent crimes: forcible rape (17%), murder (15%), and aggravated assault (15%).

- Persons between ages 10 and 49 commit most crime. In fact, in 1996, more than 95% of all arrests involved persons in this age range. Juveniles ages 10 through 17 made up 19% of this segment of the U.S. population. Compared with their proportion in the 10- to 49-year-old population, juveniles were disproportionately involved in arrests for arson, vandalism, motor vehicle theft, burglary, larceny-theft, robbery, stolen property, disorderly conduct, weapons, and liquor law violation offenses. Except for robbery, the juvenile proportion of violent crime arrests was roughly equivalent to their representation in the population of 10- to 49-year-olds.

Note: Running away from home and curfew violations are not presented in this figure because, by definition, only juveniles can be arrested for these offenses.

Data source: *Crime in the United States 1996* (Washington, DC: U.S. Government Printing Office, 1997), table 38.

involved a different juvenile (i.e., if each juvenile arrested in 1996 for a Violent Crime Index offense were arrested only once that year—which is very unlikely), then less than one-half of 1% of all persons ages 10 through 17 in the United States were arrested for a Violent Crime Index offense in 1996.

After more than a decade of consistency, the juvenile violent crime arrest rate began to increase in 1989, peaked in 1994, then fell in 1995 and again in 1996, returning to the 1991 level

Arrests per 100,000 juveniles ages 10 to 17

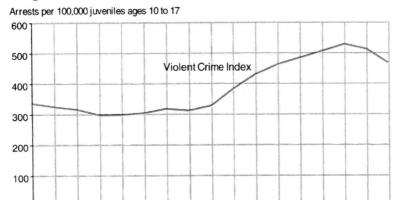

◆ Between 1994 and 1996, the juvenile arrest rate for Violent Crime Index offenses dropped 12%, to a level of 465 arrests for every 100,000 persons ages 10–17. The 1996 level is, however, about 50% above rates of the early 1980's.

Data source: Analysis of arrest data from the FBI and population data from the U.S. Bureau of the Census. [See data source note 1 for detail.]

Between 1980 and 1996, violent crime arrest rates increased substantially for all ages

Violent Crime Index arrests per 100,000 population

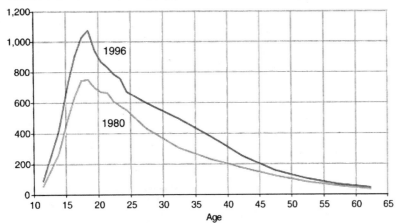

◆ There were large increases between 1980 and 1996 in juvenile violent arrest rates, with rates for younger juveniles (ages 10–14) up 68% and for older juveniles (ages 15–17) up 42%.

◆ Large increases were also found in the adult age groups. The rate for young adults (ages 18 and 19) increased 39%, while the rate for persons in their early twenties increased 28%. The largest increase in violent crime arrests in the adult population was for persons in their thirties, up 64%.

Data source: Analysis of arrest data from the FBI and population data from the U.S. Bureau of the Census. [See data source note 2 for detail.]

Juvenile arrests for property crimes remain stable

As with violent crime, the FBI assesses trends in the volume of property crimes by monitoring four offenses that are consistently reported by law enforcement agencies nationwide and are pervasive in all geographical areas of the country. These four crimes, which form the Property Crime Index, are burglary, larceny-theft, motor vehicle theft, and arson.

For the period from 1987 through 1996, during which violent crime arrests rose dramatically, juvenile property crime arrest rates (as measured by the Property Crime Index) remained relatively constant. In fact, the 1996 rate of approximately 2,400 arrests for every 100,000 youth in the United States between 10 and 17 years of age is the lowest in the 10-year period.

Most arrested juveniles are referred to court

In most States, some persons below the age of 18 are, due to their age, or by statutory exclusion of certain offenses from juvenile court jurisdiction, under the jurisdiction of the criminal justice system. For those persons under age 18 *and* under the original jurisdiction of their State's juvenile justice system, the FBI's UCR Program monitors what happens as a result of the arrest. This is the only instance in the UCR Program in which the statistics on arrests coincide with State variations in the legal definition of a juvenile.

In 1996, 23% of arrests involving youth who were eligible in their State for processing in the juvenile justice system were handled within the law enforcement agency, and then the youth was released. The FBI reports that 69% of juvenile arrests were referred to juvenile court, and 6% were referred directly to criminal court. The others were referred to a welfare agency or to another police agency. The proportion of arrests sent to juvenile court has gradually increased

Of all the Violent Crime Index offenses, juvenile arrests for murder showed the greatest decline in the last 3 years

Murder

- The rate at which juveniles were arrested for murder peaked in 1993 at a level more than double that of the early 1980's.

- Following the 1993 peak, juvenile murder arrest rates declined substantially in each of the next 3 years, for a total decline of 31%. The 1996 juvenile murder arrest rate was the lowest in the decade, but still more than 50% greater than the rate in the early 1980's.

Arrests per 100,000 juveniles ages 10 to 17

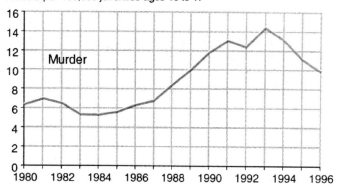

Forcible Rape

- The rate of juvenile arrests for forcible rape hit a 10-year low in 1995. The rate in 1996 was only slightly above the low point of 1995.

- Unlike aggravated assault (a crime that has many of the same attributes as forcible rape), the juvenile arrest rate for forcible rape has fluctuated within a limited range over the last two decades.

Arrests per 100,000 juveniles ages 10 to 17

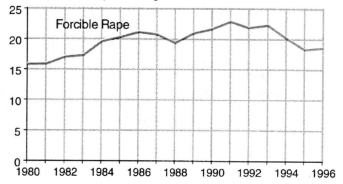

Robbery

- The juvenile arrest rate for robbery declined through most of the 1980's, reaching a low point in 1988.

- Between 1988 and 1994, the rate at which juveniles were arrested for robbery increased 70%. This arrest rate declined slightly in 1995 and by 10% in 1996.

- With these declines, the juvenile arrest rate for robbery in 1996 returned to the levels of the early 1990's and was just 7% above the 1980 rate.

Arrests per 100,000 juveniles ages 10 to 17

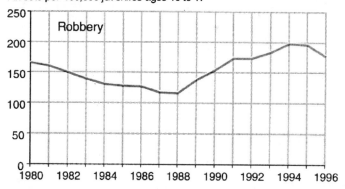

Aggravated Assault

- The rate at which juveniles were arrested for aggravated assault increased steadily between 1983 and 1994, up more than 120%.

- The aggravated assault arrest rate fell for the first time in more than a decade in 1995 (down 4%) and again in 1996 (down 9%), returning to the 1991 level.

Data source: Analysis of arrest data from the FBI and population data from the U.S. Bureau of the Census. *[See data source note 1 for detail.]*

Arrests per 100,000 juveniles ages 10 to 17

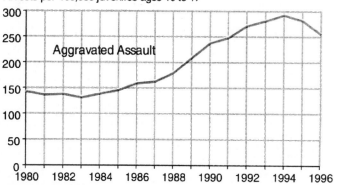

The juvenile arrest rate for property crime in 1996 was the lowest rate in a decade

Arrests per 100,000 juveniles ages 10 to 17

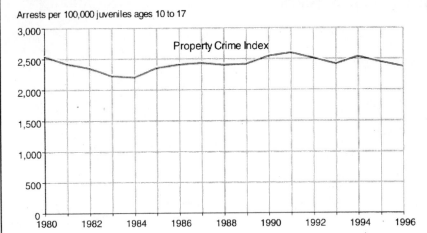

Data source: Analysis of arrest data from the FBI and population data from the U.S. Bureau of the Census. *[See data source note 1 for detail.]*

For juveniles and young adults, the property crime arrest rate changed little between 1980 and 1996, while the arrest rates for persons in their thirties and forties increased an average of nearly 50%

Property Crime Index arrests per 100,000 population

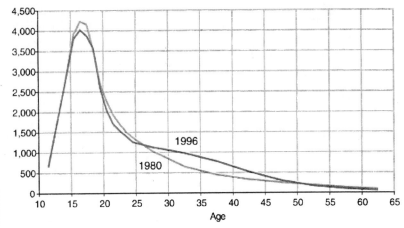

Data source: Analysis of arrest data from the FBI and population data from the U.S. Bureau of the Census. *[See data source note 2 for detail.]*

from 58% in 1980 to 69% in 1996. In 1996, the proportion of juvenile arrests sent to juvenile courts was similar in cities, suburban areas, and rural counties. The proportion of juvenile arrests sent directly to criminal court in 1996 (6%) was the highest in the last two decades.

The juvenile share of the crime problem decreased in 1996

The relative responsibility of juveniles for the U.S. crime problem is hard to determine. Studying the proportion of crimes that are cleared by the arrest of juveniles gives one estimate of the juvenile responsibility for crime.

The clearance data in the *Crime in the United States* series show that the proportion of violent crimes attributed to juveniles is lower than their proportion of arrests but has also increased in recent years. Based on clearance data, the juvenile responsibility for violent crime grew from 9% in 1986 to 14% in 1995, but dropped to 13% in 1996. Since 1986, the juvenile proportion of violent crime clearances has increased for each of the four components of the Violent Crime Index: murder (from 5% to 8%), forcible rape (from 10% to 12%), robbery (from 12% to 18%), and aggravated assault (from 9% to 12%). However, between 1995 and 1996, while the juvenile proportion of the U.S. population increased, the juvenile proportion of crimes cleared declined in each violent offense category.

The juvenile responsibility for property crime was the same in 1986 and 1996 (23%). Juvenile responsibility for the four offenses within the Property Crime Index either remained the same or increased: burglary (21% in both years), larceny-theft (from 23% to 24%), motor vehicle theft (from 20% to 22%), and arson (from 35% to 46%). The juvenile responsibility for property crimes in 1996 is near its average for the last two decades.

In contrast to their combined trend, the components of the Property Crime Index displayed substantially different juvenile arrest rate trends between 1980 and 1996

Burglary

- The juvenile arrest rate for burglary declined consistently between 1980 and 1996, with the 1996 rate 45% below that of 1980.

- Between 1980 and 1996, substantial and similar declines in burglary arrest rates were seen for all age groups below age 30. Although these levels were substantially below those of younger persons, the burglary arrest rates for persons in their thirties and forties increased by nearly one-third between 1980 and 1996.

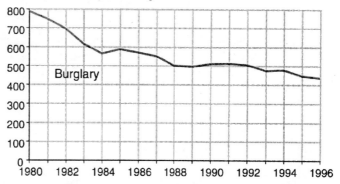

Arrests per 100,000 juveniles ages 10 to 17

Larceny-Theft

- Compared with other property offenses, the juvenile arrest rate for larceny-theft remained relatively constant between 1980 and 1996. Over this period the juvenile arrest rate for larceny-theft gradually increased, so that the 1996 rate was 10% above the rate in 1980.

- In 1996, larceny-theft arrests accounted for 70% of the FBI's Property Crime Index arrests. As a result, larceny-theft arrest trends dominate the Index and mask changes in the other offenses in the Index.

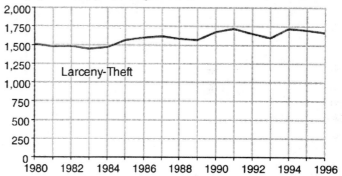

Arrests per 100,000 juveniles ages 10 to 17

Motor Vehicle Theft

- Juvenile arrests for motor vehicle theft soared between 1983 and 1990, with the rate up nearly 140% over this period.

- Between 1990 and 1996, the juvenile arrest rate for motor vehicle theft declined substantially, returning to the 1987 level. This decline compensated for half of the increase that occurred between 1983 and 1990.

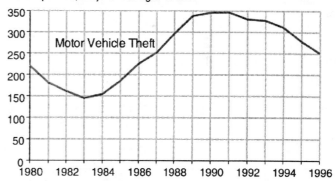

Arrests per 100,000 juveniles ages 10 to 17

Arson

- Compared with other property crimes, the number of juveniles arrested for arson is very small. During the 1980's, the rate of juvenile arrests for arson remained constant.

- Between 1990 and 1994, the rate of juvenile arson arrests increased from 26 to 34 per 100,000 juveniles ages 10 through 17. The juvenile arson arrest rate then declined in 1995 and 1996, falling back to the 1992 level.

Data source: Analysis of arrest data from the FBI and population data from the U.S. Bureau of the Census. *[See data source note 1 for detail.]*

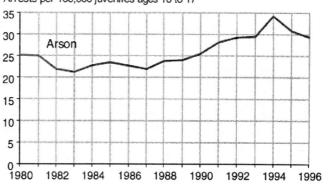

Arrests per 100,000 juveniles ages 10 to 17

Juvenile arrest rates for weapons law violations followed a pattern similar to murder arrests and declined 21% between 1993 and 1996

Arrests per 100,000 juveniles ages 10 to 17

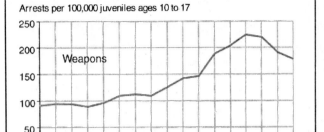

◆ From 1987 through 1993, the juvenile arrest rate for weapons law violations more than doubled. As with murder arrest rate trends, after this large increase, the juvenile arrest rate for weapons law violations declined in 1994, 1995, and 1996, with the 1996 rate dropping below the 1991 level.

Data source: Analysis of arrest data from the FBI and population data from the U.S. Bureau of the Census. *[See data source note 1 for detail.]*

After more than a decade of stability, the juvenile arrest rate for drug abuse violations increased more than 70% between 1993 and 1996

Arrests per 100,000 juveniles ages 10 to 17

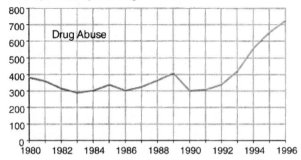

◆ Juvenile arrest rates for drug abuse increased 90% between 1980 and 1996. In comparison, arrest rates for persons in their early twenties increased about 50%, while drug abuse arrest rates for persons between ages 35 and 54 increased more than 400%.

Data source: Analysis of arrest data from the FBI and population data from the U.S. Bureau of the Census. *[See data source note 1 for detail.]*

After more than a decade of stability, the rate of juvenile arrests for curfew and loitering law violations nearly doubled between 1993 and 1996

Arrests per 100,000 juveniles ages 10 to 17

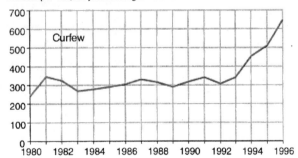

◆ In 1996, 29% of juveniles arrested for curfew and loitering law violations were females and 28% were below the age of 15.

◆ Curfew and loitering law violations differed from other offense categories in that the racial composition of juveniles arrested for these offenses was similar to that of the general U.S. population.

Data source: Analysis of arrest data from the FBI and population data from the U.S. Bureau of the Census. *[See data source note 1 for detail.]*

The increase in the juvenile arrest rate for alcohol-related offenses in 1996 came after a general pattern of decline that had lasted for a decade

Arrests per 100,000 juveniles ages 10 to 17

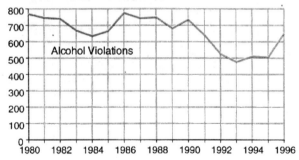

◆ Alcohol-related crimes include liquor law violations, drunkenness, and driving under the influence.

◆ Juvenile arrest rates for alcohol-related crimes increased 29% between 1995 and 1996, although the 1996 rate was still 11% below the 1990 rate.

Data source: Analysis of arrest data from the FBI and population data from the U.S. Bureau of the Census. *[See data source note 1 for detail.]*

Although Violent Crime Index arrest rates for young juveniles were much lower than those for older juveniles, the arrest rate trends for both groups were similar

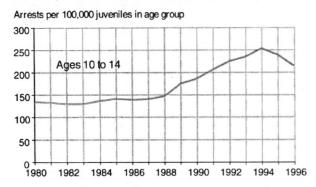

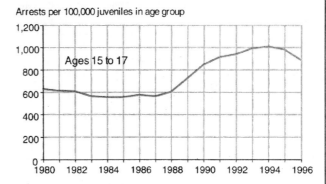

◆ The violent crime arrest rate of older juveniles (ages 15–17) has been, on average, four times greater than that of younger juveniles (ages 10–14). After this difference in magnitude has been compensated for, the violent crime arrest rate trends for younger and older juveniles are found to parallel each other from 1980 through 1996.

◆ Between 1994 and 1996, the rate declined more for younger juveniles (15%) than for older juveniles (12%).

Data source: Analysis of arrest data from the FBI and population data from the U.S. Bureau of the Census. *[See data source note 1 for detail.]*

Notes

In this Bulletin "juvenile" refers to persons below age 18. This definition is at odds with the legal definition of juveniles in 1996 in 13 States—10 States where all 17-year-olds and 3 States where all 16- and 17-year-olds are defined as adults.

These FBI data are counts of arrests within age of arrestee and offense categories from all law enforcement agencies that reported complete data for the calendar year. The proportion of the U.S. population covered by these reporting agencies ranged from 72% to 86% between 1980 and 1996.

Estimates of the number of persons in each age group in the reporting agencies' resident population assume that their population age profiles are like the Nation's. Reporting agencies' total populations were multiplied by the U.S. Bureau of the Census' most current estimate of the proportion of the U.S. population for each age group.

Data source notes

1. Analysis of arrest data from unpublished FBI reports for 1980

Based on clearance information, juveniles are responsible for a substantially smaller proportion of violent crimes than property crimes

◆ If the crimes cleared by law enforcement are representative of all crimes committed in 1996, then juveniles were responsible for 13% of all violent crimes and 23% of all property crimes. If, however, juveniles were more easily apprehended than adults, then the juvenile responsibility was less.

Data source: Compiled from *Crime in the United States* series for the years 1980 through 1996 (Washington, DC: U.S. Government Printing Office, 1981 through 1997, respectively).

through 1994 and from *Crime in the United States* reports for 1995 and 1996 (Washington, DC: U.S. Government Printing Office, 1996 and 1997, respectively); population data from the Bureau of the Census for 1980 through 1989 from *Current Popula-*

tion Reports, P25–1095 (Washington, DC: U.S. Dept. of Commerce, 1993), and for 1990 through 1996 from *Population of the U.S. and States by Single Year of Age and Sex* [machine-readable data files released April 1997].

States with high rates of juvenile Property Crime Index arrests tend to have low Violent Crime Index arrest rates

| State | Percent Reporting | 1996 Arrest Rate* | | Comparison With U.S. Rate | | State | Percent Reporting | 1996 Arrest Rate* | | Comparison With U.S. Rate | |
		Violent Crime Index	Property Crime Index	Violent Crime Index	Property Crime Index			Violent Crime Index	Property Crime Index	Violent Crime Index	Property Crime Index
Total U.S.	72%	471	2,444			Missouri	58%	473	3,106	0%	27%
Alabama	96	217	1,422	−54%	−42%	Montana	0	NA	NA	NA	NA
Alaska	89	361	3,223	−23	32	Nebraska	72	94	2,766	−80	13
Arizona	94	455	3,606	−3	48	Nevada	98	364	3,199	−23	31
Arkansas	95	303	2,243	−36	−8	New Hampshire	76	126	2,188	−73	−10
California	98	610	2,249	30	−8	New Jersey	96	655	2,182	39	−11
Colorado	74	240	2,826	−49	16	New Mexico	59	330	3,309	−30	35
Connecticut	77	524	2,731	11	12	New York	69	981	1,344	108	−45
Delaware	51	985	4,438	109	82	North Carolina	98	437	1,955	−7	−20
Dist. of Columbia	0	NA	NA	NA	NA	North Dakota	61	79	2,557	−83	5
Florida	0	NA	NA	NA	NA	Ohio	58	427	2,246	−9	−8
Georgia	61	241	1,941	−49	−21	Oklahoma	100	318	2,771	−33	13
Hawaii	100	361	3,121	−23	28	Oregon	86	330	3,987	−30	63
Idaho	98	232	4,106	−51	68	Pennsylvania	77	474	1,680	1	−31
Illinois	23	NA	NA	NA	NA	Rhode Island	95	486	2,448	3	0
Indiana	56	512	2,314	9	−5	South Carolina	99	433	2,219	−8	−9
Iowa	81	225	2,022	−52	−17	South Dakota	69	296	3,894	−37	59
Kansas	0	NA	NA	NA	NA	Tennessee	39	NA	NA	NA	NA
Kentucky	20	NA	NA	NA	NA	Texas	87	349	2,447	−26	0
Louisiana	61	478	2,854	1	17	Utah	92	265	3,735	−44	53
Maine	98	168	3,431	−64	40	Vermont	0	NA	NA	NA	NA
Maryland	79	838	3,184	78	30	Virginia	93	238	2,082	−49	−15
Massachusetts	83	515	1,058	9	−57	Washington	68	387	4,196	−18	72
Michigan	82	313	1,607	−34	−34	West Virginia	100	74	1,221	−84	−50
Minnesota	90	344	3,215	−27	32	Wisconsin	100	361	4,613	−23	89
Mississippi	23	NA	NA	NA	NA	Wyoming	58	171	3,161	−64	29

* Throughout this report, juvenile arrest rates were calculated by dividing the number of arrests of persons ages 10–17 by the number of 10- through 17-year-olds in the population. In this table only, arrest rate is defined as the number of arrests of persons under age 18 for every 100,000 persons ages 10–17. Juvenile arrests (arrests of youth under age 18) reported at the State level in *Crime in the United States* cannot be disaggregated into more detailed age categories so that the arrest of persons under age 10 can be excluded in the rate calculation. Therefore, there is a slight inconsistency in this table between the age range for the arrests (birth through age 17) and the age range for the population (ages 10–17) that are the basis of a State's juvenile arrest rate. This inconsistency is slight because just 2% of all juvenile arrests involved youth under age 10. However, this inconsistency is preferred to the distortion of arrest rates that would be introduced were the population base for the arrest rate to incorporate the large volume of children in a State's birth to 9-year-old population.

NA = Rates were classified as not available when reporting agencies represented 50% or less of the State population.

Data source: Analysis of arrest data from the FBI's *Crime in the United States 1996* (Washington, DC: U.S. Government Printing Office, 1997), tables 5 and 69, and population data from the U.S. Bureau of the Census' *Population of the U.S. and States by Single Year of Age and Sex: 1996* [machine-readable data file released in April 1997].

Technical Note

Arrest rates were calculated by dividing the number of youth arrests made in the year by the number of youth living in reporting jurisdictions. While juvenile arrest rates reflect juvenile behavior, many other factors can affect the size of these rates.

For example, jurisdictions that arrest a relatively large number of nonresident juveniles would have a higher arrest rate than a jurisdiction whose resident youth behave in an identical manner.

Therefore, jurisdictions, especially small jurisdictions, that are vacation destinations or regional centers for economic activity may have arrest rates that reflect more than the behavior of their resident youth.

Other factors that influence the magnitude of arrest rates in a given area include the attitudes of its citizens toward crime, the policies of the jurisdiction's law enforcement agencies, and the policies of other components of the justice system. Consequently, comparison juvenile arrest rates across States, while informative, should be done with caution.

In most States, not all law enforcement agencies report their arrest data to the FBI. Rates for these States are then necessarily based on partial information. If the reporting law enforcement agencies in these States are not representative of the entire State, then the rates will be biased. **Therefore, reported arrest rates for States with less than complete reporting may not be accurate.**

Acknowledgments

This Bulletin was written by Howard N. Snyder, Director of Systems Research at the National Center for Juvenile Justice, with funds provided by OJJDP to support the Juvenile Justice Statistics and Systems Development Program. Barbara Allen-Hagen is the OJJDP Program Manager for this work. The author gratefully acknowledges the assistance provided by the FBI's Criminal Justice Information Services Division, specifically, Yoshio Akiyama, Nancy Carnes, Tom Edwards, Gilford Gee, Victoria Major, and Sharon Propheter.

2. Analysis of arrest data from an unpublished FBI report for 1980 and from *Crime in the United States* 1996 (Washington, DC: U.S. Government Printing Office, 1997); population data from the U.S. Bureau of the Census for 1980 from *Current Population Reports,* P25–1095 (Washington, DC: U.S. Dept. of Commerce, 1993), and for 1996 from *Population of the U.S. and States by Single Year of Age and Sex: 1996* [machine-readable data file released April 1997].

This Bulletin was prepared under cooperative agreement number 95-JN-FX-K008 from the Office of Juvenile Justice and Delinquency Prevention, U.S. Department of Justice.

Points of view or opinions expressed in this document are those of the author and do not necessarily represent the official position or policies of OJJDP or the U.S. Department of Justice.

Storm Warning
The Coming Crime Wave Is Washed Up

By JACQUES STEINBERG

IN 1994, when a small but influential group of criminologists and politicians began fixing their gaze on the end of the 20th century, they saw a crime storm on the horizon, one teeming with a new breed of superpredators who would soon be reaching their teens.

According to their forecasts, the storm should have hit by now. Instead, the sky has been clearing.

For example, the rate of homicides committed by 14- to 17-year-olds, which leapt from 10 per 100,000 in 1985 to 30.2 in 1993, has gone down every year since, to 16.5 in 1997, said James Alan Fox, dean of the college of criminal justice at Northeastern University.

Moreover, statistics released by the Justice Department last week indicated that robberies by offenders of all ages fell a staggering 17 percent in 1997, continuing the seven-year drop in violent crime that followed the crime surge of the 1980's. That drop, criminologists say, is being driven by the falloff in the crack market and by concerted efforts by police departments across the country to seize handguns from juveniles, among other causes.

But that's not exactly what Professor Fox—along with James Q. Wilson of U.C.L.A., John J. DiIulio Jr. of Princeton University and Representative Bill McCollum of Florida, the chairman of the House subcommittee on crime—foresaw in their crystal balls several years ago. In November 1995, for example, Mr. DiIulio, a professor of politics and public affairs, suggested that a dip in crime, already perceptible then, was "the lull before the crime storm."

But if that was the case, said Franklin E. Zimring, a professor of law at the University of California at Berkeley, who was skeptical of such forecasts, "We should have our umbrellas open right now."

Professor Wilson of U.C.L.A., who doesn't recall using a weather analogy but did firmly predict rising youth crime, is more blunt than Professor Zimring.

"So far, it clearly hasn't happened," he said. "This is a good indication of what little all of us know about criminology."

At the heart of the pessimistic predictions was a historical fact: teen-agers commit a lot of crimes. Therefore, it seemed to follow, more teen-agers would mean more crime.

While it is not too late for the doomsday prognostications to come true, given that they were projected from now through 2010 and beyond, it's worth examining why they have not held so far.

Perhaps the most exaggerated factor underpinning the anticipated youth crime wave has been demographics. In January 1996, the Council on Crime in America, an organization of prosecutors and law-enforcement experts, issued a report compiled by Professor DiIulio describing violent crime as a "ticking time bomb" that would go off as the number of teenagers soared in the coming few years.

But Professor Zimring contends that too much has been made of the anticipated boom in the adolescent population. Consider that the number of Americans aged 14 to 24 is expected to grow about one percent a year from 1995 to 2010—from 40.1 million to almost 47 million—a total increase of about 16 percent. By comparison, the growth in adolescents during the baby boom, from 1960 to 1975, was 50 percent, he said.

Though the correlation between increases in the juvenile population and a rise in violent crime has been regarded as conventional wisdom, the link has hardly proven strong in recent years.

During the five years that the homicide rate among teen-age offenders has been falling, the population of adolescents has already begun to rise. And when the homicide rate among adolescents was spiking in the early 1990's, the adolescent population was flat.

Mr. Wilson, a professor emeritus in the school of management at U.C.L.A. who has written extensively about crime, now says that in foreseeing a youth crime wave, he may have focused too much on population increases at the expense of intangibles like "the perception of young people about the costs and benefits of crime."

Though rates of violent crime have been influenced by a host of more quantifiable factors—the availability of guns, the growth in the economy, the expansion of crime-prevention programs—Professor Zimring says he is uncomfortable with trying to predict the criminal potential of someone who may be just a toddler now, if born at all.

"What's been weird has been this single focus: we're only interested in kids four years old now and how many kids they're going to shoot," he said.

Howard Snyder, director of systems research for the National Center for Juvenile Justice in Pittsburgh, a longtime skeptic about the predicted crime wave, thinks many people, especially politicians, have an incentive to be pessimistic.

"People naturally have this pessimism about what's going to happen, especially with kids," he said. "If you predict the future's going to be terrible, you're in a win-win situation. If it does happen, you were right. If it doesn't, your raising the flag of concern helped turn it around."

He said the gloomy oratory has already "changed the nature of juvenile justice," by enabling many states to pass laws that make it easier to try and imprison youthful offenders as adults.

Mr. DiIulio, one of the most vocal prophets of the coming storm, did not return telephone calls last week. But Professor Fox of Northeastern, whose analysis Mr. DiIulio has cited, says that a number of signs remain ominous.

He projects, for example, that growth in the population of black males—those 14 to 17 years old, as well as to 18 to 24—will grow at a steeper rate than their white male counterparts during the first two decades of the 21st century. And if history holds, he said, young blacks will be responsible for a disproportionate share of violent crimes when compared to whites.

He suggests further that the rate of homicides committed by youths 14 to 17 years old—16.5 per 100,000 in 1997—while nearly half of what it was in 1993, remains nearly double the 20-year low of 8.5 in 1984.

Does that mean that Professor Fox continues to see bad weather on the horizon, as he did so clearly three years ago?

"We may indeed see a resurgence in youth violence," Professor Fox said. "I say 'may.' I didn't say 'will.'"

THE NEW MOOD OF MEANNESS TOWARD CHILDREN— TO BE YOUNG IS TO BE SUSPECT.

The Crackdown on Kids

ANNETTE FUENTES

When Kipland Kinkel, Mitchell Johnson and Andrew Golden reportedly unloaded mini arsenals of guns at their class-mates, they fulfilled the worst fears about young people that now dominate the nation's adult consciousness. Kinkel, 15, of Spring-field, Oregon, allegedly is responsible for the deaths of two students as a result of an incident on May 21, as well as for the deaths of his parents. Johnson, 13, and Golden, 11, were charged in connection with the March 24 deaths of four students and a teacher in Jonesboro, Arkansas. All were instantly transformed from average American boys, perhaps a bit on the wild side, into evil incarnate. Forget that Mitchell sobbed next to his mother in court, or that Drew learned to sling a shotgun from Dad and Grandpa the way many boys learn to swing a bat. "Let 'em have it" was the sentiment, with catchy phrases like "adult crime, adult time."

After the Arkansas incident, Attorney General Janet Reno scoured federal laws for some way to prosecute Johnson and Golden so they could be locked up till age 21 if convicted, a stiffer sentence than the state could mete out. One *Washington Post* Op-Ed called for states to adopt a national uniform mini-mum age for juveniles to be tried as adults for violent crimes.

The three boys are believed to have committed terrible deeds, no question. But twenty years ago, a Greek chorus would have been clamoring to understand why they went bad.

IGOR KOPELNITSKY

The events themselves would have been seen as aberrations. Redemption might have been mentioned, especially since these were not career delinquents. Instead, we have proposals like the one from Texas legislator Jim Pitts, who wants his state to use the death penalty on children as young as 11. And he's got plenty of support, because this is the era of crime and punishment and accountability for all constituencies without wealth or power to shield them. And the young are such a class of people.

In the past two decades, our collective attitude toward children and youth has undergone a profound change that's reflected in the educational and criminal justice systems as well as in our daily discourse. "Zero tolerance" is the mantra in public schools and juvenile courts, and what it really means is that to be young is to be suspect. Latino and black youth have borne the brunt of this growing criminaliza-tion of youth. But the trend has spilled over racial and ethnic boundaries—even class boundaries, to a degree. Youth, with all its innocence and vulnerability, is losing ground in a society that exploits both.

In fact, youth crime has not changed as dramatically as our perceptions of it. Data from the National Center for Juvenile Justice show that between 1987 and 1996, the number of ju-venile arrests increased 35 percent. Juvenile violent-crime ar-rests were up 60 percent, but they represent a sliver of all juvenile arrests—about 5 percent of the 1996 total of 135,100. A 1997 study by the center found that "today's violent youth commits the same number of violent acts as his/her predeces-sor of 15 years ago." As to whether criminals are getting

Annette Fuentes has just completed a Prudential Fellowship on Children and the News at Columbia University.

younger, a 1997 report from the Justice Department answers clearly: "Today's serious and violent juvenile offenders are not significantly younger than those of 10 or 15 years ago."

What's more, from 1994 to 1995 there was a 3 percent decline in juvenile arrests for violent crime, and from 1995 to 1996 there was a 6 percent decline. "I have people call me up and ask, 'Why is juvenile crime down?' " says Robert Shepherd Jr., a law professor at the University of Richmond in Virginia. "I say, 'Why was it up?' It could be just one of history's cycles. Over the thirty years I've been involved in juvenile justice issues, I've seen very little change in the incidence of violent crime by kids."

One thing that *has* changed is the prominence of guns and their role in violence. A 1997 Justice Department report looked at homicides by youths aged 13 and 14 with and without guns. In 1980 there were 74 murders committed with guns and 68 without by that age group. In 1995 gun-related murders totaled 178; there were 67 nongun murders.

Exaggerated claims about juvenile crime would be a hard sell if people weren't ready to believe the worst about young people. A 1997 report from Public Agenda, a nonprofit policy group, called "Kids These Days: What Americans Really Think About the Next Generation," found that 58 percent of those surveyed think children and teens will make the world a worse place or no different when they grow up. Even kids aged 5 to 12 weren't spared, with 53 percent of respondents characterizing them in negative terms. Only 23 percent had positive things to say about children. What America really thinks about its kids, in short, is: not much.

The generation gap is old news, but this sour, almost hateful view of young people is different. Adults aren't merely puzzled by young people; they're terrified of them. It can't be a coincidence that the shift in adult attitudes began roughly a generation after the height of political and social movements created by young people of all colors. Policy-makers now propelling anti-youth agendas remember how effective young people can be as a force for change. Demographics and the shifting nature of U.S. families also foster the anti-youth bias. According to census statistics, the number of people under age 65 has tripled since 1900, while the population aged 65 or over has increased elevenfold. One-quarter of all households are people living alone. And children are no longer integral to family structure: In 51 percent of all families there are no children under 18 living at home. Young people are easily demonized when their worlds don't coincide with ours. The sense of collective responsibility in raising children disappears as the building blocks of community change.

To an older America in a postindustrial world, children have become more of a liability than an asset. Middle-class parents calculate the cost of raising kids, including an overpriced college education, as they would a home mortgage. Low-income parents are bludgeoned by policies designed to discourage having children, from welfare reform to cuts in higher-education assistance. Young people's place in the economic order is uncertain, and a threat to those elders who are scrambling for the same jobs at McDonald's or in Silicon Valley. Says Barry Feld, professor at the University of Minnesota Law School and author of the upcoming *Bad Kids: Race and the Transformation of Juvenile Court,* "Parents raised kids so they could take care of them when they're old. As caring for the old has shifted to the public sector, the elderly no longer have that fiscal investment in their kids. They know Social Security will be there for them."

Another reason adults are willing to condemn children is that it saves them from taking responsibility when kids go wrong. Take this statistical nugget: From 1986 to 1993, roughly the same period of the youth crime "explosion," the number of abused and neglected children doubled to 2.8 million, according to the Justice Department. And just three years later, the total of all juvenile arrests was 2.8 million. What goes around comes around.

Historically, U.S. criminal law followed the definitions of adulthood and childhood laid down by William Blackstone in his *Commentaries on the Laws of England* (1765–69). Children up to 7 were considered incapable of criminal responsibility by dint of their immaturity. At 14, they could be held as responsible as adults for their crimes; the years in between were a gray area of subjective judgment on culpability. But by 1900, reformers had created a separate system of juvenile courts and reform schools based on the principles that delinquency had social causes and that youth should not be held to adult standards. Eighteen was generally held as the entryway to adulthood.

The current transformation in juvenile justice is no less radical than the one 100 years ago. This time, though, we are marching backward to a one-size-fits-all system for youth and adults in which punishment, not reform, is the goal. From 1992 to 1995, forty-one states passed laws making it easier to prosecute juveniles in adult criminal court, and today all fifty states have such laws. In more than half the states, children under 14 can be tried in adult court for certain crimes. In thirteen states, there is no minimum age at which a child can be tried in adult court for felonies. New York permits prosecution of a 7-year-old as an adult for certain felonies. The Hatch-Sessions bill now in the U.S. Senate continues the assault on youthful offenders. It would use block grants to encourage states to toughen further their juvenile justice procedures. One provision eliminates the longstanding mandate to separate incarcerated juveniles and adults. "You're going to see more suicides and assaults if that happens," says Robert Shepherd.

Violent crimes like those in Oregon and Arkansas are a rarity, but they've become the rationale for a widespread crack-

> *Violent crimes like those in Oregon and Arkansas are a rarity, but they've become the rationale for a crackdown on young people.*

4. Crackdown on Kids

down on youth at school and on the streets. If Dennis the Menace were around, he'd be shackled hand and foot, with Mr. Wilson chortling as the cops hauled his mischievous butt off to juvenile hall. In Miami recently, a 10-year-old boy was handcuffed, arrested and jailed overnight because he kicked his mother at a Pizza Hut. His mother protested the police action—it was a waitress who turned him in. The boy now faces domestic battery charges in juvenile court.

Last October at the Merton Intermediate School in Merton, Wisconsin, four boys aged 12 and 13 were suspended for three days and slapped with disorderly conduct citations and fines (later dropped) by the local sheriff after they yanked up another boy's underwear "wedgie style." "The boys were playing, wrestling around in the schoolyard, and there was a pile-on," says Kevin Keane, an attorney who represented one of the boys. "One kid was on the ground and the others gave him a wedgie. He wasn't hurt or upset, and they all went back to class." But the principal learned about the incident and termed it a sexual assault.

Anti-youth analysts prefer to think more juvenile arrests means more kids are behaving recklessly. But it's just as plausible to argue that the universe of permissible behavior has shrunk. Look at curfews, which were virtually unknown twenty years ago. Curfews generated 185,000 youth arrests in 1996—a 113 percent increase since 1987. Disorderly conduct arrests of youth soared 93 percent between 1987 and 1996, with 215,000 arrests in 1996 alone.

Public schools are at ground zero in the youth crackdown. A report released in March by the National Center for Education Statistics surveyed 1,234 public schools on crime and security measures. Three-fourths have "zero tolerance" policies on drugs, alcohol and weapons, which means ironclad punish-ment for any transgression. Six percent of the schools surveyed use police or other law enforcement on campus at least thirty hours a week, while 19 percent of high schools have stationed cops full time. Public schools are even using dogs to search for illegal drugs. The Northern California A.C.L.U. filed suit in March 1997 against the Galt, California, school district on behalf of two students and a teacher who were subjected to dog searches during a course on criminal justice. "It's a real state police-prison element introduced into the schools," says A.C.L.U. lawyer Ann Bick. "It tells kids, 'We don't trust you.' And they'll live down to those expectations."

If the goal is to change behavior, draconian policies aimed at young people have been a dismal failure. Half a dozen studies have shown that transferring juveniles to adult courts not only doesn't deter crime, it's more likely to spur recidivism. But if the goal of the crackdown on youth is to divert attention from the real crimes plaguing the nation—child poverty, failing educational systems, 15 million kids without health insurance—then it's a success. New York City Mayor Rudolph Giuliani uses that strategy brilliantly: In January a child was killed by a brick falling from a badly managed school construction site, and reading scores were once again abysmally low. What were Giuliani's issues? Uniforms for students and deployment of police in the schools.

The criminalization of young people makes no sense, of course. Kids are a national treasure and natural resource, the bearers of our collective dreams and hopes. But logic and humanity don't often determine public policies or opinion. We are sowing the seeds, the dragon's teeth, of our own comeuppance. Erasing the line between youth and adulthood without granting youths the same constitutional protections and rights of citizenship as adults sets up a powerful contradiction. And sooner or later, to paraphrase Malcolm X, the chickens will come home to roost.

Part 1. The nature and severity of juvenile crime

In hard numbers, juvenile crime significantly increased between 1984 and 1993. During that period, arrests of people under age 18 for murder and non-negligent manslaughter increased by 167.9 percent. Arrests for aggravated assault increased by 98.1 percent. Arrests for forcible rape increased by 9 percent. Arrests for other assaults increased by 112 percent. And arrests for weapons possession rose by 125.6 percent.[1]

Juvenile arrests for certain property crimes are also on the rise. Between 1984 and 1993, arrests for stolen property increased by 42.6 percent. In fact, although those between the ages of 13 and 18 comprised only 8 percent of the population in 1989, they were arrested for 31 percent of the thefts (larceny), 34 percent of the burglaries and 41 percent of the motor vehicle thefts that year.

At best, if arrest rates remain stable at 1993 levels, juvenile arrests will rise 22 percent between now and the year 2010, an increase attributable to population growth as children of the "baby boom" generation reach adulthood. At worst, if the past decade's growth trend in juvenile arrests continues at the same level, arrest rates will more than double by 2010.[2]

Recidivism rates among juvenile offenders have *not* increased, but a relatively small percentage of juvenile offenders are chronic and frequent recidivists, accounting for the vast majority of juvenile offenses. Most studies indicate that only about one-third of juvenile offenders ever commit a second offense. Moreover, a very small percentage of juvenile offenders, varying from as low as 5 percent to as high as perhaps 25 percent, are so-called "chronic offenders," responsible for the majority of juvenile crime and racking up multiple arrests and adjudications.[3] Several recent studies, for example, conclude that chronic, hard-core juvenile recidivists account for over 65 percent of robberies by juveniles, over 65 percent of rapes, over 60 percent of aggravated assaults, over 70 percent of motor vehicle thefts, and over 60 percent of homicides.[4] The disproportionality of juvenile offenses committed by chronic juvenile offenders leads some juvenile justice researchers to decry the erosion of confidentiality standards for information relating to the large majority of nonchronic juvenile offenders.

The increase in juvenile crime is taking place at a time when crime overall is going down after decades of steady increase. The FBI's "Uniform Crime Reports" for 1995 reported a 3 percent decrease in serious crime from 1994, with murder down 7 percent, forcible rape down 5 percent and robbery down 6 percent.[5] Many factors may be responsible for the adult crime trend: the implementation of community policing concepts; a greater willingness among neighborhood residents to reclaim their streets; stiffer mandatory minimum sentences; "three strikes" provisions; or an abundance of new prison space. Whatever the reason, the adult trend, so far, is not having a noticeable impact on youths between the ages of 10 and 17.

Why? The deteriorating social and economic conditions of American cities is a possible factor. In 1992, 14.6 million juveniles lived in families with incomes below the poverty level, 42 percent more than in 1976. Poverty rates for black and Hispanic teenagers were far higher than those for their Caucasian counterparts.[6] In 1960, one child in 20 was born to an unmarried mother. By 1990, it was one in four. During this period, the

---

[1] U.S. Department of Justice, Bureau of Justice Statistics, *Sourcebook of Criminal Justice Statistics: 1994* (Washington, D.C.: Government Printing Office, 1994) p. 383 [hereafter Sourcebook]. *And see,* U.S. Department of Justice, Office of Juvenile Justice and Delinquency Prevention, *Juvenile Offenders and Victims: A National Report,* by Howard N. Snyder and Melissa Sickmund, National Center for Juvenile Justice (Washington, D.C.: Government Printing Office, August 1995) [hereafter Juvenile Offenders and Victims Report]. This report uses the term "arrest" to encompass a variety of juvenile detentions, charges and prosecutions.

[2] Juvenile Offenders and Victims Report, p. 111, *supra* note 1.
[3] *See,* Ibid., pp. 49–50. *And see,* P. Tracy, M. Wolfgang and R. Figlio, *Delinquency Careers in Two Birth Cohorts* (New York: Plenum Press, 1990) pp. 38–40.
[4] Juvenile Offenders and Victims Report, pp. 50–51, *supra* note 1.

[5] U.S. Department of Justice, Federal Bureau of Investigation, *Crime in the United States, 1995, Uniform Crime Report,* (Washington, D.C.: Government Printing Office, October 1996) pp. 11, 14, 24, 27.
[6] Juvenile Offenders and Victims Report, p. 7, *supra* note 1.

From *Privacy and Juvenile Justice Records: A Mid-Decade Status Report,* May 1997, pp. 4-7. Reprinted by permission of the National Institute of Justice, National Criminal Justice Reference Service.

proportion of children living in two-parent families declined from 85 percent to 73 percent.[7]

A recent study of young felons age 12 to 18 in Ohio's juvenile prison system further illustrates that most young people who are chronic offenders are also the victims of starkly substandard social and economic conditions. The Ohio study found, for example, that:

- 90 percent of Ohio juvenile incarcerates have substance abuse problems with marijuana, crack, heroin or alcohol;
- 5 percent are homeless;
- Approximately 30 percent have mental disorders;
- 75 percent of the girls and 50 percent of the boys have been sexually assaulted;
- Almost 25 percent of these young offenders have their own children;
- More than 6 out of 10 offenders lived with single mothers; and

- More than 8 out of 10 youthful offenders incarcerated in Ohio come from households with incomes below $10,000 per year.[8]

As an Ohio prison official concluded, "These kids are the throw-aways of society."[9]

There may be, of course, other explanations beyond poverty and neglect. The easy availability of powerful handguns and semiautomatic weapons may have turned youthful dispute resolution into a matter of deadly confrontation. Arguments and jealousies that once were straightened out with words and fists could now end in gunfire.

Since 1983, gun homicides committed by juveniles have nearly tripled.[10] Drug use among high school seniors, while nowhere near the record levels of the 1970s, is on the rise after a decline in the late 1980s and early 1990s.[11] Drug arrest rates for black

juveniles paralleled those of whites from the mid-1970s to the mid-1980s. The advent of crack cocaine, however, changed all that: black drug arrests now are five times higher than equivalent rates for whites.[12]

In addition to these traditional kinds of sociological explanations, more elusive causes have been suggested for the recent surge in juvenile violence. Jose E. Castillo, chief juvenile probation officer in Bexar County, Texas, put it this way: "In the past, kids would kill for a reason—someone made them angry. Now, there is just a lot of indiscriminate violence. They don't care who they hurt, and weapons have become more sophisticated and powerful."[13] Violence in popular music, television, movies and video games may also contribute to what many see as an alarming sense of dehumanization.

---

[7] Ibid., p. 10.

[8] Thomas, "Next Stop: Prison," *Washington Post,* 18 March 1996, p. A1 [hereafter *Washington Post*].
[9] Ibid.
[10] Juvenile Offenders and Victims Report, p. 58, *supra* note 1.
[11] Ibid., p. 59.

[12] Ibid., p. 120.
[13] "Kids Who Kill," *San Antonio Express-News,* 20 November 1995, p. 1 [hereafter *San Antonio Express-News*].

Part II. Juvenile justice system history and development

The proper mix of social and law enforcement programs necessary to address juvenile crime remains hotly contested in Washington and in State capitols. But whatever the ultimate outcome, the effect of this debate on the maintenance of juvenile records already is considerable. A system initially designed to be a confidential social service record repository is under pressure to become a modern, interactive criminal history database. This is far from what the Illinois State legislature had

in mind in 1899 when it established the Nation's first independent juvenile court system, in which "children were not to be treated as criminals nor dealt with by the process used for criminals."[14]

The juvenile court was one of the many products of the "Progressive

Movement" of the late 1800s. To the Progressives, crime was the result of external forces, not of the exercise of an individual's free will. Their goal was to reform the offender, not punish the offense. This concept of the "Rehabilitative Ideal" was the kernel of the Progressive justice reforms, including the formation of the juvenile court.[15]

The Progressives saw children as "corruptible innocents" who needed "special attention, solicitude and instruction."[16] As this view gained cur-

---

[14] Privacy and Juvenile Justice Records Report, p. 11.
[15] Barry C. Feld, *Criminalizing Juvenile Justice: Rules of Procedure for the Juvenile Court,* 69 MINN. L. REV. 141, 142–48 (1984).
[16] Ibid., p. 144.

rency, it seemed logical to establish a separate court system to apply the Rehabilitative Ideal to juveniles.

This concept owed much of its existence to the Victorian ideal of childhood as a special period in life that requires extra protection from the harsh realities of the adult world. In some measure, however, the concept is also a reaction to the world of the early 19th century in which there was considerably less tolerance for the misdirection of youth. Stoking the wrath of reformist organizations such as the Society for the Prevention of Juvenile Delinquency were cases like *State v. Guild,* a New Jersey court opinion published in 1828. It tells of a 12-year-old boy named James Guild, on trial for killing a woman named Catherine Beakes. He was found guilty and subsequently executed by hanging.[17]

The Illinois juvenile court of 1899 embraced the British doctrine of *parens patriae* (the State as parent). States became overseers of children whose natural parents had failed to carry out their supervisory responsibilities. The juvenile court was there not to punish the child, but to serve a benevolent role.[18] The U.S. Supreme Court in 1967 summarized it this way: "The early conception of the Juvenile Court proceeding was one in which a fatherly judge touches the heart and conscience of the erring youth by talking over his problems, by paternal advice and admonition and in which in extreme situations, benevolent and wise institutions of the State provided guidance and help, to save him from a downward career."[19]

By 1910, a total of 32 States had followed Illinois' lead in establishing either juvenile courts or juvenile probation services. By 1925, there were only two States that had not gone this route.[20] The reform-minded legal thinkers and courts of this era were guided by two bedrock principles. First, juveniles lack the *mens rea* (criminal intent) necessary under law to establish criminal culpability and, no matter how dastardly the crime they may have committed, juveniles can be treated, rehabilitated and reformed. The second principle flowed logically from the first: Impressionable, malleable children, not yet hardened to the criminal way of life, were not truly responsible for their actions in the same way adults would be had they committed the crimes at issue. Youthful wrongs, therefore, should not condemn a child to the same lengthy, numbing process of punishment that an adult in similar circumstances would face.[21]

Juvenile judges were not to be tied down to some rigid formula of fitting punishment to crime. In a less formal way, the benevolent court could fashion a solution to a juvenile's individual circumstances, combining legal and extra-legal methods of addressing the problems at hand. Since this was not an adversarial system, the constitutional guarantee of due process was thought to be out of place. Treatment plans could consist of differing mixes of probation and "training schools." But first and foremost, dispositions were always to be tailored to "the best interests of the child." A child eventually would either be reformed or lapse into the adult criminal justice system, where the clock essentially would be reset to zero.

The juvenile justice recordkeeping system at this stage closely paralleled the predominant philosophy of shielding the child. Confidentiality became paramount precisely because nonculpable juveniles could not and should not be branded for life with crimes for which they were not truly guilty. Also, children had little chance of rehabilitation if their names and misdeeds were exposed to public ridicule. A law review commentary in 1909 stressed that the importance of confidentiality was, "To get away from the notion that the child is to be dealt with as a criminal; to save it from the brand of criminality, the brand that sticks to it for life; to take it in hand and instead of first stigmatizing and then reforming it, to protect it from the stigma—this is the work which is now being accomplished (by the juvenile court)."[22]

An entire set of euphemisms grew up around the notion of protecting children, not prosecuting them. Police never arrest juveniles; they are "taken into custody." Authorities "refer" juveniles to juvenile court, never book or arraign them.

The treatment model as a concept of juvenile justice prevailed more or less through the 1950s. By then, a number of factors were combining to change the picture. News accounts of juvenile gangs and Hollywood's spotlighting of "J.D.s" in films like "Rebel Without a Cause" and "Blackboard Jungle" left many people wondering whether all juveniles could be rehabilitated. "Gang-style ferocity—once the evil domain of hardened adult criminals—now enters chiefly in cliques of teenage brigands. Their individual and gang exploits rival the savagery of veteran desperadoes of bygone days," said no less an authority than FBI Director J. Edgar Hoover in 1957.[23] More importantly, the frequency and severity of juvenile crime eroded confidence in the belief that juveniles lacked the criminal culpability necessary to be judged "guilty" of crimes. At the same time, persistent and severe recidivism associated with the most serious juvenile offenders undermined faith in the belief that juveniles are promising candidates for rehabilitation.

In 1966, the U.S. Supreme Court effectively abandoned the idea that ju-

---

[17] Ibid., p. 142.
[18] Juvenile Offenders and Victims Report, p. 70, *supra* note 1.
[19] *In re Gault,* 387 U.S. 1, 25–26 (1967).

[20] Janet E. Ainsworth, *Re-imaging Childhood and Reconstructing the Legal Order: The Case for Abolishing the Juvenile Court,* 69 N.C.L. REV. 1083, 1096–97 (1991). By 1945, every State had a juvenile court. Edmund F. McGarrell, *Juvenile Correctional Reform, Two Decades of Policy and Procedural Change* (Albany: State University of New York Press, 1988) p. 6.
[21] Joseph J. Senna and Larry J. Siegel, *Juvenile Law—Cases and Comments* (St. Paul, Minn.: West Publishing Co., 1976) pp. 2–3.

[22] Mack, *The Juvenile Court,* 23 Harv. L. REV. 104, 109 (1909).
[23] *FBI Law Enforcement Bulletin,* February 1957, 26, quoted in Privacy and Juvenile Justice Records Report.

venile courts were friendly and informal sources of counseling for wayward juveniles. In *Kent v. United States,* the Nation's highest court said juveniles are entitled to much the same adversarial-type system of due process that is standard in adult criminal courts. This benchmark case involved a 16-year-old accused of forcible entry, robbery and rape. The juvenile judge issued a waiver to adult court without ruling on a jurisdictional motion by the 16-year-old's lawyer. The Supreme Court said that, "While there can be no doubt of the original laudable purpose of juvenile courts, studies and critiques in recent years raise serious questions as to whether actual performance measures well enough against theoretical purpose to make tolerable the immunity of the process from the reach of the constitutional guaranties applicable to adults." [24]

One year later, in 1967, the Court, in *In re Gault,* took the *Kent* rationale a step further. The Court tossed out the doctrine of *parens patriae,* ruling its history murky and its constitutional underpinning doubtful. The Court said that juveniles are entitled to the four basic elements of due process: the right to notice, the right to counsel, the right to question witnesses and the right to protection against self-incrimination. *In re Gault* also challenged the importance of juvenile record confidentiality. "[T]he summary procedures of Juvenile Courts are sometimes defended by a statement that it is the law's policy 'to hide youthful errors from the full gaze of the public and bury them in the graveyard of the forgotten past.' This claim of secrecy, however, is more rhetoric than reality." [25]

---

[24] *Kent v. United States,* 383 U.S. 541, 555 (1966).
[25] *In re Gault,* 387 U.S. 1, 24 (1967).

The Extent of Female Delinquency

Meda Chesney-Lind and *Randall G. Shelden*

Like all criminal and delinquent behavior, female delinquency encompasses a very wide range of disparate activities. Girls can be labeled as delinquent for the commission of crimes (e.g., burglary, larceny, assault), but they also can be brought into the juvenile justice system, and in many states treated as delinquent, for committing what are called "status offenses." These are offenses for which only juveniles can be taken into custody and include an array of behaviors (running away from home, being a truant, violating a curfew, being incorrigible or "beyond control"). Status offenses play a major and controversial role in female delinquency.

The purpose of this chapter is to explore the question "What is female delinquency, and how much is there?" This chapter examines data from a variety of sources to determine not only how much female delinquency exists but also its manifestations. Throughout this discussion, many comparisons are made. We lay out differences between the dimensions of girls' offending as measured by anonymous, self-report studies and those that emerge from portraits drawn by official agencies such as the police and the juvenile courts. We also look at gender differences in delinquency and trends in girls' delinquency over time.

RECENT TRENDS: NATIONAL ARREST DATA

Each year the Federal Bureau of Investigation (FBI) compiles crime data from over ten thousand law enforcement agencies in the United States and publishes these figures

From *Girls, Delinquency, and Juvenile Justice*, 1st ed., 1992, pp. 7-27. © 1991 by Wadsworth Publishing, a division of International Thomson Publishing (fax: 800/730-2215). Reprinted by permission.

in *Crime in the United States: Uniform Crime Reports.* The report includes information on characteristics of persons under the age of eighteen arrested for a variety of offenses. The 1995 arrest figures (Table 1) reveal that there are considerable gender differences in official delinquency (that is, the picture of delinquency derived from statistics maintained by law enforcement officers). Most obvious is that far fewer girls than boys are arrested for delinquent behavior. Although 482,039 arrests of girls occurred in 1995, arrests of males outnumber female arrests by a 3:1 ratio, meaning that three boys are arrested for every girl.

Boys are also far more likely than girls to be arrested for violent crimes and serious property offenses. The male-to-female ratio for violent index crimes (homicide, forcible rape, robbery, aggravated assault) is about 6:1, and the ratio for the most serious index property crimes (burglary, motor vehicle theft, and arson) is about 3:1. Males are also far more likely to be arrested for such offenses as possession of stolen property, vandalism, weapons offenses, and "other assaults." Because of these sorts of arrest patterns, serious violent and property offenses have traditionally been considered "masculine" offenses.

Girls, in contrast, are more likely to be arrested for running away from home and prostitution. Over half (58 percent) of those arrested for running away are girls (about a 1.4:1 ratio). The male-to-female ratios are also much closer for such offenses as larceny–theft (2:1), forgery (2:1), fraud (3:1), and embezzlement (roughly equal at just over a 1:1 ratio), although with the notable exception of larceny–theft, very few youths are arrested for any of these offenses.

Girls are also more likely to approach boys in the commission of other "deportment" and status offenses. For instance, the male-to-female ratio for both curfew violations and liquor laws is about 2.5:1. However, boys do outnumber girls by a considerable margin among those arrested for drug law violations (about 7:1).

Arrest statistics also can provide a portrait of the character of both female and male official delinquency. The distribution of arrests within each sex cohort (Table 1) shows that the bulk of offenses for which both males and females are arrested are relatively minor and that many do not have a clearly defined victim. For example, larceny–theft dominates both boys' and girls' delinquency, but most of these arrests, particularly for girls, are for shoplifting (Cameron, 1953; Steffensmeier and Steffensmeier, 1980; Shelden and Horvath, 1986). One out of five arrests of males and one out of four arrests of girls were for this one offense. In contrast, only 6.5 percent of boys' arrests and 3.2 percent of girls' arrests in 1995 were for serious violent crime.

Table 1. Arrests of Persons under 18, by Sex, 1995

	Male		Female	
	NUMBER	PERCENT	NUMBER	PERCENT
Total	**1,399,547**	100.0	**482,039**	**100.0**
Index Crimes				
Homicide	2,245	*	138	*
Forcible Rape	3,769	*	84	*
Robbery	37,978	2.7	3,863	0.8
Aggravated Assault	46,695	3.4	11,418	2.4
Burglary	84,229	6.0	9,255	1.9
Larceny–Theft	238,889	17.1	114,778	23.8
Motor Vehicle Theft	48,719	3.5	8,490	1.8
Arson	6,283	0.4	874	0.2
Total Violent	90,687	6.5	15,503	3.2
Total Property	378,100	27.0	133,397	27.7
Total Index	468,787	33.5	148,900	30.9
Part II Offenses				
Other Assaults	106,028	7.6	40,515	8.4
Forgery/Counterfeiting	3,928	0.3	2,175	0.5
Fraud	13,242	0.9	4,676	1.0
Embezzlement	520	*	376	*
Stolen Property	25,799	1.8	3,559	0.7
Vandalism	84,206	6.0	10,007	2.0
Weapons	36,161	2.6	3,148	0.7
Prostitution	510	*	466	0.1
Other Sex Offenses	10,380	0.7	800	0.2
Drugs	116,627	8.3	16,696	3.5
Gambling	1,038	*	55	*
Offenses Against the Family	2,585	0.2	1,492	0.3
DUI	8,074	0.6	1,491	0.3
Liquor Laws	55,548	4.0	22,421	4.7
Drunkenness	12,009	0.9	2,243	0.5
Disorderly Conduct	82,793	5.9	26,512	5.5
Vagrancy	2,329	0.2	283	*
Curfew and Loitering	72,649	5.2	30,787	6.4
Runaway	74,713	5.3	101,657	21.1
All Other Offenses	221,621	15.8	63,780	13.2

SOURCE: U.S. Department of Justice, FBI, *Crime in America, Uniform Crime Reports,* 1995: 213.
* Less than 0.1 percent.

Status offenses play a more significant role in girls' arrests than boys' arrests. Status offenses accounted for 27.5 percent of all girls' arrests in 1995, but only about 10.5 percent of boys' arrests—figures that remained relatively stable during the past decade (and over previous decades as well). Arrests of girls for one status offense alone, running away, account for just over one-fifth of all girls' arrests (21 percent), compared with only one-twentieth of boys' arrests (5.3 percent). The arrest figures for two status offenses include only running away and curfew violation in the FBI report. This understates the extent of status offense arrests because

the category "all other offenses" (which includes other status offenses, such as "incorrigibility," "unmanageable," and truancy) is an important component of both male and female delinquency: 13.2 percent of girls' arrests and 15.8 percent of boys' arrests fall into this category. Hawaii data suggest that about three-quarters of girls who are arrested for this offense are actually arrested for incorrigibility or "injurious behavior," compared with only one-third of the boys (Chesney-Lind, 1987: 210).

Both girls and boys are arrested in large numbers for alcohol-related offenses, but burglary and vandalism (which account for

Table 2. Rank Order of Arrests for Juveniles, 1985 and 1995
(figures based upon percent distribution within each sex cohort)

Male		Female	
1985	1995	1985	1995
(1) Larceny–Theft (20.2)	Larceny–Theft (17.1)	Larceny–Theft (26.4)	Larceny–Theft (23.8)
(2) All Other (16.8)[1]	All Other (15.8)	Runaway (20.2)	Runaway (21.1)
(3) Burglary (10.0)	Drugs (8.3)	All Other (15.4)	All Other (13.2)
(4) Vandalism (6.6)	Other Assaults (7.6)	Liquor Laws (7.3)	Other Assaults (8.4)
(5) Liquor Laws (5.8)	Burglary (6.0)	Other Assaults (4.9)	Disorderly Conduct (5.5)

	Male		Female	
	1985	1995	1985	1995
Arrests for Serious Violent Offenses[2]	4.9	6.5	2.1	3.2
Arrests for All Violent Offenses[3]	9.6	14.1	7.0	11.6
Arrests for Status Offenses[4]	8.2	10.5	24.6	27.5

SOURCE: *Uniform Crime Reports,* 1971, 1981, 1995.

[1]"All Other" refers to a variety of offenses, usually state and local ordinances. Among the most common include public nuisance, trespassing, failure to appear on warrants, contempt of court, and. for juveniles especially, violation of various court orders (e.g., probation, parole) and certain status offenses. This category does not include traffic offenses.
[2]Arrests for murder, robbery, rape, and aggravated assault.
[3]Also includes arrests for other assaults, a Part II crime.
[4]Arrests for curfew and runaway.

12 percent of boys' offenses) are relatively unimportant in girls' delinquency (accounting for only 4 percent of their arrests). Generally, official delinquency is dominated by less serious offenses, and this is particularly true of female delinquency. A ranking of offenses that account for the greatest number of girls' and boys' arrests over time (Table 2) shows this clearly. For the past two decades, boys were most likely to have been arrested for larceny–theft. That offense is also important in girls' arrests, accounting for over a quarter of all girls' arrests in 1980 and 1995 and just under a quarter in 1970. Running away also dominates girls' arrests, constituting just over one-fourth in 1970 and about one out of five in 1980 and 1995. Thus, running away and larceny–theft have dominated girls' delinquency arrests since 1970, and together these two offenses have accounted for roughly one-half of all female arrests.

The delinquency of boys does not show that degree of concentration. For example, the top five arrest categories in 1995 accounted for nearly three-quarters (72 percent) of all girls' arrests but only slightly over half (54.8 percent) of the total for boys.

This discussion brings up other salient questions: What are the trends in female delinquency? Are there more female delinquents today? Are they more likely than their counterparts of a previous time period to commit "masculine offenses"? FBI data for the past few decades reveal some interesting patterns. First, the number of girls arrested rose dramatically during the 1960s and early 1970s—between 1960 and 1975, for example, by around 250 percent (Federal Bureau of Investigation, 1976: 183). Statistics like these, particularly when coupled with increases in the arrests of girls for nontraditional offenses, such as a 503.5 percent hike in the arrests of teenage girls for serious, violent crimes, encouraged many to believe that the women's movement had triggered a crime wave among young women (Adler, 1975). The controversy—both theoretical and empirical—that emerged around what some have called the "liberation hypothesis" is an important one. The impact the perspective had on theories about girls' crime will be discussed later in this book. Here, we examine the arrest trends in further detail to determine what the data actually show about the amount and character of girls' delinquency since 1970.

Examining the data in Tables 3 and 4, we see several trends. First, although for some offenses the rate of increases for girls has been higher than that for boys, such increases are due in part to the relatively low base rate for the girls in 1970. Further, for the most part, as arrests for girls have gone up, so too have the arrests for boys. In other words, the patterns appear to be similar for both sexes. Second, while it could be argued that for some crimes girls are "catching up" the fact of the matter is that boys clearly outnumber girls for most major crimes, with the exception of larceny–theft.

What does need to be explored in some detail here are the recent increases in girls' arrests for violent offenses. As noted in both Tables 3 and 4, both in terms of rates per 100,000 and the proportion of arrests accounted for by girls, arrests for these kinds of offenses have increased. The increases are greatest for two specific offenses in particular: aggravated assaults and "other assaults," especially since the 1980s. However, almost equally high increases occurred for boys. The arrest rates for girls for aggravated assault increased by 118 percent between 1970 and 1980, by 112 percent between 1980 and 1995, and by 364 percent from 1970 to 1995. For boys, though, increases of 103 percent between 1970 and 1980, 45 percent between 1980 and 1995, and 195 percent between 1970 and 1995 occurred. Thus, both girls and boys showed rather large increases for this crime (Table 4). For the offense "other assaults," girls' arrest rates increased by 83 percent between 1970 and 1980, by 142 percent between 1980 and 1995, and by 343 percent between 1970 and 1995. For boys, these increases were 75 percent, 80 percent, and 215 percent, respectively. In other words, arrests for violent crime have increased rather dramatically during the past two decades for juveniles in general, both boys and girls.

There are several possible explanations for the increases in arrests for these two violent offenses. First, many of these increases could be attributed to the increase in girls' involvement in gang-related offenses. However, at the same time, the increase in actual *arrests* could also be an artifact of increased police attention to the gang problem, rather than a real increase in violent behavior. Second, some of the increase could be attributed to increasing attention toward the problem of domestic violence, which has resulted in more arrests for both males and females. Third, and perhaps more important, there is evidence to suggest that in recent years many of the arrests on these charges may be because of greater attention to normal adolescent fighting and/or girls fighting with parents.[1] In past times such aggression was ignored or dealt with informally. Fourth, some of this increase is undoubtedly a reflection of a real increase in violence, which may be a reflection of larger and more structural problems in modern society that are causing greater violence among both male *and* female youth (e.g., poverty, violence at home, lack of hope, poor educational and occupational opportunities, the increase in the amount and sophistication of modern weaponry, and the increasing norm accepting the carrying and/or use of weapons in our society).

Labeling girls as "violent" or "more violent" than at some point in the past is a process of social construction. Feminist criminologists have criticized traditional schools of criminology for assuming that male delinquency, even in its most violent forms, was somehow an understandable if not "normal" response to their situations. Girls who shared the same social and cultural milieu as delinquent boys but who were not violent were somehow abnormal or "over-controlled" (Cain, 1989). Essentially, law-abiding behavior on the part of at least some boys and men is taken as a sign of character, but when women avoid crime and violence, it is an expression of weakness (Naffine, 1987). The other side of this equation is that *if* girls engage in even minor forms of violence, they are somehow more vicious than their male counterparts. In this fashion, the construction of an artificial, passive femininity lays the foundation for the demonization of young girls of color, as has been the case in the media treatment of girl gang members. . . . Also, from the media we often get the interpretation that when there are increases in male violence the response is something like "so what else is new?" but when there's an increase in girls' violence something fundamental is wrong or there is a "new breed" of "violent women" roaming the streets and threatening the social order.

Many now suspect that changes, both upward and downward, in juvenile arrests are greatly affected by demographic changes in the age distribution of the American population. Increases in delinquency occurred as the baby-boom generation moved through adolescence (and the crime-generating ages of fifteen through twenty-four), and decreases occurred the next few years during the "baby-bust" generation. There is concern that surges may accompany the 1990s as the children of the baby-boom generation enter adolescence, though most experts do not expect a major change in the character or rates of delinquency until the year 2000 (Steffensmeier and Harer, 1987).

If we consider the girls' share of all juvenile arrests, a more complex picture emerges. As noted in Table 3, the share has remained more or less stable at between 22 and 26 percent between 1986 and 1995. There were gains made in most of the Part I crimes, although their overall contribution to these arrests increased by about 5 percent between 1986 and 1995. Perhaps the most significant increase came with the category of "larceny-theft." While girls constituted about one-fourth of all arrests for this offense in 1986, they accounted for almost one-third in 1995, while their share of all Part I property crimes went from 20 percent in 1986 to just over one-fourth in 1995.

A decrease occurred in girls' share of arrests for drugs, with an overall decrease of about two percent between 1986 and 1995, continuing a downward trend that began in the mid-1970s. Between 1986 and 1995 the girls' share of arrests showed growth in seven Part I crime categories (for an overall increase of five percent) and in eight categories of Part II offenses, but in all categories the [share] was less than five percent.

More important, the increases seen during this past quarter of a century in the tra-

ditionally female areas of crime were not signaling an upward spiral in girls' illegal activities. As an illustration of this, consider larceny-theft. In 1970 about 26 percent of all juveniles arrested for this offense were females; by 1980, about the same percentage of such arrestees were female. By 1995, the percentage went up by only about 6 percent. For the crime of fraud, the female share increased by about 5 percent from 1970 to 1986, then decreased by about 2 percent between 1986 and 1995.

Turning to consideration of arrests of girls for nontraditional, "masculine" offenses, girls under eighteen constituted 10.9 percent of all those arrested for violent index offenses in 1986 and 14.6 percent in 1995. This means the change that did occur in the female share of index offenses is largely explained by increases in girls' arrests for property crimes, notably larceny-theft. Indeed, arrests of girls made up 20.5 percent of all the index property crime arrests in 1986 and 26.1 percent in 1995. So girls' share of all index crimes went from 19.3 percent in 1986 to 24.1 percent in 1995, but almost none of the increase is explained by arrests for serious violent offenses (see Table 3).

During the same period, girls' share of arrests for curfew violation climbed steadily, while their share of runaway arrests remained virtually the same. The shift occurred during a period when various national and state legislative initiatives encouraged the diversion from official processing of youth suspected of committing status offenses.

Still another way of looking at arrest trends is rates per 100,000 population (aged five to seventeen). Because there are more males than females within this cohort, rates can provide a more reliable comparison of differences between female and male delinquency. Table 4 gives arrest rates for each offense category for the years 1970, 1980, and 1995 and reflects much the same pattern seen in the raw arrest data, though the shifts in girls' delinquency are far less dramatic because the rates control for changes in population size. Arrest rates for both males and females increased significantly between 1970 and 1980 for almost all offenses, but then either leveled off or decreased after 1980. The relative gap between males and females has narrowed for several offense categories during the past twenty-five years; however, most of the narrowing began to take place after 1965 and continued until the early 1980s. During most of the 1980s the rates remained fairly stable, but beginning in the latter part of the decade (around 1988) an increase was observed for both males and females. Between 1980 and 1995 the arrest rates for girls increased for most index crimes, with the exception of burglary, yet similar patterns can be seen for boys' arrest rates. Despite these changes, male arrest

Table 3. Girls' Share of all Juvenile Arrests, 1986 and 1995, Index Crimes and Selected Part II Offenses

	1986	1995
Part I Crimes		
Homicide	6.8	5.8
Rape	1.7	2.2
Robbery	6.9	9.2
Aggravated Assault	15.4	19.6
Burglary	7.7	9.9
Larceny–Theft	26.7	32.4
Motor Vehicle Theft	10.9	14.8
Arson	10.3	12.2
Total Violent	10.9	14.6
Total Property	20.5	26.1
Total Index	19.3	24.1
Selected Part II Crimes		
Other Assaults	23.0	27.6
Fraud	24.3	26.1
Stolen Property	9.3	12.1
Vandalism	9.1	10.6
Weapons	6.4	8.0
Drugs	14.1	12.5
Liquor Laws	26.0	28.8
Disorderly Conduct	18.6	23.2
Curfew	24.8	29.8
Runaway	57.8	57.6
All Other	20.4	22.3
Total Arrests	22.2	25.6

SOURCE: FBI, 1972: 126; 1981: 199; 1996: 213.

rates continue to be considerably higher than female rates for most offenses, especially the most serious offenses (e.g., homicide, rape, robbery, aggravated assault, burglary).

A similar but more detailed analysis of arrest trends of young people was undertaken by Steffensmeier and Steffensmeier (1980), although for an earlier period of time (1965–1977). They, too, noted that female rates rose in most offense categories, with large increases occurring in the categories of larceny–theft, liquor law and narcotic drug law violations, and running away. However, male arrest rates also rose during the same period, showing a pattern generally similar to that of the female arrest rates. The trend continued well into the 1980s and early 1990s. In other words, patterns of both male and female arrests have, with few exceptions, paralleled each other; when one goes up, so does the other.

In general, what the Steffensmeiers noted (and what our more recent data show) is that the offenses that have accounted for large increases in female arrests are "traditionally female" and are in areas where changes in enforcement practices have also been occur-

Table 4. Juvenile Arrest Rates (per 100,000 population aged 5–17), 1970, 1980, 1995

	Female			Male		
	1970	1980	1995	1970	1980	1995
Part I Crimes						
Homicide	*	*	*	5	6	9
Rape	*	*	*	11	17	15
Robbery	8	12	16	99	160	153
Aggravated Assault	11	24	51	64	130	189
Burglary	25	58	43	498	819	388
Larceny Theft	298	466	526	818	1265	1055
Motor Vehicle Theft	14	25	41	240	212	241
Arson	1	4	4	18	30	22
Total Violent	19	38	70	179	314	407
Total Property	337	553	615	1556	2326	1714
Total Index	356	590	684	1735	2640	2121
Part II Crimes						
Other Assaults	40	73	177	149	261	469
Forgery	5	12	10	18	26	17
Fraud	3	9	20	12	22	54
Embezzlement	*	1	1	*	3	2
Stolen Property	5	13	16	62	128	119
Vandalism	20	39	49	262	431	409
Weapons .	3	6	17	59	91	181
Prostitution	3	9	2	1	3	2
Other Sex Offenses	8	3	4	29	42	49
Drugs	65	70	60	216	340	435
Gambling	*	*	*	6	7	5
Offenses Against Family	*	3	6	2	5	10
DUI	*	13	6	16	108	33
Liquor Laws	47	134	102	210	442	244
Drunkenness	20	25	9	123	150	46
Disorderly Conduct	79	90	123	363	401	385
Vagrancy	9	3	3	41	13	12
Curfew	80	67	118	292	207	279
Runaway	335	355	351	300	243	251
All Other	209	244	295	631	948	1001
Total	1289	1761	2054	4538	6510	6124

SOURCE: FBI. 1971: 126; 1981: 199; 1996: 213.
* Less than 1 per 100,000.

ring. For example, the authors remarked that stores today are more likely to insist on the arrest of people they suspect of shoplifting than they were in the past. With respect to the arrests of young women for specific violent "masculine" crimes (murder, aggravated assault, robbery, other assaults, and weapons offenses), there was a slight contraction of the gap between males and females; however, much of the apparent female gain was due to an increase in the arrests of girls for "other assaults" that are "relatively nonserious in nature and tend to consist of being bystanders or companions to males involved in skirmishes" (Steffensmeier and Steffensmeier, 1980: 70). Juvenile crime, like its adult counterpart, is still mainly a male issue. Note that in 1995 the male rate for violent crime arrests was almost six times greater than the female rate.

By way of summary, although the number of youths arrested in the United States swelled remarkably during the 1970s, the increases did not signal major changes in the character of official delinquency. Patterns of female juvenile arrests have remained the same during the past twenty-five years, except that the relative gap between males and females has diminished for some offenses. Females have typically been arrested for the following offenses: running away, larceny–theft (mostly shoplifting), liquor law violations, curfew violations, disorderly conduct, other assaults, and the catchall category "all other offenses" (which, for girls, may include many arrests for certain status offenses). Males, in contrast, have been less likely to be arrested for status offenses and more likely to be arrested for property offenses (especially burglary and vandalism) and drug offenses.

Arrest statistics, though, tell only part of the story, for several shortcomings characterize the reports published annually by the FBI. An obvious problem is that the FBI's figures are based upon police contacts that result in an arrest. However, the police do not arrest all of those who have committed an offense (see Hagan, 1987: 29–31, and Barlow, 1987: 88–111). . . . [P]olice officers "contact" many more youths than they arrest. These two facts make it possible that arrest statistics are as much a measure of police behavior as they are of criminal behavior. For a more complete picture of the extent of female delinquency, it is also necessary to examine a very popular alternative source of information on the volume of delinquency: self-report surveys. In such surveys people respond anonymously to questionnaires or participate anonymously in interviews about their delinquent activities, especially about acts that never come to the attention of the police.

SELF-REPORT SURVEYS

Researchers have long used self-report surveys to attempt to gain information about the extent of juvenile delinquency. Typically, the surveys reveal that female delinquency is more common than arrest statistics indicate and that there are more similarities than official statistics suggest between male and female juvenile delinquency. They also show males are more involved in delinquency, especially the most serious types of offenses. These findings point to some possible gender biases operating within the juvenile justice system because the picture of female delinquency that emerges from the self-report data shows about as many boys as girls committing status offenses.

Concerning the volume of unreported female delinquency, Cernkovich and Giordano (1979) found that although the ratio of male to female arrestees was approximately 4:1 in the late seventies, that ratio was twice as large as the mean ratio of 2.18:1 that they found in their self-report data. Similar findings have also been reported in other self-report studies (Canter, 1982: 374).

In a comprehensive review of self-report studies published between 1955 and 1977, Steffensmeier and Steffensmeier (1980) noted that male–female differences tend to be greater for crimes of violence and serious property crimes. Males and females report similar rates (especially in more recent surveys) for such offenses as truancy, driving without a license, running away from home, and minor forms of theft. The fact that males and females are about equally as likely to admit running away is interesting because females are much more likely to be arrested (as already indicated) and to be referred to the juvenile court for this offense. . . . This interpretation is underscored by a study conducted by Teilmann and Landry (1981), who compared girls' contribution to arrests for runaway and incorrigibility with girls' self-reports of these two activities. They found about a 10 percent overrepresentation of girls among those arrested for runaway and an astounding 31 percent overrepresentation in arrests for incorrigibility.

These findings were confirmed and amplified by a reanalysis of National Youth Survey data (Canter, 1982) that indicated that both male and female delinquency did rise during the 1967–1977 decade—especially in the offense categories of marijuana use, truancy, and alcohol use—but the increases were similar for both males and females. In other words, there was no evidence that the character of girls' delinquency changed during a decade characterized by considerable discussion of women's roles. Instead, reports from this national probability sample of 1,725 youths aged thirteen to sixteen showed parallel increases in the involvement in certain delinquent behaviors but stability in the sex differences in delinquent behavior.

It might be useful to consider in some detail a picture of female delinquency drawn from self-report surveys. One good example is the just-mentioned National Youth Survey reanalysis by Canter (1982). Examining categories of offenses over time, the study found much similarity between female and male delinquency and found that there was no behavior in which girls were significantly more involved than boys—even in offenses traditionally ascribed to girls (such as prostitution and running away from home).

These findings might lead one to the conclusion that delinquency is almost exclusively a male problem, but that is not really the case. For example, no statistically significant differences appeared in boys' and girls' involvement in 40 percent of the behaviors examined. Even when differences did appear, they were such that, in the author's words, "their statistical significance overstates their practical significance" because there was considerable overlap between male and female distributions and "males and females display comparable patterns of offenses in terms of proportions as well as means" (Canter, 1982: 380). What this suggests is that, as in many other areas of research into gender differences, emphasis on the ways in which male and female behavior differs often obscures the fact that the behaviors engaged in by most youths are actually very similar; it is only at the extremes that a gender difference emerges.

This perspective on gender differences should be kept in mind as we review more closely a self-report survey of midwestern youths by Cernkovich and Giordano (1979) that provides details on female delinquency and how it differs from male misbehavior. By examining behaviors in which boys clearly dominate and those in which girls and boys are involved to like extents, we can

more rewardingly discuss differences and similarities in self-reported delinquent behavior. Table 5 divides self-reported delinquency into three categories: one in which the proportion of males admitting commission of the offense exceeds the female proportion by a considerable margin, one in which the proportion of males only moderately exceeds females, and one in which almost equal numbers of girls and boys admit having committed the offense.

Turning to male-dominated offenses, it can be seen that the category includes almost all of the violent offenses. Boys are more likely to report involvement in gang fighting, carrying a hidden weapon, strong-arming students and others, aggravated assault, hitting students, and sexual assault.

Boys are also disproportionately involved in serious property crimes; they are much more likely to report involvement in thefts of more than $50, and they are somewhat more likely to report lesser thefts (between $5 and $50). However, other property crimes show fewer gender differences than one might expect: motor vehicle theft shows a male-to-female ratio of 2.6:1; burglary, 3.88:1; and joyriding, 2.37:1 (all based upon the proportion of youths ever committing the offenses). These gender gaps are certainly of a smaller magnitude than those found in official statistics. Of interest, too, is the male dominance in some offenses that are considered traditionally "feminine," such as prostitution and sexual intercourse.

Concerning offenses in which differences in the proportions of males and females involved are less marked, some surprises appear. For example, vandalism is often seen as a "male" offense, but if one considers damaging family property, almost as many girls commit that offense as boys (male/female, 1.5:1). The strong-arming of teachers (1.8:1) and even hitting of teachers (1.9:1) show less gender difference than one might anticipate. Finally, boys dominate slightly in the selling of drugs and the procurement of alcohol (although when frequency is considered, boys tend to commit more of these acts than girls do).

In regard to offenses in which the gender difference is minimal, girls are about as likely as males to have used a variety of drugs (alcohol, marijuana, barbiturates, amphetamines, and cocaine). They are also about as likely to have run away from home, skipped classes, and engaged in disorderly conduct, as well as to have hit their parents.

The unexpected similarity in girls' and boys' violence against parents highlights another problem with some of the offense categories used in arrest statistics: categories can obscure significant differences in specific behaviors and in responses to these behaviors. Consider, for example, property damage. The National Youth Survey found that girls damage family property and males tend to damage other kinds of property (e.g.,

school property). A similar pattern appears in the area of assault, with girls closing the gender gap when simple assault against parents is considered. This pattern suggests that the setting in which delinquent behavior occurs and the relationship between victim and assailant differ for males and females in many offenses. These differences may have important implications for reporting, and for reactions of juvenile justice officials.

To return again to the data in Table 5, it should be noted that for certain offenses there were almost no gender differences. Two of these were status offenses, such as running away from home (male/female ratio, .99:1) and defying parental authority (.97:1), which often result in a charge of "incorrigibility or unmanageability" in the juvenile court. These offenses are interesting because they focus on the critical role of family relationships in the generation and labeling of female and male delinquency. . . . [A]lthough both boys and girls commit these offenses, many "delinquent" acts that bring girls into the juvenile justice system are the result of problems, conflicts, and disagreements between girls and members of their families. Boys, although they admit these behaviors, appear less likely to be officially arrested and processed for them.

Cernkovich and Giordano also found that various sex offenses, drug (including alcohol) use, minor forms of theft, disturbances, and school-related offenses tend to be about equally committed by male and female adolescents. As does the National Youth Survey, the data in their study show how similar males and females are in offense patterns. For twenty-four of the thirty-six delinquent acts included, the male/female ratio was less than 2:1. More recent surveys confirm the lack of gender differences in most drug and alcohol use. For instance, the most recent annual survey of high school seniors conducted by the Institute for Social Research (University of Michigan) found that in 1993, 87 percent of the males and 87.2 percent of the females said that they had used alcohol. Males were slightly more likely to say they had smoked marijuana (38.9 percent vs. 31.2 percent of the females), used cocaine (7.5 percent of the males and 4.6 percent of the females), and used heroin (1.5 percent of the males and 0.7 percent of the females) (Maguire and Pastore, 1994: 325–326).

The Cernkovich and Giordano survey also focused on frequency of delinquency. For males, offenses committed more than once were most likely to be skipping school, disobeying parents, sex with the opposite sex, use of alcohol and marijuana, gambling, and disturbing the peace. For females, an almost identical list appears: skipping school, disobeying parents, sex with the opposite sex, and use of alcohol and marijuana. The authors stressed that for both males and females, the most serious offenses were committed only once.

Table 5. Self-Reported Delinquency, by Sex

	Percent Engaging in Act One or More Times		
	MALE	FEMALE	RATIO
Acts Predominantly Male (2:1 ratio or greater)			
Theft of Car Parts	20.4	3.2	6.37
Robbery	5.0	0.9	5.55
Car Theft	5.5	1.1	5.00
Sex for Money	5.3	1.1	4.82
Burglary (unoccupied)	16.5	3.7	4.86
Burglary (occupied)	9.7	2.3	4.22
Property Destruction (>$10)	20.3	5.9	3.44
Joyride	18.1	6.1	2.97
Theft (>$50)	12.7	4.6	2.76
Gang Fight	38.9	14.5	2.68
Property Destruction (<$10)	36.6	16.1	2.27
Carry Weapon	34.3	17.1	2.01
Acts Moderately Male (ratio 1.5 to 1.99)			
Attack Someone with Fists	47.8	25.1	1.90
DVI Marijuana	40.1	21.8	1.85
Sell Marijuana	35.2	19.5	1.80
Use Weapon to Attack Someone	11.6	6.6	1.76
DUI Liquor	38.1	21.8	1.75
Extortion	13.6	8.3	1.64
Drive Without Permission	41.7	25.4	1.64
DUI Hard Drugs	11.7	7.2	1.62
Acts About Equally Male and Female (ratio <1.5)			
Gamble	85.3	60.8	1.40
Use Fake ID	34.8	26.5	1.31
Theft ($2–$50)	33.9	26.0	1.30
Sex with Same Sex	4.2	3.3	1.27
Sex with Opposite Sex	77.7	62.0	1.25
Sell Hard Drugs	11.6	9.5	1.22
School Probation/Suspension/Expulsion	31.8	26.6	1.19
Theft (<$2)	66.5	58.2	1.14
Drink Alcohol	82.8	72.6	1.14
Smoke Marijuana	67.2	58.7	1.14
Disturb the Peace	71.6	68.9	1.04
Skip School	81.7	80.8	1.01
Ran Away from Home	16.0	16.1	0.99
Defy Parents' Authority	40.7	42.1	0.97
Disobey Parents	89.6	93.6	0.96
Use Hard Drugs	14.8	19.3	0.77

SOURCE: Cernkovich and Giordano, 1979: 136–137.

Other studies confirm the overall pattern found in the two studies discussed so far and add additional details about male dominance among the more serious offenses. In one study, a sample of 1,735 fifteen-year-olds in a midwestern county showed that males were about four times as likely as females to commit burglary and auto theft, six times as likely to commit a theft of between $50 and $500, and about three times as likely to commit an aggravated assault (Figueira-McDonough, Barton, and Sarri, 1981). Similarly, Kratcoski and Kratcoski (1975) found that males were five times as likely to commit a theft of $50 or more, six times as likely

to commit a burglary, and three times as likely to commit a robbery. However, both surveys found great similarity when it came to minor offenses.

More recent self-report data tells the same basic story. Table 6 shows data collected from the annual survey of high school seniors by the University of Michigan (Maguire and Pastore, 1994: 312–313). As shown here, males are far more likely than females to commit most of these offenses, with the exception of "argued/had fight with parents," for which females had the edge, however slight (such an offense could no doubt result in a referral to juvenile court on

a charge of "unmanageable" or "incorrigible" or some similar status offense). According to this survey, males are far more violent in their actions than females, in addition to being involved in more serious property offenses. Aside from arguing and/or having fights with parents, girls were most often involved in minor property offenses. Curiously, relatively few of these youths were ever arrested and taken to the police station, especially the girls.

What is interesting to note about this particular annual survey is that we have access to data going back to 1981. An examination of 1981 data compared to 1993 data is that with a small number of exceptions there have been few changes in the percent of seniors reportedly engaging in such behaviors. In fact, for *every* one of the offenses noted in Table 6 except for "damaged property at work," there have been *decreases* in the proportion of both boys and girls engaging in such behavior since the year 1981!

Self-report studies, then, suggest that female delinquency is more prevalent than official statistics lead one to believe. The content of girls' delinquency is similar to male delinquency in that most are of minor seriousness, but girls commit offenses far less frequently than do boys. Some researchers (Hindelang, 1979) have suggested that it is frequency rather than character of delinquent behavior that explains the dominance by boys in the arrest statistics. That might account for the prominence of boys among those arrested for violent offenses, but not for the overrepresentation of girls among youths charged with status offenses and prostitution.

DELINQUENT CAREERS

The past several decades have witnessed considerable interest in delinquent "careers." Most of the research has been longitudinal, which means that a sample of youths is examined over a given period to explore the extensiveness of their involvement in delinquent behavior. Most studies have measured delinquency by using contact with police or courts (Visher and Roth, 1986), which, as we have seen, may exaggerate the gender difference in delinquency; nonetheless, they provide an important perspective on girls' official delinquent careers.

Longitudinal research has revealed not only that adolescent males are more actively involved in delinquent behavior (in terms of number and seriousness of offenses that bring them to official attention) but also that their "careers" go on longer than those of females. In one of the most comprehensive studies, Tracy, Wolfgang, and Figlio (1985) examined the arrest records of all youths born in Philadelphia in 1958 who resided there between their tenth and seventeenth birthdays, a total of 28,338 youths. (See

Wolfgang, Figlio, and Sellin, 1972, for an earlier study of an all-male Philadelphia birth cohort.) They found that whereas 32.8 percent of the males had at least one police contact before their eighteenth birthday, this was true for only 14.1 percent of the females. Male delinquency, as measured by arrest, was also more serious. The male offense rate overall was four times greater than that for females, but the ratio was almost 9:1 for index offenses and 14:1 for violent index offenses. Girls were also one-and-a-half times more likely to be "one-time delinquents" (Tracy, Wolfgang, and Figlio, 1985: 6).

Other studies use data from the National Survey of Health and Development (Mulligan et al., 1963; Douglas et al., 1966; Wadsworth, 1979), which followed 5,362 children drawn from a cohort born between March 3 and March 9, 1946, in England, Wales, and Scotland. These studies found lower arrest rates for both boys and girls than was the case in the Philadelphia cohort; 18 percent of the males but only 3 percent of the females were "convicted or cautioned by the police" by their eighteenth birthday. The national survey also followed both male and female offenders into their adult years; Wadsworth reports (1979: 103) that by age twenty-one only 2 percent of the girls, compared with 15.3 percent of the boys, had an adult arrest. Some years later, Ouston (1984), using a later (1959–1960) inner-city London birth cohort, found figures closer to those of the Philadelphia researchers: 29 percent of the males and 6 percent of the females had arrest records (see also Edwards, 1973).

Shannon (1982) gives us a sense of changes in delinquent careers, as measured by arrest, over time by using data from three birth cohorts (1942, 1949, 1955) in Racine, Wisconsin. In the 1942 cohort, 41.0 percent of the males and 8.7 percent of the females had at least one arrest; in the 1949 cohort, 47.3 percent and 15.1 percent, respectively; in the 1955 cohort, 44.1 percent and 22.2 percent.

These studies have found that boys' delinquent careers (usually as measured by police contact or arrest) are longer than girls' careers. Moreover, males are more likely to extend their delinquent careers into their adult lives and are more likely to begin their careers at an earlier age. There is also some indication that studies done with more recent cohorts show larger numbers of girls being contacted or arrested by police. However, there may be a problem sketching out the shape of delinquent careers by using official contacts as a measure of delinquency because arrests are, in a sense, measures of police attitudes and practices as well.

Fortunately, the dynamics of self-reported female delinquency have also been explored using the National Youth Study data. Ageton (1983) followed a sample of

Table 6. High School Seniors Reporting Involvement in Delinquent Activities in the Last 12 Months, 1993, by Gender (percent engaging at least once)

	Male	Female
Argued/had fight with parents	84.5	92.0
Hit instructor/supervisor	6.7	1.7
Got into serious fight in school or at work	21.6	13.0
Took part in fight with group of friends against another group	29.0	14.5
Hurt someone badly enough to need bandages or doctor	21.4	5.0
Used gun or knife or other weapon to get something from a person	8.1	1.0
Took something not belonging to you worth under $50	40.1	23.5
Took something not belonging to you worth over $50	17.5	4.4
Took something from a store without paying for it	37.6	23.3
Took car not belonging to you or someone in your family	8.8	3.8
Went into some house/building when you weren't supposed to be there	34.1	17.5
Set fire to someone's property on purpose	5.9	0.9
Damaged school property on purpose	11.5	2.0
Was arrested and taken to police station	14.5	4.5

SOURCE: K. Maguire and A. L. Pastore (eds.), *Sourcebook on Criminal Justice Statistics, 1993* (Washington. DC: U.S. Department of Justice, Bureau of Justice Statistics, 1994): 312–313.

girls aged eleven through seventeen through the years 1976 to 1980 (when they were between fifteen and twenty-one) and ascertained diminished incidence of offending as they matured. The decline was particularly marked in connection with assaultive crimes: the proportion of females involved fell from 36 percent to 12 percent. One particular item is noteworthy: hitting other students was by far the most common kind of aggressive offense engaged in by the girls (this behavior is also one of the most commonly included in the FBI category known as "other assaults" that has shown an increase in recent years) (Ageton, 1983: 562).

Although the National Youth Study does not enable us to examine status offenses in any great detail, a study by Datesman and Aickin (1984) gives us a look at this important subgroup. The two researchers examined offense specialization and escalation among status offenders by means of a sample of offenders referred to a Delaware family court. Some persons, especially juvenile court officials, have argued that court intervention with status offenders is justified because without it, these youths will "escalate" into more serious offenderhood.

Datesman and Aickin also investigated both self-report and official delinquency data in this sample (N = 634) and followed up the offenders three years later. Both kinds of data indicated that it would be reasonable to create a "specialized status offender group," at least among those whose first referral to court was for a status offense; this was particularly true for girls (Datesman and Aickin, 1984: 1273). Further, the researchers discovered that status offenders rarely returned to court (between 60 percent and 80 percent did not, depending upon the specific offense);

when they did return, it was almost always for another status offense. This was, again, particularly true for female offenders. Almost identical findings were reported in a longitudinal study of juvenile court referrals in Las Vegas (Shelden, Horvath, and Tracy, 1989).

In total, these studies suggest that girls' official delinquent careers are shorter and involve less serious offenses than do the careers of boys. Even in areas having to do with typically "female" offenses, such as status offenses, girls appear to desist after one referral to court rather than continuing to commit offenses. There is also some indirect indication that in recent years more and more girls have been contacted by police. Because self-report delinquency studies point to no great change in girls' behavior, such arrests may be a result of changes in police behavior....

RACIAL DIFFERENCES

There are many important racial differences in female delinquency. Rates of involvement in delinquent activity (as measured by both official and self-report data) show black males with the highest level, followed by white males, black females, and white females. Some studies indicate a rate of involvement for black females very close to that for white males. For instance, Tracy Wolfgang, and Figlio (1985) found that 18.5 percent of the black females had at least one arrest, compared to 22.7 percent of the white males. In contrast, about 9 percent of the white females had at least one arrest. They also noted that 6.0 percent of the black females had at least one arrest for an index

Table 7. Race and Sex Differences for Selected Offenses (based upon self-report data)

| | Percent Committing | | | |
| | MALE | | FEMALE | |
Offense	WHITE	BLACK	WHITE	BLACK
Theft ($50+)	16.5	17.3	1.7	6.5
Auto Theft	9.7	7.3	0.8	1.7
Burglary	16.8	12.9	4.9	4.3
Aggravated Assault	10.2	15.4	3.1	8.9
Robbery	4.1	7.9	0.7	5.3

SOURCE: Hindelang, Hirschi, and Weis, 1981: Appendix B.

crime, compared to 8.9 percent of the white males. For nonindex offenses, the percentages were 15.7 percent and 19.9 percent, respectively. Data from this most recent Philadelphia birth cohort to be studied have been used in two unpublished dissertations (Facella, 1983; Otten, 1985).

One of the most interesting findings was that among both white and nonwhite females, running away from home and a category called "missing person" constituted almost one-half of all offenses (46.3 percent for white females, 46.5 percent for nonwhite females). Both white males and females were proportionately much more likely than their nonwhite counterparts to be arrested for victimless and public-order offenses, such as drug offenses and public disturbances (Otten, 1985: 105–106). Finally, there were differences between white and nonwhite females concerning delinquent careers. Among the nonwhite females, 8.1 percent were "chronic recidivists" (five or more arrests); among white females, 4.9 percent (Facella, 1983: 218–219).

An analysis of delinquent careers based upon a longitudinal study of 863 youths first referred to juvenile court in 1980 in Las Vegas found significant racial differences, but slightly less evidence that those differences override gender differences (Shelden, 1987). Specifically, the total participation rates per 1,000 population aged ten to seventeen in Clark County were highest for nonwhite males (40.1 percent), followed by white males (20.8 percent), nonwhite females (14.1 percent), and white females (9.9 percent). A reasonable inference is that nonwhite females are closer to white females than they are to nonwhite males.

Self-report studies shed additional light on this subject. For instance, Jensen and Eve (1976) reported that 2 percent of the black females committed theft of $50 or more, compared with 1 percent of the white females; for auto theft, however, there was no difference, with 4 percent of each group reporting the offense. Hindelang, Hirschi, and Weis (1981), in their self-report study, found

that black females were much more likely than white females to admit committing theft of $50 or more, auto theft, aggravated assault, and robbery, but that both black and white girls were about equally involved in burglary. For two major offenses, robbery and aggravated assault, black females were very close to white males. The data from the latter study are illustrated in Table 7.

In the self-report study by Cernkovich and Giordano cited earlier, there were several interesting differences in the types of delinquency admitted by white and nonwhite girls. The researchers found statistically significant differences in the types of delinquent acts illustrated in Table 8.

The patterns noted here are obvious: non-white females seem, in this study, to be more likely to engage in personal crimes, and white females are more likely to be involved in drug- or alcohol-related offenses (some very serious) and status offenses. However, note that white girls engage in more delinquent behavior. Additionally, and perhaps more important, the study found that there were no significant differences for 50 percent of the acts surveyed. In other words, white females engage in more delinquent activity, but much of this is a function of their higher levels of involvement in drug-related offenses and some status offenses (Cernkovich and Giordano, 1979).

The National Youth Survey also reviewed racial differences in female delinquency. Its findings, too, suggest caution in interpretation of data. First, NYS researchers discovered that no racial differences existed between 1976 and 1980 when delinquent behavior as a whole was considered. Blacks tended to report more violent offenses, but there was a marked decline in both incidence (percentage committing at least one offense) and prevalence (total offenses committed over time) in girls' commission of such offenses. Frequency of theft increased for whites and decreased for blacks during this period, showing a 2:1 white-to-black ratio. Moreover, the racial differential was strong in 1976 but not in 1980. Indeed, although

black girls always displayed the higher scores, the white/black ratio dropped from 1.4 in 1979 to almost 1.1 in 1980 (Ageton, 1983: 577). The study also found, in following a specific cohort over time, that black girls initially reported greater involvement in theft offenses, yet by the middle of the study years, white girls surpassed black girls on almost all theft items.

The association of race with assaultive offenses is also slight, with "the overriding trend for decreasing or relatively stable involvement in assaultive crimes" as both black and white girls matured (Ageton, 1983: 565). Also, although the proportions of blacks involved in these offenses are generally higher, white girls are significantly more likely to report the hitting of parents.

Cautions about racial differences in female delinquency, particularly violent delinquency, are raised by another study. Laub and McDermott (1985) examined 1973–1981 national victimization data for personal crimes, looking for trends in crimes committed by young black women. They were specifically interested in evidence of what they called the "convergence" theory of black male and female offending—the notion that the big differences between white male and white female delinquency are not found between black male and female delinquents. Their findings did not support the notion. Despite much fluctuation during the years Laub and McDermott studied, the highest personal crime rates (per 100,000 population) were consistently for black males, followed by white males. White females had the lowest personal crime rates for all years; black females had a higher rate than white males only for 1973. The rates for black females dropped significantly between 1973 and 1977, but have since risen steadily. In contrast, white female rates have changed very little, ranging from a low of 1,062 in 1975 to a high of 1,359 in 1979. The rate for white males rose after 1975, and those of black males after 1977, following a period of significant decrease from 1973 to 1977.

Laub and McDermott also discovered considerable differences in rates for specific personal offenses: rape, robbery, aggravated assault, simple assault, and personal larceny. The highest rates for both black and white girls and for white boys were for the simple assault category, the highest rate for black males was for the robbery category, and the lowest rate was for the personal larceny category. Over time, the data showed the greatest convergence between black and white girls concerning assault, not theft crimes. Divergence from the male pattern was clear: white females had not engaged in more delinquent behavior, but white males had done so. Among blacks, the decline in female delinquency was steeper than the decline in male delinquency.

Laub and McDermott concluded that there is a convergence occurring in delinquency, a convergence of white and non-white female delinquency. The convergence is explained largely by a substantial decline in black female offending for the nine-year period they examined compared with stability in white female offending. Black girls, according to this study, do commit more personal crimes than do white girls, but even here there was considerable variation within offense categories, and the gap is shrinking.

Thus, race differences in girls' offending are not as marked as some might expect. Especially questionable are notions that black girls are far more delinquent than their white counterparts and that their delinquency is far more "masculine" in content. In fact, although there are some differences between black and white girls in delinquency content, the differences tend to be less marked as the girls mature. More to the point, black girls, like their white counterparts, are still quite likely to be arrested for traditionally female offenses.

Table 8. Offense Differences Between White and Nonwhite Females

Offenses Committed More Frequently by Nonwhite Females

Attacking someone with fists
Extortion
Using a weapon to attack someone
Carrying a weapon
Gang fight
Sex with opposite sex

Offenses Committed More Frequently by White Females

Disobeying parents	DUI liquor
Defying parents' authority	DUI marijuana
Drinking alcohol	DUI hard drugs
Using hard drugs	Property destruction under $10
Selling marijuana	Theft of car parts
Selling hard drugs	Disturbing the peace

SOURCE: Cernkovich and Giordano, 1979.

SUMMARY

This chapter has reviewed the extent of girls' involvement in delinquency. Careful measures of girls' delinquency reveal that it is more varied than official statistics indicate. Girls commit a variety of offenses but are less likely than boys to engage in serious, violent delinquency. In general, although female delinquency differs from male delinquency, some research, particularly that derived from self-report studies, suggests that there are more similarities than previously imagined in male and female delinquency. In essence, most delinquency is quite minor and the differences between boys' and girls' misbehavior are not pronounced. Discussions of delinquency that focus on very serious violent offenses tend to exaggerate the gender differences in delinquency because males are more likely to commit these offenses.

Evidence also indicates that female delinquency has changed little in the past three decades. Both official arrest statistics and self-report data suggest that the changes we have seen in girls' misbehavior have been in minor and traditionally female offenses. Girls are still arrested and referred to court for minor property offenses and status offenses. There is some evidence from cohort studies that more girls are being arrested, but there is little or no evidence that during a period characterized by much discussion about the need for changes in girls' and women's situations, there was any major change in girls' delinquent behavior.

There is also less support than some imagine for the notion that black girls are markedly more delinquent than their white counterparts. Certainly, differences exist, but they tend to appear more often in official statistics; when self-report studies are con-

sulted, white girls are slightly more delinquent than their nonwhite counterparts, although there are differences in the types of delinquency that the two groups commit.

In sum, studies of female and male delinquency, like studies of other forms of gender difference, tend to make more of dissimilarities than they do of similarities. Both are interesting from a theoretical standpoint, but to date only the gender difference in violent crime has attracted attention. Also of interest is the fact that although girls commit many offenses, only some of the offenses, notably status offenses, tend to result in arrest . . . .

NOTE

1. Although we have no hard data on this, both authors have learned from several sources inside the juvenile justice system the following trend that appears to be occurring. Because juvenile courts have been restrained in recent years from responding vigorously to cases of runaways, some police and probation officers are suggesting to parents the following: when a girl threatens to run away, the parent should stand in her way; if she runs into the parent or pushes the parent out of the way, then the parent can call the court and have the girl arrested on "simple assault" or "battery" or some other "personal" crime that would fit into the FBI category "other assaults." We have no idea how often this happens or how this could shape arrest figures that are reported to the FBI. We bring this up to illustrate that these FBI categories are just that: "categories" representing a wide variety of behaviors and different social contexts. Therefore, official arrest statistics like those discussed in this chapter should be interpreted cautiously.

BIBLIOGRAPHY

Ageton, S. 1983. "The Dynamics of Female Delinquency, 1976–1980." *Criminology* 21: 555–584.

Barlow, H. 1987. *Introduction to Criminology.* Boston: Little, Brown.

Cain, M. (ed.). 1989, *Growing Up Good: Policing the Behavior of Girls in Europe.* London: Sage.

Cameron, M. 1953. *Department Store Shoplifting,* Ph.D. diss., Indiana University.

Canter, R. J. 1981. *Family Correlates of Male and Female Delinquency.* Boulder, CO: Behavioral Research Institute.

_____. 1982. "Sex Differences in Self-Report Delinquency," *Criminology* 20: 373–393.

Cernkovich, S., and P. Giordano. 1979. "A Comparative Analysis of Male and Female Delinquency." *Sociological Quarterly* 20: 131–145.

Chesney-Lind, M. 1971. "Female Juvenile Delinquency in Hawaii." Master's thesis, University of Hawaii.

_____. 1987. "Girls and Violence: An Exploration of the Gender Gap in Serious Delinquent Behavior." In D. Crowell, I. Evans, and C. O'Donnell (eds.), *Childhood Aggression and Violence.* New York: Plenum.

Datesman, S., and M. Aickin. 1984. "Offense Specialization and Escalation Among Status Offenders." *Journal of Criminal Law and Criminology* 75: 1246–1275.

Douglas, J. W., J. M. Ross, W. A. Hammond, and D. G. Mulligan. 1966. "Delinquency and Social Class." *British Journal of Criminology* 6: 294–302.

Edwards, A. 1973. "Sex and Area Variations in Delinquency Rates in an English City," *British Journal of Criminology* 13: 123–137.

Facella, C. A. 1983. *Female Delinquency in a Birth Cohort.* Ph.D. diss., University of Pennsylvania.

Figueria-McDonough, J., W. Barton, and R. Sarri. 1981. "Normal Deviance: Gender Similarities in Adolescent Subcultures." In M. Warren (ed.), *Comparing Male and Female Offenders,* Newbury Park, CA: Sage.

Hagan, F. E. 1987. *Introduction to Criminology,* Chicago: Nelson-Hall.

Hindelang, M. J. 1979. "Sex Differences in Criminal Activity." *Social Problems* 27: 143–196.

Hindelang, M. J., T. Hirschi, and J. Weis. 1981. *Measuring Delinquency,* Newbury Park, CA: Sage.

Jensen, G., and R. Eve, 1976. "Sex Differences in Delinquency," *Criminology* 13: 427–448.

Kratcoski, P. C., and J. E. Kratcoski. 1975. "Changing Patterns in the Delinquent Activity of Boys and Girls." *Adolescence* 10: 83–91.

Laub, J., and M. J. McDermott. 1985. "An Analysis of Serious Crime by Young Black Women." *Criminology* 23: 81–98.

Maguire, K., and A. I. Pastore (eds.). 1994. *Sourcebook on Criminal Justice Statistics, 1993.* Washington, DC: U.S. Department of Justice, Bureau of Justice Statistics.

Mulligan, D. G., J. W. Douglas, W. A. Hammond, and J. Tizard. 1963. "Delinquency and Symptoms of Maladjustment." *Proceedings of the Royal Society of Medicine* 56: 1083–1086.

Naffin, N. 1987. *Female Crime: The Construction of Women in Criminology.* Sydney, Australia: Allen and Unwin.

Otten, L. A. 1985. *A Comparison of Male and Female Delinquency in a Birth Cohort.* Ph.D. Diss., University of Pennsylvania.

Ouston, J. 1984. "Delinquency, Family Background, and Educational Attainment." *British Journal of Criminology* 24: 2–26.

Shannon, L. W. 1982. *Assessing the Relationship of Adult Criminal Careers to Juvenile Careers.* Washington, DC: U. S. Department of Justice.

Shelden, R. G. 1976, *Rescued from Evil: Origins of Juvenile Justice in Memphis, Tennessee, 1900–1917,* Ph.D. diss., Southern Illinois University, Carbondale.

———. 1987. "The Chronic Delinquent; Gender and Racial Differences." Paper presented at the annual meeting of the American Society of Criminology, Montreal.

Shelden, R. G., and J. Horvath. 1986. "Processing Offenders in a Juvenile Court: A Comparison of Male and Female Offenders." Paper presented at the annual meeting of the Western Society of Criminology, Newport Beach, California.

Shelden, R. G., J. Horvath and S. Tracy. 1989. "Do Status Offenders Get Worse? Some Clarifications on the Question of Escalation," *Crime and Delinquency* 35: 202–216.

Steffensmeier, D. J., and M. D. Harer. 1987. "Is the Crime Rate Really Falling? An Aging U.S. Population and Its Impact on the Nation's Crime Rate, 1980–1984." *Journal of Research in Crime and Delinquency* 24: 23–48.

Steffensmeier, D. J., and R. H. Steffensmeier. 1980. "Trends in Female Delinquency: An Examination of Arrest, Juvenile Court, Self-Report, and Field Date." *Criminology* 18: 62–85.

Teilmann, K., and P. Landry. 1981. "Gender Bias in Juvenile Justice." *Journal of Research in Crime and Delinquency* 18: 47–80.

Tracy, P. E., M.E. Wolfgang, and R. M. Figlio. 1985. *Delinquency in Two Birth Cohorts.* Washington, DC: U.S. Department of Justice.

Visher, C. A., and J. A. Roth. 1986. "Participation in Criminal Careers." In A. Blumstein et al. (eds.), *Criminal Careers and Career Criminals,* Vol. I, Washington, DC: National Academy Press.

Wadsworth, M. 1979. *Roots of Delinquency.* New York: Barnes and Noble.

Wolfgang, M. E., R. M. Figlio, and T. Sellin. 1972. *Delinquency of a Birth Cohort.* Chicago: University of Chicago Press.

LAW & JUSTICE

JUVENILE OFFENDERS:

Should They Be Tried in Adult Courts?

The "get tough" approach to dealing with young law violators seen throughout the criminal justice system is society's reaction to violent, uncaring youths.

by Michael P. Brown

CHILDREN have been described as our future, our greatest resource, and our hope for a better tomorrow. For many Americans, though, children invoke fear. They represent violence, a segment of society lacking in self-control and devoid of ethics and morals, and the failure of the family to instill traditional values—chief among them being the value of human life and respect for others.

Fear of crime, especially random violence perpetrated by young Americans, is among the nation's greatest concerns. It has served as the motivation for countless numbers of people to change their lifestyles, take self-defense classes, install home security systems, and carry handguns for protection. Moreover, fear of crime has influenced politicians and laypersons to adopt the position that a conservative jus-

Dr. Brown is professor of criminal justice, Ball State University, Muncie, Ind.

tice system, which seeks to punish and deter, holds the most promise in curtailing juvenile crime. Waiving juveniles to criminal (*i.e.*, adult) court and imposing criminal penalties, according to the conservative position, are effective ways for society to express outrage for the transgressions of "out-of-control" youth and to placate its desire for retribution. Others, however, contend that treating juveniles as adults is going too far. Although many of these juveniles are incarcerated for their crimes, which the law allows, they often are the easy victims of homosexual rape and other forms of violence at the hands of hardened adult criminals.

The criminal sanctioning of juvenile offenders is not a contemporary phenomenon. Juveniles have been punished as adults for centuries. Prior to the 17th century, for instance, children were seen as being different from adults only in their size. Hence, they were held essentially to the same behavioral standards as adults. Youngsters were perceived of as being miniature adults and, therefore, subject to the same punishments as offenders who were decades their senior. Childhood was considered to end at about age five.

It was not until the 17th century that European church and community leaders successfully advanced the notion that children were weak and innocent and in need of the guidance, protection, and socialization of adults. Consequently, childhood was prolonged, education became a priority, and societal norms emerged specifying age-appropriate behavior. Youngsters no longer were viewed as miniature adults. For the first time in recorded history, they were a separate and distinct group.

By the 18th century, English common law characterized those under the age of seven as being incapable of forming criminal intent. For an act to be considered criminal, there must be *actus reus* (the criminal act itself), *mens rea* (the intent to commit the criminal act), and *corpus delicti* (the interaction between the act and the intent to commit it). Therefore, since youths were considered to be incapable of forming *mens rea,* they were legally unable to commit a crime or to be criminally sanctioned. Between the ages of seven and 14, children were presumed to be without criminal intent unless it could be proven that they knew the difference between right and wrong. At age 14, they legally were considered adults, capable of forming criminal intent and therefore justly sentenced to serve time in jail and prison alongside other adults.

By the early 1800s, there was the belief that juvenile and adult offenders should be incarcerated separately. At that time, special correctional institutions for youthful offenders were established in the U.S. It was not until 1899, though, that the first juvenile court was established. This uniquely American institution was based on the premise that youthful offenders should be treated differently than their adult counterparts. Instead of deciding guilt or innocence, the court would ascertain whether youths were in need of treatment. Under the driving philosophy of the new court, *parens patriae*, it would serve as the benevolent parent—all-knowing and all-loving, wanting only that which is in the best interest of children. Consequently, instead of harsh, punitive sanctions that sought to deter, the court would seek long-term behavioral change by providing the guidance youths so woefully lacked from their natural parents. Sentences were to be customized to meet the needs of each juvenile so as to optimize the rehabilitative effects of court intervention.

For most juveniles, the *parens patriae* doctrine still serves as the foundation upon which their sentences are based. Such an orientation is not deemed appropriate, however, for those juveniles waived to criminal court. Provisions that allow juveniles to be waived are, on the one hand, in contrast with the original intent and purpose of the juvenile justice system. On the other, they are consistent with the manner in which youthful offenders were sanctioned in the past.

The present-day controversy surrounding waivers appears to be a consequence of at least two factors converging. First, the definitions of childhood and age-appropriate behavior are in a state of flux. Young people are said to be more predisposed toward violence today than they were in the past. National crime data sources seem to support this notion. Violent juvenile crime has increased by nearly 70% since 1986. Moreover, the violence perpetrated by juveniles is portrayed by the mass media as being more heinous than at any other time in history. People are fearful of falling victim to a generation that seemingly holds beliefs and values that diverge drastically from those of normative society.

Second, the "get tough" approach to dealing with law violators—as seen throughout the criminal justice system—increasingly is being applied to juvenile offenders as well. Although a conservative approach to juvenile crime is not new, it is in sharp contrast to the predominant way in which the juvenile justice system has responded to youthful offenders in the U.S. for nearly 100 years. While it is true that waivers have been in existence for more than 70 years, they are used more today than in the past. This has drawn attention to how society's response to juvenile offenders is changing from primarily being oriented toward rehabilitation to increasingly becoming prone to subjecting juveniles to conservative criminal court practices.

"Legal adults"

Every state and the District of Columbia have at least one provision (some states have as many as three) to waive certain juveniles to criminal court. Juveniles may become "legal adults" through judicial waiver, prosecutorial discretion, or statutory exclusion. A judicial waiver involves the juvenile court waiving jurisdiction over a case and sending it to criminal court for prosecution. In all but three states, juvenile court judges have been entrusted with the power to waive juveniles to criminal court. Prosecutorial discretion (also known as concurrent jurisdiction) refers to the prosecutor deciding in which court—juvenile or criminal—charges will be filed. Ten states and the District of Columbia give prosecutors this authority. Statutory exclusion involves state legislatures designating certain offenses for which criminal prosecution is required. Thirty-six states and the District of Columbia have enacted legislation that excludes certain offenses from juvenile court jurisdiction.

> "... The majority of those juveniles waived to criminal court will re-enter society stigmatized by their criminal label...."

Age and offense seriousness traditionally have been the criteria by which juveniles are waived to criminal court. Twenty-one states and the District of Columbia have no minimum age requirements for transferring juveniles to criminal court. Among the remaining 29 states, minimum age requirements range from seven to 16. The largest proportion of cases waived to criminal court are serious crimes such as murder; offenses involving serious personal injury (such as aggravated assault); property crimes; public order offenses (such as disorderly conduct, obstruction of justice, and weapons offenses); and drug offenses. Additionally, some minor offenses (such as fish and game violations), which do not fall within the jurisdiction of the juvenile court, are tried in criminal court. Moreover, some states permit juveniles to be waived if their current charge is a felony and there is evidence of prior felony convictions. Furthermore, most states have a provision that allows juveniles to be waived to criminal court if there is reason to believe that offenders are not amenable to treatment.

Using the most recent available data, the Office of Juvenile Justice and Delinquency Prevention (JJDP) reports that, from 1985 to 1994, the number of delinquency cases waived to criminal court rose from 7,200 to 12,300, a 71% increase. Despite this growth, the percentage of cases waived to criminal court during this 10-year period remained relatively constant, ranging from a low of 1.2% to a high of 1.5% of all formally handled delinquency cases.

Over this span, the types of offenses waived to criminal court have changed considerably. While 54% of the cases waived in 1985 were for property crimes, the percentage dropped to 37% by 1994. Cases involving murder and personal injury rose from 33 to 44%. The percentage of drug offenses more than doubled, from five to 11%. Public order offenses remained relatively constant—nine percent in 1985 and eight percent in 1994.

The percentage of cases involving youthful offenders under the age of 16 increased from six to 12%. Males consistently have comprised the majority of cases waived to criminal court—95% in 1985 and 96% in 1994. Of the juveniles waived to criminal court in 1985, 57% were white, 42% black, and two percent of other racial and ethnic groups. By 1994, the percentage of white and black juvenile offenders became more similar (49 and 48%, respectively), and youths from other racial and ethnic groups increased to four percent. (Figures have been rounded off to nearest full percentage point.)

Waiving juveniles to criminal court often is justified on the grounds that they are deserving of more punitive criminal court sanctions and that the "get tough" approach to fighting crime will serve to deter future criminal conduct. Decades of research has yielded mixed findings regarding whether juveniles are sentenced more harshly by criminal courts and are less likely to recidivate. Most studies indicate that juveniles waived to criminal court do not receive substantially more punitive sanctions. In fact, many studies have reported that juveniles are more likely to receive probation instead of incarceration. Of those incarcerated, most receive terms of confinement comparable to those imposed in juvenile court. Moreover, research has revealed that juveniles waived to criminal court are no less likely to recidivate than those sanctioned in juvenile court.

The methods by which the justice system responds to unlawful conduct are not determined in a vacuum. They are a reflection of societal attitudes. In the past, waiving juveniles to criminal court was considered an option after all other avenues of treatment in the juvenile court had been explored. Today, the situation is drastically different. The conservative environment that currently exists not only makes it more acceptable, it is an expectation that judges and prosecutors will act decisively by waiving certain juveniles to criminal court. Hence, waivers no longer are viewed as a last resort. In fact, the use of waivers has been expanded to include first-time juvenile offenders. The establishment of exclusionary statutes, requiring certain juveniles to be waived automatically, eliminates the possibility of the exercise of discretion by those who know youngsters best—juvenile court judges and prosecutors. It is estimated that exclusionary statutes have resulted in more juveniles waived to criminal court than judicial waivers and prosecutorial discretion combined.

Waiving juveniles to criminal court is not the answer to the crime situation. At best, waivers are a short-term solution to a complex social condition that will not be simplified by transferring juveniles to the jurisdiction of the criminal court. At best, they merely serve to mollify the public's desire for retribution. After all, the majority of those juveniles waived to criminal court will re-enter society stigmatized by their criminal label and, in all likelihood, more dangerous than they were before being sanctioned as adults. This is especially true of youths who have served time in prison alongside adults.

Nevertheless, it is unlikely that waivers will be repealed. Therefore, it is incumbent upon decision-makers to make an informed, socially responsible use of waivers. In so doing, they would be restricted to those who pose the greatest risk to the safety and security of society—violent youth such as murderers, rapists, and robbers who show no apparent promise for reformation.

As for the others, juvenile court intervention holds the most promise for transforming troubled youths into productive, law-abiding adults. The OJJDP, based upon the results of numerous studies, has proposed a multifaceted strategy for dealing with youthful offenders:

Strengthen the family unit. Parents are primarily responsible for instilling in their children socially redeeming morals and values. Parenting classes may be necessary when mothers and/or fathers lack the skills, abilities, and maturity to socialize their offspring properly. When a functional family is nonexistent, a surrogate one should be established to fill that void in a child's upbringing.

Support core social institutions. Capable, productive, and responsible youths are influenced positively by schools, religious institutions, and community-based organizations. Social institutions impart law-abiding beliefs and values and offer youths legitimate opportunities for economic gain.

Promote delinquency prevention. Communities must be proactive by responding to children who are at risk of committing delinquent acts. Although youths have a responsibility to live within the boundaries of the law, social institutions have a similar responsibility to engage youngsters in activities that encourage productive, law-abiding behavior.

Encourage an effective and immediate justice system response to delinquency. When delinquency occurs, the justice system must respond immediately to prevent future such actions and suppress escalation in their seriousness. The justice system should act in concert with conventional social institutions to enlist the influences that the family and religious organizations, for instance, have on the lives of youths.

Identify and control those youths who already are serious offenders. Youths who have not responded to traditional juvenile court intervention efforts or have demonstrated an unwillingness to abide by the rules of nonsecure community-based treatment efforts should be isolated in secure juvenile facilities for the protection of society. Deviating somewhat from the OJJDP's proposal, this intervention effort would be restricted to nonviolent offenders.

The alternative to waiving juveniles to criminal court is a comprehensive community response to juvenile unlawfulness that views juvenile and criminal justice as components of a larger whole—society. Moreover, it sees crime as a community problem with a community solution, instead of viewing it solely as a justice system problem with a justice system solution.

Many people will resist the notion of instituting alternatives to criminal court waivers. A community response to juvenile crime requires the commitment of the entire society. Therefore, it needs more effort than simply waiving juveniles to criminal court. Nevertheless, it holds the promise of returning children to their natural and rightful position as our future, our greatest resource, and our hope for a better tomorrow.

Unit 2

Unit Selections

Key Points to Consider

❖ In view of the 1999 events in Littleton, Colorado, its preceding models and its successor incidents, can any rational and comprehensive theory of behavior be applied? Is this an issue of anomie? Of role models? What are the main contributing factors that we can scientifically measure?

❖ Is the search for root causes going to produce better understanding of human conduct?

❖ In view of political pressures, can good science enter the discussion of delinquent behavior causation?

❖ With a better understanding of the causes of behavior that is defined as delinquent, can we anticipate changes in our juvenile justice system and our correctional philosophy?

 **Links** | **www.dushkin.com/online/**

11. **Birth and the Origins of Violence** *http://www.birthpsychology.com/violence/index.html*
12. **Brain Development and Learning** *http://www.tyc.state.tx.us/prevention/braindev.htm*
13. **Partnerships against Violence Network** *http://www.pavnet.org*
14. **A Student's Perspective on Childhood Maltreatment and Juvenile Delinquency** *http://www.concentric.net/~dfillmer/Delinquency.htm*

These sites are annotated on pages 4 and 5.

Unit 2 presents a mixture of scientific evidence that points to various factors that influence behavior that is considered to be delinquent. The list is not complete by any means. The popular culture, especially in the visual media and in rap music, has been cited as a corruptor of children and juveniles. Lack of community support has been tendered, along with the existence of genetic predispositions, single-parent families, poverty, racial discrimination, lack of opportunity, the school system, lack of personal responsibility, lack of moral values (especially this past year), a lenient juvenile justice system, and on and on.

One of the major problems of amateur criminologists is seeking the "causes" of crime. But that is a waste of time and energy for, except in the radical view that law causes crime, the only thing that is "caused" is behavior. It is only *after the fact* that any behavior is considered to be delinquent or a crime. This is verified by the fact that sometimes people are excused for doing what would otherwise be called a crime when the behavior is considered in retrospect.

By and large, examination of existing research in juvenile delinquency discloses a tendency to emphasize select approaches or explanations. Many scholars in criminology have written almost identically that proponents of various theories of behavior defined as delinquent still too often insist that the truth is to be found only in their own special fields of study, and that, *ex hypothesis,* research done by those in other disciplines can contribute very little to the understanding and management of the delinquency/crime problem. Like the blind men and the elephant of the fable, each builds the entire subject in the image of that piece of it which he happens to have touched.

Given the problems described, however, it makes sense that we use a multifactor approach or an integration of theories. It is necessary not merely to account for the statistical factors that are so powerful such as age, gender, and peers, but also to account for the individual traits such as levels of toxicity, life experiences, and learning. In addition, today's children go through many more doorways (new social situations) than their predecessors. They are exposed earlier and more forcefully to the complete culture—for better or worse. They experience the relative impact of family, peers, media, home, neighborhood, school, and other elements of the environment quite early in life. Again, as several of our colleagues have argued in so many different ways, the person at any given

time reflects the hammer of the environment pounding incessantly on the anvil of heredity.

The study of delinquency and crime reflects the dominance (since the 1920s and 1930s) of the sociological perspective and the continuing and understandable reluctance of that community to surrender "turf." Unfortunately, this limited sociological perspective has been translated into policies that fail to account for our current knowledge about the causes of behavior. We are not burdened today, however, by the limits of the tools of the past greats of criminological inquiry such as Quetelet, Lombroso, Sheldon, Goring, and the Gluecks. We carry their scientific spirit forward. Modern neurological and biological sciences keep pushing the frontiers of knowledge about the chemical and other physical influences on human behavior. Our tools are so much more sophisticated—unimagined by these pioneers. Instead of looking at the shape of skulls from without, we now look within by way of brain scans and MRIs as the brain processes events electrochemically.

The articles in this unit are only a small sample of the diverse approaches to delinquency. They were selected because they are in some way pioneering.

LOOKING FOR SOLUTIONS

Frustrated Officials Find Standard Answers Don't Suffice

By Christi Parsons

A DAY AFTER two black-clad teenagers killed a teacher and a dozen classmates in Colorado, a stunned Illinois lawmaker stood on the House floor to give a long, wandering speech most uncharacteristic of the chamber.

"I look for blame in many areas," state Rep. Lee Daniels (R-Elmhurst) told fellow legislators. "I thought, 'You know, I am going to go back to the House floor and I am going to move to pass every piece of legislation that I can pass so that I can protect my children and your children and the children of the future . . .'

"I don't care what it is . . . This violence must stop. I look for the answers. And I don't have them . . ."

Accustomed to purposeful addresses and clear calls to action, several listeners privately commented afterward that they had no idea what Daniels had been trying to say.

Nevertheless, in meandering around the topic, Daniels aptly if inadvertently summed up what many of his colleagues say they have been feeling in the wake of the school shooting: confusion fraught with intense frustration.

Such sentiments rarely are acknowledged in political circles. Lawmakers and other elected officials usually respond to incidents of national tragedy as if they know precisely what they are doing. In fact, their response to such instances of violence has be-

come almost predictable: They offer up new gun control measures and talk about increasing penalties for gun violence.

But this time around, the course of public action isn't so clear. The nation already has witnessed four such school shootings, and none of the solutions that ensued has done much to make people feel any safer.

With their quiver of legislative arrows now seeming so useless, public policymakers are beginning to come to some startling—and, for some, dreadful—conclusions.

First, it might be time to try something entirely new. Second—and most frightening—nothing they do can guarantee the safety of schoolchildren or anyone else.

"Look at all we've done to make airports secure. And you still find people on planes with guns," said state Rep. Lou Lang (D-Skokie), a liberal lawmaker and frequent sponsor of gun control legislation. "It's frustrating, but we start [out] with the notion that it might be impossible to rid schools of the violence."

Lawmakers with near-opposite views about the role of government in society echo the thought.

"We have passed legislation creating safe school zones, enhancing penalties for just about anything imaginable that happens within 1,000 feet of a school," said state Sen. Ed Petka (R-Plainfield), a staunch conser-

vative and opponent of gun control. "Certain areas have police officers stationed right in the schools themselves . . .

"The one thing we really can't control is in the heart of a person."

Of course, the shared belief hasn't stopped lawmakers from trying. The Colorado shooting gave new impetus to bills pending in the Illinois legislature, including several to increase penalties for people who fire guns near schools and to prevent minors from gaining access to firearms.

In Washington, U.S. Sen. Dick Durbin (D-Ill.) and others were promoting passage of stricter gun laws as one way to help prevent such school violence.

And across the nation, other policymakers displayed an urge to keep current tough gun laws in place. In the Colorado, Alabama and Florida legislatures, the shooting prompted lawmakers to withdraw measures expanding the right to carry guns or protecting gunmakers from legal liability for gun violence.

But amid the usual clamor that followed the shooting was the murmur of a quieter conversation, one that suggested small signs of interest in trying something other than the old methods. Surprisingly, it involved some of the people most likely to turn to get-tough measures for answers.

Late in the week, for example, the Clinton administration launched the

"Safe Schools/Healthy Students Initiative," a $300 million program to promote school and community mental health treatment and early childhood psycho-social and emotional development programs.

And at a national meeting of state attorneys general held in Chicago in the wake of the shooting, one top prosecutor introduced the idea—novel for prosecutors to ponder—that community leaders start considering how counseling and intervention programs might be used to head off school violence.

Mike Moore of Mississippi, the president of the National Association of Attorneys General, said he thinks that only part of the solution can be found in the law.

"Students (have) said they need real counselors," Moore said. "Not just counselors who also handle money in the Coke machine or handle the band or do something else, but a counselor that talks to them, somebody who understands their problems. . . .

"These kids many times just need someone they can really trust and talk to."

With that in mind, the attorneys general have taken the unusual step of including discussions on early childhood development on the agenda for their national conference on Youth and School Violence in early May.

Do those voices in political leadership indicate a change in thinking on the subject? Some experts who work with high school students hope so.

They suggest that instead of simply toughening laws, politicians might also consider investing more money in programs aimed at helping solve basic problems of youth in crisis and teaching young people to resolve conflict peacefully.

Indeed, some studies indicate that early childhood education for at-risk youth can reduce the likelihood that they will run into trouble with the law later in life.

Poor 3- and 4-year-olds randomly selected for an educational preschool program in Ypsilanti, Mich., were only one-fifth as likely as others to have become chronic lawbreakers by age 27, according to a study published by the not-for-profit High/Scope Educational Research Foundation in 1993.

Studies also show that intervention programs in the teenage years can make a difference, experts say.

"We have a choice on how we expend our resources," said Douglas Breunlin, vice president for programs and academic affairs at the Family Institute at Northwestern University, where experts study relationships among people.

"We could invest resources to prevent violence and we could invest resources to create peace," Breunlin said. "We live in a violent society, and we can't just snap our fingers and make it go away so that people can feel protected.

"I'd rather see an 'advisory program' funded in a school than five more security guards or a metal detector."

Many schools have such advisory programs, in which students get together with a trained adult adviser and other students on a regular basis and talk about such things as their personal development, goals and how to get along with others.

"One day the adviser might say, 'Today we're going to talk about what you do when you get angry,' " said Breunlin. "Or, 'Today we're going to talk about prejudice.' "

Besides teaching all students how to get along better during difficult teenage years, he said, the programs also give adults more chances to spot problems with particular students early on.

But such set-ups aren't cheap. Some schools spend as much as $1 million a year on theirs, Breunlin said.

Officials at all levels of government are often reluctant to talk about spending a lot of money on things like counseling.

To illustrate the point, consider Gov. George Ryan's response this week to a question about whether schools ought to have full-time psychologists on staff.

He shrugged off the suggestion, saying, "You can overdo those kinds of things and kids go the other way.

"When I was in school, there were traumatic things that happened, and nobody sat down and held your hand and said, 'Poor old Joe got killed last night.' "

Still, people may be ready for at least a modest step in that direction, suggests former U.S. Sen. Paul Simon, director of the Institute for Public Policy at Southern Illinois University.

Already, the recent spate of school shootings has made it plain that the consequences of ignoring the psychological root of teenage problems can be deadly.

"When students express extreme views and wear strange clothing, what they're doing is sending a signal, 'I have emotional problems,' " said Simon.

"School superintendents and counselors and teachers are realizing more and more that they ought to pay attention to this and get help for these kids."

But in the end, even those with the most faith in programs and legal mandates must acknowledge the limitations of their power to solve the problem.

Some believe the answer is to be found only in the church, the synagogue or the mosque.

Others look to the home or the prison for solutions.

Many, like Daniels, are simply baffled as to which way to turn.

"God bless our children," he said as he concluded his plaintive speech last week. "And God help us all that we find the right way."

Christi Parsons is a Tribune staff writer based in Springfield.

WHY THE YOUNG KILL

Are certain young brains predisposed to violence? Maybe—but how these kids are raised can either save them or push them over the brink. The biological roots of violence.

BY SHARON BEGLEY

THE TEMPTATION, OF COURSE, IS TO seize on one cause, one single explanation for Littleton, and West Paducah, and Jonesboro and all the other towns that have acquired iconic status the way "Dallas" or "Munich" did for earlier generations. Surely the cause is having access to guns. Or being a victim of abuse at the hands of parents or peers. Or being immersed in a culture that glorifies violence and revenge. But there isn't one cause. And while that makes stemming the tide of youth violence a lot harder, it also makes it less of an unfathomable mystery. Science has a new understanding of the roots of violence that promises to explain why not every child with access to guns becomes an Eric Harris or a Dylan Klebold, and why not *every* child who feels ostracized, or who embraces the Goth esthetic, goes on a murderous rampage. The bottom line: you need a particular environment imposed on a particular biology to turn a child into a killer.

It should be said right off that attempts to trace violence to biology have long been tainted by racism, eugenics and plain old poor science. The turbulence of the 1960s led some physicians to advocate psychosurgery to "treat those people with low violence thresholds," as one 1967 letter to a medical journal put it. In other words, lobotomize the civil-rights and antiwar protesters. And if crimes are disproportionately committed by some ethnic groups, then finding genes or other traits common to that group risks tarring millions of innocent people. At the other end of the political spectrum, many conservatives view biological theories of violence as the mother of all insanity defenses, with biology not merely an explanation but an excuse. The conclusions emerging from interdisciplinary research in neuroscience and psychology, however, are not so simple-minded as to argue that

violence is in the genes, or murder in the folds of the brain's frontal lobes. Instead, the picture is more nuanced, based as it is on the discovery that experience rewires the brain. The dawning realization of the constant back-and-forth between nature and nurture has resurrected the search for the biological roots of violence.

Early experiences seem to be especially powerful: a child's brain is more malleable than that of an adult. The dark side of the zero-to-3 movement, which emphasizes the huge potential for learning during this period, is that the young brain also is extra vulnerable to hurt in the first years of life. A child who suffers repeated "hits" of stress—abuse, neglect, terror—experiences physical changes in his brain, finds Dr. Bruce Perry of Baylor College of Medicine. The incessant flood of stress chemicals tends to reset the brain's system of fight-or-flight hormones, putting them on hair-trigger alert. The result is the kid who shows impulsive aggression, the kid who pops the classmate who disses him. For the outcast, hostile confrontations—not necessarily an elbow to the stomach at recess, but merely kids vacating en masse when he sits down in the cafeteria—can increase the level of stress hormones in his brain. And that can have dangerous consequences. "The early environment programs the nervous system to make an individual more or less reactive to stress," says biologist Michael Meaney of McGill University. "If parental care is inadequate or unsupportive, the [brain] may decide that the world stinks—and it better be ready to meet the challenge." This, then, is how having an abusive parent raises the risk of youth violence: it can change a child's brain. Forever after, influences like the mean-spiritedness that schools condone or the humiliation that's standard fare in adolescence pummel the mind of the child whose brain has been made excruciatingly vulnerable to them.

In other children, constant exposure to pain and violence can make their brain's system of stress hormones unresponsive, like a keypad that has been pushed so often it just stops working.

These are the kids with antisocial personalities. They typically have low heart rates and impaired emotional sensitivity. Their signature is a lack of empathy, and their sensitivity to the world around them is practically nonexistent. Often they abuse animals: Kip Kinkel, the 15-year-old who killed his parents and shot 24 schoolmates last May, had a history of this; Luke Woodham, who killed three schoolmates and wounded seven at his high school in Pearl, Miss., in 1997, had previously beaten his dog with a club, wrapped it in a bag and set it on fire. These are also the adolescents who do not respond to punishment: nothing hurts. Their ability to feel, to react, has died, and so has their conscience. Hostile, impulsive aggressors usually feel sorry afterward. Antisocial aggressors don't feel at all. Paradoxically, though, they often have a keen sense of injustices aimed at themselves.

Inept parenting encompasses more than outright abuse, however. Parents who are withdrawn and remote, neglectful and passive, are at risk of shaping a child who (absent a compensating source of love and attention) shuts down emotionally. It's important to be clear about this: inadequate parenting short of Dickensian neglect generally has little ill effect on most children. But to a vulnerable baby, the result of neglect can be tragic. Perry finds that neglect impairs the development of the brain's cortex, which controls feelings of belonging and attachment. "When there are experiences in early life that result in an underdeveloped capacity [to form relationships]," says Perry, "kids have a hard time empathizing with people. They tend to be relatively passive and perceive themselves to be stomped on by the outside world."

These neglected kids are the ones who desperately seek a script, an ideology that fits their sense of being humiliated and ostracized. Todays pop culture offers all too many dangerous ones, from the music of Rammstein to the game of Doom. Historically, most of those scripts have featured males. That may explain, at least in part, why the murderers are Andrews and Dylans rather than Ashleys and Kaitlins, suggests Deborah Prothrow-Smith of the Harvard School of Public Health. "But girls are now 25 percent of the adolescents arrested for violent crime," she notes. "This follows the media portrayal of girl superheroes beating people up," from Power Rangers to Xena. Another reason that the schoolyard murderers are boys is that girls tend to internalize ostracism and shame rather than turning it into anger. And just as girls could be the next wave of killers, so could even younger children. "Increasingly, we're seeing the high-risk population for lethal violence as being the 10- to 14-year-olds," says Richard Lieberman, a school psychologist in Los Angeles. "Developmentally, their concept of death is still magical. They still think it's temporary, like little Kenny in 'South Park'." Of course, there are loads of empty, emotionally unattached girls and boys. The large majority won't become violent. "But if they're in a violent environment," says Perry, "they're more likely to."

There seems to be a genetic component to the vulnerability that can turn into antisocial-personality disorder. It is only a tiny bend in the twig, but depending on how the child grows up, the bend will be exaggerated or straightened out. Such aspects of temperament as "irritability, impulsivity, hyperactivity and a low sensitivity to emotions in others are all biologically based," says psychologist James Garbarino of Cornell University, author of the upcoming book "Lost Boys: Why Our Sons Turn Violent and How We Can Save Them." A baby who is unreactive to hugs and smiles can be left to go her natural, antisocial way if frustrated parents become exasperated, withdrawn, neglectful or enraged. Or that child can be pushed back toward the land of the feeling by parents who never give up trying to engage and stimulate and form a loving bond with her. The different responses of parents produce different brains, and thus behaviors. "Behavior is the result of a dialogue between your brain and your experiences," concludes Debra Niehoff, author of the recent book "The Biology of Violence." "Although people are born with some biological givens, the brain has many blank pages. From the first moments of childhood the brain acts as a historian, recording our experiences in the language of neurochemistry."

There are some out-and-out brain pathologies that lead to violence. Lesions

RISK FACTORS

Having any of the following risk factors doubles a boy's chance of becoming a murderer:

- **Coming from a family with a history of criminal violence**
- **Being abused**
- **Belonging to a gang**
- **Abusing drugs or alcohol**

Having any of these risk factors, in addition to the above, triples the risk of becoming a killer:

- **Using a weapon**
- **Having been arrested**
- **Having a neurological problem that impairs thinking or feeling**
- **Having had problems at school**

of the frontal lobe can induce apathy and distort both judgment and emotion. In the brain scans he has done in his Fairfield, Calif., clinic of 50 murderers, psychiatrist Daniel Amen finds several shared patterns. The structure called the cingulate gyrus, curving through the center of the brain, is hyperactive in murderers. The CG acts like the brain's transmission, shifting from one thought to another. When it is impaired, people get stuck on one thought. Also, the prefrontal cortex, which seems to act as the brain's supervisor, is sluggish in the 50 murderers. "If you have violent thoughts that you're stuck on and no supervisor, that's a prescription for trouble," says Amen, author of "Change Your Brain/ Change Your Life." The sort of damage he finds can result from head trauma as well as exposure to toxic substances like alcohol during gestation.

Children who kill are not, with very few exceptions, amoral. But their morality is aberrant. "I killed because people like me are mistreated every day," said pudgy, bespectacled Luke Woodham, who murdered three students. "My whole life I felt outcasted, alone." So do a lot of adolescents. The difference is that at least some of the recent school killers felt emotionally or physically abandoned by those who should love them. Andrew Golden, who was 11 when he and Mitchell Johnson, 13, went on their killing spree in Jonesboro, Ark, was raised mainly

by his grandparents while his parents worked. Mitchell mourned the loss of his father to divorce.

Unless they have another source of unconditional love, such boys fail to develop, or lose, the neural circuits that control the capacity to feel and to form healthy relationships. That makes them hypersensitive to perceived injustice. A sense of injustice is often accompanied by a feeling of abject powerlessness. An adult can often see his way to restoring a sense of self-worth, says psychiatrist James Gilligan of Harvard Medical School, through success in work or love. A child usually lacks the emotional skills to do that. As one killer told Garbarino's colleague, "I'd rather be wanted for murder than not wanted at all."

THAT THE LITTLETON MASSACRE ended in suicide may not be a coincidence. As Michael Carneal was wrestled to the ground after killing three fellow students in Paducah in 1997, he cried out, "Kill me now!" Kip Kinkel pleaded with the schoolmates who stopped him, "Shoot me!" With suicide "you get immortality," says Michael Flynn of John Jay College of Criminal Justice. "That is a great feeling of power for an adolescent who has no sense that he matters."

The good news is that understanding the roots of violence offers clues on how to prevent it. The bad news is that ever more children are exposed to the influences that, in the already vulnerable, can produce a bent toward murder. Juvenile homicide is twice as common today as it was in the mid-1980s. It isn't the brains kids are born with that has changed in half a generation; what has changed is the ubiquity of violence, the easy access to guns and the glorification of revenge in real life and in entertainment. To deny the role of these influences is like denying that air pollution triggers childhood asthma. Yes, to develop asthma a child needs a specific, biological vulnerability. But as long as some children have this respiratory vulnerability—and some always will—then allowing pollution to fill our air will make some children wheeze, and cough, and die. And as long as some children have a neurological vulnerability—and some always will—then turning a blind eye to bad parenting, bullying and the gun culture will make other children seethe, and withdraw, and kill.

With ADAM ROGERS, PAT WINGERT *and* THOMAS HAYDEN

OF ARMS AND THE BOY

ALL KIDS BATTLE DEMONS. WHY DID THESE FIVE LOSE?

By JOHN CLOUD SPRINGFIELD

WE'RE NOT MUCH FOR SATAN these days. He's too black and white for a world of grays. But there were moments in the past school year when it became difficult not to imagine a Supreme Evil One dancing behind the eyes of the kids who decided to solve their problems with guns.

Imagine 15-year-old Kipland Kinkel in rustic Springfield, Ore., chatting with two buddies on a three-way-phone call May 20—probably while his father's corpse lay on the floor, a bullet drilled through his skull. Kip said he couldn't wait to see the new *South Park* that night, according to Tony McGown, 15, who phoned him. "I wonder when Mom's gonna get home," he fretted. When she finally arrived, he allegedly said, "I love you, Mom," and then unloaded his weapon into her. It was around 6 p.m., and Kip presumably stayed with the bodies the rest of the night (and took in *South Park*, the episode in which Kenny falls into a grave and gets squashed by a tombstone). At some point, Kip apparently decided to shoot up his high school in the morning. What exactly did he think about in the darkness, as his parents' re-

mains grew cold? To know is surely to see the face of Satan.

Religion professor Elaine Pagels' 1995 book *The Origin of Satan* has been floating around a nearby library in recent days, as though the people of Lane County were searching its pages for answers. "What fascinates us about Satan is the way he expresses qualities that go beyond what we ordinarily recognize as human," Pagels writes. " . . . In his frustrated rage he mirrors aspects of our own confrontations. . . ."

But what calls Satan forth? Was it something about the four communities where the kid killers lived—in Springfield as in Pearl, Miss., West Paducah, Ky., and Jonesboro, Ark.? If police are right, together these five boys—Kinkel, Luke Woodham of Pearl, Michael Carneal of West Paducah, and Mitchell Johnson and Andrew Golden of Jonesboro—murdered 15 people and wounded 44 others. Were they simply bad seeds, genetic and spiritual misfits born without the brain chemistry that produces compassion—and, indeed, without souls?

Or was nurture to blame? Is America's gun culture at fault? Or did the

kids kill because they were molested by perverts, beaten by parents, rejected by girlfriends, despised by classmates or revved up by "role-playing games, heavy-metal music, violent cartoons/TV [and] sugared cereal," as Kip himself suggested on the Internet profile he wrote well before the shooting, foreshadowing with eerie prescience the debate to follow?

Of course we can't know for sure, but there are clues in each of these four places, common denominators among five boys headed toward the brink. It's now possible to try to reconstruct their motivations—a task made more urgent by the saturnalia of lawmaking under way. Mississippi has made murder on school property a capital crime, and Oregon may begin requiring a 72-hour holding period for kids who bring guns to school, as Kinkel did the day before the shooting. Members of Congress are pushing a bill that would crack down on dealers who sell firearms to children, and the President wants to spend a billion dollars on after-school programs, on the theory that if Kip had been at a "21st Century Community Learning Center," he wouldn't have been blasting away with the .22-cal. semiauto-

 From *Time*, July 6, 1998, pp. 58-62. © 1998 by Time Inc. Magazine Company. Reprinted by permission.

matic Dad had got him. Will any of these policies work? As Pearl and West Paducah, Springfield and Jonesboro know, there are no easy truths. Only grim ones.

BOYS EVERYWHERE ARE FRUStrated, abused, and saturated with media violence. But not all of them live in places where guns are available. Says Tom Furth, a former lawyer for Mitchell Johnson: "In Jonesboro, there are little militia boys that have guns, and you have an environment that is particularly conducive to what happened. This would not have happened in Minnesota," where his ex-client was originally from. "Mitchell might have snapped there too, but in a different context." Mitchell's partner, Drew Golden, 11, was Arkansas-raised and had reportedly attended a militia camp in California.

Kip Kinkel begged his parents for guns so often that the schoolteacher couple, partial to tennis and not gun people, finally relented. His father "felt that Kip was going to get a gun one way or another," family friend Rod Ruhoff told the Eugene, Ore., *Register-Guard,* so why not do it under parental supervision? Another friend recommended a single-shot weapon, but Bill Kinkel bought his son a semiautomatic rifle. Later, he surprised Kip with a Glock pistol. Just down the road from the Kinkel home—nestled along a rural road that feels more Ozark than Pacific Northwest—a sign warns NO HUNTING OR SHOOTING.

The other boys also had experience with firearms. Carneal learned to shoot at summer camp and on a shooting trip with his neighbor's dad (from whom he stole the murder weapon). Woodham kept a map on his wall with the bilious slogan "One Nation Under My Gun."

But a mix of boys and guns isn't an automatic formula for mayhem. Indeed, a student hailed as a hero for stopping Kinkel's rampage belongs to the National Rifle Association. There

is something else at work, a toxic combination of biology and environment. However lonely or teased or poisoned by culture, the accused boys all seem to share a deep-seated—perhaps "inherited," as a Kinkel family friend put it—sense of rage. Investigators think Kip shot his father as they argued over his dad's plan to send him to a National Guard program for troubled youths. Kip had been expelled that day for taking a gun to school, and his dad was at his wit's end. It seems that Kip was too.

Geneticists predict that a simple blood test will one day tell which tykes become terrors. For now, though, there is more folklore than science. Some kids, it is said, are simply born twisted. It's possible that these five boys possess some murderer gene within, but a look at their upbringing and surroundings yields plenty of old-fashioned misery, both within and without.

TIME examined court-ordered psychological reports on two of the boys, Woodham and Carneal, who both claim to be mentally ill. Last month jurors rejected Woodham's insanity defense and found him guilty of murdering his mother and two students in October, when he was 16. Last week, Carneal's lawyer disclosed that his client would plead guilty but seek a lenient sentence in light of his purported illness. Were Woodham and Carneal driven by madness? The three psychologists who examined Woodham disagreed over his sanity (two said he was able to distinguish right from wrong), but they agreed he had problems—narcissistic traits (which include, clinically speaking, lack of empathy and hypersensitivity to insult) and erratic coping skills. "Luke's head is apparently filled with craziness about his world . . . and himself," wrote defense psychologist Mick Jepsen, who believes Woodham suffers from a serious depressive disorder. Woodham talked of visiting demons. "The glowing one with the red cloak

came to me" the very night before the shootings, he told a court-appointed psychologist. A few hours later, Woodham went after his mother with a baseball bat and an Old Hickory butcher knife, and then his schoolmates with a rifle.

Carneal's psychiatric evaluation reveals a fluttery 14-year-old so afraid that people might see him naked that he even covered air vents when he was in the bathroom. He sometimes heard voices calling his name and possible predators tapping on windows. He slept on the family-room couch to be closer to his folks. "I always think people are talking about me," he said.

Whether Woodham and Carneal are ill, they doubtless shared with their three counterparts crushing feelings of isolation. The boys felt particularly isolated from family members and girls. "She always told me that I wouldn't amount to anything," Woodham said in his confession, speaking of his mother. "She always told me that I was fat and stupid and lazy." His 24-year-old brother, he said, "used to pick on me—beat on me—when I was little." His parents' marriage ended in acrimonious divorce. Police believe Luke's mother tried hard with her son and that he exaggerates her abusive behavior. (Neither Woodham's father nor brother have spoken to police or reporters. His brother even refused to talk to the psychologist evaluating Luke for the defense.)

For his part, Mitchell Johnson of Jonesboro apparently had never felt close enough to his parents to tell them that a neighborhood boy had sexually abused him repeatedly for at least four years. His parents had divorced, and they bickered over whether Mitchell needed counseling. Mitchell seemed to yearn for male approval. "Mitchell always wanted to prove to me that he was a tough guy," his dad, Scott Johnson, told TIME. The boy both feared and admired his tattooed stepdad, an ex-con. "Mitchell thought it was cool to be in prison," Johnson says.

The Kinkels weren't divorced, nor were the Carneals, but both Kip and

THE NUMBERS
From 1985 to 1995, the number of juveniles murdered by firearms went up
153%

Michael may have resented their accomplished and popular older sisters. Kristin Kinkel wasn't just a pretty cheerleader—she was the 100-pound spitfire who got tossed into the air to delight crowds at Hawaii Pacific University, which gave her a scholarship. Kelly Carneal graduated from Heath

I am realy sad inside about everything My thoughts and prayers are with those kids that I go to school with. I realy whant people to know the real Mitchell someday.

*Sincerly,
Mitchell
Johnson*

High just last month—only six months after her brother apparently killed three girls in the school's prayer group—as Heath's valedictorian. After the shooting, Michael told a psychiatrist that everyone talked about his sister, not about him.

Kip and Michael faced struggles in school. Family friends say Kip showed signs of intelligence but had trouble in the classroom. His parents put him on Ritalin for a time and, when he was later diagnosed with depression, Prozac. "He was a different kid," says family friend Berry Kessinger. "He was kind of hyper. He could actually be really obnoxious."

Carneal, meanwhile, cultivated a reputation as a jokester but was depressed. Boys flicked water on him in the school bathroom and stole his lunch. Students said he had "Michael germs" and baited him relentlessly. He didn't cotton to the Boy Scouts or the karate classes he briefly tried, leaving him to stew over his indignities alone. The week before his rampage, he told an evaluator, a couple of boys threatened to beat him up in the band room. When he pulled a .22-cal. handgun in response, he recalled, they taunted him: "You couldn't hurt anybody with that."

Four of the five boys were rumored to have some kind of girl trouble—most seriously Woodham, who was by all accounts "crushed," as a classmate told police, when Christina Menefee broke up with him. (Significantly, her father says Luke's mom was so overbearing she "drove them apart. . . . If they went to get ice cream, she was there.") After the split, Luke testified at trial, "I didn't eat. I didn't sleep. It destroyed me." On D-day, Christina was apparently his primary target; she died of her wounds.

Students say Carneal had a crush on one of his victims, Nicole Hadley, who didn't feel the same way about him. It was also reported that Mitchell Johnson lashed out because Candace Porter had broken up with him. But though Mitchell had talked of suicide after another girl spurned him, Johnson's attorney Furth says Mitchell denies Candace was his girlfriend. ("She's a fat pig!" Mitchell blurted to Furth when told of the idea.) Finally, students say a classmate had also broken up with Gold-

en. Ironically, kids had even called Drew and the girl, Jennifer Jacobs, "Bonnie and Clyde" when the two were a couple.

In their isolation, the boys seemed to suffer an erosion of self-esteem. Partly it was their physical awkwardness: Michael and Kip were small for their age; Mitchell and Luke were pudgy. Furth describes Mitchell as "a sensitive, soft 13-year-old"; in Arkansas, where little boys are taught to be flinty and stoic, softness is a handicap. Luke and Michael were teased about their physical appearance (both were called "gay," the latter in the school paper).

They responded by overcompensating. Mitchell's father calls him a "gang banger wannabe." Kip bragged about his guns. Though a friend says it's a myth that he was voted "Most Likely to Start World War III" by schoolmates, one gets the sense that Kip wouldn't have minded the tag. In fact, according to people close to the investigations, after their arrests both Luke and Michael expressed a morbid appreciation of their infamy.

The boys shared a fascination with forms of "alternative" popular culture. Yes, this is fraught territory: the links between pop culture and behavior are tentative and indirect at best. Still, academics who study such things widely agree that exposure to media violence correlates with aggression, callousness and appetite for violence—even among adults, to say nothing of kids, who have a harder time distinguishing real from vicarious. (And on some TV shows—say, *Cops*—there is no difference.) These studies were primarily completed before the spread of cable, Nintendo and the Internet into many a 14-year-old's bedroom. As social critic Sissela Bok writes in her new book *Mayhem: Violence as Public Entertainment:* "These sources bring into homes depictions of graphic violence . . . never available to children and young people in the past."

What of it? Listen to some of the words on Kip Kinkel's favorite CD, *Nevermind,* by Nirvana: "Death/ With violence/ Excitement/ Right here/

Died/ Go to hell . . . Take a chance/ Dead." It's not completely clear what Kurt Cobain had in mind with these lyrics, but they are lush with nihilism. Luke Woodham listened to goth rocker Marilyn Manson, and Mitchell Johnson to rapper Tupac Shakur. One doesn't have to support censoring any of these artists to see that hurt, isolated kids may not understand any intended symbolism.

There were other cultural loves. Woodham had implicated himself in a role-playing game at the behest of an older boy, Grant Boyette, now 19. "Grant said he knew I had been hurt by Christina, and he said there was a way to get revenge," Luke told a psychologist. "He said Satan was the way." He said Boyette introduced him

to Hitler and Nietzsche, beat and burned his pet dog and eventually led him to a Satanic group believed to be called the Kroth (initially named the Fourth Reich). The Kroth played an interactive game called Star Wars— sort of Dungeons and Dragons on drugs—that involved loaded guns and threats to blow up the school.

While Mitchell Johnson's mother has said her kids didn't have Nintendo, Scott Johnson says his boys rented gruesome games like Mortal Kombat (and played them at Wal-Mart). Finally, Carneal told a psychiatrist that he liked to play Quake and Doom, two gory video games.

Bok believes that media violence undermines kids' resilience and self-control, psychological mechanisms

that allow people to bounce back and to count to 10 before they lash out. Some biologists—Harvard's E.O. Wilson has pioneered this thinking—believe there is a genetic component to these traits, that kids like Luke and Kip simply lack the DNA that keeps their fingers off the trigger. In the end, Satan is certainly the easier explanation, if less intellectually satisfying. As Kurt Cobain once sang, "Now the people cry and the people moan/ . . . And try to find some place to rest their bones/ While the angels and the devils/ Fight to claim them for their own."

—With reporting by Julie Grace/ West Paducah, Sylvester Monroe/ Jonesboro and Timothy Roche/ Pearl

Early Violence Leaves Its Mark on the Brain

By DANIEL GOLEMAN

WITH rates of violence among teen-agers rising precipitously, the argument over the causes of violent behavior has never been more charged. Nature got a hearing last month at a University of Maryland meeting on possible genetic influences on violence. Last weekend, nurture had its day, at a meeting at the New York Academy of Sciences on the childhood causes of violence.

Several strands of findings presented by researchers at the weekend conference pointed to the same conclusion: brutality and cruelty to children can leave a clear mark on the chemistry of the brain. And those changes in brain chemistry may be the route by which a brutalized child becomes a violent adult. The conference also offered some glimmers of hope for changing an established inclination to violent behavior.

One animal study that was particularly telling showed that normally mild-mannered golden hamsters that were threatened and attacked when they were young, and that grew up to be cowardly bullies, had lasting changes in the brain circuitry for two neurotransmitters that regulate aggression. And parallel data from several long-range studies of large groups of children show that those who were childhood victims of

abuse or neglect were the most violent as teen-agers.

The hopeful news came from programs that seek to help these children learn to better control their aggressive impulses.

"Even if a child has a predisposition to aggression, he can learn to override it," said Dr. Karen Bierman, a psychologist at Pennsylvania State University. "The more aggressive kids just need more help from their parents, teachers and friends."

The research on golden hamsters took advantage of that species' habit of living singly, and being fiercely protective of their nesting territory— or, in this case, laboratory cage.

In the wild, adolescent hamsters ordinarily go off on their own and establish a solitary nest. But in the experiment, adolescent hamsters were placed in the cage of a mature one, thus violating its territory, for an hour a day over a week's time— about half a hamster's adolescence. The older hamsters threatened and attacked the younger ones to protect their territory from the interloper.

When those younger hamsters grew up they were given their own territories, and experimenters placed other hamsters in the cages of the traumatized ones. If an interloper was the same size, the traumatized hamster tended to cower or run.

But if the interloper was smaller and weaker, the resident hamster attacked—with a vengeance. "They were far more aggressive than normal," said Dr. Craig Ferris, a neuroscientist in the Behavioral Neuroscience Program in the psychiatry department at the University of Massachusetts Medical Center in Worcester. He conducted the study with Dr. Yvonne Delville.

In a related study, anatomical studies of adult hamsters that had gone through similar experiences showed changes in the neural circuitry for vasopressin, a brain substance involved in the regulation of aggressive impulses in hamsters. The vasopressin circuitry was diminished, with less of the substance being synthesized by the cells. That seems to make the receptors for the scarcer vasopressin more sensitive. Dr. Ferris plans to do similar anatomical studies of the hamsters that were terrorized in adolescence.

For serotonin, which plays a role in restraining aggressive impulses, the traumatized hamsters had circuitry that secreted larger amounts of the neurotransmitter, which seems to make the receptors for serotonin less sensitive. "The serotonin system is just not doing its job," Dr. Ferris said.

Exactly how all this affects the hamsters depends on what they are

From the *New York Times,* October 3, 1995, pp. C1, C10. © 1995 by The New York Times Company. Reprinted by permission.

confronting. "Normally, vasopressin facilitates aggression and serotonin inhibits it, but the system doesn't work very well in these hamsters," Dr. Ferris said. "They either get too timid or you get an explosion of aggression," depending on whether they are with an animal of equal size or one that is a potential victim.

Sluggish serotonin circuitry seems typical of more violent humans, too, according to studies in which people are injected with a dose of fenfluramine, a substance that stimulates receptors for serotonin. The injection leads to the release of prolactin, a stress hormone that can be measured in the blood; higher levels of prolactin indicate greater serotonin activity.

"We find that people who are easily angered and impulsive—prone to shouting and throwing things, for example—release less prolactin than those who are not so irritable and impulsive," said Dr. Emil Coccaro, a psychiatrist in the Clinical Neuroscience Unit at the Medical College of Pennsylvania in Philadelphia. "That implies that the less active or responsive your serotonin system is, the more impulsive and aggressive you'll be."

Several studies presented at the conference showed that children who were abused or otherwise severely stressed in childhood were far more likely than others to be violent as teen-agers or adults. And, again, some of the data implicated changes in serotonin or related neurotransmitter systems.

Dr. Cathy Spatz Widom, a psychologist at the State University of New York in Albany, identified 908 children who had been victims of criminal neglect or physical abuse that led to the filing of criminal charges. Tracking the children's criminal records over the next 20 years, she found that those who had been childhood victims of neglect went on to have 50 percent more arrests for violent crimes than did a comparison group, while for those who suffered physical abuse, the rate of

violent crimes was double that of the comparison group.

Similar findings were reported from a study of 66 aggressive boys winnowed from an overall sample of 1,037 inner-city children in Montreal. While the neighborhoods themselves tend to breed children somewhat more prone to aggression, these 66 boys were at the age 6 already the most violent among them.

Adolescent violence is traced to abuse and neglect in childhood.

"These are the boys who are always getting in trouble for fighting all through elementary school," said Dr. Richard Tremblay, a psychologist at the University of Montreal, who reported the main results of a 10-year study that assessed the boys annually. "As adolescents, these are the boys most frequently involved in crimes, especially violent ones." And, he said, they come from families that "tend to be more physically punitive with their children, beating them or using other physical punishment."

A test of pain sensitivity—an indirect measure of serotonin function—in these same boys suggested that they had lower levels of the substance, according to data presented by Dr. Jean Seguin, a colleague of Dr. Tremblay.

Louise Arseneault, a graduate student at the University of Montreal who worked on the study, presented data showing that the aggressive boys had difficulty focusing on activities and were easily distracted. The result is that they are impulsive, she said, and so "unable to inhibit bad behavior—even if they know they'll be punished for it—they don't seem to be able to stop themselves."

Boys who showed this deficiency on neuropsychological tests had the

biggest increase from the age of 13 to 14 in picking fights and other aggressive acts—a jump of 50 percent. Their main deficiency, Ms. Arseneault said, "is in self-regulation, the ability to keep yourself from fighting because you know it's bad or inappropriate."

At the weekend conference, Dr. Adrian Raine, a psychologist at the University of Southern California, reported on a study of 4,269 boys, some of whom suffered some form of birth complication and whose mothers were abusive or neglectful in infancy. He found that those boys with birth complications and abuse were three times as likely as the others to be arrested for a violent crime by the age of 18.

Particularly damaging, Dr. Raine said, is early child abuse, like shaking a child vigorously. He said, "We know that can lead to laceration of the white nerve fibers that link the prefrontal cortex to deeper brain structures like the amygdala, which are involved in the generation of aggressive impulses, while the prefrontal lobes inhibit those impulses."

The ability to control aggression is learned during childhood. The crucial importance of such childhood learning was underscored by studies done with rhesus monkeys in which some monkeys were raised by their mothers, and others spent childhood without their mothers but in the company of same-aged peers. The result of the motherless childhood was something like a rhesus version of "Lord of the Flies."

While mother-reared monkeys with low serotonin levels are more aggressive than others as juveniles, "they are also more prosocial," engaging in many friendly acts, too, said Dr. Gary Kraemer, a psychologist at the Harlow Primate Laboratory at the University of Wisconsin.

"But if they have low levels of serotonin and are raised deprived of interaction with their mom, they show inordinate, unpredictable and extreme aggression," Dr. Kraemer said. "The rhesus mother helps the young one learn to organize its responses to other monkeys."

Those results, of course, can be read as hopeful as well—since mothering has such a powerful effect on modifying aggressive impulses. And at the conference, educators presented hopeful reports on special programs to help more aggressive children learn to keep their impulses under better control.

"We see that after a year, children who are prone to aggression can learn to talk about their feelings and think of different ways of solving a difficulty instead of just hitting," said Dr. Karen Bierman, a psychologist at Penn State. "But the interventions can't be just with the child—parents and friends have to help the child find alternatives to aggression and learn a broader array of skills for resolving problems."

Dr. Bierman reported results from a curriculum used in the early grades to teach children better ways to manage their emotional impulses. In one technique, for example, teachers help children recognize the cues in their bodies that signal that they are about to lose control and lash out, and remind them to calm down instead. The children also regularly pair up with a buddy to play games, supervised by a trained neighborhood volunteer, and solve problems that commonly lead to fights at that age, for example, learning about the need to take turns.

"We think doing this repeatedly and consistently helps children build self-regulation skills for handling aggressive impulses," said Dr. Mark Greenberg, a psychologist at the University of Washington who is a colleague of Dr. Bierman. "Presum-

ably, it strengthens connections between the centers for emotional control in the prefrontal lobes and those for emotional impulse in the limbic areas."

Dr. Bierman reported that the program resulted in fewer arguments and fights in the classroom and the playground, and enabled children who were prone to aggression to control their impulses. "This, in turn, helped them to become more popular with their playmates.

"The brain circuits that regulate aggression in humans are malleable through childhood, so there may be some corrective experiences that reverse or otherwise improve any adverse impact from early abuse," Dr. Ferris said. "My hope is that we'll focus resources on these kids so they don't go down the path of social failure and inappropriate, excessive aggression."

The Real Root Cause of Violent Crime

THE BREAKDOWN OF THE FAMILY

Address by PATRICK FAGAN, Fitzgerald Fellow, Heritage Foundation

Delivered to The Center for Constructive Alternatives seminar, Hillsdale College, Hillsdale, Michigan.

February 1995

Social scientists, criminologists, and many other observers at long last are coming to recognize the connection between the breakdown of families and various social problems that have plagued American society. In the debate over welfare reform, for instance, it is now a widely accepted premise that children born into single-parent families are much more likely than children born into intact families to fall into poverty and welfare dependency.

While the link between the family and chronic welfare dependency is much better understood these days, there is another link—between the family and crime—that deserves more attention. Why? Because whole communities, particularly in urban areas, are being torn apart by crime. We desperately need to uncover the real root cause of criminal behavior and learn how criminals are formed if we are to fight this growing threat.

There is a wealth of evidence in the professional literature of criminology and sociology to suggest that the breakdown of family is the real root cause of crime in America. But the orthodox thinking in official Washington assumes that crime is caused by material conditions, such as poor employment opportunities and a shortage of adequately funded state and federal social programs.

The Violent Crime Control and Law Enforcement Act of 1994, supported by the Clinton administration and enacted last year, perfectly embodies official Washington's view of crime. It provides for billions of dollars in new spending, adding 15 new social programs on top of a welfare system that has cost taxpayers $5 trillion since the "War on Poverty" was declared in 1965. But there is no reason to suppose that increased spending and new programs will have any significant positive impact. Since 1965, welfare spending has increased 800 percent in real terms, while the number of major felonies per capita today is roughly three times the rate prior to 1960. As Republican Senator Phil Gramm rightly observes, "If social spending stopped crime, America would be the safest country in the world."

Still, federal bureaucrats and lawmakers persist in arguing that poverty is the primary cause of crime. In its simplest form, this contention is absurd; if it were true, there would have been more crime in the past, when more people were poorer. And in poorer nations, the crime rates would be higher than in the United States. History defies the assumption that deteriorating economic circumstances breed crime and improving conditions reduce it. America's crime rate actually rose during the long period of real economic growth in the early 20th century. As the Great Depression set in and incomes dropped, the crime rate also dropped. It rose again between 1965 and 1974, when incomes rose. Most recently, during the recession of 1982, there was a slight dip in crime, not an increase.

Official Washington also believes that race is the second most important cause of crime. The large disparity in crime rates between whites and blacks often is cited as proof. However, a closer look at the data shows that the real variable is not race but family structure and all that it implies in terms of commitment and love between adults and between adults and children.

A major 1988 study of 11,000 individuals found that "the percentage of single-parent households with children between the ages of 12 and 20 is significantly associated with rates of violent crime and burglary." The same study makes it clear that the popular assumption that there is an association between race and crime is false. Illegitimacy, not race, is the key factor. It is the absence of marriage and the failure to form and maintain intact families that explains the incidence of crime among whites as well as blacks.

From *Vital Speeches of the Day*, February 5, 1995. © 1995 by Patrick Fagan, Fitzgerald Fellow of the Heritage Foundation. Reprinted with permission of *Imprimis,* the monthly journal of Hillsdale College.

There is a strong, well-documented pattern of circumstances and social evolution in the life of a future violent criminal. The pattern may be summarized in five basic stages:

STAGE ONE: Parental neglect and abandonment of the child in early home life.

- When the future violent criminal is born his father has already abandoned the mother.
- If his parents are married, they are likely to divorce by the third year.
- He is raised in a neighborhood with a high concentration of single-parent families.
- He does not become securely attached to his mother during the critical early years of his life.
- His child care frequently changes.
- The adults in his life frequently quarrel and vent their frustrations physically.
- He, or a member of his family, may suffer one or more forms of abuse, including sexual abuse.
- There is much harshness in his home, and he is deprived of affection.
- He becomes hostile, anxious, and hyperactive. He is difficult to manage at age three and is frequently labeled as a "behavior problem."
- Lacking his father's presence and attention, he becomes increasingly aggressive.

STAGE TWO: The embryonic gang becomes a place for him to belong.

- His behavior continues to deteriorate at a rapid rate.
- He satisfies his needs by exploiting others.
- At age five or six, he hits his mother.
- In first grade, his aggressive behavior causes problems for other children.
- He is difficult for school officials to handle.
- He is rejected socially at school by "normal" children.
- He searches for and finds acceptance among similarly aggressive and hostile children.
- He and his friends are slower at school. They fail at verbal tasks that demand abstract thinking and at learning social and moral concepts.
- His reading scores trail behind the rest of his class.
- He has lessening interest in school, teachers, and in learning.
- By now, he and his friends have low educational and life expectations for themselves.
- These low expectations are reinforced by teachers and family members.
- Poor supervision at home continues.
- His father, or father substitute, is still absent.
- His life is now primarily characterized by his own aggressive behavior, his aggressive peers, and a hostile home life.

STAGE THREE: He joins a delinquent gang.

- At age 11, his bad habits and attitudes are well established.
- By age 15, he engages in criminal behavior. And the earlier he commits his first delinquent act, the longer he will be likely to lead a life of crime.
- His companions are the main source of his personal identity and his sense of belonging.
- Life with his delinquent friends is hidden from adults.
- The number of delinquent acts increases in the year before he and his friends drop out of school.
- His delinquent girlfriends have poor relationships with their mothers, as well as with "normal" girls in school.
- Many of his peers use drugs.
- Many, especially the girls, run away from home or just drift away.

STAGE FOUR: He commits violent crime and the full-fledged criminal gang emerges.

- High violence grows in his community with the increase in the number of single-parent families.
- He purchases a gun, at first mainly for self-defense.
- He and his peers begin to use violence for exploitation.
- The violent young men in his delinquent peer group are arrested more than the non-violent criminals. But most of them do not get caught at all.
- Gradually, different friends specialize in different types of crime: violence or theft. Some are more versatile than others.
- The girls are involved in prostitution, while he and the other boys are members of criminal gangs.

STAGE FIVE: A new child—and a new generation of criminals—is born.

- His 16-year-old girlfriend is pregnant. He has no thought of marrying her; among his peers this simply isn't done. They stay together for awhile until the shouting and hitting start. He leaves her and does not see the baby anymore.
- One or two of his criminal friends are experts in their field.
- Only a few members of the group to which he now belongs—career criminals—are caught. They commit hundreds of crimes per year.
- Most of the crimes he and his friends commit are in their own neighborhood.

For the future violent criminal, each of these five stages is characterized by the absence of the love, affection, and dedication of his parents. The ordinary tasks of growing up are a series of perverse exercises, frustrating his needs, stunting his capacity for empathy as well as his ability to belong, and increasing the risk of his becoming a twisted young adult. This experience is in stark contrast to the investment of love and dedication by two parents normally needed to make compassionate, competent adults out of their children.

When you consider some of the alarming statistics that make headlines today, the future of our society appears bleak. In the mid-1980s, the chancellor of the New York City school system warned: "We are in a situation now where 12,000 of our 60,000 kindergartners have mothers who are still in their teenage years and where 40 percent of our students come from single-parent households." But today this crisis is not confined to New York City; it afflicts even small, rural communities. Worse yet, the national illegitimacy rate is predicted to reach 50 percent within the next twelve to twenty years. As a result, violence in school is becoming worse. The Centers for Disease Control recently reported that more than 4 percent of high school students surveyed had carried a firearm at least once to school. Many of them were, in fact, regular gun carriers.

The old injunction is clearly true: Violence begets violence. Violent families are producing violent youths, and violent youths are producing violent communities. The future violent criminal is likely to have witnessed numerous conflicts between his parents. He may have been physically or sexually abused. His parents, brothers, and sisters may also be criminals, and thus his family may have a disproportionate negative impact on the community. Moreover, British and American studies show that fewer than 5 percent of all criminals account for 50 percent of all criminal convictions.

Overall, there has been an extraordinary increase in community violence in most major American cities. Between 1989 and 1990, for example, the homicide rate in Boston increased by over 40 percent; in Denver, it rose by 29 percent; in Chicago, Dallas, and New Orleans, by more than 20 percent; in Los Angeles, by 16 percent; in New York, by 11 percent.

Government agencies are powerless to make men and women marry or stay married. They are powerless to guarantee parents will love and care for their children. They are powerless to persuade anyone to make and keep promises. In fact, government agencies often do more harm than good by enforcing policies that undermine stable families and by misdiagnosing the real root cause of such social problems as violent crime.

But ordinary American are not powerless. They know full well how to fight crime effectively. They do not need to survey current social science literature to know that a family life of affection, cohesion, and parental involvement prevents delinquency. They instinctively realize that paternal and maternal affection and the father's presence in the home are among the critical elements in raising well-balanced children. And they further acknowledge that parents should encourage the moral development of their children—moral development that is best accomplished within the context of religious belief and practice.

None of this is to say that fighting crime or rebuilding stable families and communities will be easy. What is easy is deciding what we must do at the outset. Begin by affirming four simple principles: First, marriage is vital. Second, parents must love and nurture their children in spiritual as well as physical ways. Third, children must be taught how to relate to and empathize with others. And, finally, the backbone of strong neighborhoods and communities is friendship and cooperation among families.

These principles constitute the real root solution to the problem of violent crime. We should do everything in our power to apply them in our own lives and the life of the nation, not just for our sake, but for the sake of our children.

When Our Children Commit VIOLENCE

BY ANN F. CARON

WHEN I RECENTLY ASKED A GROUP OF PARENTS HOW many felt responsible for their children's behavior, only a few raised their hands. Their response was not surprising. After all, most of us assume that children are responsible for their own behavior.

But family research consistently shows that parents who feel responsible for their children's behavior are more effective parents. Likewise, the children of these parents are more likely to behave responsibly.

The tragic schoolyard slaughters in Arkansas and Oregon have escalated concerns about violence and responsibility. We cannot exonerate the boys who killed and injured classmates on the basis of their ages. Eleven, 13- and 15-year-olds know that killing people is wrong. They also know that cheating, lying, stealing and meanness to others are wrong.

What many children do not know, however, is that when they do something wrong, they harm themselves as well as others. Further, few of them know that their actions have consequences.

That is where responsible parents come in. They are the primary teachers of right and wrong to the 2-year-old and to the 18-year-old. Their children know that bad actions have bad consequences. But not all parents set those limits or follow through with those consequences. The schools cannot do the job. The church cannot do the job. Only parents can. And now

many states are deciding to fill the responsibility gap left by parents and adults.

According to a report in the *New York Times*, legislators around the country are "rushing" to enact laws that make parents responsible for their children's misdeeds. Under Arkansas law, parents of shooting victims can bring civil lawsuits against the killers' parents. Also in Arkansas, the parents of a truant child who is deemed a delinquent must perform court-ordered public service with their child. In Virginia, parents whose children are caught defacing or vandalizing property (even mailboxes) can face $2,500 in fines.

Why does government feel obligated to perform a basic parental role? When school violence was confined to inner-city schools, many blamed poverty, single-parent families and drug-infested streets. But now rural and suburban communities with two-parent families feel the repercussions of youth violence. The nation is, at last, waking up to the issue of responsibility.

Are Americans failing to raise civilized children? Are we trying so hard to be non-judgmental that we hesitate to tell our children that some issues are black and white—that some behavior is clearly wrong?

I don't agree with the popular radio psychologist Dr. Laura Schlesinger, who said in a television interview after the Arkansas shootings that children possess an "innate sense of cruelty." But I do believe that we must teach our children how to behave in a civil manner. Some children intimidate their parents, teachers and schoolmates and never feel the sting of a reprimand, a "time out" or an appropriate consequence. When as adults we don't teach our children right from wrong, they learn from an early age that anything goes. They learn that their will is primary.

"But," parents protest, "aren't children, particularly adolescents, responsible for their own behavior?" Yes and no is the answer.

By the time children are adolescents, they must assume responsibility for living up to their parents' and society's rules. But if we don't articulate or demonstrate those ideals, we leave our children with no direction or moral compass. A psychologically or physically absent parent basically abandons his or her children, and, unfortunately, no one is picking up the slack. Neither the community nor the schools can assume parental obligations. Therefore, all citizens must face the adolescent angst that arises when a child feels that no one cares. Every child who grows into a responsible adult believes that he or she really matters to someone.

When two high-school boys in my suburban community agreed to kill each other using one of their parent's guns (a murder-suicide), no adult could explain it, but their friends could. No adult had reached out to them as they struggled with anger and sexual confusion. When I interviewed students for a book I was writing, most children whose parents had divorced told me that no adult ever talked to them about the worst event in their young lives. No one showed sympathy or understanding. In other words, adults ignored the topic. Where were the so-called "godparents" or even their parents' friends? Responsible adults seem to have disappeared from the lives of adolescents. Same-age friends fill the void.

Sometimes even adults can send a child the wrong message about responsibility. A teacher at a local school, for instance, told me a student's father threatened him with a lawsuit. The teacher had given the man's son a failing grade on an essay because he had copied someone's work. The father was indignant. His wrath came not because his son cheated, but because the teacher had given him an "F." By threatening a lawsuit, the father clearly absolved his son from any responsibility. If he had doubts about the teacher's decision, he should have asked his son to write another essay in the presence of the teacher and prove his ability. But now the boy realizes that his father will do anything, even threaten a lawsuit, to cover for him.

A mother told me that she has written her daughter's essays and term papers since her daughter was in the fifth grade. Her reason? When she is assigned a research paper, the daughter "gets a headache," and the mother can't stand to watch her daughter's discomfort. At first I thought her story was unique, but now I think attempts to cover up children's failures,

mistakes or misdeeds are becoming more commonplace.

Who is teaching responsibility?

Rationalizing children's misbehavior feeds into their sense of invulnerability. Nothing bad will ever happen, no matter what they do. When a 5-year-old sneaks other children's toys into his pockets to claim as his own, he should return those items with an apology. His parents should not ignore or laugh at the incident. If 12-year-old girls maliciously tease an acquaintance, parents and teachers should not consider their taunts "just part of growing up." The parents and teachers should tell the girls that harassing classmates is unacceptable behavior.

What can caring parents and adults do to encourage their children to honestly face life, accept responsibility and live in civilized harmony? First, parents must be the authorities in parenting. In short, even if their children are 18, parents know more than their children.

These confident adults possess two major characteristics. They demand a lot of children, yet they are highly responsive to children's needs. Whether a child is a preschooler or a high-schooler, a responsible parent offers the stability of firmness and the warmth of caring love.

Some parents are there but "not there." I have talked to many children who feel like appendages to their families. They feel insignificant because no one has shown them that they are needed.

Yet, healthy children come from families that stress the interdependence of all family members. A man told me that his parents owned a restaurant, and he worked with them from the time he was nine. He knew they could not run the restaurant without him. He recalls those experiences as forming his own sense of responsibility. Now he runs a major company and is trying to figure out how to give his 12-year-old son that same sense of being essential to the family.

How can parents and adults articulate the values that lead to responsible behavior? Television and films offer many opportunities to discuss moral issues. An 8-year-old asked her mother if girls had to have sex when they went to senior prom. She had watched a popular show in which the main character was trying to decide whether she and her boyfriend should sleep together the night of her senior prom. This was an important parental moment to teach sexual values.

Violence as well as sex is endemic to film and television, and the most popular computer games feature combat action geared for young males. Parents don't have to buy those games, allow their children to attend those movies or permit guns in the house. Children who know that their homes are dedicated to non-violence learn how to solve disputes without fighting. Harvard University research confirms that children who discuss moral issues, such as sex and violence, with adults tend to make better moral and responsible decisions when they are in their late teens.

Responsible parents don't fear their children's outcry when they enforce limits. Whether the offense is shoplifting by a 9-year-old or breaking curfew expectations by a 17-year-old, these children know that if they get into trouble, their parents will not approve or cover up for them.

A boy said it well when he told me: "Let him know the rules before he goes out so he knows what he has to fulfill before he gets in trouble. If he doesn't know the rules, you can't get mad at him."

In contrast, the father of the 15-year-old Oregon boy who killed his parents and classmates confided in a stranger he met at an airport that he was "terrified" of his son. Yet, in order to win his son over, he bought him the automatic rifle that his son eventually turned on him and his wife. We will never know why this father bought his son a weapon of destruction, but the purchase itself reflected complete irresponsibility.

Part of teaching responsibility is teaching self-regulation. For instance, a mother said that during her son's senior year, she asked him daily whether he had filled out his college application. At last, frustrated by his easy-going attitude, she resolved never to ask about college again. Consequently, when his friends went off to college her son stayed home and worked. But by October, without his parents saying anything, he finished his applications and joined his classmates in college a year late. His mother reported that the best thing she ever did for him was to stop nagging him about his application. He learned that he—not his mother or his father—had the responsibility for getting into college.

But who taught him that? His parents.

A fear many adults secretly harbor is that adolescents will not like them or turn on them. When adults realize that adolescents are children who need and want guidance, this unfounded fear will abate. Their bravado, their seeming indifference and their anger do not have to break out in violence. Wise parents and adults who teach them, love them, commit to them and take responsibility for them can direct those adolescent traits.

These children know their voices are heard and, in turn, will grow up feeling responsible to themselves, to their parents and to society.

A 1954 Mundelein graduate, Ann F. Caron is a developmental psychologist, lecturer and author of Strong Mothers, Strong Sons: Raising the Next Generation of Men (*Harper Collins*); Don't Stop Loving Me: A Reassuring Guide for Mothers of Adolescent Daughters (*Harper Collins*); *and* Mothers and Daughters: Searching for New Connections (*Henry Holt and Co.*). *She and her husband, John, are parents of six adult children and live in Connecticut.*

WHERE RAMPAGES BEGIN
A special report.

From Adolescent Angst To Shooting Up Schools

By TIMOTHY EGAN

MOSES LAKE, Wash.—Well before the school shootings in Oregon and the South prompted a search to the depths of the national soul, a 14-year-old honors student named Barry Loukaitis walked into his algebra class in this hard little farm town and shot his teacher in the back and two students in the chest.

Guns and violent videos were always around the boy's house. He learned how to fire weapons from his father. And he picked up a pose from the Oliver Stone movie "Natural Born Killers," telling a friend it would be "pretty cool" to go on a killing spree just like the two lead characters in the film.

Dressed in black and armed with three of the family firearms, Barry entered Frontier Middle School in this desert town 180 miles east of Seattle on Feb. 2, 1996, and turned his guns loose on fellow ninth graders.

"This sure beats algebra, doesn't it," Barry said, according to court re-

cords, as he stood over a dying boy who was choking on his own blood. He was tackled by a teacher and hauled off to jail, where he promptly took a nap.

A sign soon appeared on a nearby school, bearing a single word: Why? Of late, that question has been asked around the nation, following a spate of multiple-victim school shootings over the last nine months that have left 15 people dead and 42 wounded. People wonder whether something aberrant and terrifying—like a lethal virus, some have called it—is in the bloodstream.

While precise answers may be elusive, the recent killing sprees share a remarkable number of common traits. The first of the rural, multiple-victim student shootings, here in Moses Lake, looks in many respects like a road map of what was to come. From this case and interviews with police officers, prosecutors, psychologists and parents of

the attackers—as well as the boys' own words—several patterns emerge:

• Each case involved a child who felt inferior or picked on, with a grudge against some student or teacher. The attackers complained of being fat or nearsighted, short or unloved—the ordinary problems of adolescence, at first glance. But in fact, most of the assailants were suicidal, and of above-average intelligence, according to mental health experts who have examined most of the children arrested for the shootings. Their killings are now viewed by some criminologists and other experts as a way to end a tortured life with a blaze of terror.

• The killers were able to easily acquire high-powered guns, and in many cases, their parents helped the children get them, either directly or through negligence. Guns with rapid-fire capability, usually semi-automatic rifles that can spray a burst of bullets in a matter of seconds, were used in the incidents with the most victims. Single-fire, bolt-action guns or revolvers would not have caused near the damage in human life, the police say.

• To varying degrees, each of the attackers seemed to have been obsessed by violent pop culture. A 14-year-old in West Paducah, Ky., was influenced by a movie in which a character's classmates are shot during a dream sequence, according to detectives. Violent rap lyrics may have influenced one of the boys in the Jonesboro, Ark., case, his mother says. In particular, a song about a stealth killing eerily matches what occurred. The killer who has confessed in Pearl, Miss., says he was a fan of violent fantasy video games and the nihilistic rock-and-roll lyrics of Marilyn Manson, as was the boy charged in the Springfield, Ore., shootings last month. The Springfield youth was so enmeshed in violent television and Internet sites that his parents recently unplugged the cable television and took away his computer, a close family friend said.

• The student killers gave ample warning signs, often in detailed writings at school, of dramatic, violent outbursts to come. The boy in Moses Lake wrote a poem about murder, saying, "I'm at my point of no return." Similar jottings were left by the boys in the South, and in Springfield. In virtually all of the cases, adults never took the threats and warning signs seriously. Or they simply overlooked them.

"When you look at the overall pattern, it's a pretty serious wake-up call," said Dr. Ronald D. Stephens, executive director of the National School Safety Center, which monitors school violence from its headquarters in Westlake Village, Calif. "We are seeing an increasing number of violent, callous, remorseless juveniles.

"What's behind it," Dr. Stephens said, "seems to be a combination of issues that range from the availability of weapons to the culture our kids immerse themselves in to the fact that many youngsters simply

have no sense of the finality of death."

People argue, in the age-old debate, either that the killers are simply bad human beings or that their actions can be linked to a corrosive family environment—nature versus nurture. Certainly, the recent shootings give plenty of new material for both sides.

Parents of the young killers place blame on the surfeit of guns, the influence of junk culture and children stressed to a snapping point. But they also look at themselves, their broken marriages, their lives of stress and hurry, and wonder how all that affected their children.

"I didn't think about Barry at all," said JoAnn Phillips, the mother of Barry Loukaitis in Moses Lake, in court testimony last year in her son's case. A few weeks before the shooting, she had told her son that she planned to divorce her husband and that she herself was suicidal, but she was oblivious to how this would affect her son.

"We are responsible for our kids, but you tell me, where did I go wrong?" Gretchen Woodward said in an interview recently in which she discussed her son, Mitchell Johnson, the seventh grader accused, along with Andrew Golden, of killing 5 and wounding 10 in Jonesboro last March. "I think there's a lot more pressure on our kids today than there was when we were growing up."

The Killings

Urban Trend Takes Rural Turn

Children have long killed children in the United States. The peak was the 1992-93 school year, when nearly 50 people were killed in school-related violence, according to the School Safety Center. Most of those killings were in urban schools, and prompted a Federal law banning guns from schools, security measures like metal detectors, and efforts to control the influence of

gangs. What is different now is that the shootings are largely rural, have multiple victims and, within the warped logic of homicide, seem to make no sense; many of the victims have been shot at random.

In looking at the 221 deaths at American schoolyards over the last six years, what leaps out is how the shootings changed dramatically in the last two years—not the number, but the type.

Most earlier deaths were gang-related, or they were stabbings, or they involved money or a fight over a girlfriend. (Boys are almost always the killers.) Then came the Moses Lake shooting in 1996. Barry Loukaitis, who confessed to the shootings and was found guilty as an adult in trial last fall, did have a target in mind when he walked into the afternoon algebra class—a popular boy who had teased him. He shot the boy to death.

But then he fired away at two other students, people against whom he said he had no grudge. He shot the teacher, Leona Caires, in the back. She died with an eraser still in her hand.

When asked in a tape-recorded session with police why he shot the others, Barry said, "I don't know, I guess reflex took over."

After Moses Lake, shootings of a somewhat similar nature followed. In February 1997 in Bethel, Alaska, a boy armed with a 12-gauge shotgun that had been kept unlocked around the home killed a popular athlete, fired shots at random and then tracked and killed the principal. Like Barry, the 16-year-old Alaskan killer thought it would be "cool," prosecutors said, to shoot up the school.

"He loved what he did," said Renee Erb, who prosecuted the youth, Evan Ramsey. "This was his moment of glory."

By the end of last year, the killings seemed to come with numbing sameness. All but one of the victims apparently were chosen at random in the shootings outside a high school in Pearl, Miss.

MOSES LAKE, WASH., FEB. 2, 1996

Three killed and one wounded when Barry Loukaitis, 14, fired on an algebra class at Frontier Middle School. He was convicted [in 1997] of murder and assault, and sentenced to two consecutive life terms without parole, plus 205 years.

BETHEL, ALASKA, FEB. 19, 1997

Two people killed, a student and the principal, when Evan Ramsey, 16, went on a shooting rampage at Bethel High School. He was convicted in February [1998] of two counts of first-degree murder and 15 counts of assault.

PEARL, MISS., OCT. 1, 1997

Three people killed and seven wounded when a boy fired on students at Pearl High School after stabbing his mother. Luke Woodham was found guilty of killing his mother, and convicted of two other murders.

WEST PADUCAH, KY., DEC. 1, 1997

Three people killed and five wounded when a student opened fire on a prayer circle inside Heath High School. Michael Carneal, 14, has been charged with the killings.

"I wasn't aiming at anyone else," said Luke Woodham, convicted this week in the shootings, in a tape-recorded confession played at his trial in Hattiesburg, Miss. "It was like I was there, and I wasn't there."

JONESBORO, ARK., MARCH 24, 1998
Five people killed and 10 wounded when two students who lay in wait in the grass opened fire on teachers and students who had filed out of Westside Middle School after an alarm had been pulled. Andrew Golden (top right), 11 and Mitchell Johnson (below right), 13, have been charged with the killings, though they cannot be tried as adults and could be released, under Arkansas law, after they reach their 18th birthdays.

SPRINGFIELD, ORE., MAY 21, 1998
Four people killed (including the parents of the alleged assailant) and 22 injured in a shooting rampage that started at home and moved to Thruston High School. Kipland Kinkel, 15, has been formally accused of the killings.

In West Paducah, Ky., three girls were killed and five other students wounded in a shooting with no apparent motive. "It was kind of like I was in a dream," the accused attacker, 14-year-old Michael Carneal, told his principal.

In March, an 11-year-old steeped in gun culture and a 13-year-old with a troubled past opened fire, in what seemed like a military assault, at students who filed out of Westside Middle School in Jonesboro, Ark.

And finally in Springfield last month—where a boy with a love of guns is accused of mowing down as many students as possible in the crowded school cafeteria, using a semiautomatic rifle taken from his

father—the victims were anyone who happened to be in the way, the police said.

People ask why this is happening now in white, rural areas, said Dr. Alan Unis, a University of Washington psychiatrist who did an examination of the Moses Lake assailant for the court. "It's happening everywhere," he said. "One of the things we're seeing in the population at large is that all the mood disorders are happening earlier and earlier. The incidence of depression and suicide has gone way up among young people."

Suicide rates for the young have increased over the last four decades and have leveled off near their all-time highs. More than 1.5 million Americans under age 15 are seriously depressed, the National Institute of Mental Health says. The number may be twice that high, in the view of the American Academy of Child and Adolescent Psychiatry.

Most of the attackers in the recent cases had shown signs of clinical depression or other psychological problems. But schools, strapped for mental health counselors, are less likely to pick up on such behavior or to have the available help, principals at the schools where the shootings happened said.

The Guns
Troubled Children And Easy Access

A depressed, insecure child is one thing, and quite common. But that same boy with a gun can be a lethal threat. In all of the recent shootings, acquiring guns was easier than buying beer, or even gas. And these children armed themselves with small arsenals, as if preparing for battle.

The Moses Lake assailant used to play at home with his family guns as if they were toys, friends testified in court. In his confession, Barry Loukaitis said he took two of his father's guns from an unlocked cabinet, and a third one—a .25-caliber semiautomatic pistol—from a family car.

The gun used in the Alaska school shootings was kept unlocked at the foot of the stairs in a foster home where Evan Ramsey was living, according to police.

The shootings in West Paducah, Jonesboro and Springfield were similar in that semiautomatic weapons—capable of firing off dozens of rounds in less than a minute—were used to kill children. Weapons of less rapid-fire capability would likely have reduced the death tolls, the police said.

In Jonesboro and Springfield, the parents of the accused assailants taught their children, at an early age, how to use guns properly, which is the general advice of the National Rifle Association. The story of how Andrew Golden, accused in the Jonesboro shooting, was given a gun by Santa Claus at age 6, and was an expert marksman in the Practical Pistol Shooters Club a few years later has been widely reported.

But less well-known is how the other accused Jonesboro killer came by his knowledge of guns. Mitchell Johnson's mother, Mrs. Woodward, said in an interview that she taught her boy how to shoot a shotgun, and then he took a three-week course.

When the boys were arrested after hitting 15 human targets at Westside Middle School, police found nine guns in their possession. Most of them had been taken from the home of Andrew's grandfather, Doug Golden, a conservation officer who says he usually kept his guns unlocked in the house.

The parents of Kipland Kinkel, the boy accused of the Springfield shootings, were not gun enthusiasts, but their son was, according to interviews with family friends. The parents agonized over the boy's gun obsession, finally giving in and buying him a weapon. The father and son took courses in marksmanship and safety, and the guns were kept under lock and key.

But given Kip Kinkel's moods and temper, the parents had debated over whether to get him a single-loading bolt-action weapon or something with more rapid-fire capability. They settled on the more powerful gun, a .22-caliber semiautomatic Ruger rifle. It was a fatal mistake, said some people who are studying the recent shootings. It was that rifle that Kip used to fire off 50 rounds at Thurston High School.

"The kid had them by the throat," said Dr. Bill Reisman, who does profiling of deviant youth behavior for law-enforcement officials and recently gave a closed-door briefing to community leaders from cities where the school shootings occurred. "They were terrified of his interest in guns, but they went out and bought him guns."

A Kinkel family friend, Tom Jacobson, who played tennis every other week with the boy's father, said the parents were looking for a way to control and connect with their volatile child. The parents, Bill and Faith Kinkel, were both killed by their son, prosecutors in Oregon said.

"These were devoted parents in a tight-knit family," Jacobson said in an interview. "Bill had tried everything with Kip. I think he just ran out of ideas."

The Culture

Too Influenced By Music and Film?

Just as easy to get as guns were videos or cassettes in which murder is a central theme, and often glorified. Jurors in the trial of Barry Loukaitis were shown a Pearl Jam video, "Jeremy," about a youth who fantasizes about using violence against classmates who taunt him. That video, along with "Natural Born Killers," a movie about a pair who kill their parents and then go on nationwide shooting spree, were among Barry's favorites, his friends testified.

At least one of the boys accused in the Jonesboro attack, Mitchell Johnson, was a big fan of gangsta rap. Friends and family members say a favorite song was one by Bone Thugs-n-Harmony, called, "Crept and We Came," about killings in a massacre-like way.

The boy also played Mortal Kombat, a popular video game that involves graphic killing of opponents, his mother said.

"There are many cultural forces predisposing kids to violent behavior," said the Rev. Chris Perry, a youth minister for Mitchell Johnson at Central Baptist Church, who has talked to the boy three times since the shootings. "There is a profound cultural influence, like gravity, pulling kids into a world where violence is a perfectly normal way to handle our emotions."

But Mitchell also loved gospel music, the preacher said, and he sang at nursing homes. Millions of children listen to violent-themed rap music, play Mortal Kombat and witness thousands of killings on television by age 10, and do not become murderers.

"Barry Loukaitis was obviously influenced by 'Natural Born Killers,'" said John Knodell, who prosecuted the Moses Lake assailant. "But there are hundreds of thousands of kids who watch these things and don't blow away their schoolmates."

The psychiatrist in the Loukaitis case, Dr. Unis, also is reluctant to blame violent cultural influences. But he and other experts say there is a syndrome at work, in which a child who sees one shootout on the news may be inspired to try something similar.

"The media or violent videos do not by themselves make the event happen," said Ms. Erb, the prosecutor in Alaska. "But it shows them a way."

The Signs

Cries for Help Often Overlooked

The boys accused of shooting classmates are portrayed as average children. But a look inside their bedrooms or journals, or a discussion with their friends shows they left ample clues of trouble to come.

Michael Carneal was known as a slight boy who played baritone sax in the school band in West Paducah. After the killings, his principal, Bill Bond, looked at some of his writing and found a child who felt weak and powerless, with an angry desire to lash out.

A week before the shooting, Michael warned classmates that "something big was going to happen" and they should get out of the way, detectives said. At least three boys accused in other cases did the same thing.

The Alaskan assailant warned specific students the night before the killings to go up on a second-floor balcony. "These kids didn't tell anyone," said the prosecutor, Ms. Erb.

"Instead, they got right up there the next day to get their view of the killings."

In his ninth-grade English class, Barry Loukaitis wrote a poem about murder that ended this way:

I look at his body on the floor,
Killing a bastard that deserves to die,
Ain't nothing like it in the world,
But he sure did bleed a lot

Kip Kinkel read a journal entry aloud in English class about killing fellow students.

Most of the attackers were also suicidal, writing notes before the killings that assumed they would die.

Luke Woodham's journal writings were particularly graphic. He left a last will and testament, leaving music cassettes to the older boy who is said by police to have influenced

him. "I do this to show society, 'Push us and we will push back,'" he wrote. "I suffered all my life. No one ever truly loved me. No one ever truly cared about me."

Dr. Reisman said parents and teachers should be alarmed by such writings. Animal abuse, arson and a sudden interest in death and darkness are red flags, he said.

Often the assailants live in the shadow of successful older siblings, Dr. Reisman added. But the most common element is deep depression, he said.

"They'll all have depression, in the state in which they do these things," Dr. Reisman said. "When they're cornered, the first thing they say is, 'Kill me.' It's suicide by cop."

Unit 3

Unit Selections

15. **The Culture of Youth,** Marvin E. Wolfgang
16. **Preventing Crime, Saving Children: Sticking to the Basics,** John J. Dilulio Jr.
17. **Great Idea for Ruining Kids,** Mortimer B. Zuckerman
18. **Boys Will Be Boys,** Barbara Kantrowitz and Claudia Kalb
19. **Crimes by Girls Flying Off the Charts,** Maureen Graham, Rita Giordano and Christine Bahls

Key Points to Consider

❖ What are the elements of the youth subculture at the beginning of millennium? How do they differ from the youth culture of 1990?

❖ What is the role of such phenomena as heavy metal, gothic, rap music, pornography, skinhead, Web waste, and other media-enhanced trends in shaping juvenile behavior?

❖ Are the gender definitions of our society truly changing? If so, how?

❖ What will be the end result of the "war" on drugs?

❖ What other forms of deviance in the community are not being adequately addressed as we focus on guns and drugs?

 **Links**   **www.dushkin.com/online/**

15. **America's Children: Key National Indicators of Child Well-Being 1998**
    http://www.childstats.gov/ac1998/ac98.htm
16. **Center for Substance Abuse Research (CESAR)**
    http://www.bsos.umd.edu/cesar/cesar.html
17. **Juvenile Female Offenders** *http://www.ojjdp.ncjrs.org/pubs/gender/*
18. **Legalization of Drugs: The Myths and the Facts**
    http://www.frc.org/insight/is95c2dr.html
19. **Tattooing and Body Piercing Amongst Contemporary Youth and Youth Culture**
    http://www.urbanprimitive.com/academia/simon/1.html

These sites are annotated on pages 4 and 5.

There is something about contemporary values and culture in the United States that distinguishes us from much of known civilization. That something is violence. And we need to understand why this is happening before we can create good policy. But violence is not the only thing. Affluence, need in the face of affluence, drugs, basic values, attitudes, integrity, and other factors are very important.

Given that in the United States morality and law are intertwined only slightly less than in the world's theocracies, we have to consider seriously how much of our problem is due to our attitudes toward behavior which we regard as criminal, though it

might be tolerated elsewhere as immoral or sick. Radical or conflict criminology approaches just that question—how much is it the law?

We consider much of what are moral vices to be criminal, and on these issues debates rage: marijuana, sexual behavior, gambling, drinking, drugs, abortion, alternative lifestyles, and so on. We enjoy our great rights and freedoms, but we pay for them with the existence of deviations. We endure a constant battle between individual liberty and social accountability. We further compound the lives of juveniles by criminalizing what is acceptable for adults.

Drugs, Sex, Law, Policy, and Other Compounding Issues

THE CULTURE OF YOUTH*

by Marvin E. Wolfgang

THE SUBCULTURE OF YOUTH

The first issue confronted in discussing youth is whether social analysts may validly refer to a given age group as constituting a culture or a subculture. The term "culture" has gone through many definitional forms since E. B. Tylor's famous statement in 1871 defining it as " . . . that complex whole which includes knowledge, belief, art, morals, law, custom, and any other capabilities and habits acquired by man as a member of society."[1]

By 1962, A. L. Kroeber and Clyde Kluckhohn had analyzed 160 definitions in English by anthropologists, sociologists, and others, and offered a synthesis that embodied the elements accepted by most contemporary social scientists: "Culture consists of patterns, explicit and implicit, by symbols, constituting the distinctive achievements of human groups, including their embodiment in artifacts; the essential core of culture consists of traditional (i.e., historically derived and selected) ideas and especially their attached values; culture systems may, on the one hand, be considered as products of action, on the other as conditioning elements of further action."[2]

In discussing the elements of culture, social scientists usually refer to life style, prescribed ways of behaving, norms of conduct, beliefs, values, behavior patterns and uniformities, as well as the artifacts which these "nonmaterial" aspects create. The writings of Franz Boas, Ralph Linton, Otto Klineberg, Pitirim Sorokin, Robert MacIver and Leslie White are only a few examples among the many important contributions to the embellishment of the meaning of culture.[3]

More recently, A. L. Kroeber and Talcott Parsons have provided a meaningful distinction between "society" and "culture" in the following way: "We suggest that it is useful to define the concept culture for most usages more narrowly than has been generally the case in American anthropological tradition, restricting its reference to transmitted and created content and patterns of values, ideas and other symbolic-meaningful systems as factors in the shaping of human behavior and the artifacts produced through behavior. On the other hand, we suggest that the term society or, more generally, social system be used to designate the specifically relational system of interaction among individuals and collectivities."[4]

The term subculture, although not the concept, did not become common in social science literature until af-

MARVIN E. WOLFGANG

A.B., 1948, Dickinson College; M.A., 1950, Ph.D., 1955, University of Pennsylvania

Marvin E. Wolfgang is the Graduate Chairman of the Department of Sociology of the University of Pennsylvania and Criminology Director of the University's Center for Studies in Criminology and Criminal Law. He is also codirector of the Study of Violence Project at the University of Puerto Rico; Criminology Editor of the Journal of Criminal Law, Criminology and Police Science; Associate Editor of *The Annals* of the American Academy of Political Science; President of the American Society of Criminology; and President of the Pennsylvania Prison Society.

Among the books he has written are: THE SOCIOLOGY OF CRIME AND DELINQUENCY (coauthor, 1962); THE SOCIOLOGY OF PUNISHMENT AND CORRECTION (coauthor, 1962); THE MEASUREMENT OF DELINQUENCY (coauthor, 1964); CRIME AND RACE: CONCEPTIONS AND MISCONCEPTIONS (1964). In addition he has contributed many articles to professional journals.

* A publication of the Office of Juvenile Delinquency, Welfare Administration, U.S. Department of Health, Education, and Welfare, 1967. Reproduced by permission.

[1] E. B. Tylor, Primitive Culture, London: John Murray, 1871, p. 1.
[2] A. L. Kroeber and Clyde Kluckhohn, A Critical Review of Concepts and Definitions, Papers of the Peabody Museum of American Archeology and Ethnology, vol. 47, No. 1, 1952.
[3] Typical statements of these authors may be found in Franz Boas, "Anthropology," in E. R. A. Seligman (ed.), Encyclopedia of the Social Sciences, New York: Macmillan Co., 1930, vol. II, p. 79; Ralph Linton, The Study of Man, New York: D. Appleton-Century, 1936, p. 78; Otto Kleinberg, Race Differnces, New York: Harper & Brothers, 1935, p. 255;

Pitirim Sorokin, Society, Culture and Personality, New York: Harper & Brothers, 1947, p. 313; Robert M. MacIver, Social Causation, Boston: Ginn & Co., 1942, pp. 269–290; Robert M. MacIver and Charles H. Page, Society: An Introductory Analysis, New York: Rinehart & Co., 1949, pp. 498 ff; Leslie White, The Science of Culture, New York: Farrar and Strauss, 1949, p. 25.

[4] A. L. Kroeber and Talcott Parsons, "The Concepts of Culture and of Social Systems," American Sociological Review (October 1958), 23: 582–583. See also the seminal article by Gertrude Jaeger and Philip Selznick, "A Normative Theory of Culture," American Sociological Review (October 1964).

From *Task Force Report: Juvenile Delinquency and Youth Crime,* 1967, pp. 145–154. Reprinted by permission of the National Institute of Justice, National Criminal Justice Reference Service.

ter World War II. Alfred McClung Lee[5] made use of the term in 1945; Milton Gordon in 1947 defined subculture as " ... a subdivision of the national culture, composed of a combination of factorable social situations such as class status, ethnic background, regional and rural or urban residence, and religious affiliation, but forming in their combination a functional unity which has an integrated impact on the participating individual.[6]

In sociological criminology, Albert Cohen,[7] in his "Delinquent Boys," describes the term by referring to the following items: The cultural patterns of subgroups; the emergence of subcultures "only by interaction with those (persons) who already share and embody, in their belief and action, the culture pattern"; the psychogenic situation of physical limitations in problems requiring solution; the fact that human problems are not randomly distributed among the roles that make up the social system; reference groups for interaction, for the sharing of values, and as the means of achieving status, recognition, and response.

Even before the publication of Richard Cloward and Lloyd Ohlin's "Delinquency and Opportunity,"[8] its significant breakdown into criminal, conflict, and retreatist subcultures, Milton Yinger[9] noted over 100 books and articles that made some use of the idea of subculture. After a comprehensive review of such terms as "situation," "anomie," and "role," which should not, he says, be confused with the meaning of subculture, Yinger introduced the concept of contraculture to refer to those subcultural groups that are at considerable variance with the larger culture.

It is not our purpose to try to add new clarity, precision, or quantifiable parameters to the meaning of subcultures.[10] We are drawing attention to the generally communicative meaning of subculture in order to indicate that youth represent a separate subculture in society. We do assume, however, that not all values, beliefs, or norms in a society have equal status, that some priority allocation of them is made which the persons in a subculture partially accept and partially deny. The representatives of a subculture may even construct antitheses to elements of the central or dominant values while still remaining within the larger cultural system.

These assumptions lead us to assert that a subculture implies that there is a cluster of value judgments, or a social value system, which is both apart from and a part of the central value system. From the viewpoint of the larger, dominant culture, the values of the subculture set the latter apart and prevent total integration, occasionally causing open or covert conflicts. The dominant culture may directly or indirectly promote this apartness, and the degree of reciprocal integration may vary, but whatever the reason for the difference, some normative isolation and solidarity of the subculture result. There are, thus, shared values that are learned, adopted, and even exhibited by participants in the subculture, and these values differ in quantity and quality from the dominant culture.

A subculture is, then, only partly different from the parent culture, the larger culture from which subcultural elements have stemmed as different offshoots of its own value system. But there must be a sufficient number and variety of significant values commonly shared between "parent" and "child" if the latter is to retain its theoretical attribution of subculture. Some of the values of a subculture may, however, be more than different from the larger culture; they may be in conflict or at wide variance with the latter. Thus, a delinquent subculture represents a contractual system that is more than merely different from the parent culture, for in its dysfunctional character it is also antithetical to the broader social system. To be part of the larger culture implies that some values related to the ends and means of the whole are shared by the part. The subculture that is only different is a tolerated deviation; what we generally refer to as the youth subculture is in fact a tolerated form of variation from the parent culture. Values shared in the subculture are often made evident in terms of conduct that is expected, ranging from permissible to required expectations in certain kinds of life situations. These conduct norms generated by the value content of the subculture (indeed, of any subculture) have not yet been subjected to much quantified measurement.

[5] Alfred McClung Lee, "Levels of Culture as Levels of Social Generalization," American Sociological Review (August 1945), 10:485–495; "Social Determinants of Public Opinion," International Journal of Opinion and Attitude Research (March 1947), 1:12–29; "A Sociological Discussion of Consistency and Inconsistency in Inter-Group Relations," Journal of Social Issues (1949) 5:12–18.
[6] Milton M. Gordon, "The Concept of the Sub-Culture and Its Application," Social Forces (October 1947), 26:40. For additional discussions by Gordon, using the term "subculture," see also "A System of Social Class Analysis," Drew University Studies, No. 2 (August 1951), pp. 15–18. Social Class in American Sociology, Durham, N.C.: Duke University Press, 1958, pp. 252–256; "Social Structure and Goals in Group Relations," Morre Berger, Theodore Abel, and Charles H. Page (eds.), Freedom and Control in Modern Society, New York: D. Van Norstrand Co., 1954. In these references, Gordon uses the term to refer to subsociety as well.
  Gordon has recently gone further and proposes a new term, ethclass, to refer to "the subsociety created by the intersection of the vertical stratifications of ethnicity with the horizontal stratifications of social class...." (Assimilation in American Life. New York: Oxford University Press, 1964, p. 51.)
[7] Albert K. Cohen, Delinquent Boys, Glencoe, Ill.; Free Press, 1955.
[8] Richard Cloward and Lloyd Ohlin, Delinquency and Opportunity, New York: Free Press of Glencoe, 1960.
[9] Milton Yinger, "Contraculture and Subculture," American Sociological Review (October 1960), 25:625–635.
[10] An effort to show how parameters of subcultures might be designed appears in Marvin E. Wolfgang and Franco Ferracuti, Subculture of Violence, London: Tavistock Publications, 1967. Some of the notions expressed in this section of the paper are contained in more detail in the Wolfgang-Ferracuti book. See also Thorsten Sellin, Culture Conflict and Crime, New York: Social Science Research Council, Bulletin 41, 1938, for some of the provocative theoretical antecedents to current ideas about subcultures; and Leslie T. Wilkins, Social Deviance, London: Tavistock Publications, 1964.

It is difficult to discuss subcultures and conduct norms without reference to social groups, for values are shared by individuals, and individuals sharing values make up groups. In most cases, when we refer to subcultures we are thinking of individuals who share common values and who socially interact in some limited geographical or residential isolation. However, value sharing does not necessarily require direct or primary social interaction. Consequently, a subculture may exist widely distributed spatially and without interpersonal contact among individuals or whole groups of individuals. Several delinquent gangs, for example, may be spread throughout a city and rarely, if ever, have contacts; yet they are referred to collectively as the "delinquent subculture," and properly so, for otherwise each gang would have be considered as a separate subculture.

If a subculture, like a culture, is composed of values, conduct norms, social situations, role definitions and performances, sharing, transmission, and learning of values, then there is sufficient reason to speak of the subculture of youth in American society. We have said that the degree of concordant and tolerated, as well as discordant and untolerated, values of various segments of youth are related to the dominant culture themes of American society. A detailed analysis of the establishment and measurement of the parameters of the youth subculture would seem to be necessary in order to establish exactly where the values vary, to measure the intensity or strength of these values among youth, and to determine the degree of commitment or allegiance that youth has to certain values that when clustered together, may be called the value system of youth. It may be contended that an age group roughly embracing 12 to 20 years represents a subcultural system, although there are, of course, other subcultures, or other transmittable value systems, within which youth functions.

Without appropriate measurements of values and value systems, it is difficult to indicate exactly where subcultures blend into one another. However, the subculture of the lower class poor, of a Negro subsociety, delinquent subcultures, and other varieties of subcultural affiliations may be assumed to have groups of individuals who represent not only separate subcultures, but also conclaves where these various subcultures overlap. The descriptive characteristics of the generic term "youth" are often of little help to the social analysts or the consumers of social observations who wish to understand the variety of youth problems. Our attention, therefore, should be drawn not merely to the ways in which an age group called youth fits functionally into the larger culture system created and maintained by adults; what is needed beyond these age-graded and age-linked descriptive features is some notion of how several subcultures combine with youth. In a more elaborate treatise, the linkages should contain an interwoven tread of theory and be embraced by meaningful sociological conceptualisms. One of the main conceptual propositions to be employed later in this paper includes protest against the lack of, and request or even demand for more power and for participation in the larger culture system and its processes.

An interesting feature in the present generation that contributes to this age-graded subculture we call youth is the massive network of communication. Instant awareness of news and the rapid spread of innovations in dress, dancing, and dating habits quickly unify people and make rapid the sharing of values and norms across the entire country. The structure of our mass communication functions to make elements in the youth subculture quickly reinforced by supportive acts and attitudes on a numerically larger scale and spatially wider arena than ever before. For example, a university sit-in protest is known abroad even while it happens, and repetitive reinforcement readily appears in other universities. The transistor radio carried by a West Berlin teenager reports same musical styles heard in Boise, Idaho. Thus, the contraction of time and the extension of space for spreading the elements attractive to and shared by youth combine to create a firm subculture of their own.

It should be remembered, however, that more new things lasting shorter periods of time create only an illusion of diversity. The young listeners to television and transistors, more sensitive than their elders to innovation, fads, and fashion, do not have alternatives of action that correspondingly increase with the number of changes they witness. Their repertoire of response may even be reduced as the youth culture grows stronger. Deviance adult models may be more evident now, but the more committed the youth become to their own subculture, the more captive they become to their conformity. The more they strive to be recognized, loved, wanted, and feared within their own group culture, the more they contribute to their own captivity. The shared mass media of magazines and electronics probably produce greater homogenization among the young than among adults, and within the youth subculture of today more than during any previous period. This generalization is applicable to the considerable variability that exists in the youth subculture, ranging from Saturday afternoon dance clubs to Florida and Bermuda springtime frolics, the free university students, the Berkeley free speech movement, and the local drugstore crowd of the "Street Corner Society."[11]

EXTENDED SOCIALIZATION AND DEPENDENCY STATUS

Gertrude Stein is alleged to have said that the United States is the oldest country in the world because it has had the most experience with modem industrial society

---

[11] William Foote Whyte, Street Corner Society, Chicago: University of Chicago Press, 1943 and 1955.

and its complex consequences. With similar perception, Dwight Macdonald[12] has said that the United States was the first to develop the concept of the teenager, a concept which is still not well accepted in Europe, and that we have had the longest experience with the subculture of youth. The way we handle a nearly "overdeveloped" society with transportation, bureaucratization, impersonal, automated living, and the way we learn to understand the new problems of youth and the existence of poverty to remind us of our social imperfection, will be lessons of value to underdeveloped or newly developed countries. Despite our longer experience with modernity and the teenage subculture, we still have lessons to learn about the problems created by both, and the particular interrelation of modern youth and modern poverty is especially important and striking in many ways.

Our youth in general are richer today than they have ever been and have more alternatives of action and more privileges. The list of privileges usurped by youth has not only increased but has shifted downward in age. The high school student of today has the accoutrements of the college student of yesteryear—cars, long pants, money, and more access to girls. This downward shift in privileges, precocious to younger ages, is a phenomenon well known to every parent whose own youth subculture was devoid of them.

Not only are our youth more privileged and richer, but they have for some time constituted an increasingly significant portion of American purchasing power. The statistics of consumption of lipsticks and brassieres, even by 12- and 13-year-olds, are well known, as are those of records, used cars, popular magazines, and transistor radios. The magnified purchasing power of young teenagers is one of the factors that tends to make them want to grow up faster or not at all, which is suggestive of Reuel Denney's credit-card viewpoint of "grow up now and pay later."[13]

The ambivalence of the analyzers regarding whether our youth become adultlike too early or behave as adolescent children too long is a scholastic debate that has not yet been resolved by empirical data. Moreover, a valid appraisal of the "youth problem" is also made difficult by the existence of conflicting cultural prescriptions for youth. We appear to want teenagers to act like young adults in our society, yet we are increasingly stretching the whole socialization process from childhood to adulthood. And the number of people involved in the subculture stretch is increasingly large. There are nearly 70 million persons in the United States under 18 years of age, or nearly one-third of the Nation's population.[14]

The number reaching age 18 each year has, however, doubled within a decade. There were 2 million in 1956 and 4 million in 1965, the result of the "baby boom" of the late forties. Of the more than 1.5 million who graduate from high school, about half will register for college, and the 25 percent of the 16–24 age group now in college will increase. One could say with Denney[15] that the age of extended socialization is already in full swing.

It is of correlative interest that the public has become disturbed by the announced figure of 7.5 million school dropouts during the 1960's, despite some queries about whether we really want to or can prevent all school dropouts. The middle-class and middle-aged producers of prescriptions for youth want to keep them in, or return them to school for reasons that extend from a genuine belief that all youth should benefit from more formal education to fears that dropout youths inundate the labor market and thereby contribute to delinquency and crime. Our society would apparently like more children to go to college, often without commensurate concern for how the extended period of dependency, socialization, and an indiscriminate density of college population may contribute to producing mediocrity of educational standards. Yet, without continued education, the dropouts are commonly dependent in other ways. As Lucius

[12] Dwight Macdonald, "Profile," The New Yorker, Nov. 22, 1957. Both this reference and the remark by Gertrude Stein are cited in Reuel Denney, "American Youth Today: A Bigger Case, A Wider Screen," in Erik H. Erickson (ed.), The Challenge of Youth, Garden City, N.Y.: Anchor Books Edition, Doubleday, 1965, pp. 155–179.

[13] Reuel Denney, op.cit.

[14] We might parenthetically remind ourselves that at the time of the signing of the Declaration of Independence, about one-half of the Nation was under 18 years of age.

[15] Denney, op. cit.

For other detailed descriptions of adolescents, teenagers, the youth subculture, etc., see the following useful examples:

F. Elkin and W. Westley, "The Myth of Adolescent Culture," American Sociological Review (1955), 20:680–684.

Hermann H. Remmers and D. H. Radler, The American Teenager, Indianapolis: Bobbs-Merrill, 1957.

Edgar Z. Friedenberg, The Vanishing Adolescent, Boston: Beacon Press, 1959.

Paul Goodman, Growing Up Absurd, New York: Random House, 1960.

Jessie Bernard (ed.), "Teen-Age Culture," Annals of the American Academy of Political and Social Science (November 1961), 338.

J. S. Coleman, The Adolescent Society, New York: Free Press of Glencoe, 1961.

Lee G. Burchinal (ed.), Rural Youth in Crisis: Facts, Myths, and Social Change, Proceedings of A National Conference on Rural Youth in a Changing Environment, Stillwater, Okla., 1963. Washington, D.C.: U.S. Government Printing Office, 1965.

David Gottlieb and J. Reeves, Adolescent Behavior in Urban Areas, New York: Macmillan and Co. 1963.

Orville G. Brin, Jr., "Adolescent Personality as Self-Other Systems," Journal of Marriage and the Family (May 1965), 27:156–162.

Erik H. Erikson (ed.), The Challenge of Youth, Garden City, N.Y.: Anchor Books Editor, Doubleday, 1965.

David Gottlieb, "Youth Subculture: Variations on a General Theme," in Muzafer W. Sherif and Carolyn Sherif (eds.), Problems of Youth: Transition to Adulthood in a Changing World, Chicago, Aldine Publishing Co., 1965, pp. 28–45.

Kenneth Keniston, The Uncommitted: Alienated Youth in American Society, New York: Harcourt Brace and World, 1965.

John Barron Mays, The Young Pretenders: A Study of Teenage Culture in Contemporary Society, London: Michael Joseph, 1965.

Blaine R. Porter, "American Teen-Agers of the 1960's—Our Despair or Hope?" Journal of Marriage and the Family (May 1965), 27:139–147.

Graham B. Blaine, Jr., Youth and the Hazards of Affluence, New York: Harper and Row, 1966.

Cervantes has very recently pointed out, although the dropout group cuts across social class, ethnic, and geographic lines, most come from the blue- and lower white-collar economic classes. In summarizing, he says: "The dropout rate nationally is between 30 and 40 percent. The rate is higher in the South than in the North; higher among boys than girls (53 percent versus 47 percent); higher in the slums than in the suburbs. Most dropouts withdraw from school during or before their 16th year. There is 10 times the incidence of delinquency among the dropouts as there is among the stayins. In view of society's educational expectations for modern youth and dropout youth's inability to get a job while 'just waiting around for something to happen,' the very state of being a dropout has all but become by definition a condition of semidelinquency."[16]

On the one hand, then, the privileges and age roles are being extended by being lowered, and young teenagers are as sophisticated or cynical, as fantasy-filled and joyriding as our older teenagers used to be. On the other hand, and at the other end of the range of the youth age, the period of their not moving into adult roles is also being extended.

This extended socialization is accompanied by the problem of poor adult models. Throughout the social classes, it appears that the search for the adult to be emulated is often a desperate and futile quest. Part of the reason for this futility is due to the very rapid social and technological changes occurring in our society which make it more difficult for the adult to perform his traditional role of model and mentor to youth. Social change is so rapid, says Kenneth Keniston,[17] that growing up no longer means learning how to fit into society because the society into which young people will someday fit has not yet been developed or even, perhaps, cannot properly be imagined. Many youth feel forced into detachment and premature cynicism because society seems to offer youth today so little that is stable, relevant, and meaningful. They often look in vain for values, goals, means, and institutions to which they can be committed because their thrust for commitment is strong. Youth can be a period of fruitful idealism, but there are few of what Erik Erikson[18] would call "objects of fidelity" for our youth; so that "playing it cool," is more than an ephemeral expression—it becomes a way of avoiding damaging commitments to goals and life styles of the parent generation which may be outmoded tomorrow. Times and viewpoints shift rapidly, and many of our children resemble world-weary and jaded adults at age 14. The social isolation, social distance, alienation, and retreat from the adult world are increased by many social and technological mechanisms operating to encourage a youth

subculture. As the numbers and intensity of value sharing in the youth subculture increase, the process of intergenerational alienation also escalates. Parents have almost always been accused of not understanding their children. What may be new is that more parents either do not care that they do not understand, or that it is increasingly impossible for them to understand. Perhaps, then, it is not that parents are poor models for the kinds of lives that the youths will lead in their own mature years; parents may simply be increasingly irrelevant models for their children. So rapid is current social change that the youth of today have difficulty projecting a concept of themselves as adults.

This double stretch in that band of the life cycle we call youth has systemic effects on definitions and dependency. As the period of socialization extends further for more people, the concept of youth embraces later ages. When to this conceptual change is added the fact of greater life expectancy and a larger proportion of our population living longer, the social and perhaps physical meaning of middle age has changed, likewise moving upward. Our society has created linguistic support for this notion by its references to young adults, older youth, young or junior executives when referring to men who are in their midthirties or early forties.

The conceptual extension of what being young means is also reflected in the perpetration of a dependency status started in youth (that is, during late adolescence and early adulthood). The child from an economically deprived family, the dropout who becomes, like his parents, economically dependent on welfare benefits, remains in his dependency condition throughout much or most of his life. Others, mostly from the middle class, shift their extended dependency from being supported by parents or educational grants to being dependent on bureaucratic systems which continue the socialization process that often leads to the pathos of the organization man.

THE MASCULINE PROTEST AND ITS TRANSFORMATION

Social scientists have long stressed the importance of the theme of masculinity in American culture and the effect that this image of the strong masculine role has had on child rearing and the general socialization process. The inability of the middle-class child to match himself to this masculine model and the neuroticism that is the consequence of this increasingly futile struggle was vividly brought to our attention years ago by Arnold Green.[19] The continuity of this masculine role in the lower classes has often been asserted and was made one

---

[16] Lucius F. Cervantes, "The Dropout," Ann Arbor: University of Michigan Press, 1965, p. 197.
[17] Kenneth Keniston, "Social Change and Youth in America," in Erik H. Erikson (ed.), The Challenge of Youth, 1965, pp. 191–222.

[18] Erik H. Erikson, "Youth: Fidelity and Diversity," in Erik H. Erikson, ibid., pp. 1–28.
[19] Arnold W. Green, "The Middle Class Male Child and Neurosis," American Sociological Review (February 1946), 11:31–41.

of the "focal concerns" in Walter B. Miller's[20] profile of the lower class milieu. There is reason to believe, however, that this once dominating culture theme is dissipating, especially in the central or middle-class culture, and that this dissipation is diffusing downwards through the lower classes via the youth subculture. It may be argued that in the United States, while the status of the sexes in many social spheres of activity has been approaching equality, there has been an increasing feminization of the general culture. Instead of females becoming more like males, males have increasingly taken on some of the roles and attributes formerly assigned to females. It is not so much that maleness is reduced as a goal motivating young boys; rather, physical aggressiveness, once the manifest feature of maleness, is being reduced and the meaning of masculinity is thereby being changed to more symbolic forms. The continued diminution of the earlier frontier mores which placed a premium on male aggressiveness has been replaced by other attributes of masculinity. The gun and fist have been substantially replaced by financial ability, by the capacity to manipulate others in complex organizations, and by intellectual talents. The thoughtful wit, the easy verbalizer, even the striving musician and artist are, in the dominant culture, equivalents of male assertiveness where broad shoulders and fighting fists were once the major symbols. The young culture heroes may range from Van Cliburn to the Beattles, but Bill the Kid is a fantasy figure from an earlier history.

It may well be true that in many lower class communities violence is associated with masculinity and may not only be acceptable but admired behavior. That the rates of violent crimes are high among lower class males suggests that this group still strongly continues to equate maleness with overt physical aggression. In the Italian slum of the Boston West End, Herbert Gans[21] describes families dominated by the men and where mothers encourage male dominance. On the other hand, lower class boys who lack father or other strong male figures, as is the case with many boys in Negro families, have a problem of finding models to imitate. Rejecting female dominance at home and at school, and the morality which they associate with women, may be the means such boys use to assert their masculinity, and such assertion must be performed with a strong antithesis of feminity, namely by being physically aggressive. Being a bad boy, Parsons[22] has said, can become a positive goal if goodness is too closely identified with feminity.

Whatever the reasons for this stronger masculine role among lower class youth, its retention will continue to result in violence, because the young male is better equipped physically to manifest this form of masculinity than the very young, the middle-aged, or the very old. Because he needs no special education to employ the agents of physical aggression (fists, feet, agility), and because he seeks, as we all do, reinforcement from others for his ego and commitment, in this case to the values of violence, a youth often plays violent games of conflict within his own age-graded violent subcultural system. So do others play games, of course; the artist when he competes for a prize, the young scholar for tenure, the financier for a new subsidiary, and a nation for propaganda advantage. But the prescribed rules for street fighting produce more deadly quarrels with weapons of guns and knives than do competitions among males who use a brush, a dissertation, or a contract.

Jackson Toby[23] recently suggested that if the compulsive masculinity hypothesis has merit, it ought to generate testable predictions about the occurrence of violence. He lists the following: "(1) Boys who grow up in households headed by women are more likely to behave violently than boys who grow up in households headed by a man. . . . (2) Boys who grow up in households where it is relatively easy to identify with the father figure are less likely to behave violently than boys in households where identification with the father figure is difficult. . . . (3) Boys whose development toward adult masculinity is slower than their peers are more likely to behave violently than boys who find it easy to think of themselves as 'men'. . . . (4) Masculine ideals emphasize physical roughness and toughness in those populations where symbolic masculine power is difficult to understand. Thus, middle-class boys ought to be less likely than working class youngsters to idealize strength and its expression in action and to be more likely to appreciate the authority over other people exercised by a physician or a business executive."[24] As Toby indicates, it is unfortunate that evidence at present is so fragmentary that these predictions are not subject to rigorous evaluation.

The male self-conception is both important and interesting. Recently Leon Fannin and Marshall Clinard[25] tested for differences between lower class and middle class boys through informal depth interviewing and by forced-choice scales. While self-conceptions were quite similar, lower class boys felt themselves to be tougher, more powerful, fierce, fearless, and dangerous than middle class boys. "It was unexpected," claim the authors, "that they (the lower class boys) did not feel themselves to be significantly more violent, hard, and pugilistic."

[20] Walter B. Miller, "Lower Class Culture as a Generating Milieu of Gang Delinquency," Journey of Social Issues (1958), 14:5–19.

[21] Herbert J. Gans, The Urban Villages, New York: Free Press of Glencoe, 1962.

[22] Talcott Parsons, "Certain Primary Sources and Patterns of Aggression in the Social Structure of the Western World," Psychiatry (May 1947), 10:167–181.

[23] Jackson Toby, "Violence and the Masculine Ideal: Some Qualitative Data," in Marvin E. Wolfgang (ed.) "Patterns of Violence," The Annals of the American Academy of Political and Social Science (March 1966), 364:19–27.

[24] Ibid., pp. 21–22.

[25] Leon F. Fannin and Marshall B. Clinard, "Differences in the Conception of Self as a Male Among Lower and Middle Class Delinquents," Social Problems (fall 1965), 13:205–214.

The middle class boys conceived themselves as being more clever, smart, smooth, bad, and loyal. The self-conceptions were also related to specific types of behavior, for the "tough guys" significantly more often "committed violent offenses, fought more often and with harsher means, carried weapons, had lower occupational aspirations, and stressed toughness and related traits in the reputation they desired and in sexual behavior."[26]

Should the lower classes become more like the middle class in value orientation, family structure, and stability, there is reason to believe the emphasis on masculine identification through physical prowess and aggression will decline. The need to prove male identity may not disappear, but even being "bad" in order to sever the linkage of morality and femininity may become increasingly difficult to perform in a purely masculine way. And if there are available, as some believe, new and alternative models for demonstrating masculinity, ways that may be neither "bad" nor physically aggressive, then we should expect masculine identity to be manifested differently, that is symbolically, even by lower class boys. As the larger culture becomes more cerebral, the refined symbolic forms of masculinity should be more fully adopted. And as the disparity in life style, values, and norms between the lower and middle classes is reduced, so too will be reduced the subculture of violence that readily resorts to violence as an expected form of masculine response to certain situations.

If this social prognosis proves correct, there may not always be functional and virtuous expertise in the masculine symbolism. We could witness, for example, a shift from direct physical violence to detached and impersonalized violence or to corruption. The dominant, middle class culture has a considerable tolerance for distant and detached violence expressed in ways that range from dropping heavy bombs on barely visible targets, to the stylized, bloodless violence of film and television heroes, and to the annual slaughter of 50,000 persons on our highways. This same culture, for reasons too complex to detail here, not only tolerates but sometimes creates structural features in its social system that seem to encourage corruption, from tax evasion to corporate crime.[27] To transform the theme of male aggressiveness may mean assimilation with the larger culture, but this may merely increase the distance between the user and consumer of violence, and increase the volume of contributors to corruption. It may be hoped, of course, that changes in the current direction of the dominant culture may later produce a more sanguine description of this whole process.

YOUTH AND VIOLENT CRIME

There is little more than faulty and inadequate official delinquency statistics to answer basic questions about the current extent and character of youth crime. Recording techniques have changed, more juvenile police officers are engaged in handling young offenders, more methods are used for registering such minor juvenile status offenses as running away from home, being incorrigible, or truant. For over a decade most city police departments have used a dichotomy of "official-nonofficial arrest" or "remedial-arrest" or "warned-arrest" for apprehending juveniles, but not for adults. Yet both forms of juvenile disposition are recorded and rates of delinquency are computed in the total. Separate treatises have been written on these matters[28] which we cannot pursue here in detail.

The public image of a vicious, violent juvenile population producing a seemingly steady increase in violent crime is not substantiated by the evidence available. There may be more juvenile delinquency recorded today, but even that is predominantly property offenses. Rather consistently we are informed by the Uniform Crime Reports, published by the Federal Bureau of Investigation, that two-thirds of automobile thefts and about one-half of all burglaries and robberies are committed by persons under 18 years of age. Among crimes of personal violence, arrested offenders under age 18 are generally low; for criminal homicide they are about 8 percent; for forcible rape and aggravated assault, about 18 percent.

What this actually means is not that these proportions of these crimes are committed by juveniles, but that among persons who are taken into custody for these offenses, these proportions hold. Most police officers agree that it is easier to effect an arrest in cases involving juveniles than in cases involving adults. Most crimes known to the police, that is, complaints made to them or offenses discovered by them, are not "cleared by arrest," meaning cleared from their records by taking one or more persons into custody and making them available for prosecution. The general clearance rate is roughly 30 percent. Thus, the adult-juvenile distribution among 70 percent of so-called major crimes (criminal homicide, forcible rape, robbery, aggravated assault, burglary, larceny over $50, auto theft) is not known and cannot safely be projected from the offenses cleared or the age distribution of offenders arrested.

In addition, very often the crude legal labels attached to many acts committed by juveniles give a false impression of the seriousness of their acts. For example, a

---

[26] Ibid., p. 214.

[27] We have borrowed from a quite different context in which Georges Sorel expressed similar ideas about the shift from force to fraud, from violence to corruption as the path to success and privilege. The first edition of Reflextions sur la violence appeared in 1906; also, Paris: M. Riviere, 1936. For additional reference to this work, see Marvin E. Wolfgang, "A Preface to Violence," in "Patterns of Violence," The An-

nals of the American Academy of Political and Social Science (March 1966), 364:1–7.

[28] See for example, Thorsten Sellin and Marvin E. Wolfgang, The Measurement of Delinquency, New York: John Wiley and Sons, Inc. 1964. A new summary of these problems from around the world may be found in T. C. N. Gibbens and R. A. Ahrenfeldt (eds.), Cultural Factors in Delinquency, London: Tavistock Publications, 1966.

"highway robbery" may be a $100-theft at the point of a gun and may result in the victim's being hospitalized from severe wounds. But commonly, juvenile acts that carry this label and are used for statistical compilation are more minor. Typical in the files of a recent study were cases involving two 9-year-old boys, one of whom twisted the arm of the other on the school yard to obtain 25 cents of the latter's lunch money. This act was recorded and counted as "highway robbery." In another case, a 9-year-old boy engaged in exploratory sexual activity with an 8-year-old girl on a playlot. The girl's mother later complained to the police, who recorded the offense as "assault with intent to ravish."

Nothing now exists in the official published collection of crime statistics to yield better information about the qualitative variations of seriousness. Weighted scores of seriousness are possible and available for producing a weighted rate of crime and delinquency, much like the operating refinements in fertility and mortality rates or in econometric analyses.[29] Without a weighted system, it is the incautious observer who is willing to assert that youth crime is worse today than a generation or even a decade ago.

Moreover, computing rates of crime or delinquency per 100,000 is an extremely unsatisfactory and crude technique. Even a rate for all persons under 18 years of age fails to account for the bulges in specific ages like 14, 15, 16, 17, 18 that have occurred because of high fertility rates shortly after World War II. Without age-specific rates, most criminologists are reluctant to make assertions about trends or even the current amount of juvenile crime and violence. Research is now underway that hopefully will provide new and more meaningful age specific rates. It would not be expected if, when these rates are computed, much of any recorded increase in violent juvenile crime for the past 8 years or so could be attributed to standard statistical error.

By making certain gross assumptions about the proportion of juvenile population between the meaningful ages of 10 and 17 for the population in cities of 2,500 and over included in the survey areas of the Uniform Crime Reports from 1958 to 1964,[30] it has been possible to provide some juvenile rates for violent or assaultive crimes against the person. Computations were performed in the following way: the population of all cities of 2,500 inhabitants and more, included in the Uniform Crime Reporting area, was summed for each of the 7 years from 1958 through 1964. (1958 was a year of important revisions in the UCR classification system, hence a safe year with which to begin the analysis.) The total populations of the United States and of the children from ages 10 through 17 were obtained for each of the 7 years from reports of the Bureau of the Census. The respective proportions of the 10- to 17-year-old population for each year were readily obtained from these census reports and then applied to the UCR survey population. The number of juveniles under 18 years of age arrested for specific offenses, divided by the population of persons aged 10 to 17, multiplied by 100,000, yielded a rate for each of the years. The table below shows these rates:[31]

Urban Rates of Crimes of Violence for Persons Arrested, Ages 10–17

	1958	1959	1960	1961	1962	1963	1964
Criminal homicide: murder and nonnegligent manslaughter	1.9	2.3	3.0	3.2	2.9	2.9	3.1
Negligent manslaughter	1.15	0.98	1.10	0.96	0.79	1.00	0.87
Forcible rape	10.0	9.8	10.9	11.4	11.2	10.3	10.0
Aggravated assault	34.4	35.8	53.2	60.1	61.6	63.0	74.5
Other assaults	95.9	118.0	118.7	126.0	139.2	153.7	163.6

Caution must be applied to these figures because of two major assumptions that had to be made: That the UCR survey population contained roughly the same proportion of persons aged 10–17 as the general population of the United States; that the overwhelming bulk of arrests of juveniles under 18 years of age, for offenses against the person, involved offenders no younger than age 10. It is assumed that little error is involved in this latter assumption because most juvenile court statutes with a lower age limit do not go below ages 6 or 7, and

[29] For details of one such weighting system, see Sellin and Wolfgang, The Measurement of Delinquency, op cit.

[30] Uniform Crime Reports, Washington, D.C.: Federal Bureau of Investigation, Department of Justice, 1958 to 1964. See also the report of the New York Division of Youth on this period, "Youth Crime—A Leveling Off?", Youth Services News (spring 1966), 17:3–5, and the succinct analysis of UCR and California data, found in Ronald H. Beattie and John P. Kenney, The Annals of the American Academy of Political and Social Science (March 1966), 364:73–85.

[31] The following data were used for computing the rates:

The UCR survey population of cities of 2,500 and more inhabitants, for the years 1958 through 1964, was: for 1958—52,329,497; 1959—56,187,181; 1960—81,660,735; 1961—85,158,360; 1962—94,014,000; 1963—94,085,000; 1964—99,326,000. (Source: UCR Reports, Tables 18, 17, 18, 21, 21, 28, 27 for the respective years.)

The U.S. population for the years 1959–64 was: 171,822,000; 177,830,000; 180,684,000, 183,756,000; 186,591,000; 189,417,000; 192,119,000. (Source:

Estimates of the Bureau of the Census, Department of Commerce, Current Population Reports, Series P-25, No. 314, August 1965.)

The percentages which the UCR survey population represented of the total U.S. population were: 29, 31, 45, 46, 50, 50, and 52 percent. (Computed.)

The U.S. child population aged 10–17 for the years 1958–64 was: 23,433,000; 24,607,000; 25,364,000; 26,023,000; 27,983,000; 29,119,000. (Source: Estimates of Bureau of Census, Department of Commerce, Current Population Reports, Series P-25.) The UCR child population aged 10–17 for the years 1958–64 was 6,798,470; 7,628,170; 11,423,800; 13,468,000; 13,999,150; 15,141,880. (Assumed and computed.)

The number of persons under 18 years of age arrested for each of the five offenses over each of the 7 years may be found on the specific tables in the UCR annual reports.

In gathering and computing these data, the author had the assistance of Bernard Cohen, Research Assistant, Center of Criminological Research, University of Pennsylvania.

very few of these offenses are ever recorded for ages below 10. Moreover, computing a rate based on the entire population under 18 years would continue the unsatisfactory practice of including in the denominator preschool and infant children.

With this caution and these assumptions, the table can nevertheless be said to show substantially the same rates in 1964 as in 1960 for murder and nonnegligent manslaughter and for rape. Murder and nonnegligent manslaughter reached a peak rate in 1961 of 3.2, was under a rate of 3.0 per 100,000 in 1962 and 1963, and was 3.1 in 1964. These slight variations are of no statistical consequence, considering the operation of chance errors.

Negligent manslaughter was highest in 1958 (1.15), had no statistically significant increase in the years since then, and in 1964 was down to 0.87. This offense mostly refers to automobile deaths, and despite the fact that more teenagers are driving today, the rate has not increased. Forcible rape has not significantly changed over the 7 years: the high was 11.4 in 1961 and has dropped to 10.3 in 1963 and 10.0 in 1964. Aggravated assault jumped from 34.4 in 1958 to 53.2 in 1960, had a relatively stable rate of 60.1 to 63.0 between 1961 and 1963 and then rose to 74.5 in 1964. Other assaults (not part of the UGR index offenses) climbed steadily from 95.9 in 1958 to 163.6 in 1964.

There is little in these figures of criminal homicide or rape that should cause alarm. Assaults appear to be the main area of violence that should cause concern. But not until better data are available from some of the studies previously mentioned can we make proper conclusions and interpretations.

Among city gangs selected for their reputation for toughness and studied in detail by detached workers, the amount of violent crime, reports Walter B. Miller, is surprisingly low. Twenty-one groups, numbering about 700 members, yielded cumulative figures of 228 known offenses committed by 155 boys during a 2-year period and 138 court charges for 293 boys during a 12-year span. Miller remarks that " . . . violence appears neither as a dominant preoccupation of city gangs nor as a dominant form of criminal activity,"[32] even among these toughest of gang members, the yearly rate of assault charges per 100 individuals per year of age was only 4.8 at age 15, 7.2 at 16, 7.2 at 17, and 7.8 at 18, after which the rates dropped through the early twenties. Violent crimes were committed by only a small minority of these gang members, represented a transient phenomenon, were mostly unarmed physical encounters between combatting males, did not victimize adult females, and were not ideological forms of behavior.[33]

It should be mentioned also that the increasingly methodologically refined studies of hidden deliquency have not clearly and consistently reported a significant reduction in the disparity of social classes for crimes of violence.[34] The incidence and frequency of crimes of violence appear to remain considerably higher among boys from lower social classes when the appropriate questions are asked about these offenses over specific periods of time. In their recent study of delinquents, Fannin and Clinard reported: "One of the more important of the tests was a comparison of the frequency with which reported and unreported robberies and assaults were committed by members of the two class levels (middle and lower). The vast majority of all lower class delinquents, 84 percent, had committed at least one such offense compared to 28 percent of the middle class (probability less than 0.01); 28 percent of the lower and 8 percent of the middle class had committed 10 or more violent offenses. Class level was also related to the frequency of fighting with other boys. Lower class delinquents fought singly and in groups significantly more often (probability less than 0.05) than middle class delinquents, with 20 percent of them averaging five or more fights per month compared to 4.0 percent."[35]

It should also be kept in mind that the proportion of the entire juvenile population under 18 years of age that, in any calendar year, is processed by the police and juvenile court is generally no higher than 3 to 5 percent. There are, however, several factors denied clarity by this kind of commonly reported statistic: (1) Arrest or juvenile-court-appearance statistics include duplicate counting of the same juveniles who have run away, been truant, or committed malicious mischief more than once during the year, and for some types of offenses this amount of duplication can be sizable; (2) the figure ignores the fact that children have been delinquent during preceding years, and that in many census tracts throughout large cities as many as 70 percent or more of all juveniles under 18 years, at one time or another during their juvenile-court-statute ages, may have been delinquent. Solomon Kobrin[36] and others have drawn attention to this perspective; Nils Christie[37] in Norway has done the most elaborate study on the topic by analyzing

[32] Walter B. Miller, "Violent Crimes in City Gangs," in Marvin E. Wolfgang (ed.), "Patterns of Violence," The Annals of the American Academy of Political and Social Science (March 1966), 364:96–112.
[33] Ibid.
For a new, detailed listing of research and theory in this area, see Dorothy Campbell Tompkins, Juvenile Gangs and Street Gangs—A Bibliography, Berkeley, Calif.: Institute of Governmental Studies at the University of California, Berkeley, 1966.
[34] See Robert Hardt and George F. Bodine, Development of Self-Report Instruments in Delinquency Research, Syracuse, N.Y.: Youth Develop-

ment Center, Syracuse University, 1965. This item is a conference report on methods of doing research on hidden delinquency and includes a good bibliography of major items in that area. See also Nils Christie, Johs. Andenacs, and Sigurd Skirbekk, "A Study of Self-Reporting Crime," in Karl O. Christiansen (ed.), Scandinavian Studies in Criminology, vol I, London: Tavistock Publications, 1965; Kerstin Elmhorn, "Study in Self-Reported Delinquency among School-Children in Stockholm," in Karl O. Christiansen (ed.), Scandanavian Studies in Criminology, vol. I, London: Tavistock Publications, 1965.
[35] Fannin and Clinard, op. cit. p. 211.

a birth cohort; and Thorsten Sellin and Marvin Wolfgang[38] are presently engaged in a large-scale research of a birth cohort of approximately 10,000 males in Philadelphia in order to compute a cohort rate of delinquency, examine their cumulative seriousness scores by age and over time, and to provide a prediction model that might aid in decisions about the most propitious time in juvenile life cycles for maximizing the effectiveness of social intervention.

The data needed to describe the volume of youth crime are inadequate at present, but an alarmist attitude does not appear justified. Age-specific and weighted rates are required before trends can be validly presented and analyzed, but because of the known rise in the present adolescent population due to high fertility rates of the late forties, there is reason to suspect that any overall increase in juvenile delinquency can be largely attributed to the population increase in the ages from 14 to 18. The absolute amount of delinquency can be expected to increase for some time, for this same reason, but there is no basis for assuming that rates of juvenile violence will increase.

Moreover, as the suburban population increases, the amount of juvenile delinquency can be expected to rise in these areas even without a rate increase. In addition, as the social class composition of suburbs changes, as it has been, from being predominantly upper class to containing more middle and lower middle class families, the rates of delinquency of the last migrating class will travel with them. And as Robert Bohlke[39] has suggested, what is often viewed as middle class delinquency is not middle class in the sense of the traditional middle class value system or life style but only in terms of the middle income group. There is considerable theoretical merit in this suggestion which should be further explored through empirical research.

Finally, with respect to delinquency, it might be said that a certain amount of this form of deviancy has always existed, will continue to exist, and perhaps should exist. In the sense discussed by Emile Durkheim,[40] crime is normal, and perhaps even, in some quantity, desirable. Not only does the existence of delinquency provide the collective conscience an opportunity to reinforce its norms by applying sanctions, but the presence of deviancy reflects the existence of something less than a total system of control over individuals. Moreover, there appear to be personality traits among many delinquents that could be viewed as virtues if behavior were rechanneled. For instance, Sheldon and Eleanor Glueck noted, in "Unravel-

ing Juvenile Delinquency,"[41] that among 500 delinquents compared to 500 nondelinquents, the delinquent boys were characterized as hedonistic, distrustful, aggressive, hostile and, as boys who felt they could manage their own lives, were socially assertive, and defied authority. The nondelinquents were more banal, conformistic, neurotic, felt unloved, insecure, and anxiety-ridden. The attributes associated with the delinquents sound similar to descriptions of the Renaissance Man who defied the authority and static orthodoxy of the middle ages, who was also aggressive, richly assertive, this-world rather than other-world centered, and was less banal, more innovative, than his medieval predecessors. The Glueck delinquents also sound much like our 19th century captains in industry, our 20th century political leaders and corporation executives. The freedom to be assertive, to defy authority and orthodoxy may sometimes have such consequences as crime and delinquency, but it is well to remember that many aspects of American ethos, our freedom, our benevolent attitude toward rapid social change, our heritage of revolution, our encouragement of massive migrations, our desire to be in or near large urban centers, and many other values that we cherish, may produce the delinquency we deplore as well as many things we desire.

THE SEARCH FOR POWER AND PARTICIPATION: YOUTH, NEGROES, AND THE POOR

We have said that to speak generically of youth overlooks variability in a pluralistic society, and we have drawn attention to some notable variations between middle class and lower class youth. There are, however, many more versions of the concatenation of variables that differentiate youth. Being young, middle class, white, and from an economically secure family generates a quite different image from being young, lower class, poor, and Negro. In sheer absolute numbers, more young people are located in the former group that in the latter and probably suffer fewer strains from culture contradictions, anomie, and psychological deprivation than do the latter. There is likely to be greater conformity to parental prescriptions in the former, more familial transmission of group values, more cohesiveness of the family. The Negro, lower class of youth drop out of school and drift into delinquency in greater proportions than do white middle class youth. Class is probably a stronger factor

[36] Solomon Kobrin, "The Conflict of Values in Delinquency Areas," *American Sociological Review* (October 1951), 16:653–661.

[37] Nils Christie, *Unge norske lovovertrebere*, Oslo, Norway: Institute Criminology, Oslo University, 1960.

[38] Thorsten Sellin and Marvin E. Wolfgang, The Extent and Character of Delinquency in an Age Cohort, research project of the Center of Criminological Research, University of Pennsylvania, sponsored by the National Institute of Mental Health.

[39] Robert H. Bohlke, "Social Mobility, Stratification Inconsistency in Middle Class Delinquency," *Social Problems* (spring 1961), 8:351–363. See also, Ralph W. England, Jr., "A Theory of Middle Class Delinquency," *Journal of Criminal Law, Criminology and Police Science* (April 1960), 50:535–540.

[40] Emile Durkheim, Rules of Sociological Method, 8th Edition, translated by Sarah A. Solvay and John H. Mueller and edited by George E. G. Catlin, Glencoe, Illinois: Free Press, 1950, pp. 65–73.

contributing to value allegiance and normative conduct than is race, which is to say that Negro and white middle class youth are more alike than are Negro middle and lower class or white middle and lower class youngsters.

Yet, with all the variabilities that might be catalogued in an empirically descriptive study of youth, there are characteristics of the life stage, status, and style of youth in general which are shared by the status of poverty and the status of being Negro in American society. All may be described as possessing a kind of structural marginality[42] that places them on the periphery of power in our society. When the multiple probabilities of being young, Negro, and poor exist, the shared attributes are more than a summation. The force of whatever problems they represent is more of multiplicative than an additive function.

Youth, Negroes, and the poor have subcultural value systems different from, yet subsidiary to the larger culture. They often share many features, such as being deprived of certain civil rights and liberties, barred from voting, and denied adequate defense counsel and equality of justice. Their current statuses are frequently subject to manipulation by an enthroned elite and their power to effect change in their futures may be minimal. They tend to have common conflicts with authority and to be dominated by females in the matriarchial structure of their own social microcosms.

All three groups know the meaning of spatial segregation, whether voluntary or compulsory. For youth, it is in schools, clubs, seating arrangements, occupations, forms of entertainment, and leisure pursuits. For the poor and for Negroes, it may be all of these as well as place of residence and other alternatives of work, play, and mobility opportunities. There are similarities in their subordinate and dependency status, and in having poor, inadequate, or irrelevant role models. The values and behavior of the dominant culture and class in American society, as adopted by Negroes, often reveal a pathetically compulsive quality; the poor have been denied access to the ends to which they subscribe, and youth is, at best, a power-muted microculture. For all three, norms seem to shift and change with more than common frequency or are not clearly designated. All three groups tend to be more romantic, nonrational, impulsive, physically aggressive, more motivated toward immediacy and directness than their counterparts in the dominant culture. There is among youth, Negroes, and the poor more deviant and criminal behavior, and a greater disparity between aspiration and achievement. At times their re-

volt against authority erupts into violence for which they feel little guilt or responsibility.

Increasingly they are self-conscious, aware of their own collectivities as subcultural systems, partly because their revolt is today a greater threat to the systems which have been established to control, govern, or manipulate them. The poor are being asked for the first time what they want and what they would like to do to help themselves or have done for them. Negroes are acting as advisers and consultants on Federal policy, and young people are being heard when they speak about Vietnam, restrictions on passports, college curricula, faculty appointments, and new notions of freedom and sexual morality.

With more clarity and conscience, the three groups are searching for meaningfulness, identity, and social justice. They are articulating their protest against powerlessness, are seeking participation in decision making processes that affect their own life conditions. That some retreat into drugs, alcohol, and other symptoms of alienation is now viewed as dysfunctional by their own majorities as well as by the establishment. That some resort to violence, whether in Watts or in Hampton Beach,[43] episodic, meant to display boredom with their condition, blatant protest, and latent power. As achievement, as a danger signal, and as a catalyst, violence for them may serve the social functions outlined by Lewis Coser.[44] But their use of violence is end-oriented and cannot be viewed as a cultural psychopathology. They desire to be recognized, not to be forgotten, because they now see themselves for the first time. They are seeking what Edmund Williamson,[45] dean at the University of Minnesota, calls the most important freedom of all—to be taken seriously, to be listened to.

One of the interesting things about American youth today, especially the older student segment, is its activistic character and increasing identification with the poor and with the civil rights movement. There is an intense morality and a demand for clear commitments. In many cases young people are directly involved in working in neighborhoods of poverty or in the Negro struggle in the South, whether in song, march, or litigation. Moreover, the idealism of youth and this identification with the process toward participation in power is being fostered by Federal support of the Peace Corps program, both foreign and domestic, and by much governmental concern and protection of young civil rights workers in the South. But the reference here to identification is not to these overlapping involvements; it is to the means for communicating their lack of participation in formulating

---

[41] Sheldon and Eleanor Glueck, Unraveling Juvenile Delinquency, Cambridge, Mass.: Harvard University Press for the Commonwealth Fund, 1950.

[42] Tamme Wittermans and Irving Kraus, "Structural Marginality and Social Worth," Sociology and Social Research (April 1964), 48:348–360. For an excellent summary of theory and research on lower class family life, see the recent work of Suzanne Keller, The American Lower Class Family, Albany: New York State Division for Youth, 1965.

[43] See the Hampton Beach Project, Paul Estaver, Director, Project Director's Report, Hampton Beach, N.H.: Hampton Beach Chamber of Commerce, n.d.

[44] Lewis A. Coser, "Some Social Functions of Violence," in Marvin E. Wolfgang (ed.), "Patterns of Violence," The Annals of the American Academy of Political and Social Science (March 1966) 364:8–18.

[45] The New York Times, Nov. 21, 1965, p. 72.

the rules of life's games. Impatience, discontent, and dissatisfaction with the state of American society[46] become healthy reflections of a new commitment, a commitment to the desire for change and for participating in the direction of change.

Obviously, there are also differences among the three groups, the most striking of which is the fact that youth is a temporary stage in a life cycle and that ultimately the structural marginality and status deprivation are overcome for many by the passage of time. The representatives of the subculture of youth are mobile, eventually leave the subculture, and with age, birth cohorts socially fold into one another. But the status designation of Negro is, except for race crossings, permanent, and the poor commonly have oppressive generational continuity. That youth in its temporariness shares with the major minority groups certain attributes of being and of the struggle for becoming is itself noteworthy, even if the youth were less affected by and conscious of their mutual interests, means, and goals. Perhaps the short sample of time represented by youth will one day be viewed in the long perspective as symbolic of the longer, but also temporary, state of deprivation and disenfranchisement of being poor or of having the status of Negro in American society.

The identity of youth with the protestation process, whether similar to or in common with the poor and the Negro, is, of course, not universal and may not even be a cultural modality. Its expression is, nonetheless, vigorous and viable. It has entered the arena of public attention and functions as a prodder for its concepts of progress. With this identity, the youth of today are unlike the "flaming youth" in the frenetic milieu of the twenties, the youth associated with the political left and the proletarian cult of the thirties, the uninformed youth of the forties, or the passive youth of the fifties. And yet, even with this identity they are without a systematic ideology. Despite the fact that they have come to realize the ad-

vantages of collective drives that prick the giants of massive and lethargic organization into action, they have developed no political affiliation. Perhaps the closest these young groups come to a focal concern is in their alerting their peers and adults to the ethical conflicts and issues embraced by society's increasing ability to reduce individual anonymity and to manipulate lives. In one sense it could be said that they jealously guard the constraints a democratic society ideologically imposes on overcontrol, invasion of privacy, and overreaction to deviancy.

There are fringes to most movements, and there are parasites attached to the youth we have been describing as healthier segments of society. Frequently the fringe looms larger than the core in the public image of youth and an excessive degree of rebelliousness is conveyed. The bulk of our youth are not engaged in a rebellion against adults, and the degree of dissimilarity between the generations has often been overstressed, as some authors have recently asserted.[47] Rather than rejecting most parental norms, the majority of those in the youth subculture are eager to participate in the larger society. Individuals resisting specific authority patterns do not constitute group rejection of dominant social norms.

Moreover, except for those suppressed beyond youth by their status of being poor or being Negro, achievement comes with aging and that convergence often leads to the collapse of a once fiery, romantic drive. And, as Peter Berger[48] has eloquently remarked, with success, prophets become priests and revolutionaries become administrators.

The gravity of time pulls hard on our muscles and ideals and too often the earlier triumph of principle gives way to the triumph of expedience. The once lambent minds of youth are frequently corroded by conformity in adulthood, and a new flow of youth into the culture is needed to invoke their own standards of judgment on our adult norms.

---

[46] On this point, see Talcott Parsons, "Youth in the Context of American Society," in Erik H. Erikson, The Challenge of Youth, 1965, pp. 110–141.
[47] Robert C. Bealer, Fern K. Willits, and Peter R. Maida, "The Myth of a Rebellious Adolescent Subculture: Its Detrimental Effects for Understanding Rural Youth," in Lee G. Burchinal (ed.), Rural Youth in Crisis,

Proceedings of a National Conference on Rural Youth in a Changing Environment, Stillwater, Okla., 1963, Washington, D.C.: U.S. Government Printing Office, 1965.
[48] Peter Berger, An Invitation to Sociology: A Humanistic Perspective, New York: Doubleday & Co., Anchor Book, 1963.

Preventing Crime, Saving Children:

Sticking To The Basics

BY JOHN J. DIIULIO, JR.

"Post-Crack," Not Post-Problem

Like media coverage of most complicated social problems, press attention to the problems of youth crime and substance abuse ebbs and flows. But make no mistake: the passing of the much publicized inner-city crack-cocaine-and-crime epidemic of the late 1980s and early 1990s is *not* synonymous with the passing of the challenges of youth crime and substance abuse, least of all in urban America. The news spotlight on juvenile crime and delinquency flickers, but the practical and moral challenges posed by millions of juveniles who murder, rape, rob, assault, burglarize, vandalize, join street gangs, deal illegal drugs or consume illegal drugs does not thereby fade.

To the contrary, an intellectually and ideologically diverse range of expert voices has been proclaiming that the challenges of youth crime and substance abuse are more pressing today than they were at the height of the crack plague. Consider, for example, reports released over the last several years by the National Research Council, the International Association of Chiefs of Police, and the Council on Crime in America.

A few years ago, the National Research Council's Panel on High-Risk Youth reported that at least seven million young Americans—roughly a quarter of adolescents aged 10 to 17—are at risk of failing to achieve productive adult lives.[1] The United States, the panel warned, is in danger of "losing generations" of low-income children who abuse illegal drugs, engage in unprotected premarital sex, drop out of school, prove unable to get and keep jobs, succumb to the blandishments of illegal drugs, commit serious crimes or become victims of serious crimes.

In 1996, the International Association of Chiefs of Police (IACP) held a major summit on youth violence. The IACP noted that the number of juvenile offenders had risen rapidly in recent years, and warned that juvenile crime "will get considerably worse as a big new group of youngsters reach their teenage years." Looking over the horizon of the next few years, the IACP envisioned more kids, more drugs, more guns and more murders.[2] According to the IACP, in 1996 crack cocaine use was down, but crack was hardly invisible on East Coast inner-city streets, heroin was making a roaring comeback (especially on the West Coast), and LSD, amphetamine, stimulant and inhalant use was rising among teenagers nationwide. Thus, in several big cities, the percentage of juveniles in custody who tested positive for illegal drug use has more than tripled since 1990.

In 1997, the bipartisan Council on crime in America stated flatly that "America's crime prevention challenge—at core a challenge of at-risk youth in need of adults—must be met, and soon." According to the Council, in 1994 there were over 2.7 million arrests of persons under age 18 (a third of them under age 15), up from 1.7 million juvenile arrests in 1991. Some 150,000 of these 2.7 million arrests were for violent crimes. In all, juveniles were responsible for an estimated 14 percent of all violent crimes and a quarter of all property crimes known to the police. Nationally, juveniles perpetrated 137,000 more violent crimes in 1994 than in 1985, and were responsible for 26 percent of the growth in violent crime over that period, including 50 percent of the increase in robberies, 48 percent of the increase in rapes, and 35 percent of the increase in murders. Juvenile violent crime arrest rates rose 5.2 percent in 1987–88 , 18.8 percent in 1988–89, 12.1 percent in 1989–90, 7.6 percent in 1990–91, and by at least 4.4 percent in every year thereafter until 1994–95, when arrests for violent crime among juveniles aged 10 to 17 fell by 2.9 percent. While such recent drops in juvenile arrest rates are obviously welcome, the Council urged all Americans to place them against the backdrop of a decade's worth of steep annual increases in youth crime and violence.

Moreover, the Council warned, America is now home to about 57 million children

From *Perspectives*, Spring 1998, pp. 24-29. © 1998 by The Council of State Governments. Reprinted by permission of the American Probation and Parole Association.

under age 15, some 20 million of them aged four to eight. The teenage population will top 30 million by the year 2006, the highest number since 1975. Thus, "no one," the Council concluded, "should feel certain that recent declines in crime will continue into the next century.

Indeed, the nation's two most widely respected criminologists, Professor James Q. Wilson of UCLA and Professor Marvin E. Wolfgang of the University of Pennsylvania, have both expressed deep concerns about present and impending youth crime and delinquency patterns and trends. According to Wilson, average Americans of every race, creed and region are right to "believe that something fundamental has changed in our patterns of crime," namely, the tangible threat of unprecedented levels of youth crime and substance abuse, including acts of violence committed by youngsters who "afterwards show us the blank, unremorseful stare of a feral, pre-social being."[4] Likewise, Wolfgang has observed that today's juvenile offenders probably do about three times as much serious crime as did the crime-prone boys born in the 1940s and 1950s, and could represent a new and especially challenging "subculture of violence."[5]

The expert understandings, statistics and warnings about youth crime and substance abuse seem broadly consistent with the well-founded worries of young Americans themselves. Any juvenile between ages 12 and 17 is more likely to be the victim of violent crime than are persons past their mid-twenties, and about half of all crimes of violence committed by juveniles are committed against juveniles.[6] A 1994 survey asked teenagers "How much of the time do you worry about being the victim of a crime?" In response, about 36 percent of white teenagers and 54 percent of black teenagers said "A lot or some of the time."[7] Apparently, the number of youngsters who are growing up scared in America—scared of other juveniles, that is—has been increasing for some time now. A 1995 Gallup Youth Survey found that between 1977 and 1994 the fraction of teenagers who regularly fear for their physical safety at school increased by 38 percent to one in four. And one teen in four said there was at least one time in the past year when they feared for their physical safety while in school classrooms or hallways, on playgrounds, or walking to and from school.[8]

Sticking to the Basics, Acting Now

The good news is that we do know a lot about youth crime and substance abuse that is relevant to saving at-risk youth—and acting now. Strategically, the key to preventing youth crime and substance abuse among our country's expanding juvenile population is to improve the real, live, day-to-day connections between responsible adults and young people—period. Whether it emanates from the juvenile justice system or from the community, from government agencies or from civil institutions, from faith-based programs or secular ones, from nonprofits or for-profits or public/private partnerships, from structural theorists or cultural theorists, from veteran probation officers or applied econometricians, no policy, program or intervention that fails to build meaningful connections between responsible adults and at-risk young people has worked, or can.

Of all the factors we have found as contributing to delinquency, the clearest and most exhaustive evidence concerns the adequacy of parenting. Parents who are incompetent, abusive, or rejecting, parents who fail to maintain adequate supervision over their children, and parents who, indeed, are little more than children themselves, have direct effects on anti-social behavior of their children.

It is all well and good to acknowledge both the multivariate character of social problems, and the myriad legal, political, administrative, financial and other difficulties of replicating what works. But it is also all too easy to let such intellectually de rigeur acknowledgments of social complexity become convenient covers for academic excuse-mongering, inaction and, of course, calls for more grants for more basic research, more research symposia, more conferences—more of everything save more human and financial support of people and existing programs that actually put responsible adults into the daily lives of the at-risk kids of inner-city Detroit, Philadelphia, and other major metropolitan regions.

James Q. Wilson has argued that uncovering "the subtle interaction between individual characteristics and social circumstances requires policy-related research of a sort and on a scale that has not been attempted before."[9] I agree. But there is already a voluminous private foundation-funded literature on understanding and reducing violence.[10] There is also a huge and still-growing government-funded literature on the literally dozens of "contexts and factors" that determine crime patterns.[11]

Besides, easily the most persistent, policy-relevant and common-sensical finding of the literature is that most disadvantaged youth who commit crimes and abuse drugs begin as neglected or maltreated children in need of responsible adults. In the words of a 1996 draft report of an American Society of Criminology task force on juvenile delinquency:

Of all the factors we have found as contributing to delinquency, the clearest and most exhaustive evidence concerns the adequacy of parenting. Parents who are incompetent, abusive, or rejecting, parents who fail to maintain adequate supervision over their children, and parents who, indeed, are little more than children themselves, have direct effects on anti-social behavior of their children. Inadequacy of parenting cannot be viewed in isolation as the sole cause of delinquency. However, its association with other factors is critical in predicting future delinquency.[12]

Likewise, in a magisterial, still unsurpassed and only slightly dated 500-plus-page summary of the scientific literatures on criminal behavior, Wilson and the late Richard J. Hernstein concluded that "after all is said and done, the most serious offenders are boys who begin their careers at a very early age."[13] Numerous empirical studies have indeed found that most juveniles who engage "in frequent criminal acts against persons and property . . . come from family settings characterized by high levels of violence, chaos, and dysfunction."[14] For example, a study that compared the family experiences of more violent and less violent incarcerated juveniles found that 75 percent of the former group had suffered serious abuse by a family member, while "only" 33 percent of the latter group had been so abused; and 78 percent of the more violent group had been witnesses to extreme violence, while 20 percent of the less violent group had been witnesses.[15]

Similarly, a recent ethnography of nearly 200 young West Coast street gangsters and felons found that, almost without exception, the kids' families "were a social fabric of fragile and undependable social ties that weakly bound children to their parents and other socializers." Nearly all parents abused alcohol and illegal drugs or both. Most young street criminals and drug abusers had no father in the home; many had fathers who were in prison or jail. Parents who were present in the home often "beat their sons and daughters—whipped them with belts, punched them with fists, slapped them, and kicked them."[16] Much the same was found in a 1996 study that reconstructed the entire juvenile and adult criminal histories of a randomly selected sample of 170 Wisconsin prisoners from Milwaukee: "Most inmates were raised in dysfunctional families.... Drug and alcohol abuse was common among inmates, their parents, and siblings."[17]

Of course, today's at-risk child in need of meaningful connections with responsible adults is also tomorrow's young adult in need of a meaningful, living-wage job. At least with respect to the crime- and drug-abuse-reduction value of legitimate work opportunities, "liberal and conservative criminologists do not differ all that much about the causes of street crime."[18] There is almost universal agreement among crime analysts that "jobs matter," and that in the big-city neighborhoods that so many at-risk youth and the adults in their lives call home, jobs have virtually disappeared.[19] And there is also almost complete agreement among employment and training experts that, regardless of how bright or bleak general economic conditions may be, the most effective way—and perhaps the only way—to help no- and low-skill urban youth get and keep jobs is to "stick to basics: adult caring and guidance, plenty of legitimate things to do in a youth's spare time, and real help in connecting to employers. This is the stuff of successful human, citizen and worker development."[20]

Unfortunately, on youth crime, substance abuse and related social problems, sticking to the basics is anything but common, and anything but easy. The very conceptual and moral simplicity of the hard work that needs to be done—that is, the hard person-, place-, and institution-specific work of building meaningful connections between responsible adults and at-risk young people—makes getting it done very hard indeed. One little-acknowledged reason is that in the elite social policy, foundation and research communities, most financial, reputational and other rewards have been, and continue to be, skewed in favor of peddling "original" and esoteric (if often emptily erudite) ideas and "comprehensive" (if hardly feasible) top-down program strategies and designs.

But if we really care about getting a handle on our present and impending youth

crime and substance abuse problems, then the time has come to proceed inductively, building meaningful connections between at-risk youth and responsible adults via existing community-based programs; focusing on the highly particular and often banal barriers to helping at-risk youth in particular places with particular people at particular times; having the money to fix a broken pipe that flooded the inner-city church basement where a "latch-key" ministry operates; finding a way to transport a young job-seeker from a public housing site to a private job site; getting police and probation officers in a particular neighborhood to work together on a daily basis; funding an incremental expansion of a well-established national or local mentoring program; and so on.

In fact, the youth crime and delinquency problem is highly concentrated where America's most severely at-risk youth are concentrated, namely, on the predominantly minority inner-city streets of places like Newark, New Jersey, not on the predominantly white tree-lined streets of places like Princeton, New Jersey. This is hardly a new social fact. For example, in 1969, a presidential commission on violent crime broadcast it far and wide.[21] Still, the concentration of at-risk youth and associated social ills in America's big cities easily ranks among the most often ignored, distorted or forgotten of all policy-relevant social realities.

The concentration of crime and delinquency among low-income urban minority youth is especially striking for crimes of violence, including murder. In 1995, a nationwide total of 21,597 murders were reported to police, a total 7 percent lower than the 1994 total, and representing a national murder rate of 8 per 100,000 inhabitants. But 77 percent of murder victims in 1995 were males, 48 percent were black, and 12 percent were under age 18. Moreover, recent studies find that males ages 14 to 24 are roughly 8 percent of the country's total population, but they constitute over a quarter of all homicide victims and nearly half of all murderers. Between 1985 and 1992, for example, black males ages 14–24 remained just above 1 percent of the population but increased from 9 to 17 percent of the murder victims and from 17 to 30 percent of the assailants.[22]

One thing is tragically clear: "Homicide for young black males is very concentrated geographically," and remained so throughout the epidemic increases of the last decade.[23] As a 1994 study of youth violence concluded: "The violence now occurring within our cities is a national scourge. The fact that minority youth are disproportionately its victims makes it a tragedy as well as a disgrace."[24]

There is growing evidence of a substantial overlap between the highly concen-

trated populations of young crime victims and the highly concentrated populations of young offenders. For example, in an ongoing analysis of youth homicides in Boston, Professor Anne Morrison Piehl of Harvard University has found that about 75 percent of both offenders and victims of youth homicides (victim age 25 or younger) have criminal histories consisting of at least one arraignment. "In fact," Piehl observes, "among those with criminal histories, the victims and offenders were virtually indistinguishable in terms of criminal records. This finding suggests several things: the distribution of victimization may be even more concentrated than commonly believed, and strategic innovations based on law enforcement may be able to diffuse violent situations because there is leverage over both potential victims and potential offenders."[25]

Few "Guppies," Few "Great Whites"

But, as you well know, most juvenile offenders with whom the justice system deals are neither violent nor incorrigible.[26] Metaphorically speaking, today the system must handle relatively more young "Great White Sharks" (serious, violent, and predatory juvenile criminals) and relatively fewer "Guppies" (mere first-time midemeanants or delinquents) than it did in previous decades. Still, most juvenile offenders are neither Great Whites nor Guppies, and, for that reason, and even with the passage of so-called get-tough laws in many states, the system still rightly responds by putting the vast majority of juvenile offenders on probation, not behind bars.

For example, in 1993 public juvenile detention, correctional and shelter facilities held a total of over 60,000 juveniles (89 percent of them male, 43 percent of them black)—the largest number of juveniles in such public facilities on any given day since these data on juveniles in public facilities were first compiled in 1974. There were 1,025 facilities with a median population capacity of 24 and a mean capacity of 57—clearly not the huge, 500-plus bed juvenile reformatories of old. From 1991 to 1993, the one-day population of juveniles in publicly operated facilities increased by 5 percent. And note: the one-day population figures grossly minimize the actual amount of traffic in and out of these facilities each year. In 1993, for example, about 674,000 juveniles were admitted to these facilities, and 669,000 were released from their custody.[27]

Still, even today, it is probation authorities, not custodial institutions, that remain the true "workhorses" of the juvenile justice system. In 1993, 520,600 cases disposed by juvenile courts resulted in probation—a 21 percent increase over the 428,500 cases handled via probation in 1989. Probation has long been, and continues to be, the most severe disposition in over half (56 percent) of adjudicated delinquency cases. Between 1989 and 1993, the number of adjudicated juvenile cases placed on formal probation rose by 17 percent to 254,800. Over the same period, the number of juvenile probation cases involving a "person offense" such as homicide, rape, robbery, assault or kidnapping, soared by 45 percent to 53,900.[28]

As you also are well aware, alcohol, illegal drugs and substance abuse are clearly implicated in youth crime. The trouble almost always begins—both for the at-risk children and often for their parents as well—with child maltreatment in the home or a severe lack of positive adult-child relationships. Recently, a number of popular books have spoken to this harsh social reality in the vivid way that only first-rate journalism can.[29] In one such account, we are treated to the following summary of the research on at-risk youth, juvenile crime and related social ills:

Boiled down to its core (the research teaches) that most adolescents who become delinquent, and the overwhelming majority who commit violent crimes, started very young.... They were the impulsive, aggressive, irritable children.... If children know someone is watching them and that they may get caught, they are less likely to get into trouble.[30]

Even some older children who have gone badly astray and gotten "caught" (even incarcerated) can be saved if they are not only watched or monitored in the future, but mentored or ministered to as needed by responsible adults. Weigh the following synopses of a representative armful of relevant research monographs published over the last decade or so:

• Since 1986, the National Institute of Justice and the National Institute of Alcohol Abuse and Alcoholism have been conducting an ongoing examination of 1,575 child victims identified in court cases of abuse and neglect from 1967 to 1971. By 1994, almost half the victims (most of whom were then in their late twenties or early thirties) had been arrested for some type of nontraffic offense. About 18 percent had been arrested for a violent crime. Substance abuse rates were elevated, especially among women who were maltreated as children. Blacks who had been abused or neglected as children had higher crime rates than whites with the same background: 82 percent of black males had been arrested for some type of nontraffic offense; half of black males had at least one arrest for violence. For all child victims, in terms of future criminality, neglect appeared to be as damaging as physical abuse. The rate of

arrest for violent crimes of those who had been neglected as children was almost as high as the rate for those who had been physically abused. Overall, maltreatment of children increased their chances of delinquency and crime by about 40 percent.[31]

• A 1985 study based on a representative national sample of 7,514 adolescents aged 12 to 17 compared delinquency rates of children in single-parent (mother-only) households to rates of children in two-parent households. Delinquency was measured in terms of number of arrests, school disciplinary problems (truancy, for example), and similar indicators. By all measures, the children in single-parent households were more likely to be delinquent.[32]

• A major re-analysis of data from a classic study of crime and delinquency confirmed the primacy of family factors: "Despite controlling for these individual difference constructs, all family effects retained their significant predictive power. And once again mother's supervision had the largest of all effects on delinquency, whether official or unofficial. A major finding of our analysis is that the family process variables are strongly and directly related to delinquency ... family processes of informal social control still explain the largest share of variance in adolescent delinquency."[33]

• A study of the relationship between adolescent motherhood and the criminality of her offspring revealed a birds-of-a-feather phenomenon. About "25 percent of boys with criminal fathers also have a criminal mother, compared to 4 percent in the case of non-criminal fathers. Similarly, 67 percent of boys with criminal mothers also have a criminal father, compared to just 19 percent when the mother is not convicted.... Our results suggest that the children latest in the birth order of women who begin childbearing early are at greatest risk of criminality. This finding appears to reflect the coming together of the deleterious impacts of poor parenting and role modeling and diminished resources per child."[34]

• A study of urban street criminals concluded: "An abundance of scholarly research shows that anti-social and delinquent tendencies emerge early in the lives of neglected, abused, and unloved youngsters, often by age nine. My ethnographic data support these findings and show that, once these youngsters leave home and go on the street, they are at best difficult to extricate from street culture...."[35]

• A study of "resilient youth"—the half of all high-risk children who do not engage in delinquency or drug use—indicated that child "maltreatment itself has for a long time been associated with problematic outcomes for children.... Considerable research in both criminology and child

development suggests that family deviance, including criminality and substance abuse of family members, affects developing children because such parents are likely to tolerate and model deviance for children."[36]

Four decades ago, child psychologist Emmy Werner began studying the offspring of desperately poor, alcoholic and abusive Kauai, Hawaii parents. She was hoping to discover how these dysfunctions were passed from one generation to the next. Instead, she found that about a third of the children reached adulthood virtually unscathed—healthy, happy, employed, without substance abuse problems, and so on. So she shifted her attention to these abuse-and-neglect survivors, hoping to discover what made them so resilient and capable of beating the social odds. In 1992, a major storm flattened Kauai, leaving over 15 percent of its residents homeless and many others scrambling to find money for repairs, avoid bankruptcy, and fend off deep depression. But most of the study's resilient youth, then in their thirties, were not among the homeless, the foreclosed, or the depressed. They had heeded storm warnings, prepared their properties, saved for a stormy day, and bought insurance. For them, successfully riding out the storm was, as it were, an old habit. During the social hurricanes of their early lives, Kauai's resilient youth had responsible nonparental adults enter their lives, and through relationships with these adults the children had developed not only a sense of self-worth and respect for others, but, in Werner's words, personalities as "planners and problem solvers and picker-uppers." As she argued in her book, the crux of the Kauai story is consistent with the bottom line of the basic research on resilient youth: caring adults are the bedrock of a young person's behavior toward self and others, as well as the primary avenue for securing those skills, services, and opportunities (such as jobs) that are key to a civil and self-sufficient life.[37]

Thus, our brisk walk through the literatures on the concentrations and causes of youth crime and substance abuse returns us to the core strategic principle: no approach that does not build connections between responsible adults and at-risk youth has worked, or should rationally be expected to work. Again, no one can reasonably deny that, whatever the state of adult-child relationships, growing up in neighborhoods with few opportunities for healthy play and employment is a breeding ground for youth crime and substance abuse. But improving those opportunities, without first ensuring that there is adequate parental or nonparental adult caring, supervision, guidance and support, is unlikely to prevent or reduce youth crime and substance abuse, and hence unlikely to forestall the adult dysfunctions and criminal activities that fuel the "cycle of violence."

The single most consistent and powerful finding in the evaluation literature on youth development interventions is that positive effects accrue while at-risk children are in the programs, and sometimes for a few years thereafter, but diminish or dwindle to nothing by the time the child reaches adulthood. Many have met this finding as a counsel of despair. Logically, however, all the finding says is that the young generally do better when they are being helped by adults than when that help has stopped—better with and while in Head Start than without and after it; better when they stay in structured drug treatment than when they drop out of it; better during a summer education and training program than two summers later when they are older, more challenged, and unhelped by responsible adults; and so on. Many social programs do not so much "fail" as "stop." The obvious need, therefore, is to translate a series of short-term, non-stop positive adult-child connections into that long-term developmental success known as responsible, self-sufficient adulthood. To employ a football metaphor, winning at at-risk youth development is impossible when your most ill-equipped players have coaches or quarterbacks but only on alternate game days, are only occasionally given playbooks or schedules, and, should they even bother to keep playing, get invited to take the field as a team only during the first and third quarters of a four-quarter game. Or, shift the context from at-risk youth in need of responsible adults to children living with both parents in the best of all possible emotional, material and cognitive early life circumstances. Even for well-loved, advantaged children in their teens, we know that when their circumstances change for the worse—when, for example, their family breaks up or falls suddenly on economic hard times—the youth are more likely to experience a wide variety of life troubles than are comparable youth who remained, as it were, in the 'advantaged childrens' program. In short, the plural of short-term is long-term.

Likewise, many well-intentioned persons have concluded that unless interventions into the lives of at-risk youth are quite early, intensive and expensive, not much good can come of them. To some, "early" means while still in dirty diapers, and certainly no later than ages seven or eight. This perspective is, to be sure, a useful corrective to unfettered optimism about social programs, especially, perhaps, where our country's most severely at-risk youth are concerned. But there are, alas, few unfettered optimists still walking the social planet, and the "dirty diapers or doom" perspective is grossly inconsistent with recent findings on the efficacy of mentoring

programs like Big Brothers Big Sisters. Moreover, it is largely beside the point: whether or not we think we can help at-risk youth who are out of dirty diapers, the fact is that there are millions of them out there and on the way. In particular, intellectual confidence that these children are beyond help, even if it were justified (and I think it is most certainly not justified), would constitute no real answer to challenges posed by youth criminals and substance abusers—our youngest, most needy, and potentially our most dangerous fellow citizens.

The 3 M's of Youth Crime and Substance Abuse Prevention

The nation's at-risk youth population, including the segment of it that is involved in illegal activities, is not an undifferentiated mass. The best way, I believe, to think about and relate to present and potential juvenile offenders is with respect to their varying needs for adult supervision and guidance.

Specifically, I believe that some at-risk juveniles—for example, truants, petty thieves or kids who have had non-violent run-ins with their peers, neighbors and the law—need little more than a dedicated probation officer or a caring adult volunteer looking over their shoulder. They need monitoring. Other at-risk juveniles need responsible adults in their lives on a deeper, more intensive level, helping them with their personal problems, offering a sympathetic ear and a guiding hand. They need mentoring. Still other juveniles are among the nation's most severely at-risk children—abused and neglected as infants and toddlers, exploited for sex, drugs and money as adolescents, and already involved in (or quite likely to become involved in) serious, organized or predatory street crime as teenagers and young adults. Their badly broken lives and spirits cry out for a type and a degree of adult help that is holistic, personal and challenging. They need some type of ministering.

Over the last two years, I have spent most of my time working on the "3rd M"—ministering. I believe that local churches represent the single best hope for reaching some of our most severely at-risk youth, and I have witnessed, if you will, the capacity of "super-preachers" to stop potential "super-predators" before it's too late. But preachers and church volunteers need the support of prosecutors, probation and police to succeed.

In conclusion, a recent report from the Bureau of Justice Statistics indicates that, at present, the lifetime risks of a black male going to prison or jail in America are 1 in 3 versus 1 in 20 for the population as a

whole.[38] Strategies that put responsible adults into the lives of at-risk youth can change both odds for the better. But how much have monitoring, mentoring and ministering-type efforts proliferated to date? These programs are far from being taken to scale and need lots of human and financial help if they are to make a real difference. Precious little is now being done by private foundations to bolster this strategic, street-level approach to youth crime and substance abuse.

Endnotes

1. National Research Council, Panel on High-Risk Youth, Losing Generations (National Academy Press, 1993).

2. Youth Violence in America: Recommendations from the IACP Summit (International Association of Chiefs of Police, 1996), section III, tables 11 and 12.

3. Council on Crime in America, Preventing Crime, Saving Children (Center for Civic Innovation, Manhattan Institute, 1997), pp. 1–3.

4. James Q. Wilson, "Crime and Public Policy," in Wilson and Joan R. Pertersilia, Crime (Institute for Contemporary Studies, 1995), p. 20.

5. Marvin E. Wolfgang, "From Boy to Man, From Delinquency to Crime," University of Pennsylvania, Wharton School, Public Policy and Management Crime Policy Seminar Series, October 17, 1996, and personal correspondence of February 11, 1997; also see Wolfgang and Franco Ferracuti, The Subculture of Violence (Tavistock, 1967), esp. pp. 158–161.

6. Juvenile Offenders and Victims (U.S. Office of Juvenile Justice and Delinquency Prevention, June 1996), pp. 20, 47. Note: These estimates of youth crime and youth victimization in America are based on data gathered via the U.S. Bureau of Justice Statistics (BJS) and the National Crime Victimization Survey (NCVS). Unfortunately, the NCVS undercounts youth crime and youth victimization because it does not survey persons age 12 or younger; see John J. DiIulio, Jr. and Anne Morrison Piehl, "What the Crime Statistics Don't Tell You," Wall Street Journal, January 8, 1997, p. A22. Experts disagree about how severe the NCVS undercount is, but for some crimes it is clearly substantial. For example, other BJS data indicate that as many as 1 in 6 rape victims are age 12 or younger, but the NCVS does not capture these rapes; see Child Rape Victims 1992 (Bureau of Justice Statistics), June 1994. Likewise, it has been estimated that the NCVS undercounts the number of gun-shot victims by a factor of three; see Philip J. Cook, "The Case of the Missing Victims," Journal of Quantitative Criminology, 1985, pp. 91–102.

7. New York Times/CBS News Poll, as reported in The New York Times, July 10, 1994, p. 16.

8. George H. Gallup with Wendy Plump, Growing Up Scared in America (George H. Gallup International Institute, 1995), p. 2.

9. James Q. Wilson, On Character (American Enterprise Institute), p. 179; also see Wilson et al., Understanding and Controlling Crime (Springer-Verlag, 1986), and Wilson and Joan R. Petersilia, eds., Crime, op. cit.

10. For example, see 1993 Report of the Harry Frank Guggenheim Foundation: Research for Understanding and Reducing Violence, Aggression and Dominance (The Harry Frank Guggenheim Foundation, 1993).

11. For example, see "Understanding the Roots of Crime," National Institute of Justice Journal (National Institute of Justice, November 1994), p. 14.

12. "Critical Criminal Justice Issues," Task Force Reports from the American Society of Criminology, compiled by National Institute of Justice, draft, 1996, p. 2. 1 am grateful to Ross D. London for supplying a copy of this draft document.

13. James Q. Wilson and Richard J. Hernstein, Crime and Human Nature (Simon and Shuster, 1985), p. 509.

14. David M. Altschuler and Troy L. Armstrong, "Intensive Aftercare," in Armstrong, ed., Intensive Interventions with High-Risk Youths (Criminal Justice Press, 1991), p. 48.

15. Ellen Schall, "Principles for Juvenile Detention," in Francis X. Hartmann, ed., From Children to Citizens, vol. 2 (Springer-Verlag, 1987), p. 350.

16. Mark S. Fleisher, Beggars and Thieves (University of Wisconsin Press, 1995).

17. John J. DiIulio, Jr. and George Mitchell, Who Really Goes to Prison in Wisconsin? (Wisconsin Policy Research Institute, April 1996), pp. 2, 3.

18. Jerome H. Skolnick, "Passions of Crime," The American Prospect, March–April 1996, p. 92.

19. For example, see the following: Richard Freeman, "Crime and the Economic Status of Disadvantaged Young Men," in George Peterson and Wayne Vroman, eds., Urban Labor Markets and Job Opportunity (Urban Institute Press, 1992); Freeman, "Why Do So Many Young Men Commit Crimes and What Might We Do About It?," Journal of Economic Perspectives, Winter 1996, pp. 25–42; Jeffrey Grogger, "The Effect of Arrests on Employment and Earnings of Young Men," Quarterly Journal of Economics, February 1995, pp. 51–71; Joel Waldfogel, "The Effect of Criminal Conviction on Income and the Trust 'Reposed in the Workmen'," Journal of Human Resources,

1994, pp. 62–81; William Julius Wilson, When Work Disappears (Knopf, 1996).

20. Gary Walker, "Back to Basics: A New/Old Direction for Youth Policy," Public/Private Ventures News, Spring 1996, p. 3; and Gary Walker, testimony before the U.S. Subcommittee on Employment and Training, March 11, 1997.

21. Violent Crime: The Challenge to Our Cities (George Braziller, 1969). The commission's central findings were reinforced a few years later by the results of a major longitudinal study; see Marvin E. Wolfgang et al., Delinquency in a Birth Cohort (University of Chicago, 1972).

22. Trends in Juvenile Violence (Bureau of Justice Statistics, March 1996), p. 2.

23. Ibid, p. 30.

24. Violence in America: Mobilizing a Response (National Academy Press, 1994), p. ix.

25. Anne Morrison Piehl, personal correspondence of March 1997; also see Piehl et al., "Youth Gun Violence in Boston," in Law and Contemporary Problems, forthcoming 1997. 1 am grateful to Professor Piehl for supplying us with a copy of this draft essay, and for her additional insights.

26. For example, see James Alan Fox, "The Calm Before the Juvenile Crime Storm?," Population Today, September 1996, pp. 4, 5, and "Yes, the Federal Government Should Have a Major Role in Reducing Juvenile Crime," Congressional Digest, August–September 1996, pp. 206, 208, 210, and 212; and see DiIulio, "Our Children and Crime," Keynote Address, International Association of Chiefs of Police, April 25, 1996; testimony before the U.S. Senate Subcommittee on Children and Families, "Juvenile Crime: An Alarming Indicator of America's Moral Poverty," July 18, 1996; and "Stop Crime Before It Starts," The New York Times, July 25, 1996.

27. Juveniles in Public Facilities, 1993 (Office of Juvenile Justice and Delinquency Prevention, May 1995), p. 1, and Juveniles in Public Facilities, 1991 (Office of Juvenile Justice and Delinquency Prevention, September 1993), p. 1.

28. Juvenile Probation: Workhorse of the Juvenile Justice System (Office of Juvenile Justice and Delinquency Prevention, March 1996).

29. For example, see Fox Butterfield, All God's Children (Knopf, 1995), and Leon Dash, Rosa Lee: A Mother and Her Family In Urban America (Basic Books, 1996).

30. Butterfield, ibid., p. 327–328.

31. The cycle of Violence (National Institute of Justice, 1992), and The Cycle of Violence Revisited (National Institute of Justice, 1996).

32. Sanford M. Dornbusch et al., "Single Parents, Extended Households, and the Control of Adolescents," Child Development, 1985, pp.326-341. Also see the following: Anthony Pillay, "Psychological Disturbances in Children of Single Parents," Psychological Reports, 1987, pp. 803–806; Laurence Steinberg, "Single Parents, Stepparents, and Susceptibility of Adolescents to Antisocial Peer Pressure," Child Development, 1987, pp. 269-275 and Brigitte Mednick et al., "Patterns of Family Instability and Crime," Journal of Youth and Adolescence, 1990, pp. 201-220. I am grateful to Boston probation officer Milton Britton for directing our attention to these additional studies.

33. Robert J. Sampson and John H. Laub, Crime in the Making (Harvard University Press, 1993), pp.95-96.

34. Daniel S. Nagin et al., "Adolescent Mothers and the Criminal Justice System," unpublished paper, Carnegie Mellon University, December 15, 1995, pp. 28, 30.

35. Fleisher, Beggars and Thieves, op. cit., pp. 262–263.

36. Carolyn Smith et al., "Resilient Youth: Identifying Factors That Prevent High-Risk Youth from Engaging in Delinquency and Drug Use," Current Perspectives on Aging and the Life Cycle, 1995, p. 221.

37. Emmy Werner and Ruth Smith, Overcoming the Odds: High-Risk Children from Birth to Adulthood (Cornell University Press, 1992), and Joseph P. Shapiro, "Invincible Kids," U.S. News & World Report, November 11, 1996.

38. I am grateful to Dr. Allen Beck of the Bureau for supplying a draft copy of this document.

This article was based on an address given to the National District Attorneys Association on July 14, 1997.

John J. DiIulio, Jr. is a Professor of Politics and Public Affairs at Princeton University and a Douglas Dillon Senior Fellow at the Brookings Institute.

Great idea for ruining kids

The case for legalizing some drugs is seductive—and completely wrong

BY MORTIMER B. ZUCKERMAN / EDITOR-IN-CHIEF

We are at a critical stage in the intermittent war on drugs. The plausible case for allowing sick patients access to marijuana for the relief of pain, approved by California and Arizona voters, has given impetus to those who would legalize drugs altogether. They are dangerously wrong. If marijuana is to be approved for hospital medicine, it is essential that general use be more rigorously curtailed. The narrow window of legitimacy in medicine will be a menace if it becomes a wide-open door.

The argument of the legalizers is that America has lost the drug war. No matter how many fast boats, helicopters, and antinarcotics teams we have, illegal drug use continues and so does the criminal apparatus that supports the trade. If drugs were legalized at low prices the gangs and peddlers would be out of business and the killings and extortions would disappear. In a democracy, in short, it is a mistake to criminalize the behavior of so many people. It promotes crime and weakens respect for the rule of law.

There are many things amiss with this analysis. The drug war is not being lost. In 1979, some 25 million had tried drugs sometime in the preceding month. Today that figure is 11 million. Why? Because of stricter drug laws, stronger societal disapproval, and an increased awareness of the devastation drugs can produce.

Within the brighter general picture, there is an ominous trend. Drug use has increased threefold among young teens in the past five years. They think they are immune and can limit their involvement to soft drugs. That is a delusion—like trying to be a little bit pregnant. The earlier and more frequently an adolescent uses a soft drug the more likely it is he will go on to the hard drugs. This is surely an argument for more vigilance, not less. Legalization would jeopardize a whole generation.

The legalizers respond that if drugs were legal, it would not increase the number of addicts, since anyone who wants a drug can get it now. This does not square with the facts. Drugs are not accessible at all. According to

Millions more teens will surely become addicts if drugs are legally and socially acceptable.

research, fewer than 50 percent of high school seniors and young adults under 22 believed that they could obtain cocaine "fairly easily" or "very easily." Only 39 percent of the adult population reported that they could get cocaine. So, after legalization, you could double or triple the number of people who would have access to drugs and who would assuredly use them—exactly the history of alcohol when Prohibition ended.

An even more absurd legalization argument is that young people could be excluded from the free market for drugs. How could we do that when we have been unable to keep legal drugs—tobacco and alcohol—out of the hands of children? Five million children smoke and 12 million teens drink. Nor should we overlook that the stigma of illegality has been important in discouraging kids from experimenting. In separate studies, 60 percent to 70 percent of New Jersey and California students reported that "fear of getting in trouble with the authorities was a major reason why they did not use drugs." Another study found that "the greater the perceived likelihood of apprehension and swift punishment for using marijuana, the less likely adolescents are to smoke it."

Imagine the prospect that the number of drug users would approach the number of alcohol abusers (more than 18 million) or tobacco addicts. One expert estimates that legalizing cocaine would increase the number of addicts 10-fold to about 20 million. If millions become addicted in a period when drugs are illegal, socially unacceptable, and generally difficult to get, then millions more will surely become addicts when drugs are legally and socially acceptable and easily obtainable.

We should always be suspicious of simple solutions to complex problems. Legalization is such a bromide. The National Center on Addiction and Substance Abuse at Columbia University had it right: "Drugs are not a threat to American society because they are illegal; they are illegal because they are a threat to American society." They should remain that way.

From *U.S. News & World Report*, February 24, 1997, p. 68. © 1997 by U.S. News & World Report. Reprinted by permission.

Boys will be Boys

Developmental research has been focused on girls; now it's their brothers' turn. Boys need help, too, but first they need to be understood.

BY BARBARA KANTROWITZ AND CLAUDIA KALB

I T WAS A CLASSIC MARS-VENUS ENCOUN-ter. Only in this case, the woman was from Harvard and the man—well, boy—was a 4-year-old at a suburban Boston nursery school. Graduate student Judy Chu was in his classroom last fall to gather observations for her doctoral dissertation on human development. His greeting was startling: he held up his finger as if it were a gun and pretended to shoot her. "I felt bad," Chu recalls. "I felt as if he didn't like me." Months later and much more boy-savvy, Chu has a different interpretation: the gunplay wasn't hostile—it was just a way for him to say hello. "They don't mean it to have harsh consequences. It's a way for them to connect."

Researchers like Chu are discovering new meaning in lots of things boys have done for ages. In fact, they're dissecting just about every aspect of the developing male psyche and creating a hot new field of inquiry: the study of boys. They're also producing a slew of books with titles like "Real Boys: Rescuing Our Sons From the Myths of Boyhood" and "Raising Cain: Protecting the Emotional Life of Boys" that will hit the stores in the next few months.

What some researchers are finding is that boys and girls really are from two different planets. But since the two sexes have to live together here on Earth, they should be raised with special consideration for their distinct needs. Boys and girls have different "crisis points," experts say, stages in their emotional and social development where things can go very wrong. Until recently, girls got all the attention. But boys need help, too. They're much more likely than girls to have discipline problems at school and to be diagnosed with attention deficit disorder (ADD). Boys far outnumber girls in special-education classes. They're also more likely to commit violent crimes and end up in jail. Consider the headlines: Jonesboro, Ark.; Paducah, Ky.; Pearl, Miss. In all these school shootings, the perpetrators were young adolescent boys.

Even normal boy behavior has come to be considered pathological in the wake of

the feminist movement. An abundance of physical energy and the urge to conquer—these are normal male characteristics, and in an earlier age they were good things, even essential to survival. "If Huck Finn or Tom Sawyer were alive today," says Michael Gurian, author of "The Wonder of Boys," "we'd say they had ADD or a conduct disorder." He says one of the new insights we're gaining about boys is a very old one: boys will be boys. "They are who they are," says Gurian, "and we need to love them for who they are. Let's not try to rewire them."

Indirectly, boys are benefiting from all the research done on girls, especially the landmark work by Harvard University's Carol Gilligan. Her 1982 book, "In a Different Voice: Psychological Theory and Women's Development," inspired Take Our Daughters to Work Day, along with best-selling spinoffs like Mary Pipher's "Reviving Ophelia." The traditional, unisex way of looking at child development was profoundly flawed, Gilligan says: "It was like having a one-dimensional perspective on a two-dimensional scene." At Harvard, where she chairs the gender-studies department, Gilligan is now supervising work on males, including Chu's project. Other researchers are studying mental illness and violence in boys.

While girls' horizons have been expanding, boys' have narrowed, confined to rigid ideas of acceptable male behavior no matter how hard their parents tried to avoid stereotypes. The macho ideal still rules. "We gave boys dolls and they used them as guns," says Gurian. "For 15 years, all we heard was that [gender differences] were all about socialization. Parents who raised their kids through that period said in the end, 'That's not true. Boys and girls can be awfully different.' I think we're awakening to the biological realities and the sociological realities."

But what exactly is the essential nature of boys? Even as infants, boys and girls behave differently. A recent study at Children's Hospital in Boston found that boy babies are more emotionally expressive; girls are more reflective. (That means boy babies tend to

cry when they're unhappy; girl babies suck their thumbs.) This could indicate that girls are innately more able to control their emotions. Boys have higher levels of testosterone and lower levels of the neurotransmitter serotonin, which inhibits aggression and impulsivity. That may help explain why more males than females carry through with suicide, become alcoholics and are diagnosed with ADD.

The developmental research on the impact of these physiological differences is still in the embryonic stage, but psychologists are drawing some interesting comparisons between girls and boys (chart). For girls, the first crisis point often comes in early adolescence. Until then, Gilligan and others found, girls have an enormous capacity for establishing relationships and interpreting emotions. But in their early teens, girls clamp down, squash their emotions, blunt their insight. Their self-esteem plummets. The first crisis point for boys comes much earlier, researchers now say. "There's an outbreak of symptoms at age 5, 6, 7, just like you see in girls at 11, 12, 13," says Gilligan. Problems at this age include bed-wetting and separation anxiety. "They don't have the language or experience" to articulate it fully, she says, "but the feelings are no less intense." That's why Gilligan's student Chu is studying preschoolers. For girls at this age, Chu says, hugging a parent goodbye "is almost a nonissue." But little boys, who display a great deal of tenderness, soon begin to bury it with "big boy" behavior to avoid being called sissies. "When their parents drop them off, they want to be close and want to be held, but not in front of other people," says Chu. "Even as early as 4, they're already aware of those masculine stereotypes and are negotiating their way around them."

It's a phenomenon that parents, especially mothers, know well. One morning last month, Lori Dube, a 37-year-old mother of three from Evanston, Ill., visited her oldest son, Abe, almost 5, at his nursery school, where he was having lunch with his friends. She kissed him, prompting another boy to comment scornfully: "Do you know what your mom just did? She kissed you!" Dube acknowledges, with some sadness, that she'll have to be more sensitive to Abe's new reactions to future public displays of affection. "Even if he loves it, he's getting these messages that it's not good."

There's a struggle—a desire and need for warmth on the one hand and a pull toward independence on the other. Boys like Abe are going through what psychologists long ago declared an integral part of growing up: individualization and disconnection from parents, especially mothers. But now some researchers think that process is too abrupt. When boys repress normal feelings like love because of social pressure, says William Pollack, head of the Center for Men at Boston's McLean Hospital and author of the forthcoming "Real Boys," "they've lost contact with the genuine nature of who they are and what they feel. Boys are in a silent crisis. The only time we notice it is when they pull the trigger."

No one is saying that acting like Rambo in nursery school leads directly to tragedies like Jonesboro. But researchers do think that boys who are forced to shut down positive emotions are left with only one socially acceptable outlet: anger. The cultural ideals boys are exposed to in movies and on TV still emphasize traditional masculine roles—warrior, rogue, adventurer—with heavy doses of violence. For every Mr. Mom, there are a dozen Terminators. "The feminist movement has done a great job of convincing people that a woman can be nurturing and a mother and a tough trial lawyer at the same time," says Dan Kindlon, an assistant professor of psychiatry at Harvard Medical School. "But we haven't done that as much with men. We're afraid that if they're too soft, that's all they can be."

And the demands placed on boys in the early years of elementary school can increase their overall stress levels. Scientists have known for years that boys and girls develop physically and intellectually at very different rates (time-line). Boys' fine motor skills—the ability to hold a pencil, for example—are usually considerably behind girls. They often learn to read later. At the same time, they're much more active—not the best combination for academic advancement. "Boys feel like school is a game rigged against them," says Michael Thompson, coauthor with Kindlon of "Raising Cain." "The things at which they excel—gross motor skills, visual and spatial skills, their exuberance—do not find as good a reception in school" as the things girls excel at. Boys (and girls) are also in academic programs at much younger ages than they used to be, increasing the chances that males will be forced to sit still before they are ready. The result, for many boys, is frustration, says Thompson: "By fourth grade, they're saying the teachers like girls better."

A second crisis point for boys occurs around the same time their sisters are stumbling, in early adolescence. By then, say Thompson and Kindlon, boys go one step further in their drive to be "real guys." They partake in a "culture of cruelty," enforcing male stereotypes on one another. "Anything tender, anything compassionate or too artistic is labeled gay," says Thompson. "The homophobia of boys in the 11, 12, 13 range is a stronger force than gravity."

Boys who refuse to fit the mold suffer. Glo Wellman of the California Parenting Institute in Santa Rosa has three sons, 22, 19 and 12. One of her boys, she says, is a "nontypical boy: he's very sensitive and caring and creative and artistic." Not surprisingly, he had the most difficulty growing up, she says. "We've got a long way to go to help boys . . . to have a sense that they can be anything they want to be."

In later adolescence, the once affectionate toddler has been replaced by a sulky stranger who often acts as though torture would be preferable to a brief exchange of words with Mom or Dad. Parents have to try even harder to keep in touch. Boys want and need the attention, but often just don't know how to ask for it. In a recent national poll, teenagers named their parents as their No. 1 heroes. Researchers say a strong parental bond is the most important protection against everything from smoking to suicide.

For San Francisco Chronicle columnist Adair Lara, that message sank in when she was traveling to New York a few years ago with her son, then 15. She sat next to a woman who told her that until recently she would have had to change seats because she would not have been able to bear the pain of seeing a teenage son and mother together. The woman's son was 17 when his girlfriend dumped him; he went into the garage and killed himself. "This story made me aware that with a boy especially, you have to keep talking because they don't come and talk to you," she says. Lara's son is now 17; she also has a 19-year-old daughter. "My daughter stalked me. She followed me from room to room. She was yelling, but she was in touch. Boys don't do that. They leave the room and you don't know what they're feeling." Her son is now 6 feet 3. "He's a man. There are barriers. You have to reach through that and remember to ruffle his hair."

With the high rate of divorce, many boys are growing up without any adult men in their lives at all. Don Elium, coauthor of the best-selling 1992 book "Raising a Son," says that with troubled boys, there's often a common theme: distant, uninvolved fathers, and mothers who have taken on more responsibility to fill the gap. That was the case with Raymundo Infante Jr., a 16-year-old high-school junior, who lives with his mother, Mildred, 38, a hospital administrative assistant in Chicago, and his sister, Vanessa, 19. His parents divorced when he was a baby and he had little contact with his father until a year ago. The hurt built up—in sixth grade, Raymundo was so depressed that he told a classmate he wanted to kill himself. The classmate told the teacher, who told a counselor, and Raymundo saw a psychiatrist for a year. "I felt that I just wasn't good enough, or he just didn't want me," Raymundo says. Last year Raymundo finally confronted his dad, who works two jobs—in an office and on a construction crew—and accused him of caring more about work than about his son. Now the two spend time together on weekends and sometimes go shopping, but there is still a huge gap of lost years.

Black boys are especially vulnerable, since they are more likely than whites to grow up in homes without fathers. They're often on their own much sooner than whites.

The Wonder (and Worry) Years

There may be no such thing as *child* development anymore. Instead, researchers are now studying each gender's development separately and discovering that boys and girls face very different sorts of challenges. Here is a rough guide to the major phases in their development.

Boys

0–3 years At birth, boys have brains that are 5% larger than girls' (size doesn't affect intelligence) and proportionately larger bodies—disparities that increase with age.

4–6 years The start of school is a tough time as boys must curb aggressive impulses. They lag behind girls in reading skills, and hyperactivity may be a problem.

Age 1	2	3	4	5	6	7

Girls

0–3 years Girls are born with a higher proportion of nerve cells to process information. More brain regions are involved in language production and recognition.

4–6 years Girls are well suited to school. They are calm, get along with others, pick up on social cues, and reading and writing come easily to them.

Trouble Spots: Where Boys Run Into Problems

Not all boys are the same, of course, but most rebel in predictable patterns and with predictable weapons: underachievement, aggression and drug and alcohol use. While taking chances is an important aspect of the growth process, it can lead to real trouble.

When Johnny Can't Read

Girls have reading disorders nearly as often as boys, but are able to overcome them. Disability rates, as identified by:

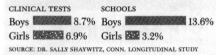

CLINICAL TESTS		SCHOOLS	
Boys	8.7%	Boys	13.6%
Girls	6.9%	Girls	3.2%

SOURCE: DR. SALLY SHAYWITZ, CONN. LONGITUDINAL STUDY

Suicidal Impulses

While girls are much more likely to try to kill themselves, boys are likelier to die from their attempts.

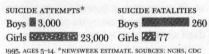

SUICIDE ATTEMPTS*		SUICIDE FATALITIES	
Boys	3,000	Boys	260
Girls	23,000	Girls	77

1995, AGES 5–14. *NEWSWEEK ESTIMATE. SOURCES: NCHS, CDC

Binge Drinking

Boys binge more on alcohol. Those who had five or more drinks in a row in the last two weeks:

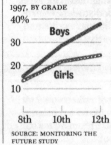

1997, BY GRADE

40%
30
20
10

Boys
Girls

8th   10th   12th

SOURCE: MONITORING THE FUTURE STUDY

Aggression That Turns to Violence

Boys get arrested three times as often as girls, but for some nonviolent crimes the numbers are surprisingly even.

Arrests of 10- to 17-year-olds: ■ Boys ▨ Girls

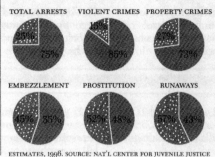

TOTAL ARRESTS — 25% / 75%
VIOLENT CRIMES — 15% / 85%
PROPERTY CRIMES — 27% / 73%
EMBEZZLEMENT — 45% / 55%
PROSTITUTION — 52% / 48%
RUNAWAYS — 57% / 43%

ESTIMATES, 1996. SOURCE: NAT'L CENTER FOR JUVENILE JUSTICE

Eating Disorders

Boys can also have eating disorders. Kids who used laxatives or vomited to lose weight:

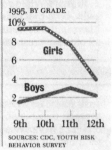

1995, BY GRADE

10%
8
6
4
2

Girls
Boys

9th   10th   11th   12th

SOURCES: CDC, YOUTH RISK BEHAVIOR SURVEY

Black leaders are looking for alternatives. In Atlanta, the Rev. Tim McDonald's First Iconium Baptist Church just chartered a Boy Scout troop. "Gangs are so prevalent because guys want to belong to something," says McDonald. "We've got to give them something positive to belong to." Black educators like Chicagoan Jawanza Kunjufu think mentoring programs will overcome the bias against academic success as "too white." Some cities are also experimenting with all-boy classrooms in predominantly black schools.

Researchers hope that in the next few years, they'll come up with strategies that will help boys the way the work of Gilligan and others helped girls. In the meantime, experts say, there are some guidelines. Parents can channel their sons' energy into constructive activities, like team sports. They should also look for "teachable moments" to encourage qualities such as empathy. When Di-ane Fisher, a Cincinnati-area psychologist, hears her 8- and 10-year-old boys talking about "finishing somebody," she knows she has mistakenly rented a violent videogame. She pulls the plug and tells them: "In our house, killing people is not entertainment, even if it's just pretend."

Parents can also teach by example. New Yorkers Dana and Frank Minaya say they've never disciplined their 16-year-old son Walter in anger. They insist on resolving all disputes calmly and reasonably, without yelling. If there is a problem, they call an official family meeting "and we never leave without a big hug," says Frank. Walter tries to be open with his parents. "I don't want to miss out on any advice," he says.

Most of all, wise parents of boys should go with the flow. Cindy Lang, 36, a full-time mother in Woodside, Calif., is continually amazed by the relentless energy of her sons, Roger Lloyd, 12, and Chris, 9. "You accept the fact that they're going to involve themselves in risky behavior, like skateboarding down a flight of stairs. As a girl, I certainly wasn't skateboarding down a flight of stairs." Just last week, she got a phone call from school telling her that Roger Lloyd was in the emergency room because he had fallen backward while playing basketball and school officials thought he might have a concussion. He's fine now, but she's prepared for the next emergency: "I have a cell phone so I can be on alert." Boys will be boys. And we have to let them.

With KAREN SPRINGEN *in Chicago,*
PATRICIA KING *in San Francisco,*
PAT WINGERT *in Washington,* VERN E. SMITH
in Atlanta and ELIZABETH ANGELL *in New York*

7–10 years While good at gross motor skills, boys trail girls in finer control. Many of the best students but also nearly all of the poorest ones are boys.

11–13 years A mixed bag. Dropout rates begin to climb, but good students start pulling ahead of girls in math skills and catching up some in verbal ones.

14–16 years Entering adolescence, boys hit another rough patch. Indulging in drugs, alcohol and aggressive behavior are common forms of rebellion.

8	9	10	11	12	13	14	15	16

7–10 years Very good years for girls. On average, they outperform boys at school, excelling in verbal skills while holding their own in math.

11–13 years The start of puberty and girls' most vulnerable time. Many experience depression; as many as 15% may try to kill themselves.

14–16 years Eating disorders are a major concern. Although anorexia can manifest itself as early as 8, it typically afflicts girls starting at 11 or 12; bulimia at 15.

SOURCES: DR. MICHAEL THOMPSON, BARNEY BRAWER. RESEARCH BY BILL VOURVOULIAS—NEWSWEEK

Young and Violent

Crimes by girls flying off the charts

In the last decade, the FBI recorded a 114 pct. increase in arrests of girls for violent offenses.

By Maureen Graham,
Rita Giordano
and Christine Bahls
FOR THE INQUIRER

By the time Adelle Steele was 14, the Kennett Square girl had been arrested 10 times for theft and assault. Once, while in a treatment facility, she kicked, punched and helped tie up a teacher, then tried to run away.

Steele, now 15, was arrested for stealing a car and for numerous assaults, including beating up her sister, after which she pushed over a full-sized refrigerator. The reason: "I just wanted to fight. I'd hit, and they'd fall."

Steele, a teenager who is alternately sweet and strong-willed, is at the forefront of a national surge in violent crimes committed by girls and young women. Today's female teenagers are fighting more, forming their own gangs, using weapons regularly, and robbing with greater frequency than at any time in recent American history, according to FBI statistics.

Between 1986 and 1996, the number of girls younger than 18 arrested nationwide for violent crimes—murder, rape, robbery, aggravated assault—increased 114 percent, according to FBI statistics. In the same period, the number of boys arrested for violent crime increased 39 percent.

In interviews, teenage girls who have been arrested for crimes say there is lit-tle difference between boys and girls when it comes to breaking the law.

"Girls are just as aggressive as guys, sometimes more," said Brenda Hall, a suburban New Jersey 19-year-old now serving time for armed robbery. "Whatever guys are doing, girls are doing—holding a gun, fighting, joining a gang."

Some law enforcement authorities say they are beginning to see a pattern of "macho" attitudes and behavior among girls.

In interviews, teenage girls in Pennsylvania and New Jersey described running illegal drug operations and carrying weapons—either for protection or to commit crimes. They said they engage in violent fights either to stake claim to a boyfriend or because someone has shown them disrespect. If they need money, they rob or burglarize. Some said they are not afraid to carry a gun.

Crime statistics show that in 1996, nearly one of every four juveniles arrested was a girl. In 1985, one in every nine juveniles arrested for a violent crime was female. Between 1992 and 1996, there was a 20 percent increase in the number of girls arrested for robbery, while the number of boys arrested for robbery rose 6 percent. Theft arrests for girls were 25 percent higher, while the increase among boys was 2 percent.

According to police, prosecutors and juvenile counselors, the same forces at work among boys who commit crimes are now affecting girls: A lack of parental guidance; a notion that they will not be held accountable for their actions; over-indulgence by parents; an increase in drug use; greater access to guns; and a desire for excitement.

Case workers also see a parallel between greater freedom in the workplace for women and the growing number of female juvenile offenders. In the same way that women in recent years have stepped into roles traditionally held by men, girls now feel freer to commit crimes.

"When women began to take nontraditional jobs and became more independent, it crossed over into the world of juvenile crime," said Cleet Davis, who directs the Florence Crittendon girls detention center in Trenton. "Girls began to feel they could be their own bosses. They didn't need the boys to sell the drugs, they could have their own gangs. I hear it all the time."

Twenty years ago roles were different, said Don Haldeman, a probation officer in Delaware County. "Girls weren't allowed to be violent. Society wouldn't accept it at all. They were brought up on that, and they bought into that. Now they don't. All the walls have crashed and they're free to do whatever the boys do."

Philip W. Harris, a criminal justice professor at Temple University who is working with the city to keep track of some juvenile offenders, said female delinquents are shedding traditional roles.

"Girls sense they don't have to play these charming little-girl roles anymore," Harris said.

Heather Corbett, 16, of Pennsauken, served time for assault. She said girls in school get into serious fights every week.

"Some of them feel like they have to fight," she said. "They don't want people to think they're punks. They fight because some girls think they're being disrepected. They're losing their pride. If somebody calls you a bitch, you will fight."

Kaveen Dudley, 16, of Mizpah, N.J., is serving time for assaulting a girl in the Oak Crest High School cafeteria. She said the girl had been telling other girls she was contacting Kaveen's boyfriend with a pager. As a result of the assault, the victim lost her peripheral vision.

"I lunged," Dudley said. "I was out of it. I don't know what happened. I was kicking her and stuff. I didn't have to react, but I wanted to. I wasn't angry. I was just fighting."

Leah Miller, 18, of Atlantic County, is serving time for drug possession. She said she has cut school, taken drugs, and participated in robberies. She said she has gone to a local park with a group of boys to steal. She said she held all the guns, because there was no female officer on the local police force, and she could not be frisked.

"I was having fun," Miller said. "Once I got into the fast life, they wasn't stopping me."

Authorities say dealing with girls is more difficult than dealing with boys.

"The girls are the toughest, they are more incorrigible," said Anthony Guarna, chief juvenile probation officer in Montgomery County.

"The girls are more bullheaded," said Lisa Douple, a Bucks County public defender.

Law enforcement officials and case workers say that each year, the crimes by some girls have become more violent.

"Girls are using razors and baseball bats as weapons now," said Ellen Cohill, who runs Valentine, a facility for delinquent girls in Bordentown, N.J. "They are very angry, and they are very aggressive. It's vicious."

Police, who once took a benign approach with delinquent girls, now arrest them.

Her last free day: Tears, goodbyes—and hope

The day of her high-school prom, Brenda Hall went to jail. A judge sentenced her in May to 10 years in prison for her role in three robberies in Gloucester County. She must serve a minimum of three years and three months. The day before, she took her little sister to Pizza Hut in her mother's Dodge Stratus and said goodbye to family and friends at an emotional barbecue. Her mother baked a cake, and wrote in frosting, "Say a prayer for Brenda." Brenda wiped that away and in its place spelled out "good luck" with pieces of candy.

The next morning, her parents nailed her bedroom door shut so that her three siblings wouldn't raid her belongings. She went to court, heard the sentence, and wept. Her first night in Gloucester County Jail, she was beaten by other inmates. She was moved to Salem County Jail and then the state women's prison in Clinton. A few days later, she was nostalgic. "The last few weeks I was home, I started appreciating things more," she said. But she was positive. "I'm really optimistic. My mom told me that when I get out, I get her Stratus!"

—By April Saul

"The guys hesitate to arrest girls. It goes back to the mentality of their being female," said Detective Jim Waltrop of Lansdale. "The younger officers are starting to realize that the girls are as violent as the boys, but the older officers still have this thought that this is somebody's daughter, will be somebody's mother."

Another contributor to crimes by girls is childhood abuse.

Adelle Steele's mother, Roxanne, said her daughter was routinely and severely beaten by her father, who died in 1994.

"The abuse issues and the subsequent anger were always there," said William Ford, chief juvenile probation officer of Bucks County.

But in recent years, case workers say, girls have expressed their anger in more violent and criminal ways.

"If there are 20 girls in a detention room, 18 of those have been raped or sexually abused," said Davis, of the girls' center. Davis, who has supervised the detention center since 1991, said girls come to her angry and frustrated.

"If she's raped at 12, by 13 she's out on the street raising hell," Davis said.

"They've just lost their way," said Alisa Brown of Big Sisters of Philadelphia. "You can't help them with the delinquency issues until you deal with the other things."

The 1995 lavender Dodge Neon was a teenager's dream.

Brenda Hall was given the car by her parents as a reward for good grades, for volunteer church work, and for tending to her three younger brothers and sisters. She was the "good daughter," with not a hint of problems in her background.

In 1997, Hall used the Dodge as a getaway car in a series of armed robberies in Gloucester County, she said. She took part in cuffing and terrorizing a gas station attendant with a sawed-off shotgun. She said she also planned the burglary of a bagel store, where she and two other youths stole more than $10,000.

In a three-month period, the high school senior whom everyone considered level-headed committed violent crimes. She pleaded guilty to three robberies, and in May was sentenced to 10 years, facing a minimum of three years and three months.

There are few answers to why and how Hall started her life of crime. Her parents, Carol and Harry Hall of Franklin Township, say they are still searching. They think part of the problem is that they spoiled her and gave her too much freedom too soon.

"It was so much of everything," Brenda Hall said. "It was fitting in. It was being accepted." And at first, she said, "It was so exciting."

A somewhat overweight young woman with curly red hair, Hall never really liked herself, she said. As a child, her classmates would tease her about her weight and call her ugly. She did "everything right," trying to please everyone, she said.

By her senior year her friends were dating, but she had no one. She desperately sought out friends, she said, and met a 16-year-old boy and an 18-year-old girl, both of whom had juvenile criminal records.

They told her of exploits that seemed glamorous. Before long, she joined them.

"I didn't want to be the one person to say no," she recalled.

Her purple Neon gave Hall instant acceptance. Neither of her new friends, Jason Nigro and Sharin Stallings, had a car. Whenever the three went out, Hall drove. One night in March 1997, the three planned to rob a Heritage store in Franklin Township, Hall and Nigro said in separate interviews. (Stallings declined to be interviewed.) Hall drove. They stole more than $200.

Within two weeks, they had planned a second robbery.

Hall was working part time at Don's Bagels in Glassboro. Don Brasco, the owner, had deducted $35 from her pay because money was missing from the cash register, she said. Denying that she took the money and angered that Brasco had charged her for it, she suggested to Stallings and Nigro that they rob the bagel store, Hall said. She sketched the inside of the bakery and gave them her key.

They were expecting to get a couple hundred dollars. Instead, they said, beneath the floorboards they found thousands of dollars. Amazed, they grabbed what they could—$10,000—and left.

In celebration, they rented a limousine and went to South Street in Philadelphia.

Realizing how much trouble she could get into, she told Nigro and Stallings she wanted out. Stallings objected, she said, telling Hall she would tell Hall's parents everything if she didn't continue to help.

Several weeks later, the three decided to rob a Franklin Township gas station.

Tom Severance was working that night when Hall and Nigro drove to the back of the station. Severance said a young woman, later identified as Stallings, approached him and told him that she and her friend were having car trouble.

"I went in the back, and the hood of the car was up," Severance said. "When I saw two girls in trouble, I just started to help."

He recalled seeing movement out of the corner of his eye. Then, a masked person appeared holding a shotgun. It was Nigro.

"You know what I want," Nigro said, according to Severance.

Forced to lie on the ground, Nigro and Stallings searched him, he said. Then Nigro told him to get up. "We're going for a walk."

"I was scared," Severance said in an interview. "I wondered whether I was go-ing to get shot. It was scary looking down the barrel of that shotgun and not knowing what they were going to do."

Hall stayed in her car, waiting to provide the getaway, she said. They ordered him to take money out of the cash register, and give it to them. It was about $100. They then tied Severance to a tree and drove away.

Nigro and Stallings pleaded guilty on three robbery charges and are in jail.

For Barbara Washington, fighting was a way of life.

Once, she went after a man with a knife and a brick. Fighting was a regular occurrence at school. But when Washington committed an assault so brutal that the victim was hospitalized, the Darby girl, who had just turned 15, found herself in court.

Despite the seriousness of the charge, she stood before the judge alone.

"Where are the parents?" demanded Juvenile Court Judge A. Leo Sereni.

Informed that they had been subpoenaed, the usually gentlemanly jurist exploded.

"This court will not tolerate noncompliance of parents!" Sereni said. He ordered bench warrants for the parents, called for child welfare to investigate the home, and kept Washington in detention.

Everyone in the courtroom snapped to attention. Except Barbara Washington.

It was not the first time she had stood alone.

Washington remembers the time her mother left her and her half-brother, Danny. She was 5, he was 10.

"She left us at some lady's house and she never came back," Washington said. "The lady kicked us out." She ended up on the street, she said. "My brother was carrying me on his back. I had no shoes on."

At 12, Washington struck a small boy who wouldn't play her way, she said. When the boy's father objected and hit Barbara on the back, she said she went after the father with a knife. Then she hit the father over the head with a brick.

She said she even fought when in detention. She remembers fighting because a girl was "talking trash." She punched the girl, knocking her onto a couch.

Washington said she often hit her mother. She learned to fight from her brother, who taught her at an early age to fight back.

"I was taught that nobody hits me," she said.

Washington's first arrest occurred in 1997. She said she was "helping" a 13-year-old friend, who was arguing with a woman. Washington said she bashed the woman's head seven times with a hard object.

"It just happened," she said, adding that she "went blank" when she assaulted the woman. At the time, Washington said she felt "nothing." Later, she said, she felt sorry.

The woman, badly bruised and terrified, was hospitalized. Washington and her friend were found guilty in juvenile court of aggravated assault.

Throughout Washington's short life, her parents have been often too mired in their own criminal entanglements, imprisonments and bouts of substance abuse to allow for a decent childhood, they said.

At one point, Washington lived with Shirley Carmichael, a school cleaning woman who was her half-brother's maternal grandmother. Carmichael said of Washington: "I don't blame little Barbara. I blame her mother, I blame her father."

At Quakertown High School, Joanna Seifert had a tough time making friends, she said. She did not belong to any clubs but maintained good grades. "I felt a little different," she said. "I had low self-esteem."

Then, in the summer of 1996, when she was 16, her grandfather bought her a black 1985 Porsche 944. The car quickly became her pride and joy, she said. Every week, she would vacuum and shine it in her grandparents' driveway.

At school, the car stood out as a singular attraction, she said. And Seifert, a quiet, hard-to-read, reticent girl, was becoming noticed by fellow classmates.

"I liked to show it off," she said.

She also liked to drive fast. Within months after she got the car, she got a ticket for tailgating; soon after that, she got a speeding ticket. And after that, she hit a van and was cited for reckless driving. A stop-sign violation followed. She said her grandparents paid most of the fines.

On the evening of Aug. 1, 1997, she left her part-time job at a Quakertown movie theater to visit a friend, she said. Traveling 50 m.p.h. in a 10 m.p.h. zone, she struck and killed a pedestrian.

Afraid of facing the consequences, she said, she sped away. But a witness gave state police her license number.

By midnight, she had been arrested at her grandparents' house, the place she had called home for most of her life. She was charged with involuntary manslaughter, homicide by vehicle and related offenses.

On Nov. 14, Bucks County Common Pleas Court President Judge Isaac Garb ordered her to a residential treatment facility near Harrisburg.

Her probation officer, Mark Maryott, told the court that Seifert's "family situation has caused very serious problems, and her drug usage has compounded the situation.

"She truly lacks any insight into her problems. Anything short of this [placement] won't be effective with her," Maryott said.

When Seifert was 8, and her sister 11, their parents separated after a stormy marriage. The children chose to move in with their maternal grandparents.

Seifert said that she did not feel abandoned, and was not angry at her parents. "I love them, I just don't feel close," she said.

In late 1996, Seifert said, she became friends with some kids she considered to be "cool."

"The popular kids were the bad kids, and I wanted the recognition," she said. "Once I had that, I didn't have low self-esteem."

By April last year, after experimenting with a host of drugs, including heroin, she decided to push her popularity one step further by selling drugs, she said.

"Basically, I had a variety store going on," she said.

Supplying friends, she would travel to Philadelphia for cocaine and marijuana. She bought acid in the Quakertown area, she said.

Using the cellular phone her grandfather bought her for her birthday, Seifert conducted business from her car and in friends' houses. She was rarely home.

"I would go home to sleep and shower, and sometimes I would stay out all night," Seifert said. "Sometimes I would go from the crack house to work. I would call my grandmother and tell her I was all right. She would be on the phone crying."

She recalled the night she killed a man with her car:

Driving fast through a development, she headed toward a woman in the street who was yelling, "Slow the H down!"

"I put my brakes on, to swerve around her," Seifert said. A man, Harold Winkler, was in the street. "All I seen was the middle portion of his body," Seifert said. Winkler was struck by the side of the car; the impact dented the door. Flying in the air, he landed, head first, on the curb.

"To me, it was like, I pushed him away," Seifert said. "I was scared of what happened; I was scared of the woman in the street. I knew I would get in a lot of trouble. I was trying to get away from it."

She said she sped home, then went to a pizzeria to meet her friend. They headed for Allentown and bought crack cocaine.

From the treatment facility, she said the only thing she regretted about the accident was that Winkler died.

"I'm basically a thrill seeker," she said. "I was just living it up."

The *Inquirer* interviewed and received consent from the parents or legal guardians of all subjects under 18 to be named and fully quoted in this series.

For More Information

■ People who need help with troubled children can call these 24-hour hotlines: In New Jersey, Contact 609 at 609-317-0022. In Pennsylvania, the Philadelphia crisis intervention unit at 215-686-4420 or Contact 215 at 215-879-4402.

Unit 4

Unit Selections

Key Points to Consider

❖ What are our expectations of community policing with regard to juveniles? Should we change our expectations and thus change police policy?

❖ The public health model suggests that guns are a driving force in the epidemic of violence. What should we consider legal and illegal for juveniles regarding their possession and use of guns? How much should this reflect the laws regarding adults and guns? Is there a difference?

❖ Is our understanding of gangs adequate to allow formation of public policy about them? Discuss.

❖ Some citizens of Cicero, Illinois, have voted to create a "gang-free community" and expel gang members who violate the community. What policy implications does this movement have?

DUSHKINONLINE **Links**   **www.dushkin.com/online/**

These sites are annotated on pages 4 and 5.

It was determined more than 30 years ago in benchmark research by Piliavin and Briar that police discretion in dealing with juveniles was strongly influenced by a few "readily observable criteria," including the juvenile's prior offense record, ethnicity, grooming, and demeanor. Today, police still have great latitude in encounters with juveniles, which may be enhanced by community policing philosophies.

It was observed back then that police discretion was an extension of the juvenile court philosophy that held that when making decisions about youth, more weight should be placed on their character than on the immediate offense. Of course, with the rise of the justice model, this view, too, was modified to a stance that dictates, even for juveniles, that if you do the crime you will do the time.

Still, who becomes an officially recognized delinquent is usually decided by a police officer's judgment. So police define juveniles' behavior in terms of existing laws—laws that are today becoming harsher and harsher as panic develops.

Criminology has studied this phenomenon under the theoretical approach of "labeling," in which it is recognized that the official agents of society—the courts and the police especially—are the main labelers. It must be recognized, in defense of police, that this labeling is not taking place in a vacuum. Bad labels (stigmas) are contingent also on social attitudes, legislatures, media, and interest groups such as community leadership, activist organizations, and lobbying and support groups.

If there is a war on crime, then the police are the front line of the war. Indeed, the introduction of community policing has enhanced the importance of the police officer, who, while not at war in this model, is the main line of community control.

Reference
Piliavin, Irving, and Briar, Scott, "Police Encounters with Juveniles," *American Journal of Sociology*, 70, 2, September 1964, 206–214.

Police, Juveniles, and the Law

Tokyo's Teen Tribes

The Sydney Morning Herald

It's past midnight in Shibuya, a funky entertainment district popular with Tokyo's younger generation. Three high-school boys are lying unconscious outside a busy bar. Two teenage girls in party gear are throwing up. A third, who looks about 16, is striking erotic poses in the middle of the street while three boys grope her breasts and buttocks. Ten yards away, a uniformed officer studiously ignores the scenes of drunken teenage debauchery that have become an almost nightly event in this part of town.

Welcome to the world of the *kogyaru,* the *femio kun,* the *boso zoku*—the new tribes of Japan's younger generation who are worrying the wits out of their parents with their wild behavior.

International surveys show that Japanese youngsters are more discontented with their materialistic society than kids in other countries. They also tend to be more apathetic and less ambitious. The latest poll, conducted by the government's Management and Coordination Agency, found that only 44 percent of Japanese under 20 were happy with their lives—a far lower percentage than in the United States, Europe, and even Russia.

Rebelling against what psychiatrist Masao Miyamoto calls the "straitjacket society" where kids have their whole lives predetermined for them by the time they reach junior high school at 13—Japanese youth are shocking the authorities with their sex, drugs, and rock 'n' roll. Particularly the sex.

A national survey of 3,600 14- and 15-year-olds by the National Congress of Parents' and Teachers' Associations confirmed every parent's worst fears. One quarter of the girls admitted that they had frequented *terekura* ("telephone clubs"), the 500-odd dating agencies in Tokyo, where frustrated men pay for introductions to schoolgirls. The girls boast they can earn $700 or more in cash and gifts for a date.

Two thirds of the students said they regularly drank alcohol (the drinking age in Japan is 20), one in six said they had shoplifted, and 7 percent said they used drugs—an extraordinarily high figure in a country where possession of even one marijuana joint almost invariably brings a stiff jail sentence.

Hiroshi Itakura, a professor of criminal law at Tokyo's Nihon University, says the survey showed Japanese youngsters had "an undeveloped sense of right and wrong and a general attitude of permissiveness." He asserts: "Someday this will lead to Japan's ruin."

The schoolgirl date-club phenomenon sprang into the headlines last year when three 15-year-olds confessed that they had picked up a 43-year-old office worker through a club and gone with him to a love hotel—one of thousands of specialized hotels in Tokyo that rent rooms with video cameras by the hour. There the girls squirted him in the eyes with a teargas canister and fled with his wallet containing $1,500. The man told police he thought the girls were treating him to some kinky S&M and didn't realize he was being robbed until too late.

In the uproar that followed, police were ordered to crack down on the clubs. Teachers and police rounded up no fewer than 526 schoolgirls—some as young as 13—and charged more than 100 of them with prostitution. The clubs, however, soon resumed business.

Not far from the Shibuya bar, two casually dressed 16-year-olds named Yuko and Akiko are primping at a street corner, waiting for someone to pick them up. They are typical *kogyaru* (literally "child/girls"), attending school by day, partying by night.

Yuko denies selling her body but cheerfully admits she sleeps with strangers who sometimes leave her money. She sold her school knickers, along with a photo of herself wearing them, to one of the *buru sera* sex shops in Tokyo for $95. *Buru sera* means "sailor's bloomers," and the stores are the latest craze among Tokyo's dirty old men, who are also willing to pay liberally for schoolgirls' fingernails, vials of saliva, and used tampons.

Both girls say they use drugs—amphetamines, marijuana, hash, and LSD. The latest craze is inhaling capsules of a liquid used to clean video-recorder heads.

Although Japan still has an enviably low rate of drug use, police figures show a dramatic increase among the young. Last year, police arrested more than 10,000 juveniles for drug use or dealing; most of the arrests involved paint-thinner

From *World Press Review,* January 1996, pp. 39-40. Originally published in the *Sydney Morning Herald,* Sydney, Australia. © 1996 by Ben Hills. Reprinted by permission.

abuse. Inhalation of thinners has been blamed for a rash of deaths among teenagers and for last New Year's Eve's suicide attempt by five junior-high-school girls who leapt from an apartment building. Three were killed and two terribly injured.

The *boso zoku* ("reckless tribe") have been around Tokyo since the early 1970s. Now, however, bikers and their rivals in hotted-up cars are giving police and law-abiding drivers a bigger headache than ever. Wearing black leather and chains, and sporting tattoos and rings through their ears, noses, tongues, bellybuttons, nipples, and genitals, the reckless riders turn sections of Tokyo's Shuto expressway into a raceway. More than a third of the 1,000-odd motorcycle deaths last year involved teenagers, and police are now pushing for tougher laws to try to cut down on the mayhem.

Then there are the *femio kun* ("feminine lads"). Although they deny they are gay, anywhere else in the world they would be regarded as having a severe case of gender confusion. Wearing berets over their short "monkey-hair" cuts and carrying dainty backpacks, these kids parade around the streets wearing necklaces and makeup and dressed in tight skivvies over lacy blouses, miniskirts or billowing bell-bottom trousers, and platform shoes.

A whole new industry has sprung up to cater to this latest subculture, and social commentators are falling over themselves to explain the appeal of the androgynous look. "They [the feminine lads] are very popular with the girls," says one young woman. "They are not macho or threatening—it's like having a pet to play with."

No one has yet come up with a snappy name like Generation X to describe the kaleidoscope of subcultures. The term most commonly used by tut-tutting TV commentators is *shiji machi sedai*, which translates clumsily as "a generation awaiting instruction." Nor can any two sociologists agree on the causes, or consequences, of Japan's youth rebellion.

Author Hideo Kato, 65, blames frustration over the Japanese education system, under which a child's education and hence career has already been mapped out by the time he or she—particularly she—leaves primary school. Teenage suicide is common—almost 3,000 deaths in the past decade—under the relentless pressure to succeed at school.

Hideo Kato says: "When their future is decided for them in this way, there is often a gap between their parents' expectations and what their teachers say is possible. They develop an inferiority complex and a shaky sense of identity. The future is not worth thinking about, so they pursue the pleasures of the moment—that's why they sell their bodies or their underwear. They don't care any more what society thinks."

—*Ben Hills (with research by Mayu Kanamori), "Sydney Morning Herald" (centrist), Oct. 7, 1995.*

Law enforcement and juvenile crime

For delinquents, law enforcement is the doorway to the juvenile justice system. Once a juvenile is apprehended for a law violation, it is the police officer who first determines if the juvenile will move deeper into the justice system or will be diverted.

Law enforcement agencies track the volume and characteristics of crimes reported to them and use this information to monitor the changing levels of crime in their communities. Not all crimes are reported and most of those that are reported remained unsolved. Consequently, the reported crime information cannot shed much light on the problem of juvenile crime. However, law enforcement

agencies also report arrest statistics that can be used to monitor the flow of juveniles and adults into the justice system. These arrest statistics are the most often cited source of information on juvenile crime trends.

This chapter describes the volume and characteristics of juvenile crime from the perspective of law enforcement. Information is presented on the number of juvenile arrests made annually, the nature of these arrests, and arrest trends. Violent crime, property crime, drug, and weapons arrests and trends are presented. Juvenile arrests and arrest trends are also compared with those of adults. The data presented in this chapter were originally

compiled by the Federal Bureau of Investigation as a part of its Uniform Crime Reporting Program.

Acknowledgments

This chapter was written by Howard Snyder. The county-level arrest maps were produced by Dennis Sullivan using data extrapolated from a data file prepared by the Inter-university Consortium for Political and Social Research at the University of Michigan, which was based on a data file provided by the FBI.

Information from the FBI's Uniform Crime Reporting Program is the most often cited source for juvenile crime and arrest trends

Since the 1930's police agencies have reported to the Uniform Crime Reporting (UCR) Program

Each year thousands of agencies voluntarily report the following data to the FBI:

- Number of reported Index crimes.
- Number of arrests and the most serious charge involved in each.
- Age, sex, and race of arrestees.

- Proportion of reported Index crimes cleared by arrest and the proportion cleared by the arrest of persons under age 18.
- Dispositions of juvenile arrests.
- Detailed victim and assailant information in homicide cases.

In 1992 law enforcement agencies with jurisdiction over 95% of the U.S. population contributed data on reported crimes, while 84% of the country was represented in the reported arrest data.

What can the UCR data tell us about crime and young people?

The UCR data can provide estimates of the annual number of arrests of young people for various offense categories. It can detail these arrests by sex, race, and urban, suburban, and rural areas. It can estimate changes in arrests over various time periods and the proportion of crimes cleared by youthful arrests. The UCR can also compare the relative number of adult and youthful arrests within offense categories and over time.

 From *Juvenile Offenders and Victims, A National Report,* 1995, pp. 97-122. Reprinted by permission of the National Institute of Justice, National Criminal Justice Reference Service.

UCR data document the number of crimes reported, not the number of crimes committed

The UCR Program monitors the number of Index crimes (see side bar) that come to the attention of law enforcement agencies. Although this information is useful in trending the volume of crime committed, it must be recognized that not all crimes are brought to the attention of law enforcement. Reported crime figures cannot be used to measure the number or the proportion of crimes committed by juveniles.

Crimes are more likely to be reported if they involve an injury or a large economic loss. For example, the National Crime Victimization Survey found that 92% of motor vehicle

What are the Crime Indices?

The designers of the UCR Program wanted to create an index (similar in concept to the Dow Jones Industrial Average or the Consumer Price Index) which would be sensitive to changes in the volume and nature of reported crime. They decided to incorporate specific offenses into the index based on several factors: likelihood of being reported, frequency of occurrence, pervasiveness in all geographical areas of the country, and relative seriousness.

The *Crime Index* is divided into two components: the *Violent Crime Index* and the *Property Crime Index:*

Violent Crime Index—includes murder and nonnegligent manslaughter, forcible rape, robbery, and aggravated assault.

Property Crime Index—includes burglary, larceny-theft, motor vehicle theft, and arson.

Crime Index—includes all eight crimes included in the *Violent Crime Index* and *Property Crime Index.*

While some violent crimes such as kidnapping and extortion are excluded, the Violent Crime Index contains what are generally considered to be serious crimes. In contrast, a substantial proportion of the crimes in the Property Crime Index are generally considered less serious crimes, such as shoplifting, theft from motor vehicles, and bicycle theft, all of which are included in the larceny-theft category.

thefts were reported in 1992, while police received reports on 70% of robberies with injury, 52% of simple assaults with injury, and 29% of attempted robberies without injury. Consequently, changes in reported crime may reflect changes in the number of crimes committed, in the willingness of victims to report these crimes to law enforcement agencies, or in the inclination of the police to make a record of the incident. At least part of the increase in reported crime statistics in the past 20 years can be attributed to an increase in the willingness of victims to report crimes to police.

UCR data document the number of arrests made, not the number of persons arrested

A person can be arrested more than once in a year. Each arrest is counted separately in the UCR. One arrest can represent many crimes. A person arrested for allegedly committing 40 burglaries would show up in the UCR data as one arrest for burglary. One crime may also result in multiple arrests. For example, three youth may be arrested for one burglary. This situation of multiple arrests for a single crime is more likely to occur for juveniles than for adults because juveniles are more likely than are adults to commit crimes in groups.

UCR records only the most serious offense for which a person was arrested

Arrest counts and trends for less serious offenses must be carefully interpreted. For example, an arrest of a person for both robbery and weapons possession would appear in the UCR data as one robbery arrest. The count of weapons arrests reflects only those arrests in which a weapons charge was the most serious offense charged.

How should clearance and arrest data be interpreted?

Let's try to answer the question: "What proportion of all burglaries are committed by juveniles?" The UCR reports that 20% of all burglaries cleared in 1992 were cleared by the arrest of persons under age 18 and that 34% of persons arrested for burglary in 1992 were under age 18. How do we reconcile these very different percentages?

First, can we be certain that the 13% of all burglaries that were cleared in 1992 are like all the burglaries committed? It could be argued that juveniles are less skilled at avoiding arrest. If so, cleared burglaries are likely to contain a greater percentage of juvenile burglaries than would those that are not cleared.

But even if we assumed that the offender characteristics in the 13% of cleared burglaries are similar to those of the 87% not cleared, how do we reconcile that large difference between the juvenile clearance and arrest percentage (18% vs. 34%)?

The key to this difference can be found in the fact that, more so than adults, juveniles tend to commit crimes in groups. Assume a police department cleared five burglaries, one committed by a pair of juveniles and the other four committed individually by four different adults. The juvenile proportion of burglaries cleared would be 20% (1 in 5), while 33% of persons arrested for burglary would be a juvenile (2 in 6).

Clearance and arrest statistics answer different questions. If you want to know how much crime was committed by juveniles, the clearance data give a better indication because they count crimes, not arrestees. However, if you want to know how many persons entered the justice system, use the arrest data.

UCR documents the result of a juvenile arrest

Local agencies report to the FBI how they disposed of arrestees who are classified as juveniles in their jurisdictions. This is the only information in the UCR Program that is sensitive to the States' statutory juvenile/adult distinction. The UCR permits agencies to characterize the disposition of the arrest into five categories: handled within the department and released; transferred to another police agency; or referred to a welfare agency, a juvenile court, or a criminal court.

Clearance statistics provide a different perspective than do arrest statistics

A crime is considered *cleared* once someone is charged with that crime. If a person is arrested and charged with committing 40 burglaries, UCR would record 40 burglary clearances. If three people are arrested for robbing a liquor store, UCR would record one robbery cleared. Knowing the number of crimes reported as well as the number of crimes cleared in a year provides an understanding of the proportion of crimes for which an arrest was made.

A much greater proportion of violent than property crimes are cleared by arrest

	Percent of all crimes cleared
Violent Crime Index	45%
Murder	65
Forcible rape	52
Robbery	24
Aggravated assault	56
Property Crime Index	18%
Burglary	13
Larceny-theft	20
Motor vehicle theft	14
Arson	15

Source: FBI. (1993). *Crime in the United States 1992.*

UCR captures the proportion of crimes cleared by juvenile arrest

UCR data also document the proportion of cleared crimes that were cleared by the arrest of persons under age 18. This is the only source of information in the UCR that specifies the percentage of crime committed by juveniles.

Assessments of the juvenile contribution to the U.S. crime problem are often based on the proportion of arrests that are juvenile arrests. Clearance and arrest statistics give a very different picture of the juvenile contribution to crime. An understanding of this difference is important if one wishes to use the UCR data properly.

In 1992 juveniles accounted for 13% of all violent crimes reported to law enforcement agencies and 18% of all violent crime arrests

How much of the crime problem is caused by juveniles?

Arrest proportions accurately characterize the ages of individuals entering the justice system. The fact that juveniles were 15% of all persons arrested for murder in 1992 implies that 15% of all persons entering the justice system on a murder charge were juveniles, not that the juveniles committed 15% of all murders.

Because juveniles are more likely than adults to commit crime in groups, arrest percentages are likely to exaggerate the juvenile contribution to the crime problem. The FBI clearance data provide a better assessment of the juvenile contribution to crime.

Juveniles were responsible for 13% of all violent crimes in 1992 and 23% of all property crimes

The juvenile contribution to the crime problem in the U.S. in 1992 varied considerably with the nature of the offense. Based on 1992 clearance data, juveniles were responsible for:

- 9% of murders.
- 12% of aggravated assaults.
- 14% of forcible rapes.
- 16% of robberies.
- 20% of burglaries.
- 23% of larceny-thefts.
- 24% of motor vehicle thefts.
- 42% of arsons.

Crimes with greater discrepancies between the arrest and clearance proportions may be those in which group behavior is more common. For example, while the discrepancy is small for forcible rape, it is relatively large for motor vehicle theft, burglary, murder, and robbery.

Arrests for Violent Crime Index offenses monitor violence levels in the juvenile population

The Violent Crime Index combines four offenses (murder/nonnegligent manslaughter, forcible rape, robbery, and aggravated assault). The Index is dominated by arrests for two of the four offenses—robbery and aggravated assault. In 1992, 93% of juvenile Violent Crime Index arrests were for robbery and aggravated assault.

21. Law Enforcement and Juvenile Crime

Thus, a jurisdiction with a high juvenile Violent Crime Index arrest rate does not necessarily have a high juvenile arrest rate in each component of the Index. For example, while New Jersey had one of the highest juvenile Violent Crime Index arrest rates in 1992, its juvenile murder arrest rate was below the national average.

After more than a decade of relative stability, the juvenile violent crime arrest rate soared between 1988 and 1992

The increase in the juvenile arrest rate for violent crimes began in the late 1980's

During the period from 1973 through 1988 the number of juvenile arrests for a Violent Crime Index offense (murder and nonnegligent manslaughter, forcible rape, robbery, and aggravated assault) varied with the changing size of the juvenile population. However, in 1989, the juvenile violent crime arrest rate broke out of this historic range.

The years between 1988 and 1991 saw a 38% increase in the rate of juvenile arrests for violent crimes. The rate of increase then diminished, with the juvenile arrest rate increasing little between 1991 and 1992. This rapid growth over a relatively short period moved the juvenile arrest rate for violent crime in 1992 far above any year since the mid-1960's, the earliest time period for which comparable statistics are available.

The juvenile violent crime arrest rate increased substantially in all racial groups in recent years

In 1983 the violent crime arrest rate for black youth was nearly 7 times the white rate. Between 1983 and 1992 the white arrest rate increased

more than the black arrest rate increased (82% vs. 43%). As a result, in 1992 the rate of violent crime arrests for black youth was about 5 times the white rate.

Over the 10-year period from 1983 through 1992, the violent crime arrest rate for youth of other races increased 42%, nearly equal to the increase in the black rate.

Females were involved in 1 in 8 juvenile violent crime arrests in 1992

From the 1960's through most of the 1980's, the percentage of juvenile violent crime arrests involving females fluctuated between 9% and 11%. Between 1983 and 1992 the female arrest rate increased 83%, while the male rate increased 49%. As a result, females accounted for 13% of all juvenile violent crime arrests in 1992.

Juvenile responsibility for violent crime has increased in the past few years

During the 1970's and 1980's the proportion of violent crimes cleared by juvenile arrest declined with the de-

clining juvenile population in the U.S. In fact, the juvenile responsibility for violent crime reached its lowest level in 20 years in 1987. After this low point, the responsibility of juveniles for violent crime began to increase, with the rate moving up 4 percentage points between 1987 and 1992, returning to the levels of the early 1970's.

In 1992, as in previous years, the juvenile proportion of all violent crime arrests was above their clearance proportion—18% of violent arrests compared with 13% of violent crimes cleared. Therefore, while juveniles may have been responsible for about 1 in 8 violent crimes in 1992, juveniles accounted for more than 1 in 6 persons entering the justice system charged with a violent offense.

After a decade of gradual increase, the juvenile arrest rate for weapons violations increased 75% between 1987 and 1992

A weapons law violation was the most serious charge in 54,000 juvenile arrests in 1992

There were more juvenile arrests for weapons law violations in 1992 than

for murder, forcible rape, and robbery combined. A weapons law violation was the most serious charge in 54,000 juvenile arrests. Many more juvenile arrests actually involved a weapons law violation but, following the FBI's reporting procedures, an arrest is

classified under the most serious offense involved (e.g., aggravated assault, robbery, forcible rape, and murder).

107

Juvenile arrests for weapons law violations more than doubled between 1983 and 1992

Between 1983 and 1992 the adult arrests increased 21%, while juvenile arrests increased 117%. During this same time period, juvenile murder arrests rose 128% and aggravated assault arrests rose 95%, while arrests for other assaults increased 106%. These large increases in juvenile ar-

rests reflect a growing involvement of juveniles in violent crime.

As juveniles age, the probability that their murderer will use a firearm increases substantially

The proportion of victims killed by firearms in 1992 varied with the age of the victim:

- 4% of victims under age 1.
- 15% of victims ages 1–4.
- 37% of victims ages 5–9.
- 72% of victims ages 10–14.
- 85% of victims ages 15–17.

With some notable exceptions, percentage increases in juvenile and adult arrests have been roughly similar over the past 10 years

Persons arrested in 1992 were, on average, older than those arrested in 1972

Between 1972 and 1992 the average age of the U.S. population increased by nearly 3 years. Generally following this increase in the general population, the average age of persons arrested in 1992 for larceny-theft, forcible rape, and burglary was nearly 4 years older than those arrested in 1972.

The increase in the average age of those arrested for a drug abuse viola-

tion was greater than the increase in the general population; those arrested for a drug abuse violation were nearly 6 years older.

Even with the aging of the U.S. population, the larger percentage increases in juvenile arrests for murder and weapons law violations resulted in a decline in the average age of arrestees in these crime categories. On average, 1992 arrestees were nearly 3 years younger than those arrested for these crimes in 1972.

Offense	Average age of arrestees	
	1972	1992
Violent Crime Index	26.2	27.6
Murder	29.7	27.2
Forcible rape	24.8	28.6
Robbery	22.0	24.1
Aggravated assault	29.0	28.8
Property Crime Index	21.1	25.1
Burglary	19.9	23.5
Larceny-theft	21.8	26.2
Motor vehicle theft	20.1	21.8
Arson	20.5	22.8
Weapons	29.1	26.0
Drug abuse	22.3	28.5

Source: FBI. (1993). *Age-specific arrest rates and race-specific arrest rates for selected offenses 1965–1992.*

Although adults were responsible for most of the recent violent crime increases, juveniles contributed more than their fair share

Users of reported crime and arrest statistics face difficult interpretation problems

Violent crime is increasing and, based on their representation in the general population, juveniles are responsible for a disproportionate share of this increase. But is it accurate to say that juveniles are driving the violent crime trends?

The number of violent crimes reported to law enforcement agencies increased 23% between 1988 and 1992. Knowing that over this same period, juvenile arrests for violent crime grew 47%, while adult arrests for violent crimes increased 19%, it is easy to conclude that juveniles were responsible for most of the increase in violent crime. However, even though the percentage increase in juvenile arrests was more than double the adult increase, the growth in violent crime

cannot be attributed primarily to juveniles.

An example shows how this apparent contradiction can occur. Of the 100 violent crimes committed in 1988 in a small town, assume that juveniles were responsible for 10, and adults for 90. If the number of juvenile crimes increased 50%, juveniles would be committing 15 (or 5 more) violent crimes in 1992. A 20% increase in adult violent crimes would mean that adults were committing

108 (or 18 more) violent crimes in 1992. If each crime resulted in an arrest, the percentage increase in juvenile arrests would be more than double the adult increase (50% versus 20%). However, nearly 80% of the increase in violent crime (18 of the 23 additional violent crimes) would have been committed by adults.

Large percentage increases can yield relatively small overall changes. Juvenile arrests represent a relatively small fraction of the total; consequently, a large percentage increase in juvenile arrests does not necessarily translate into a large contribution to overall crime growth.

Adults responsible for 70% of recent increase in violent crimes

In 1988 the FBI reported juveniles were arrested in 9% of the violent crimes for which someone was arrested; this juvenile clearance percentage was 13% in 1992. If it is assumed that juveniles were responsible for similar percentages of the unsolved violent crimes in these years, then it is possible to estimate the number of crimes committed by juveniles and by adults in 1988 and 1992.

From FBI reported crime and clearance statistics, it was estimated that ju-

veniles committed 108,000 more Violent Crime Index offenses in 1992 than in 1988, while adults committed an additional 258,000. Therefore, juveniles were responsible for 30% of the growth in violent crime between 1988 and 1992. Between 1988 and 1992 juveniles were responsible for 26% of the increase in murders, 41% of the increase in forcible rapes, 39% of the increase in robberies, and 27% of the increase in aggravated assaults. Juveniles contributed less to the increase in murder than to the increases in other violent crimes.

If trends continue as they have over the past 10 years, juvenile arrests for violent crime will double by the year 2010

Age-specific arrest rates provide a clearer picture of arrest trends

The media and the public often use arrest trends to assess the relative changes in juvenile and adult criminal behavior. Arrest trends are simple to report—*juvenile violent crime arrests up 47% in past 5 years*—but they are notoriously difficult to interpret. First, interpretations are complicated by population changes, which can be considerable, even over a short time period, for the few high-crime-generating age groups. For example, how differently would the increase in juvenile arrests from 1983 to 1992 be viewed if it were known that the number of 16- and 17-year-olds in the U.S. population declined by 10% over this period?

Also, juvenile and adult arrest trends lump everyone into one of two groups. This ignores important variations within the groups that may provide important information to understand these trends.

A better method for comparing arrest patterns is to compare annual, age-specific arrest rates—for example, the number of arrests of a typical

group of 100,000 17-year-olds in 1983 and in 1992. Arrest rates control for the impact of population growth or decline on arrests. They also break down the juvenile and adult groups into smaller pieces so that changes in younger and older juveniles and adults can be studied independently. Age-specific arrest rates can also be used to project the number of future arrests if certain assumptions are made and projections of population growth are available.

How many juvenile violent crime arrests will there be in the year 2010?

Estimates of future juvenile arrests for violent crime vary widely. The accuracy of these estimates relies on the appropriateness of each estimate's underlying assumptions and the accuracy of existing data. For this report, two sets of estimates were developed using different assumptions. Both sets are based on age-specific arrest rates

Juvenile arrest projections vary with the nature of underlying assumptions

Offense	Juvenile arrests in 1992	Projections assuming no change in arrest rates from 1992 to 2010		Projections assuming annual changes in arrest rates equal to the average increases from 1983 to 1992	
		Juvenile arrests in 2010	Increase over 1992	Juvenile arrests in 2010	Increase over 1992
Violent Crime Index	129,600	158,600	22%	261,000	101%
Murder	3,300	4,100	23	8,100	145
Forcible rape	6,300	7,700	22	10,400	66
Robbery	45,700	56,600	24	72,200	58
Aggravated assault	74,400	90,200	21	170,300	129

■ If juvenile arrest rates remain constant through the year 2010, the number of juvenile arrests for violent crime will increase by one-fifth; if rates increase as they have in recent history, juvenile violent crime arrests will double.

Note: Both series of estimates control for racial variations in population growth.

and projected population growth (controlling for racial differences).

The first set of estimates assumes that the rates of juvenile violent crime arrests in 2010 will be equal to the rates in 1992. Under this assumption, the number of violent juvenile crime arrests is projected to increase 22% between 1992 and 2010. This increase corresponds to the projected growth in the juvenile population ages of 10 to 17. Projected increases would be nearly equal in all offense categories.

In contrast to the "constant rate" assumption underlying the first set of projections, the second set of estimates assumes that juvenile violent crime arrest rates will increase annually between 1992 and 2010 in each offense category as they have in recent history (i.e., from 1983 to 1992).

Assuming both population growth and continuing increases in arrest rates, the number of juvenile violent crime arrests is expected to double by 2010. The projected growth varies across crime categories. If current trends continue, by the year 2010 the number of juvenile arrests for murder is expected to increase 145% over the 1992 level. Projected increases are less than half as great for forcible rape (66%) and robbery (58%).

The increase in violent crime arrest rates is disproportionate for juveniles and young adults

Violent crime arrest rates have increased in all age groups

Over the 10-year period from 1983 to 1992, arrest rates for Violent Crime Index offenses increased substantially for juveniles as well as adults. Juveniles had the largest increases (averaging nearly 60%), but even the rates for persons ages 35 to 39 increased 47%.

The Violent Crime Index treats each of its four offenses equally—an arrest for aggravated assault is counted the same as an arrest for murder. While this may be reasonable statistically, these four crimes raise different concerns and should be understood separately.

Aggravated assault arrest rates increased most for juveniles and young adults

In 1992 arrests for aggravated assault were 68% of all Violent Crime Index arrests. Thus, changes in violent crime arrest rates primarily reflected changes in aggravated assaults. As with violent crime overall, aggravated assault arrest rates increased substantially between 1983 and 1992 in all age groups, with juvenile rates up about 100% and the rates for persons in their twenties up about 60%.

Forcible rape arrest rates increased far less than other violent crimes

In contrast to the overall violent crime and aggravated assault patterns, forcible rape arrest rates for juveniles grew between 1983 and 1992 by a relatively small 20%, while actually declining for persons in their twenties.

Robbery arrest rates increased much less than aggravated assault arrest rates

Robbery arrest rates increased in all age groups from 1983 to 1992. However, the growth was less than half of violent crime overall. The age groups with the smallest increases were those in their early twenties, with the juvenile increases similar to those of persons above age 25.

Murder rates declined in most age groups from 1983 to 1992

In 1992 persons above age 25 were arrested for murder at substantially lower rates than they were in 1983. For example, the murder arrest rate for persons ages 35–45 declined nearly 25% over the 10-year period.

In stark contrast, murder arrest rates for juveniles and young adults soared, with increases far greater than in any other violent crime category. The average increase for juveniles was double the average increase for young adults.

The fact that murder arrests for all adults increased just 9% between 1983 and 1992 masks two very different trends within the adult age group. The substantial declines in murder arrest rates for adults above their mid-twenties almost offset the very large increases in murder arrests of young adults.

As in all violent crimes, 18-year-olds had the highest arrest rate for murder in 1992. However, the pattern of age-related growth in murder arrest rates was not mirrored in any other violent offense, but was paralleled in weapons arrests.

High juvenile violent crime arrest rates do not imply high property crime arrest rates

The three States with the highest juvenile arrest rates for Property Crime Index offenses (Utah, Wisconsin, and Washington) were ranked 19th, 25th, and 21st in juvenile arrests for Violent Crime Index offenses. States with high adult violent and property crime arrest rates do, however, tend to have high corresponding juvenile arrest rates.

In contrast to their violent arrest trends, juvenile arrest rates for property crimes were stable between the mid 1980's and 1992

Juvenile property crime arrest rates were at their lowest point in the past 20 years in 1984

Law enforcement agencies made 29% fewer arrests of juveniles for Property Crime Index offenses (burglary, larceny-theft, motor vehicle theft, and arson) in 1983 than in 1974. Only about half of this decline can be explained by the 15% drop in the size of the U.S. population ages 10–17 during the same time period.

After these years of decline, the number of property arrests began to increase in 1985. Between 1983 and 1992, the number of juvenile arrests for a property crime increased 11%, while the juvenile population remained relatively constant. This increase was far less than the 57% growth in juvenile violent crime arrests during the same period.

The contrasting growth of violent and property arrest rates is common to all race groups

While property crime arrest rates of black youth have remained constant, the white arrest rate increased 16% in the 10-year period between 1983 and 1992. The relative stability in property crime arrest rates between 1983 and 1992 is in sharp contrast to the much larger increases in violent crime arrest rates for the same period—the 82% increase in violent crime arrests for white youth and the 43% increase for black youth. Similarly, while the violent crime arrest rate for youth of other races increased 42%, their property crime arrest rate increased only 5% over the 10-year period from 1983 through 1992.

Recently the female arrest rate for property crimes increased more than the male rate

Between 1983 and 1992, while the number of juvenile male arrests for a property offense increased 7%, the number of juvenile female arrests increased 27%. The greater involvement of females in property crime arrests was not limited to the juvenile population; a similar increase is found in the adult arrest statistics.

The juvenile responsibility for property crimes changed little between 1983 and 1992

Based on clearance data, juveniles committed about 1 in 5 property crimes between 1983 and 1992. However, over this 10-year period about 1 in 3 persons arrested for a property offense was a juvenile. The arrest proportion is larger than the clearance proportion because juveniles are more likely than adults to commit crimes in groups and may be more easily apprehended.

Property Crime Index arrest trends are dominated by the less serious larceny-theft offenses

Two-thirds of all juvenile Property Crime Index arrests in 1992 were for larceny-theft. Consequently, the Index trends follow closely the trends in larceny-theft. Over the past 20 years, the juvenile arrest trends for the more serious offenses of burglary and motor vehicle theft have been very different from the Index. Juvenile burglary arrest rates have dropped precipitously over the past 20 years, while motor vehicle theft arrest rates declined sharply before returning to, and then surpassing, their earlier levels.

The 1980's witnessed a significant change in patterns of juvenile arrests for drug abuse violations with the emergence of crack

From the mid 1970's through the mid 1980's juvenile drug abuse arrest rates dropped by half

During this period the magnitude of arrest rates for whites and blacks were similar; in fact from 1973 through 1980, the white arrest rate for drug abuse violations was higher than the rate for blacks. The decline in drug arrest rates from 1975 to 1985 can be attributed to a change in the rate at which juveniles, particularly

	Juvenile arrests per 100,000		
	1975	1985	1990
Marijuana			
White	436	285	131
Black	313	378	199
Other	246	160	25
Cocaine/Heroin			
White	14	42	68
Black	36	121	766
Other	21	7	6

Source: FBI. (1992). *Crime in United States 1991.*

white juveniles, were arrested for marijuana offenses.

While the arrest rate for white youth continued to decline, the black rate grew substantially after 1985. The overall growth in the black rate was driven by huge increases in cocaine/heroin arrests.

In 1980 juveniles accounted for 19% of the drug abuse violation arrests; by 1992 the juvenile proportion had declined to 8%

Over this same period the female proportion of juvenile drug arrests

also declined from 16% to 11%. Both of these changes are likely to be related to the decline in arrests for marijuana.

What do police do with the juveniles they arrest?

Most large law enforcement agencies have specialized units concentrating on juvenile justice issues

A national survey of law enforcement agencies conducted in 1990 asked large police departments and sheriffs' departments (those with 100 or more sworn officers) about the types of special units they operate. A large proportion reported that they had special units targeting juvenile justice concerns, although neither the level of staffing nor the effectiveness of these units were addressed.

Special units	Type of agency	
	Police	Sheriff
Drug education in schools	93%	82%
Juvenile crime	89	59
Child abuse	79	65
Missing children	74	61
Gangs	60	47
Domestic violence	45	40

Sources: Reaves. B. (1992). Sheriffs' departments 1990. *BJS Bulletin.* Reaves, B. (1992). State and local police departments, 1990. *BJS Bulletin.*

A large proportion of these agencies also reported that they had written policy directives for handling juveniles (95% of police and 86% of sheriffs' departments) and for handling domestic violence/spousal abuse events (93% of police and 77% of sheriffs' departments).

On a typical day about 750 juveniles are admitted to police lockups

Lockups are the temporary holding facilities maintained by law enforcement agencies. Twenty-nine percent of local police departments in 1990 operated a lockup facility separately from a jail. While the average capacity of these lockups was 8 inmates, the range was quite broad. While the average capacity of lockups was only 5 in communities with populations under 10,000, the average capacity of lockups was more than 160 in communities with populations more than 1 million.

The national survey asked departments that administered these facilities for the number of juveniles they had admitted on Friday, June 29, 1990. It was estimated that approximately 750, or 4% of persons admitted to lockups on this day, were classified by State law as juveniles. Assuming that, on average, about 6,000 juveniles were arrested per day in 1990, this means that roughly 1 in 10 were placed in lockups. While most stays are short, this volume of admissions implies that a substantial portion of all juveniles in custody are held in police lockups.

Most juveniles arrested in 1992 were referred to court for prosecution

The FBI's Uniform Crime Reporting Program asks law enforcement agen-

cies to report their responses to the *juveniles* they take into custody. This is the only component of the UCR Program that is sensitive to State variations in the definition of a juvenile. Consequently, in New York, law enforcement agencies report their responses to those persons arrested who were younger than age 16 at the time of arrest; in Illinois and Texas the reports are for arrestees younger than age 17, while in most other States the reports captured the dispositions of arrests of persons younger than age 18.

Thirty percent of juveniles taken into custody by law enforcement in 1992 were handled within the department and released. These juveniles were warned by police and then released, usually to parents, other relatives, or friends. In some jurisdictions, the law enforcement agency may operate its own diversion programs that may provide some intervention services to juveniles. Another 3% of arrested juveniles were either referred to another law enforcement agency or to a welfare agency.

The remaining juveniles, more than 2 in 3 arrested, were referred to court intake, the next step in the justice system. Most of these juveniles (93%) were referred to a juvenile court or a juvenile probation department. However, law enforcement agencies reported in 1992 that 7% were referred to criminal courts for prosecution as an adult.

Juveniles arrested in small cities and in rural areas were more likely than those in large urban centers to be referred to a criminal court. For example, in 1992 only 1.4% of juveniles referred for prosecution in cities with populations more than 250,000 were sent to criminal courts, compared with 9.6% in rural counties and 12.4% in cities with populations less than 10,000.

Sources

Bureau of Justice Statistics. (1993). *Highlights from 20 Years of Surveying Crime Victims.* Washington, DC: BJS.

Federal Bureau of Investigation. (1984). *Crime in the United States 1983.* Washington, DC: Government Printing Office.

Federal Bureau of Investigation. (1985). *Crime in the United States 1984.* Washington, DC: Government Printing Office.

Federal Bureau of Investigation. (1986). *Crime in the United States 1985.* Washington, DC: Government Printing Office.

Federal Bureau of Investigation. (1987). *Crime in the United States 1986.* Washington, DC: Government Printing Office.

Federal Bureau of Investigation. (1988). *Crime in the United States 1987.* Washington, DC: Government Printing Office.

Federal Bureau of Investigation. (1989). *Crime in the United States 1988.* Washington, DC: Government Printing Office.

Federal Bureau of Investigation. (1990). *Crime in the United States 1989.* Washington, DC: Government Printing Office.

Federal Bureau of Investigation. (1991). *Crime in the United States 1990.* Washington, DC: Government Printing Office.

Federal Bureau of Investigation. (1992). *Crime in the United States 1991.* Washington, DC: Government Printing Office.

Federal Bureau of Investigation. (1993). *Crime in the United States 1992.* Washington, DC: Government Printing Office.

Federal Bureau of Investigation. (1994). *Age-specific arrest rates and race-specific arrest rates for selected offenses 1965– 1992.* Washington, DC: Government Printing Office.

Inter-university Consortium for Political and Social Research, University of Michigan. (1994). *Uniform Crime Reporting Program data [United States]. County-level detailed arrest and offense data, 1992* [machine-readable data file]. Washington, DC: FBI [producer]. Ann Arbor, MI: ICPSR [distributor].

Reaves, B. (1992). State and local police departments, 1990. *BJS Bulletin.* Washington, DC: Bureau of Justice Statistics.

Reaves, B. (1992). Sheriffs departments 1990. *BJS Bulletin.* Washington, DC: Bureau of Justice Statistics.

Technical Note

While juvenile arrest rates reflect juvenile behavior, many other factors can affect the size of these rates.

Arrest rates are calculated by dividing the number of youth arrests made in the year by the number of youth living in the jurisdiction. Therefore, jurisdictions that arrest a relatively large number of nonresident juveniles would have a higher arrest rate than a jurisdiction whose resident youth behave in an identical manner.

Jurisdictions, especially small jurisdictions, that are vacation destinations or that are centers for economic activity in a region may have arrest rates that reflect more than the behavior of their resident youth.

Other factors that influence the magnitude of arrest rates in a given area include the attitudes of its citizens toward crime, the policies of the jurisdiction's law enforcement agencies, and the policies of other components of the justice system. Consequently, the comparison of juvenile arrest rates across jurisdictions, while informative, should be done with caution.

In most areas not all law enforcement agencies report their arrest data to the FBI. Rates for these areas are then necessarily based on partial information. If the reporting law enforcement agencies in these jurisdictions are not representative of the complete jurisdiction, then the rates will be biased. For example, if the only agencies that report in a county are urban agencies, the country's reported rate will only reflect activity in the urban section of the county. Reported rates for jurisdictions with less than complete reporting may not be accurate.

In the cited reports, the FBI calculates juvenile arrest rates by dividing the number of arrests of persons under age 18 by the population ages 0 through 17. While this is consistent, the majority of the population in this age range is below 10, while few arrestees are below age 10. For this report, the FBI's reported arrest rates were modified to make them more sensitive to changes in that part of the juvenile population that is likely to generate the arrest figures. Specifically, the reported arrest rates were recalculated using a population base of persons ages 10 through 17.

Fighting Crime, One Kid at a Time

By Isabelle de Pommereau

Special to The Christian Science Monitor
JERSEY CITY, N.J.

Detective Calvin Hart's unmarked black Chevy screeches to a halt near a bleak 13-story building. The high-rise is one of six in Curries Woods, a massive public housing complex infested with crime and drugs.

It's stop No. 1 on the detective's night-long patrol in Jersey City, N.J., a multi-ethnic city of 230,000. Detective Hart is a full-time juvenile cop, and his job tonight—and every night—is to keep an eye on troubled youths.

"Get your behind home," Hart warns a teenager on the roam. There's a tinge of affection in his voice. Malik, the teenager, retorts with a cunning smile. He's no stranger to Hart. The boy's uncle was a childhood friend of the detective's who was killed in a drug-related dispute not long ago.

Hart represents an emerging breed of cop dedicated solely to what has long been considered the nation's most intractable urban crime problem: juvenile delinquency.

While the overall crime rate is falling across most of the United States, crimes committed by youths continue unabated. Now, in growing numbers, cities like Reno, Nev., Memphis, and New York are recognizing the important role youth-focused community cops can play in helping kids stay on the right track.

"There's an outreach effort by police departments to have police officers not just show up when there's a problem, but be an intricate part of the fabric of the community and be there at all times to participate," says Steve Riddell of the National Council of Juvenile and Family Court Judges, at the University of Nevada in Reno.

For Hart, this new role means serving as the first-ever juvenile-intervention officer for Jersey City's 10 public housing projects, coordinating the city's new curfew law, and, perhaps most significant, being a near-father figure to hundreds of streetwise youths.

'He's in the real world'

As Hart unlocks the door of Curries Woods' Building 3, he points to the peep holes in the plywood front—the glass was shattered long ago. Children drilled the holes, he says, so they could keep a lookout for the police.

The lobby is a world of decay. The floor is strewn with cigarette butts and half-eaten fried chicken legs. The air smells of urine. And every inch of the walls is covered with graffiti. But Hart's presence immediately warms this sordid setting.

"Uncle Calvin!" exclaims a young girl bundled head to toe in a yellow coat. Lacovia Huggins breaks away from a cluster of friends to hug the detective.

"Hey darlin', how are you doing?" asks Hart. The police officer knows the stories of the girls on his beat. Too often those stories include early pregnancy, absent fathers, domestic abuse, and drugs.

If Hart's mission seems personal, that's because in many ways it is. For him, Jersey City is more than a police beat, it's home.

Born and raised here, he grew up with the parents and grandparents of the young people he now supervises.

"He's not an outsider even though he's on the police force. He's in the real world," says Jeanette Drayton, guidance counselor at a Jersey City elementary school where Hart often lectures on drug prevention. "He was brought up here. He sees the problems kids face everyday—he has empathy."

His style is distinctive: He is a follow-through cop. He arrests drug users but gets them into drug treatment. He puts convicted youths in jail but visits them in their cells and helps find them jobs when they're released. He plays basketball with the older kids, picks up the smaller children at school, and calls their mothers and school principals if trouble looms.

Still, Hart says he has sent many to jail, and he's seen a few die violently.

A veteran narcotics and homicide detective, Hart has the skills experts say are crucial for fighting juvenile crime. These include knowing when and how to use force and, more important, knowing how to connect with the kids on his beat.

The teens here have dubbed him The Creeper, a term of grudging respect for his ability to be "everywhere at once."

"He's about the only cop that gets respect out here," says Carmen Strickland, a teenage resident of Curries Woods.

Changing role of youth officers

A consensus is emerging among police departments and law-enforcement experts that officers like Hart have a central role to play in interrupting young criminal careers, if they can successfully form partnerships not only with teens but also with the community's schools, churches, and parents.

The concept of youth-focused policing has become popular in the past few years, and versions of it are being attempted in cities and towns around the country.

In Reno, Deputy Police Chief Ondra Berry says his first priority is for offi-

'I went through it all—sleeping in abandoned buildings, standing in the soup lines—and I wouldn't wish it to my worst enemy. That's why I do what I do. It's . . . my way of giving back and making sure that the kids don't do the same.'

—Detective Calvin Hart

cers to connect with young people. In the Bronx, Sgt. Ricardo Aguirre is enlisting the help of his fellow officers to work with troubled youths through a counseling program he created called "Keep Our Kids Alive."

At a conference in Reno this week, more than 1,300 judges, law-enforcement officials, and other juvenile-crime experts are meeting to discuss the importance of youth-beat officers and the changing face of juvenile justice.

While many experts say they are encouraged by the successes they've observed, they also believe that police departments must learn better ways to recruit and train juvenile cops.

"We have turned the philosophy [of juvenile policing] around, but what we haven't turned around is who we bring to be police officers and how we train them," says John Firman of the International Association of Chiefs of Police in Alexandria, Va.

"We're still looking for guys who're driving cars and firing guns," Mr. Firman says. "But the involvement of the officer has to be a personal one, a commitment to understanding the kids' lives."

From alcoholic to role model

In Jersey City, Detective Hart doesn't just try to understand kids' lives, he's "here to save lives," he says. And he knows what saving lives means, because he saved his own. For years, he was an alcoholic, and the addiction cost him his home, jobs, and family.

"I went through it all—sleeping in abandoned buildings, standing in the soup lines, and I wouldn't wish it to my worst enemy," Hart remembers. As a result, his wife, Linda, divorced him and took their baby daughter with her when she left.

Several years after Linda left, Hart says he finally got tired of leading a self-destructive life. With the encouragement and support of a close friend who was a Jersey City police officer, Hart conquered his alcoholism. The friend also inspired him to become a cop.

"That's why I do what I do," Hart says. "It's kind of my way of giving back and making sure that the kids don't do the same [things I did]."

"I became the oldest rookie in the Jersey City Police Department I know," he jokes.

To make things complete, Linda came back and they remarried. They have another daughter and are also raising his niece.

In the Jersey City Police Department, Hart rose fast. Within a year, he was promoted to narcotics detective, then to homicide detective. The housing authority recruited him to help rid the Curries Woods complex of its drug scourge. Major drug busts helped improve life for the 712 families living there, he says.

But Hart also achieved something deeper—he got residents to trust the police, at a time when distrust was running high. Last year, he became the housing authority's first juvenile-intervention officer.

"He's like a father to the projects," says Ms. Strickland.

Make no mistake about it, however. Calvin Hart can be just as tough as he is friendly, and the kids know it.

"If you do something wrong, [Uncle Calvin] takes you where you're supposed to go," says Monique Richburg.

She learned that firsthand when she was arrested for delivering drugs. "He'll come get you, knock at your door. [But] he won't be nasty [or] forceful—others will probably beat you up."

A friend for struggling parents

Stop No. 2 tonight is the Curries Woods weekly parenting session at 7:30 p.m. It's a haven of warmth and cleanliness in Building 6, which was renovated recently as part of a multimillion-dollar effort to make 40-year-old Curries Woods more hospitable.

When Hart arrives, he's greeted with laughter and hugs. Many of the mothers here know the detective both as their friend and as the only positive male role model their children have ever had.

"When it comes to him talking to the little ones, he can do it," says Maxine Warner, who went to school with Hart and now relies on him as a friend to her grandchildren, whose father isn't around.

Many parents and guardians here know that their children will listen to Hart, if to nobody else. Claretha Roach, for example, brings her young son, Jamal—who has been cursing at his mother—to the meeting so Hart can talk to him.

"I know how to whip him," Hart says grinning.

But Hart needs only words and his broad shoulders to impress Jamal. He invites the boy to sit near him on a big couch, and then begins firing questions at him: What does Jamal want to do when he grows up?

Be a basketball star, responds the boy.

How many points does he score? Hart asks. Does he know that out of 100,000 high school basketball players, only about 600 make it to the top? And what will happen if Jamal isn't one of them?

Jamal looks at the officer intently. Hart tells Jamal he'd better stick with school; in fact, he'll pick him up at school tomorrow. A smile creeps across Jamal's face.

Tough when he has to be

It's about 10:30 p.m. now, and stop No. 3 is Curries Woods' Building 4, a grim high-rise soon to be demolished. As Hart makes his way toward the door, the teenagers outside spot him coming.

But rather than scatter at his approach, the kids flock to him.

"Colleer," Hart yells to a boy with a baby face and braided hair. "You back in school?"

Silence.

"If you don't know, who does know?"

Silence still.

In a voice filled with exasperation, Hart warns the teen that he'll have a word with him tomorrow. It was, after all, the detective who locked up Colleer's two older brothers, who were major drug pins. And now, Hart worries that Colleer is selling "wet"—a mixture of marijuana and PCP—to younger kids.

But Hart's cheerfulness quickly comes back when Elliott Smith shows up. Hart and Mr. Smith enjoy each other's company.

"He used to be slinging [selling drugs] out here," Hart says. Smith explains that, after he did jail time, it was the detective who recommended him for a temporary job as a warehouse worker. Now, Hart hopes to get Smith a permanent job at the city recycling plant. "It's minimum wage, but it's work history," says Hart.

At home on the streets

As midnight approaches, Hart is back in his Chevy and heading toward Martin Luther King Drive. Once bustling with shoppers, the street now teems with drug activity day and night. It went downhill when its middle class fled, along with its banks and stores.

Hart recognizes many of the young people clustered on the corners, some brazenly offering drugs. He knows who controls what.

One corner is powered by the brothers of a girl who was caught carrying drugs.

"She did a favor, and she got caught," Hart says. He ponders aloud: "How can you let your sister get trapped like this?"

As the car moves along, he points to another corner where a young girl is standing alone. "This girl is a hooker," Hart says. "I put her in drug rehab, but she came right back [to drugs and prostitution]."

Cruising along this grim street, the detective reveals his dreams of restoring the neighborhood to the bustling center it was when he was a boy.

He points to where his grandfather's restaurant used to be; now it's part of a public-housing complex. On another corner stands a dilapidated building that used to be the Rainbow Shop, where Hart would buy stockings for his mother.

"This was the showplace at one time," he says with some excitement.

When Hart reaches a ramshackle building next to the St. Stephen Holiness Church, he stops the car.

The boarded-up house used to be his aunt's. Now, Hart owns it, and he plans to turn it into a computer learning center for kids and cops.

"We talk a lot about space for kids, things for them to do," Hart muses, "and we don't live up to our bargain."

Kids and Guns: From Playgrounds to Battlegrounds

by Stuart Greenbaum

Late last year an 11-year-old boy was shot and killed. An 18-year-old allegedly killed the boy because he had shorted him on drug money (Thomas and Martin, 1996). The shooting should have rocked the Chicago neighborhood where it took place, except that this kind of thing happens all too often.

The lethal mix of children and guns has reached a crisis in the United States. Teenage boys are more likely to die of gunshot wounds than from all natural causes combined. The number of children dying from gunshot wounds and the number of children committing homicides continue to rise at alarming rates (McEnery, 1996).

Guns are now the weapon of choice for youth. As can be seen in the figure in the following box, "Juvenile Gun Homicides," gun homicides by juveniles have tripled since 1983, while homicides involving other weapons have declined. From 1983 through 1995, the proportion of homicides in which a juvenile used a gun increased from 55 percent to 80 percent (Snyder and Finnegan, 1997).

Disputes that would previously have ended in fist fights are now more likely to lead to shootings. A 1993 Louis Harris poll showed that 35 percent of children ages 6 to 12 fear their lives will be cut short by gun violence (Louis Harris and Associates, Inc.,

Stuart Greenbaum is president of Greenbaum Public Relations, a Sacramento, California, firm that specializes in public interest concerns, including high-risk youth services. A 20-year veteran of public safety communication, Mr. Greenbaum is a cofounder and past communications director of the National School Safety Center at Pepperdine University.

1993). A 1990 Centers for Disease Control and Prevention study found that one in five 9th through 12th graders reported carrying a weapon in the past month; one in five of those carried a firearm (Centers for Disease Control and Prevention, 1991).

Buying guns illegally is relatively easy for juveniles.

"No corner of America is safe from increasing levels of criminal violence, including violence committed by and against juveniles," Attorney General Janet Reno has observed. "Parents are afraid to let their children walk to school alone. Children hesitate to play in neighborhood playgrounds. The elderly lock themselves in their homes, and innocent Americans of all ages find their lives changed by the fear of crime" (Coordinating Council on Juvenile Justice and Delinquency Prevention, 1996).

The number of murdered juveniles increased 47 percent between 1980 and 1994, according to figures from *Juvenile Offenders and Victims: 1996 Update on Violence* (Snyder et al., 1996). The Summary, which cites data from the Federal Bureau of Investiga-

From *Juvenile Justice*, September 1997, pp. 3-10. Reprinted by permission of the U.S. Department of Justice, Office of Juvenile Justice and Delinquency Prevention.

tion's Uniform Crime Reporting Program, notes that from 1980 through 1994 an estimated 326,170 persons were murdered in the United States. Of these, 9 percent (30,200) were youth under age 18. While there was a 1-percent increase from 1980 through 1994 in the total number of murders, the rate of juveniles murdered increased from five per day to seven per day. Fifty-three percent of the juveniles killed in 1994 were teenagers ages 15 to 17, while 30 percent were younger than age 6. In 1994, one in five murdered juveniles was killed by a juvenile offender.

Programs to get guns out of the hands of young people are being put into place.

Recently, however, there has been good news. Between 1994 and 1995, juvenile arrests for murder declined 14 percent, resulting in the number of juvenile murder arrests in 1995 being 9 percent below the 1991 figure. Overall arrests for violent juvenile crime decreased 3 percent between 1994 and 1995—the first decline in 9 years. These efforts must continue,

however, as even these reduced rates are substantially higher than 1986 levels (Snyder, 1997).

Often, teenagers turn guns on themselves. In 1991, 1,889 teens ages 15 to 19 committed suicide–a rate of 11 per 100,000 (Allen-Hagen et al., 1994). Between 1980 and 1994, the suicide rate for 15- to 19-year-olds rose 29 percent, with an increase in firearms-related suicides accounting for 96 percent of the rise (Centers for Disease Control and Prevention, 1996). The risk of suicide is five times greater for individuals living in households with guns than for those in households without guns (Kellerman et al., 1992).

What is causing this epidemic of violence and how can it be stopped? The deterioration of the traditional family and the impact of drugs, gangs, poverty, and violence in the media are among the factors cited as contributing to the violent behavior of today's teens. Many of these children–victims and perpetrators–come from one- or no-parent families (McEnery, 1996).

Guns are readily available to juveniles. Although Federal law mandates that a person must be at least 18 years old to purchase a shotgun or rifle, and at least 21 years old to buy a handgun, law enforcement officials and youth themselves report that buying guns illegally is relatively easy for juveniles. Increasingly, juveniles believe they need guns for protection or carry them as status symbols. As more guns appear in the community, a local arms race ensues.

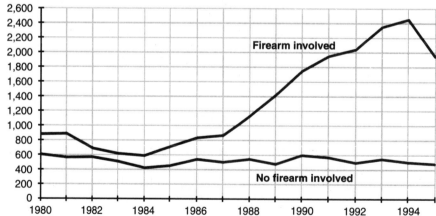

Juvenile Gun Homicides

Gun homicides by juveniles have tripled since 1983, while homicides involving other weapons have declined.

Number of homicides

Firearm involved

No firearm involved

◆ From 1983 through 1995, the proportion of homicides in which a juvenile used a gun increased from 55 to 80 percent.

Source: Snyder, H.N., and T.A. Finnegan. 1997. *Easy Access to the FBI's Supplementary Homicide Reports: 1980–1995* (data presentation and analysis package). Washington, DC: U.S. Department of Justice, Office of Justice Programs, Office of Juvenile Justice and Delinquency Prevention.

This article describes some promising steps that have been taken to curb the violence endangering our youth and our communities. It also provides information about a number of initiatives that have focused on gun violence in particular.

U.S. Attorneys Join the Fight

Local, State, and national programs to get guns out of the hands of young people are being put in place. In a report to the Attorney General and the President, U.S. Attorneys outlined the following ways in which they are supporting State and local programs:

◆ Disrupting the markets that provide guns to youth.

◆ Taking guns out of the hands of young people through coordination with State and local law enforcement officials.

◆ Working with State and local prosecutors to enhance enforcement of their laws.

◆ Encouraging and providing financial support for State and local efforts to trace the sources of guns taken from juveniles.

◆ Launching targeted enforcement efforts in places where young people should feel safe, such as their homes, schools, and recreation centers.

◆ Participating in prevention efforts directed at juveniles in our communities through mentoring, adopt-a-school (in which schools are "adopted" by civic groups or businesses), and Neighborhood Watch programs.

◆ Promoting increased personal responsibility and safety through public outreach and information on the consequences of juvenile handgun possession (Office of Juvenile Justice and Delinquency Prevention, 1996).

These approaches, also supported by other components of the U.S. Department of Justice (DOJ), are critical elements of a comprehensive youth gun violence reduction strategy.

To advance the U.S. Attorneys' violence prevention efforts and to help States and local jurisdictions respond to the problem of juvenile firearms violence, the Office of Juvenile Justice and Delinquency Prevention (OJJDP) published *Reducing Youth Gun Violence: An Overview of Programs and Initiatives* (Office of Juvenile Justice and Delinquency Prevention, 1996). This report provides information on a wide array of strategies–from school-based prevention to gun market interception. In addition to program descriptions, the report includes a directory of youth gun violence prevention organizations and a bibliography of research, evaluation, and publications on youth and guns.

Promising Programs

Many State and local programs designed to take guns out of the hands of teenagers have proven successful. In the Kansas City (Missouri) Gun Experiment, the U.S. Attorney's Office and the Kansas City Police Department worked with local agencies to focus law enforcement efforts on high-crime neighborhoods. Under this initiative, developed with Weed and Seed funding from the Bureau of Justice Assistance, traffic law violators were routinely stopped, as were youth violating curfews and individuals involved in other infractions of the law. During these stops, police looked for violations that established legal authority to search a car or pedestrian for illegal guns. These special gun-interception teams were 10 times more cost-effective than regular police patrols.

The experience of victimization by violence is far too common among children.

The success of the Kansas City Gun Experiment is striking. An evaluation funded by the National Institute of Justice (NIJ) found that crime in the 80-block target neighborhood, which had a homicide rate 20 times the national average, was cut in half in 6 months. Significantly, the program did not merely displace crime to other locations. Gun crimes did not increase in any of the seven surrounding patrol beats. The active involvement of community and religious leaders in the development of the program resulted in broad support for the program in the community, which had objected to past police crackdowns on guns (Sherman et al., 1995).

In Boston, where juveniles in high-risk neighborhoods frequently carry guns, NIJ has launched a problem-solving project to devise, implement, and assess strategic interventions to disrupt illicit firearms markets and deter youth violence. Its initial focus was analyzing the supply and demand for guns. Strategic interventions by police, probation, and parole officers have presented gang members–prevalent among both victims and offenders–with a clear choice: Stop the flow of guns and stop the violence or face rapid, focused, and comprehensive law enforcement and corrections attention. Although it is too soon to evaluate the long-term effectiveness of this strategy, its immediate impact is encouraging; youth violence in Boston appears to have been substantially reduced (Kennedy, 1997).

Child abuse and neglect nearly doubled between 1986 and 1993.

NIJ's promising initiative in Boston was highlighted at OJJDP's August 1996 national satellite teleconference, Reducing Youth Gun Violence, which was viewed by more than 8,000 participants at 271 downlink sites. The teleconference, which is available on videotape from OJJDP's Juvenile Justice Clearinghouse, also featured the Detroit-based Handgun Intervention Program, carried out by volunteers in Michigan's 36th District Court, and the Shock Mentor Program, a collaborative effort among Prince George's County, Maryland, Public Schools, the Washington, D.C., chapter of Concerned Black Men, Inc., and Prince George's Hospital Center.

Partnerships To Reduce Juvenile Gun Violence

Based on a review of research and programs conducted by OJJDP and summarized in *Reducing Youth Gun Violence: An Overview of Programs and Initiatives*, OJJDP has started a new initiative, Partnerships To Reduce Juvenile Gun Violence. This effort is intended to increase the effectiveness of existing youth gun violence reduction strategies by enhancing and coordinating prevention, intervention, and suppression strategies and by strengthening linkages among the community, law enforcement, and the juvenile justice system. Its comprehensive approach addresses three critical factors: juveniles' access to guns, the reasons young people carry guns, and the reasons they choose to use guns to resolve conflicts. Partnerships have been forged through recent OJJDP grants to the Center for Community Alternatives in Syracuse, New York; the City of East Baton Rouge, Louisiana; the Council on Alcoholism and Drug Abuse of Northwest Louisiana; and Youth ALIVE!, which services Oakland and Los Angeles, California.

OJJDP is funding an evaluation of Partnerships To Reduce Juvenile Gun Violence to document and analyze the process of community mobilization, planning, and collaboration needed to develop a comprehensive approach to combating youth gun violence.

The fundamental challenge in reducing juvenile firearm possession is to convince youth that they can survive in their neighborhoods without being armed. Community-based programs such as those listed above are working to dispel the perception by many juveniles that the authorities can neither protect them nor maintain order in their neighborhoods. A number of communities have implemented programs that address the risk of victimization, improve school safety, and foster a secure community environment.

Victimization and the Cycle of Violence

The experience of victimization by violence is far too common among children in America. A survey of inner-city high school students revealed that 45 percent had been threatened with a gun or shot at, and one in three had been beaten up on their way to school (Sheley and Wright, 1993). According to a survey released by the U.S. Department of Health and Human Services, child abuse and neglect nearly doubled between 1986 and

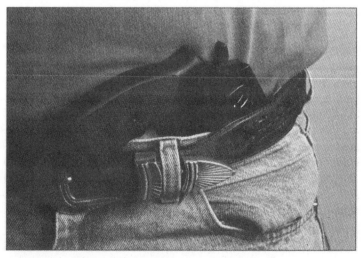

1993 (Sedlak and Broadhurst, 1996). Investigations by child protective services agencies in 49 States determined that more than 1 million children were victims of substantiated or indicated child abuse and neglect in 1995 (National Center on Child Abuse and Neglect, 1997).

OJJDP and NIJ have supported several studies focusing on this cycle of violence. The research indicates a relationship between experiences of childhood violence and subsequent delinquent behavior. OJJDP's Rochester (New York) Youth Development Study found that children who had been victims of violence were 24 percent more likely to report engaging in violent behavior as adolescents than those who had not been maltreated in childhood (Thornberry, 1994). An NIJ longitudinal study of childhood victimization found that child abuse increases the likelihood of future delinquency and adult criminality by nearly 40 percent (Widom, 1992).

With funding support from OJJDP, the New Haven (Connecticut) Department of Police Services and the Yale Child Study Center established the Child Development-Community Policing (CD-CP) program to address the adverse impact of continued exposure to violence on children and their families and to interrupt the cycle of violence affecting so many of our children. Reflecting New Haven's commendable commitment to community policing, the program brings law enforcement and mental health professionals together to help children who are victims, witnesses, and (in some instances) perpetrators of violent acts. The CD-CP program serves as a model for police-mental health partnerships across the Nation and is being replicated under the CD-CP grant in Buffalo, New York; Charlotte, North Carolina; Nashville, Tennessee; and Portland, Oregon (Marans and Berkman, 1997). In fiscal year 1997, OJJDP is enhancing the CD-CP program to provide training to school personnel, probation and parole officers, and prosecutors.

Public Information Campaigns

Researchers have found that long-term public education campaigns on violence prevention, family education, alcohol and drug prevention, and gun safety curriculums in schools are effective in helping to reduce delinquency (American Academy of Pediatrics, 1992; Centers for Disease Control and Prevention, 1991; Christoffel, 1991; DeJong, 1994). This may be especially true for education campaigns to prevent gun violence, because public awareness of positive activities can reduce fear, which is a powerful factor in juveniles choosing to carry guns. Involving teenagers in the development and operation of these programs is a critical ingredient to a program's success (Treanor and Bijlefeld, 1989). The public and private sectors, including the media, also can play significant roles in program design and implementation.

The goal of public information and education efforts should be threefold: to change public perceptions about youth violence and guns, to educate the community about the problem, and to convince youth and adults that their involvement is essential to the success of any program to curb possession and use of guns by youth. Public information campaigns can empower citizens to reach informed judgments about effective ways of preventing firearms violence by and against juveniles.

Public information campaigns can empower citizens to reach informed judgments.

Public information campaigns to reduce gun violence should:

◆ Provide accurate information to key policymakers about the causes, nature, and extent of juvenile delinquency and victimization, particularly gun-related violence.

◆ Communicate that juvenile gun violence and victimization are preventable.

◆ Publicize strategies and results of successful programs and encourage their replication.

◆ Motivate individuals, government agencies, and community service organizations to work collaboratively to address the problem as a key to ensuring public safety.

A number of public information campaigns have been launched or are being developed. In California, the statewide Campaign To Prevent Handgun Violence Against Kids has produced 30-second television public service announcements (PSA's) in English and Spanish; communicated critical information on youth gun violence to elected officials, media leaders, and public agencies; and received thousands of calls through its hotline and information service (Office of Juvenile Justice and Delinquency Prevention, 1996).

To assist communities in their public education efforts, the Center to Prevent Handgun Violence collaborated with Disney Educational Productions (1994) to produce *Under the Gun: A Story About Violence Prevention.* The video, intended for educational and law enforcement agencies, refutes the notion that guns are glamorous and that carrying guns makes communities safer.

OJJDP and the Bureau of Justice Assistance are funding a public-private partnership to create and market PSA's with a three-part message designed to persuade young people to turn away from violence, educate parents and other community residents about solutions to youth violence, and show teens, parents, and youth-serving professionals how they can become part of the solution.

Conclusion

As disturbing as youth gun violence is, it need not be inevitable. It is preventable–as many programs throughout the United States are beginning to demonstrate. With the public alarmed about the problem, public servants and practitioners might bear in mind the Greek philosopher Solon's words, "There can be no justice until those of us who are unaffected by crime become as indignant as those who are."

References

Allen-Hagen, B., M. Sickmund, and H.N. Snyder. 1994 (November). *Juveniles and Violence: Juvenile Offending and Victimization.* Fact Sheet. Washington, DC: U.S. Department of Justice, Office of Justice Programs, Office of Juvenile Justice and Delinquency Prevention.

American Academy of Pediatrics, Committee on Adolescence. 1992. Firearms and adolescence. *Pediatrics* 89(4):784–787.

Centers for Disease Control and Prevention. 1996 (November). *National Summary of Injury Mortality Data, 1987–1994.* Atlanta, GA: Centers for Disease Control and Prevention, National Center for Injury Prevention and Control.

Centers for Disease Control and Prevention. 1991. Weapon carrying among high school students: United States, 1990. *Morbidity and Mortality Weekly Report* 40(40):681–684.

Christoffel, K.K. 1991. Toward reducing pediatric injuries from firearms: Charting a legislative and regulatory course. *Pediatrics* 88(2):294–305.

Coordinating Council on Juvenile Justice and Delinquency Prevention. 1996 (March). *Combating Violence and Delinquency: The National Juvenile Justice Action Plan.* Report. Washington, DC: U.S. Department of Justice, Office of Justice Programs, Office of Juvenile Justice and Delinquency Prevention.

DeJong, W. 1994 (November). *Preventing Interpersonal Violence Among Youth: An Introduction to School, Community and Mass Media Strategies.* NIJ Issues and Practices. Washington, DC: U.S. Department of Justice, Office of Justice Programs, National Institute of Justice.

Disney Educational Productions. 1994. *Under the Gun: A Story About Violence Prevention.* Burbank: The Walt Disney Company.

Kellermann, A.L., F.P. Rivara, G. Somes, D.T. Reay, J. Francisco, G. Banton, J. Prodzinski, C. Fligner, and B.B. Hackman. 1992. Suicide in the home in relation to gun ownership. *New England Journal of Medicine* 327:467–472.

Kennedy, D.M. 1997 (March). *Juvenile Gun Violence and Gun Markets in Boston.* Research Preview. Washington, DC: U.S. Department of Justice, Office of Justice Programs, National Institute of Justice.

Louis Harris and Associates, Inc. 1993. *A Survey of Experiences, Perceptions and Apprehensions About Guns Among Young People in America.* New York, NY: Louis Harris and Associates, Inc., and LH Research, Inc.

Marans, S., and M. Berkman. 1997 (March). *Child Development-Community Policing: Partnership in a Climate of Violence.* Bulletin. Washington, DC: U.S. Department of Justice, Office of Justice Programs, Office of Juvenile Justice and Delinquency Prevention.

McEnery, R. Today's schoolyard bully just might be armed. *Asbury Park Press.* Feb. 28, 1996.

National Center on Child Abuse and Neglect. 1997. *Child Maltreatment 1995: Reports from the States to the National Child Abuse and Neglect Data System.* Washington, DC: U.S. Department of Health and Human Services, National Center on Child Abuse and Neglect.

Office of Juvenile Justice and Delinquency Prevention. 1996 (May). *Reducing Youth Gun Violence: An Overview of Programs and Initiatives.* Program Report. Washington, DC: U.S. Department of Justice, Office of Justice Programs, Office of Juvenile Justice and Delinquency Prevention.

Sedlak, A.J., and D.D. Broadhurst. 1996 (September). *Third National Incidence Study of Child Abuse and Neglect.* Washington, DC: U.S. Department of Health and Human Services, National Center on Child Abuse and Neglect.

Sheley, J.F., and J.D. Wright. 1993 (December). *Gun Acquisition and Possession in Selected Juvenile Samples.* Research in Brief. Washington, DC: U.S. Department of Justice, Office of Justice Programs, National Institute of Justice and Office of Juvenile Justice and Delinquency Prevention.

Sherman, L.W., J.W. Shaw, and D.P. Rogan. 1995 (January). *The Kansas City Gun Experiment.* Research in Brief. Washington, DC: U.S. Department of Justice, Office of Justice Programs, National Institute of Justice.

Snyder, H.N. 1997 (February). *Juvenile Arrests 1995.* Bulletin. Washington, DC: U.S. Department of Justice, Office of Justice Programs, Office of Juvenile Justice and Delinquency Prevention.

Snyder, H.N., and M. Sickmund. 1995 (August). *Juvenile Offenders and Victims: A National Report.* Washington, DC: U.S. Department of Justice, Office of Justice Programs, Office of Juvenile Justice and Delinquency Prevention.

Snyder, H.N., M. Sickmund, and E. Poe-Yamagata. 1996 (February). *Juvenile Offenders and Victims: 1996 Update on Violence.* Statistics Summary. Washington, DC: U.S. Department of Justice, Office of Justice Programs, Office of Juvenile Justice and Delinquency Prevention.

Snyder, H.N., and T.A. Finnegan. 1997. *Easy Access to the FBI's Supplementary Homicide Reports: 1980–1995* (data presentation and analysis package). Washington, DC: U.S. Department of Justice, Office of Justice Programs, Office of Juvenile Justice and Delinquency Prevention.

Thomas, J., and A. Martin. Notorious block's deadly legacy, West Adams Street's world of fear, drugs, death. *Chicago Tribune.* Nov. 23, 1996.

Thornberry, T. 1994 (December). *Violent Families and Youth Violence.* Fact Sheet. Washington, DC: U.S. Department of Justice, Office of Justice Programs, Office of Juvenile Justice and Delinquency Prevention.

Treanor, W.W., and M. Bijlefeld. 1989. *Kids and Guns: A Child Safety Scandal.* Washington, DC: American Youth Work Center and Educational Fund to End Handgun Violence.

Widom, C.S. 1992 (October). *The Cycle of Violence.* Research in Brief. Washington, DC: U.S. Department of Justice, Office of Justice Programs, National Institute of Justice.

A Sad Fact of Life

Gangs and their activities are spreading into small-town America

BY ARTHUR G. SHARP

Gang activity is regularly a hot item for the media. Does it deserve such prominence, or does it receive such attention merely to boost audience interest?

Magali Kupfer, a leader in the Meriden, CT, Hispanic community stated at a conference in 1994 that the way gang violence is portrayed by police and politicians and then reported in the news media has made the problem a racial issue. Kupfer told a reporter for the Hartford Courant that the "politicians and the police departments are really overreacting."

Regardless of who is right in the debate over how the news is reported, gangs do exist—but in how many communities?

In a recent poll, 26% of law enforcement administrators said that gangs are more a topic for the media to dwell on rather than a real problem, at least in their communities. Another 13% were not sure. The remaining 61% stated that gangs are real problems.

That percentage agrees closely with the number of respondents (52%) who said they have gang problems in their communities. Gangs are becoming more widespread, according to 74% of those polled, and are also spreading into rural areas.

While 55% think that gangs are more a problem of bigger cities than small communities, 41% said they are not. Significantly, 59% of the respondents believe that vigorous anti-gang programs by large city departments will have a spillover effect into smaller communities. Only 4% said they were not. That is not good

news for administrators in small communities, some of whom are feeling the pressure from gangs already.

Ronald Glidden, Chief of Police in Lee, MA, noted that his small community is a stopping-off point for transient gang members traveling from Hartford, CT, and Springfield, MA, to Pittsfield and North Adams, two small cities in the Berkshire Mountains of western Massachusetts. North Adams' population is only 16,800; Pittsfield's is 48,600. Lee has a population of 6,500 served by an 11-member police force. Springfield, on the other hand, has a population of 160,000 and a 527-member police department. Hartford is home to 130,000 citizens; its police force comprises 460 members.

Why is Lee seeing more gang members? The answer is simple. Both Springfield and Hartford are placing a lot of pressure on gangs operating in their cities. The gangs have been forced to seek new territory and smaller communities seem likely places to go. That explains in part why smaller communities are becoming way stations for gang activity.

A September 10, 1994, article in the Salisbury, MD, Daily Times highlighted the problem of gangs uprooting themselves and expanding their activities. The writer said that gang activity was on the increase in Maryland, in large part due to enforcement actions in cities like Chicago and Los Angeles. There were reports circulating in Maryland that organized gangs in out-of-state loca-

tions were seeking to expand their activities in the state because it was basically "virgin territory."

Shortly before the report appeared, police in Torrington, CT, heard rumors involving gang activity in their city of 33,000 people. A newspaper in a nearby city, the Waterbury Republican-American, printed a story about the rumors that fueled the situation. The Torrington department called in officers specifically to augment evening shifts but the rumors never came to fruition.

Were there gang members in Torrington? No one knows for sure. What exactly is a "gang member" anyway?

There is some difference of opinion over exactly what constitutes a "gang." The definition does have some bearing on how large a problem communities have with groups of youths. For example, Police Chief Jim Uhde, North Lauderdale, FL. said that the world "gang" is "overused and hysterically taken out of context."

He stressed that "Most of our problems involve groups, not nearly 'gangs,' as we know them, of young 'wanna-be' punks just trying to act bad." Similarly, Chief Tad Leach, Lincolnwood, IL, questions the use—or overuse—of the word "gang."

Lincolnwood, with 11,300 people and a 34-member police force, is a suburb bordering the north side of Chicago, which is one of the major gang centers in the United States. Chicago's infamous Gangster Disciples, with a murderous history dating to the 1970s, has extended its territory over much of the city's

From *Law and Order*, July 1996, pp. 64-68. © 1996 by Law and Order. Reprinted by permission.

south side and beyond, including several suburbs. It is not surprising, then, that gangs operate in communities like Lincolnwood. That is where the definition of gangs becomes important.

Leach explained gang activity as "street gang members claiming neighborhoods as 'turf' and doing activities which promote the gang's ends." He added that "We do have some crime committed by individuals who are gang members but do not reside in our village."

Perhaps police administrators can differentiate between real gang members and "wanna-be's." Media representatives, however, may not.

In some reporters' minds, all crimes committed by youths can be attributed to what they define as "gangs." As they report on "gang activities," real or imagined, the problem becomes magnified in the public's mind. That puts more pressure on law enforcement.

Administrators agree that gangs in general and crimes perpetrated by young people are problems. There is, after all, a clear connection between gang activities and overall crime rates. (It is important to note, though, that many gang members are well out of their teens. Therefore, they hardly qualify for "youthful offender" status.)

While 48% of the poll respondents theorized that eliminating gang problems in their jurisdictions would significantly reduce their overall crime rates, 35% said it would not. Unfortunately, many administrators believe that a total solution to the gang problem is out of their hands. There are simply too many forces at play in the total picture.

Chief Rudolf Rossmy, Vernon, CT, observed, "Gangs and their activities are a sad fact of life and know no boundaries, whether local or state. Local media dwelling on the subject accomplishes two things: it gives credence to gangs causing real problems and feeds on gang members, and the articles create havoc for the community, resulting in fears that are mostly unfounded."

He concluded that "Police need the community in a partnership to control gangs and their activity and should not have to face community paranoia and/or lack of cooperation." That is exactly the approach many police agencies are using to combat gangs and media involvement in their activities.

Chief Dave Scates of Couer D'Alene, ID, emphasized the need for partnerships between law enforcement and the community. "Police alone cannot deal with the problem of gangs," he said. "It takes a concerted community effort. Unfortunately, in too many cases the problem has been dumped into our lap."

He suggested that people often refuse to recognize the insidious emergence of gangs as influences in their communities. "In some cases," he noted, "community members feel law enforcement is crying wolf. By the time they awake, the problem is deeply rooted."

Police Agent Matthew D. Reed, Administrative Services, South Windsor, CT, concurs with Scates. "We are fortunate—or unfortunate, depending on how you look at it—that a number of upper-level gang members reside in our town," he said. "They tend to keep their activity out of their 'back yard' and we do not have a significant gang activity as a result. The potential, however, is significant."

He does not look forward to that potential being realized. "Communities all around us are constantly battling the activity and it is most likely only a matter of time before we become overwhelmed. Unfortunately, it's a topic no one locally discusses."

If the media publicizes an unpopular topic such as gangs and their activities and nobody wants to listen, when the problem finally erupts the community may be unprepared. "When and if a problem occurs in the future, the police agency will be playing 'catch up,' " Reed said.

Of the agencies contacted, 51% sponsor or participate in special programs aimed at deterring young people's involvement in gang activity. About the same percentage (52%) operate anti-gang forces or their

equivalents. They support massive education programs to warn young people about the dangers of involving themselves in gang activities. But, they do question the efficiency of such programs.

Only 18% of the respondents said they feel intensive education programs are effective. Granted, 66% acknowledged they are to some extent, but the question lingers as to whether police agencies should concern themselves more with enforcing laws and apprehending criminals rather than involving themselves in sociological activities. As 82% of the respondents emphasized, the basic underlying sociological reasons contributing to gang activities, e.g., high unemployment and too many single-parent families, are beyond law enforcement's control.

At the same time, 41% said that the gang problem can be eliminated—or at least limited—if young people are given more job and activity opportunities. In their absence, however, sociological problems prevail across all economic strata in contemporary society. These problems affect virtually everyone, as Chief Thomas L. Hennies of Rapid City, SD, suggested.

In his city of 60,000 people, the 100 department members have to deal with Native-American gang activity. "Most gang activity is perceived to involve Blacks, Hispanics, or Asians—at least from a national perspective. Gangs are not just a 'big city' problem," he stressed. "The factors that contribute to the emergence of the gang subculture are everywhere in American society."

In Hennies' opinion, "Gangs are simply a manifestation of many of the social ills that plague our country. The problem must be addressed from a community standpoint, not solely from within the criminal justice system."

One part of the puzzle which administrators are looking closely at is strengthening juvenile offender laws and applying more stringent punishments. In most cases, they do not want more laws. They want stricter enforcement of those that exist.

Chief Emery E. Brejle, Glasgow, MT, pointed out, "Typically, laws increasing punishments for a particular offense are passed by politicians who are more interested in appearing to do something about crime than they are in actually dealing with the complex problems surrounding criminal behavior." He admitted that "There are isolated examples where increasing punishments for a particular offense are effective, but they are the exception." Nevertheless, 89% of the respondents said that juvenile offender laws have to be toughened as one step toward curbing gang problems.

The respondents indicated that current enforcement of youth-related crimes is too lenient and they are frustrated by the courts' treatment of youthful offenders. For instance, 57% reported it is common in their jurisdictions for officers to apprehend gang members only to find them back on the streets within a matter of hours. In many administrators' opinions, there is simply not enough of a deterrent for youthful offenders.

To underline that viewpoint, Assistant Chief Ron Ward, Lawton, OK, related a story that happened in his jurisdiction. Two gang members were caught in a stolen car but only the driver was arrested. The passenger asked the arresting officer if he would tell the driver to call him later that afternoon after he was released. "They know they are not going to spend much time being held, and nothing is going to happen to them," Ward said. "Until this changes, the justice system is doomed to failure."

Perhaps part of the answer, then, is to reach young people before they get involved in gang activities. The town of Hurlock, MD, applied for a $50,000 state grant to improve the seven-member police department's image among local youths. Mayor

Don Bradley emphasized that the grant was not made to change any negative images of the police department. Instead, he noted, youths without respect for police is a national problem.

If the mayor and police chief of a town of 1,700 people are concerned with the lack of respect youths have for officers in their community, then the problem must be real! It is no wonder, then, that law enforcement agencies are looking for help in their attempts to combat gangs.

The federal government can be a source of help, and 43% of the respondents said they would like to see more federal involvement in trying to eliminate the gang problem. Newly-appointed Chief Paul Meara of Springfield, MA, said "Since gangs are a problem to every city and town, federal involvement is very important for networking, information, and money."

There is no doubt that the federal government can have a major impact on gang operations. The results, which receive ample exposure in the press, are encouraging.

In March, the federal government convicted eight members and associates of a Chicago gang of drug conspiracy. The convictions could mean life sentences for the defendants. A Hartford gang member who hid the gun used in a fatal drive-by shooting received a 135-month prison sentence for his participation. These sentences are significant, since federal prisoners must serve at least 85% of their sentences. That, according to one State of Connecticut probation officer, is a definite wake-up call to gang members.

The probation officer stated that gang members who visit her change their attitudes considerably when they learn that they may be charged with federal crimes. "They do not have a lot of respect for state laws," she said. "They know that state-

mandated prison sentences are short—if they are levied at all. However, federal sentencing policies do make them sit up and take notice."

Is stricter enforcement the answer? Some administrators believe so. A resounding 80% of the poll respondents said they would like to see harsher prison sentences meted out to convicted gang members, regardless of their ages. Only 2% would not.

Sergeant Dave Horton of the San Francisco Police Department stressed that "Our agency believes in strict enforcement of laws—especially gang-related laws (186.22 of the California Penal Code)—and prosecution of incidents involving violence." He tempered his statement somewhat by saying, "The San Francisco Police Department also believes that we must work with community groups to help prevent violent gang activity."

Perhaps the San Francisco approach to dealing with gang activity epitomizes law enforcement's strategy in combating youth crime. It blends strict police activity with community involvement. After all, gang activity is real. Based on law enforcement administrators' opinions, it is not a creation of the media. The combination of strategies being employed today against gang crime by law enforcement agencies is probably the best approach, although the administrators are always open to new weapons in the battle.

It would be a real benefit if the media reported profusely on law enforcement's successes in combating gang-related crime, rather than concentrating on the negative activities of gangs and their mystique.

Arthur Sharp, a professional writer and educator, writes regularly for LAW and ORDER. His surveys have been conducted among agency executives on topics of current concern to law enforcement.

Criminal Behavior of Gang Members and At-Risk Youths

Summary of a presentation by C. Ronald Huff, Ohio State University

During the past decade, the problem of gang-related crime has become a significant policy issue in the United States. According to recent estimates, more than 16,000 gangs are active in this country, with at least half a million members who commit more than 600,000 crimes each year. Two recent studies conducted by researchers at Ohio State University were designed to address three critical questions:

- What is the nature and magnitude of self-reported criminal behavior among youth gang members?
- What is the nature and magnitude of such behavior among at-risk youths—those who are not yet gang members?
- What is the effect of gang membership on criminal behavior?

To answer these questions, the National Institute of Justice funded research in three communities—Aurora, Colorado; Denver, Colorado; and Broward County, Florida—and the Office of Juvenile Justice and Delinquency Prevention (OJJDP) funded research in Cleveland, Ohio. Also, as part of the OJJDP grant, researchers in Columbus, Ohio, tracked leaders of youth gangs to determine what happens to gang leaders over time.

Gang membership leads to criminal behavior

The Colorado-Florida and Cleveland studies obtained self-reported data through one-time confidential interviews. In each community, researchers interviewed 50 gang members and 50 youths who were at risk of becoming gang members, developing as close a demographic match between the two groups as possible. They selected interviewees through referrals from local youth-serving organizations, rather than from police databases of arrestees. Questions focused on

criminal and noncriminal activities of the youths and their peers.

The data on criminal activity showed differences between the behavior of gang members and at-risk youths. For example, individual gang members in both studies reported that they had stolen cars (Colorado-Florida, 58.3 percent; Cleveland, 44.7 percent); aggregate rates for auto theft—reflecting statements that members of their gang had stolen cars—were much higher (Colorado-Florida, 93.6 percent; Cleveland, 82.6). Auto theft rates among at-risk youths were markedly lower (Colorado-Florida, 12.5 percent; Cleveland, 4.1 percent). The researchers found similar contrasts when looking at violent crimes. About 40 percent of gang members in the Cleveland sample said they had participated in a drive-by shooting, compared with 2 percent of at-risk youths. In the Colorado-Florida study, 64.2 percent of gang members said that members of their gang had committed homicide, whereas 6.5 percent of at-risk youths said that their friends had done so.

Although both gang members and at-risk youths admitted significant involvement with guns, gang members were far likelier to own guns, and the guns they owned were larger caliber. More than 90 percent of gang members in both studies reported that their peers had carried concealed weapons; more than 80 percent reported that members of their gang had carried guns to school. In contrast, about one-half of at-risk youths in both studies had friends who had carried a concealed weapon; about one-third of at-risk youths said their friends had carried guns to school.

In both studies, gang members were more involved with selling drugs (Colorado-Florida, 76.9 percent; Cleveland, 72.3 percent) than were at-risk youths (Colorado-Florida, 6.4 percent; Cleveland, 9.1 percent). When asked what level of legitimate wages would induce them to stop selling drugs, about one-quarter of

From *Research Preview, National Institute of Justice,* October 1998, pp. 1-9. Reprinted by permission of the National Institute of Justice, National Criminal Justice Reference Service.

the young people in both studies cited an amount little higher than that earned in fast-food restaurants; approximately half of the interviewees, both gang members and at-risk youths, said they had held jobs in the past year.

Gang leaders engage in more serious criminal behavior

The second component of the Ohio study focused on the criminal activity of identified gang leaders in Columbus. The researchers analyzed the arrest records of 83 gang leaders in the years 1980 to 1994. Membership of 78 of these leaders was distributed among five gangs; the rest belonged to other gangs.

During these 15 years, the 83 gang leaders accumulated 834 arrests, 37 percent of which were for violent crimes (ranging from domestic violence to murder). Property crimes and drug-related offenses also figured prominently. The researchers identified a clear pattern of arrest charges in each of the five prominent gangs. A gang's peak arrest rate for property crimes occurred about 1.5 years before its peak arrest rate for violent crimes; the peak arrest rate for drug crimes followed about 3 months later. The researchers theorized that violent crimes increased as the gangs began engaging in drug activity and may have been connected to the establishment of the drug trade. The increasingly violent activities took their toll on the gangs: By the end of the period studied, a disproportionate number of the gang leaders had died.

Steps to prevention and control

These studies identified a close relationship between gang membership and criminal behavior. Gang membership exposed youths to an increased risk of physical violence and death—often including an assaultive initiation ritual—even though most gang members joined for a sense of belonging and security. In contrast, many young people told the researchers that they suffered no physical reprisal for refusing to join a gang. The research demonstrated that the benefits of resisting a gang far outweigh those of joining. Creative prevention that fosters feelings of belonging in the community as a whole might dissuade many of these youths from joining gangs. Also, since half the young people interviewed had held a job, programs that expand job opportunities in the legitimate economy could induce some to stop selling drugs.

Finally, the Columbus study noted a decline in the arrest rate of gang leaders, which the researchers attributed in part to a reallocation of police resources away from gang activities toward specifically drug-related activities: Drugs and gangs are not synonymous, and the assignment of personnel to drug teams reduced the ability of the police to monitor gang activity.

This summary is based on a presentation at the National Institute of Justice (NIJ) by C. Ronald Huff, Ph.D., Director of the School of Public Policy and Management and the Criminal Justice Research Center at Ohio State University, to an audience of researchers and criminal justice practitioners. The research, for which Dr. Huff was principal investigator, was conducted with NIJ support (grant #91-IJ-CX-K013). Support was also received from the State of Ohio's Office of Criminal Justice Services (grant #91-JJ-C01-0682), with funds from the Federal Juvenile Justice and Delinquency Prevention Act, administered by the Office of Juvenile Justice and Delinquency Prevention. The seminar, *Criminal Behavior of Gang Members*, is available as a 60-minute videotape.

Unit Selections

Key Points to Consider

❖ There are some who think the juvenile court as evolved from its start 100 years ago is not longer viable. What do you think and why?

❖ If the juvenile court does not protect juveniles, who will?

❖ What are the desirable qualities of persons who comprise the juvenile courts?

❖ What juvenile programs exist in your jurisdiction? Are there any alternatives? Are they all doing their job?

❖ What can the "restorative justice" movement do for the juvenile court and for influencing juvenile behavior?

 **Links**   **www.dushkin.com/online/**

These sites are annotated on pages 4 and 5.

Juvenile delinquency statutes have traditionally assumed that there are qualitative differences (for example, differences in the thought processes, experience, and knowledge base) between the behavior of children, teens, young adults and adults. Today, to put it mildly, this assumption is under scrutiny, or, to put it more vigorously, this assumption is in the process of being obliterated. Note, for example, the willingness of legislatures and the media and the public to "hang 'em high," "lock 'em up and throw away the key," or otherwise relegate our troublesome—and especially our threatening—youth to adult penal institutions and similar levels and types of penal sanctions, including the death penalty. As Sellin and Wolfgang indicated more than 30 years ago, "the general public does not see the differences in the seriousness of crimes based on the age of the offender" (1964).

Unit 5 deals with these issues that are implicit in almost every contemporary discussion of our "delinquency problem."

We are torn between trying to save our youth and trying to protect ourselves from the most malicious and destructive among them. We examine and reexamine the fine lines that enable us to make the calls when they need to be made. The juvenile court is the place where, like it or not, those calls are made. Most of us do not have the courage or knowledge to do so; we leave it to our juvenile judges. This might be a great argument for more citizen participation in the decision-making process, for community boards, neighborhood panels, and so on. That is not, however, a comfortable solution, given the inertia that many citizens have about

actually doing something constructive about our problems.

As we read the articles in this unit, we ask several questions (Hershey and Gottfredson, 1993) about juveniles. We think here in terms of *most* juveniles, not *all* juveniles:

1. Is the criminal behavior of juveniles less serious?

2. Are juveniles as responsible as adults?

3. Are juveniles more amenable to treatment than adults?

4. Is there a class of undesirable behaviors (status offenses) that only juveniles can commit?

5. Is it possible to implement penal sanctions against juvenile misbehaviors without jeopardizing their entire life chances and therefore creating our own worst nightmare?

6. Who is ultimately responsible for youth who are misguided (parents, state, community, religion, etc.)?

7. Can juveniles be isolated from the corrupting influences of the world around them and especially of the institutions in which they might be placed with severely disturbed youth or adults?

References

Hershey, Travis, and Gottfredson, Michael, in T. Booth, (Ed.), *Juvenile Justice in the New Europe*, University of Sheffield, 1993.

Sellin, Thorsten, and Wolfgang, Marvin, *Measurement of Delinquency*, New York: Wiley, 1964.

**Bureau of Justice Statistics
Special Report**

State Court Processing Statistics, 1990–94

Juvenile Felony Defendants in Criminal Courts

By
Kevin J. Strom and **Steven K. Smith**
BJS Statisticians
Howard N. Snyder
National Center for Juvenile Justice

In the Nation's 75 largest counties, juveniles handled as adults in criminal courts represented about 1% of all felony defendants. State statutes define which persons are under the original jurisdiction of the juvenile court system. In 1994, 39 States and the District of Columbia defined the upper age limit of juvenile court jurisdiction at age 17. The remaining 11 States set the upper age limit below age 17. Three States (Connecticut, New York, and North Carolina) defined 16- and 17-year-olds as adults. Eight States (Georgia, Illinois, Louisiana, Massa-

---

**Jointly Published with the
Office of Juvenile Justice and
Delinquency Prevention**

Highlights

**Juvenile defendants
in criminal courts**

• In the Nation's 75 largest counties, juveniles transferred to criminal courts represented about 1% of all felony defendants.

• Juveniles transferred to criminal court were generally violent felony offenders. Two-thirds were charged with a violent offense, including about 11% with murder, 34% with robbery, and 15% charged with felony assault.

• 63% of juveniles transferred to criminal courts were black males, 29% were white males, 3% were black females, and 2% were white females.

• 59% of juveniles transferred to criminal courts were convicted of a felony, and 52% of those convicted of a felony were sentenced to prison.

• About a third of juveniles in criminal courts sentenced to State prison received a sentence of 4 years or less. The average prison sentence for juveniles convicted in criminal courts was about 9 years; for those convicted of a violent offense, the average prison sentence was nearly 11 years.

Defendants in juvenile courts

• In the 75 largest counties, nearly 2% of juveniles age 15 or older formally handled in juvenile courts were transferred to criminal courts by judicial waiver. Among those referred to juvenile court for murder, 37% were judicially waived to criminal court.

• Of juveniles formally processed in juvenile courts, 48% were white males; 36%, black males; 7%, white females; and 5%, black females.

• 55% of juvenile defendants formally processed in juvenile courts were adjudicated delinquent.

• Among juvenile defendants adjudicated delinquent, 40% received a disposition of residential placement and 50% received formal probation.

Juvenile defendants in the 75 largest counties, 1990, 1992, and 1994

Characteristic	Criminal court	Juvenile court
Male	92%	88%
Female	8	12
White	31%	55%
Black	67	41
Other	2	4
Most serious arrest charge		
Violent	66%	24%
Property	17	46
Drug	14	13

From *Bureau of Justice Statistics Special Report,* September 1998, pp. 1-11. Reprinted by permission of the National Institute of Justice, National Criminal Justice Reference Service.

Table 1. Characteristics of juvenile defendants in criminal and juvenile courts in the Nation's 75 largest counties, 1990, 1992, and 1994

Characteristic	Percent of juveniles in —	
	Criminal court	Juvenile court
Sex		
Male	92%	88%
Female	8	12
Race		
White	31%	55%
Black	67	41
Other	2	4
Age at arrest		
14 and under	8%	--
15	24	36
16	27	35
17	40	26
18 or over	--	3

Note: 1,638 juvenile defendants were prosecuted as adults in the Nation's 75 largest counties during May 1990, 1992, and 1994. 370,424 defendants were formally processed in juvenile courts in a selected number of the Nation's 75 largest counties in 1990, 1992, and 1994. Data on sex of defendants were available for 99% of the cases; on defendants' race, for 85%. General offense categories include offenses other than those displayed. --Adult court sample includes only defendants under 18. Juvenile court sample includes only defendants age 15 or older.

Table 2. Most serious arrest charge for juvenile felony defendants in criminal courts, 1990, 1992, and 1994

Most serious arrest charge	Percent of juvenile defendants in the criminal courts of the Nation's 75 largest counties
All offenses	100%
Violent offenses	66%
Murder	11
Rape	3
Robbery	34
Assault	15
Property offenses	17%
Burglary	6
Theft	8
Drug offenses	14%
Public-order offenses	3%

Note: 1,638 juvenile defendants were prosecuted as adults in the Nation's 75 largest counties during May 1990, 1992, and 1994. Data for most serious arrest charge available for 100% of all cases. Detail may not add to total because of rounding. General offense categories include offenses other than those displayed.

Table 3. Most serious referral offense for juvenile defendants age 15 or older in juvenile courts, 1990, 1992, and 1994

Most serious referral charge	Percent of defendants in juvenile courts of the Nation's 75 largest counties
All offenses	100%
Violent offenses	24%
Murder[a]	--
Rape[b]	1
Robbery	6
Assault	15
Property offenses	46%
Burglary	13
Theft	22
Drug offenses	13%
Public-order offenses	18%

Note: 370,424 defendants were formally processed in juvenile courts in a selected number of the Nation's 75 largest counties in 1990, 1992, and 1994. These defendants were not transferred to criminal court for prosecution. Data for most serious referral charge were available for 100% of all cases. Detail may not add to total because of rounding. The juvenile court sample represents counties from the National Juvenile Court Data Archive that were included in the Nation's 75 largest counties. General offense categories include offenses other than those displayed.
--Less than .05%.
[a]Murder includes manslaughter.
[b]Rape includes other violent sex offenses.

chusetts, Michigan, Missouri, Texas, and South Carolina) defined 17-year-olds as adults.

Each State legislature, however, has put in place mechanisms that enable persons classified as juveniles in the State to be transferred to the adult justice system and handled in criminal court. These mechanisms include judicial waiver, concurrent jurisdiction, and statutorily excluding certain offenses from juvenile court jurisdiction. (See box, "Mechanisms by which juveniles can reach criminal court.")

Juveniles in criminal and juvenile courts

This report presents data on juveniles prosecuted as felony defendants in criminal courts within the Nation's 75 largest counties. Comparable data are also presented on juvenile defendants formally processed in the juvenile court system in a selected number of the Nation's 75 largest counties.

Every 2 years the Bureau of Justice Statistics (BJS) gathers information on a sample of felony defendants through the State Court Processing Statistics (SOPS) project. Data for this report were combined from the 1990, 1992, and 1994 data collections. An estimated 7,110 defendants under age 18 faced charges in criminal court during May in the 3-year period—about a fourth (23%) of whom, based on age, would be considered juveniles by State law. Juvenile court data were provided by the National Center for Juvenile Justice (NCJJ).

The National Juvenile Court Data Archive provided data on more than 370,000 juvenile defendants formally processed in juvenile courts in a selected number of counties among the Nation's 75 largest. (See *Methodology* for description of sampled counties from the NCJJ.)

Most serious arrest charge

Criminal court

Among juveniles prosecuted in criminal courts in the Nation's 75 largest

counties, two-thirds were charged with a violent felony offense—including robbery (34%), assault (15%), and murder (11%) (table 2). About a sixth were charged with a felony property offense. For the remainder of juveniles in criminal courts, the most serious arrest charge was a drug (14%) or a public-order offense (3%). Public-order offenses include weapons charges, driving-related charges, and other violations of social order. Juvenile court

Juvenile court

An estimated 24% of the defendants in juvenile courts in the Nation's 75 largest counties were referred for violent offenses, about 18% for public-order offenses, and 13% for drug-related offenses (table 3). Slightly less than half of the defendants in juvenile courts were referred for property offenses (46%)—including theft (22%) and burglary (13%).

Demographics

Criminal court

In the Nation's 75 largest counties, 92% of juveniles in criminal courts were male, with the proportion of male offenders varying slightly by offense type (table 4).

Females, who represented about 8% of all juvenile defendants in criminal courts, were charged with a violent offense in over 70% of cases (not shown in table). Over half of female defendants in criminal court were charged with robbery (55%).

Two-thirds of the juveniles in criminal courts were black, almost a third were white, and the remaining defendants were members of other racial groups.

Black males comprised 7 in 10 violent juvenile defendants in criminal courts (not shown in a table). About 65% of juvenile murder defendants in criminal court were black males, 72% of rape defendants, 78% of robbery defendants, 61% of assault defendants, and 65% of defendants charged with other types of violent crime.

Three-fourths of juvenile drug offenses in criminal court involved a black male defendant, as did two-thirds of public-order charges. White males comprised the majority of juveniles charged with burglary (82%).

Juvenile court

As in criminal court, juvenile defendants in juvenile courts were largely male (88%). By offense, males comprised the largest percentages among defendants referred to juvenile court for rape (98%), burglary (94%), and murder (94%) (table 5).

Fifty-five percent of defendants processed in juvenile courts were white, 41% were black, and 4% were members of other racial groups. Whites accounted for 59% of the murder defendants referred to juvenile court, 51% of assault defendants, 69% of burglary, 56% of theft, and 59% of public-order defendants. Black defendants comprised 53% of defendants re-

ferred to juvenile court for rape, 60% of robbery, and 59% of drug defendants.

Overall, black males accounted for about a third of defendants in juvenile courts (not shown in a table). About 40% of violent defendants in juvenile court were black males compared to 70% of violent juveniles in criminal courts. White males accounted for the majority of juvenile

defendants referred to juvenile courts for murder (55%) and burglary (64%).

Pretrial release and detention

Criminal court

Overall, about half of juveniles prosecuted in criminal courts were released prior to the final disposition of their

Table 4. Sex and race of juvenile felony defendants in criminal court, by most serious arrest charge: 1990, 1992, and 1994

Most serious arrest charge	Percent of juvenile felony defendants in the 75 largest counties						
	Sex			Race			
	Total	Male	Female	Total	White	Black	Other
All offenses	100%	92%	8%	100%	31%	67%	2%
Violent offenses	100%	92%	8%	100%	25%	73%	2%
Murder	100	96	4	100	25	69	6
Rape	100	89	11	100	28	72	0
Robbery	100	87	13	100	16	82	3
Assault	100	97	3	100	39	61	0
Property offenses	100%	95%	5%	100%	63%	31%	6%
Burglary	100	100	0	100	82	13	4
Theft	100	95	5	100	49	42	9
Drug offenses	100%	92%	8%	100%	19%	81%	0%
Public-order offenses	100%	89%	11%	100%	23%	77%	0%

Note: 1,638 juvenile defendants were prosecuted as adults in the Nation's 75 largest counties during May 1990, 1992, and 1994. Data on sex and race of defendants were available for 99% of all eligible cases. Detail may not add to total because of rounding. Zero indicates no cases in the sample. General offense categories include offenses other than those displayed.

Table 5. Sex and race of juvenile defendants in juvenile court, by most serious referral charge: 1990, 1992, and 1994

Most serious referral charge	Percent of defendants in juvenile courts of the Nation's 75 largest counties						
	Sex			Race			
	Total	Male	Female	Total	White	Black	Other
All offenses	100%	88%	12%	100%	55%	41%	4%
Violent offenses	100%	86%	14%	100%	48%	48%	4%
Murder[a]	100	94	5	100	59	36	5
Rape[b]	100	98	2	100	44	53	3
Robbery	100	92	8	100	37	60	3
Assault	100	82	18	100	51	45	4
Property offenses	100%	88%	12%	100%	61%	35%	4%
Burglary	100	94	6	100	69	26	5
Theft	100	83	17	100	56	40	4
Drug offenses	100%	92%	8%	100%	40%	59%	1%
Public-order offenses	100%	87%	13%	100%	59%	37%	4%

Note: 370,424 defendants were formally processed in juvenile courts of the Nation's 75 largest counties in 1990, 1992, and 1994. These defendants were not transferred to criminal court for prosecution. Data on sex of defendants were available for 100% of cases and for race of defendants, for 88% of all eligible cases. Detail may not add to total because of rounding. The juvenile court sample represents counties from the National Juvenile Court Data Archive that were included in the Nation's 75 largest counties. General offense categories include offenses other than those displayed.
[a]Murder includes manslaughter.
[b]Rape includes other violent sex offenses.

Table 6. Juvenile felony defendants in criminal court released before or detained until case disposition, by most serious arrest charge, 1990, 1992, and 1994

Most serious arrest charge	Juvenile defendants in the criminal courts of the Nation's 75 largest counties		
	Total	Detained until case disposition	Released before case disposition
All offenses	100%	49%	51%
Violent offenses	100%	56%	44%
Murder	100	87	13
Rape	100	53	47
Robbery	100	45	55
Assault	100	53	47
Property offenses	100%	26%	74%
Burglary	100	34	66
Theft	100	25	75
Drug offenses	100%	37%	63%
Public-order offenses	100%	81%	19%

Note: 1,638 juvenile defendants were prosecuted as adults in the Nation's 75 largest counties during May 1990, 1992, and 1994. Data on pretrial release were available for 93% of all eligible cases. Details may not add to total because of rounding. General offense categories include offenses other than those displayed.

Table 7. Juvenile defendants age 15 or older detained at any time prior to case disposition in juvenile court, by most serious referral charge, 1990, 1992, and 1994

Most serious referral charge	Defendants in juvenile courts of the Nation's 75 largest counties		
	Total	Detained[a]	Released
All offenses	100%	35%	65%
Violent offenses	100%	43%	57%
Murder[b]	100	78	22
Rape[c]	100	44	56
Robbery	100	55	45
Assault	100	38	62
Property offenses	100%	29%	71%
Burglary	100	35	65
Theft	100	28	72
Drug offenses	100%	40%	60%
Public-order offenses	100%	35%	65%

Note: 370,424 defendants were formally processed in juvenile courts of the Nation's 75 largest counties in 1990, 1992, and 1994. These defendants were not transferred to criminal court for prosecution. Data on pretrial release were available for 71% of all eligible cases. Details may not add to total because of rounding. The juvenile court sample represents counties from the National Juvenile Court Data Archive that were included in the Nation's 75 largest counties. General offense categories include offenses not shown.
[a]Includes those who did not post bail.
[b]Murder includes manslaughter.
[c]Rape includes other violent sex offenses.

case (table 6). Public-order (19%) and violent (44%) juvenile defendants were the least likely to be released pretrial, while property (74%) and drug (63%) defendants were the most likely.

About half of juveniles in criminal courts charged with robbery (55%), assault (47%), or rape (47%) were released pretrial. Thirteen percent of juvenile murder defendants in criminal courts were released prior to case disposition.

Juvenile court

Over half of violent defendants in juvenile courts were released pretrial (57%), as were about two-thirds of those charged with property (71%), drug (60%), or public-order (65%) offenses (table 7). Among defendants referred to juvenile courts, 22% of murder defendants, 45% of robbery, and 56% of rape defendants were released pretrial.

Table 8. Adjudication outcome for felony defendants defined as juveniles, by most serious arrest charge, 1990, 1992, and 1994

Most serious arrest charge	Percent of felony defendants defined as juveniles in the 75 largest counties							
		Convicted				Not convicted		
	Total	Felony Total	Plea	Trial	Misde-meanor	Total[a]	Dis-missed	Other outcome[b]
All offenses	64%	59%	51%	8%	5%	27%	25%	9%
Violent offenses	59%	56%	47%	9%	4%	31%	29%	10%
Murder	58	56	37	19	3	31	24	10
Rape	54	54	54	0	0	38	39	8
Robbery	58	56	48	8	2	30	29	12
Assault	63	53	46	7	9	30	26	7
Property offenses	74%	61%	59%	3%	13%	19%	16%	7%
Burglary	77	64	64	0	13	19	9	4
Theft	76	59	54	6	16	16	16	8
Drug offenses	70%	68%	56%	12%	2%	24%	24%	6%
Public-order offenses	91%	91%	91%	0	0	9%	9%	0%

Note: 1,638 juvenile defendants were prosecuted as adults in the Nation's 75 largest counties during May 1990, 1992, and 1994. Eleven percent of all eligible cases were still pending adjudication at the end of the 1-year study period and are excluded from the table. Data on adjudication outcome were available for 85% of those cases that had been adjudicated. Detail may not add to subtotal because of rounding. General offense categories include offenses other than those displayed. Zero indicates no cases in the sample.
[a]Total not convicted includes acquittals.
[b]Includes other outcomes such as diversions and deferred adjudication.

Adjudication

Criminal court

Nearly two-thirds of juvenile defendants in criminal courts were con-

victed (table 8). About 9 in 10 of the convictions were for felonies. By general offense category, conviction rates in criminal court were 91% for public-order offenses and 59% for violent of-

fenses. About 74% of juvenile property defendants in criminal court and 70% of defendants charged with drug offenses were convicted. Juvenile defendants in criminal court charged with public-order or drug charges were the most likely to have received a felony conviction.

In most cases where the juvenile was not convicted in criminal court, it was because the charges against the defendant were dismissed by the prosecutor or the court. Dismissal occurred in about a fourth of juvenile felony cases in criminal court. Nearly 40% of defendants charged with rape had their cases dismissed. Overall, about 2% of juvenile defendants in criminal court were acquitted, including 7% of murder defendants and 11% of burglary defendants. About 9% of juvenile cases in criminal court had other outcomes such as diversion or deferred adjudication.

Fifty-one percent of juvenile defendants in criminal court pleaded guilty to a felony, and an additional 5% pleaded guilty to a misdemeanor. About 10% of juvenile cases adjudi-

cated within 1 year went to bench or jury trial. A fifth of the trials ended in an acquittal, while the remainder resulted in a guilty verdict.

Regardless of the method of adjudication, defendants who were convicted were usually convicted of the original arrest charge. This was most likely to be the case when the original offense was violent. Among those charged with murder and later convicted, 84% were convicted of the original arrest charge. The corresponding percentages were also high for robbery 87%) and assault (76%).

Juvenile court

Among juvenile defendants formally processed in the juvenile court system, 55% were adjudicated delinquent (table 9). Juvenile adjudication patterns differed little by offense type, as at least half or more in each major offense category were found delinquent. Among defendants referred to juvenile court for public-order offenses, 59% were found delinquent, as were

51% of those referred for violent offenses.

Conviction and delinquent adjudication

Criminal court

Overall, about 9 in 10 juvenile convictions in criminal court were felonies, with over half representing violent convictions and a fifth property convictions (table 10). The remainder of juvenile defendants were convicted of drug-related offenses (15%), public-order offenses (5%) or misdemeanor offenses (8%). By conviction offense, 25% of juveniles in criminal court were convicted of robbery, 7% were convicted of burglary, 15% of drug offenses, 14% of felony assault, and 10% of theft.

Juvenile court

Nearly half of defendants in juvenile courts were adjudicated delinquent for a property offense, about a fifth for a violent offense, and a fifth for a public-order offense (table 11).

Table 9. Adjudication outcome for defendants age 15 or above in juvenile courts, by most serious referral offense, 1990, 1992, and 1994

Most serious referral offense	Defendants in juvenile courts of the Nation's 75 largest counties		
		Adjudicated	
	Total	Delinquent	Not delinquent
All offenses	100%	55%	45%
Violent offenses	100%	51%	49%
Murder[a]	100	58	42
Rape[b]	100	55	45
Robbery	100	55	45
Assault	100	48	52
Property offenses	100%	55%	45%
Burglary	100	56	44
Theft	100	57	43
Drug offenses	100%	55%	45%
Public-order offenses	100%	59%	41%

Note: 370,424 defendants were formally processed in juvenile courts of the Nation's 75 largest counties in 1990, 1992, and 1994. These defendants were not transferred to criminal court for prosecution. Data on adjudication outcome were available for 100% of the eligible cases. The juvenile court sample represents counties from the National Juvenile Court Data Archive that were included in the Nation's 75 largest counties. General offense categories include offenses not shown.
[a]Murder includes manslaughter.
[b]Rape includes other violent sex offenses.

Table 10. Juvenile felony defendants in criminal court, by conviction offense, 1990, 1992, and 1994

Most serious conviction offense	Juvenile defendants in the criminal courts of the Nation's 75 largest counties Percent
All offenses	100%
All felonies	92%
Violent offenses	51%
Murder	6
Rape	2
Robbery	25
Assault	14
Property offenses	21%
Burglary	7
Theft	10
Drug offenses	15%
Public-order offenses	5%
Misdemeanors	8%

Note: 1,638 juvenile defendants were prosecuted as adults in the Nations' 75 largest counties during May 1990, 1992, and 1994. Data on conviction offense type were available for 100% of cases involving defendants who had been convicted. Detail may not add to total because of rounding. General offense categories include offenses not shown.

Table 11. Defendants age 15 or older adjudicated delinquent in juvenile court, by most serious adjudication offense, 1990, 1992, and 1994

Most serious referral offense	Defendants in juvenile courts of the Nation's 75 largest counties Percent
All offenses	100%
Violent offenses	22%
Murder[a]	--
Rape[b]	1
Robbery	6
Assault	14
Property offenses	46%
Burglary	13
Theft	22
Drug offenses	13%
Public-order offenses	19%

Note: 370,424 defendants were formally processed in juvenile courts of the 75 largest counties in 1990, 1992, and 1994. These defendants were not transferred to criminal court. Data on adjudication charge available for 100% of all eligible cases. Details may not add to total because of rounding. General offense categories include offenses not shown. The juvenile court sample represents counties from the National Juvenile Court Data Archive that were included in the 75 largest counties.
--Less than .05%.
[a]Murder includes manslaughter.
[b]Rape includes other violent sex offenses.

Sentencing

Criminal court

Overall, 68% of convicted juveniles in criminal court were sentenced to incarceration in a State prison or local jail (table 12). Over half of juvenile felony convictions resulted in a sentence to State prison, while over half of juvenile misdemeanor convictions resulted in a sentence to local jail.

Seventy-nine percent of juveniles convicted of violent offenses in criminal court were sentenced to incarceration, with nearly 7 in 10 violent convictions resulting in a sentence to State prison. Half of juveniles in criminal court convicted of drug offenses were sentenced to incarceration, with 34% sentenced to State prison.

Thirty-one percent of juveniles convicted in criminal court were sentenced to probation, and about 1% received other nonincarceration sentences. Forty-six percent of those convicted of drug offenses were sentenced to probation, while 21% of those convicted of violent offenses had a similar outcome. By specific offense type, three-fourths of juveniles in criminal court convicted of burglary were sentenced to probation.

Juvenile court

In juvenile court during this period, 40% of delinquent defendants were sentenced to residential placement, 50% were sentenced to probation, and 10% to other sanctions (table 13). Over half of defendants adjudicated delinquent for murder (77%) and robbery (57%) were sentenced to residential placement.

Among defendants adjudicated delinquent in juvenile court, half were sentenced to probation. Fifty-four percent of those adjudicated delinquent for property offenses and 47% of those adjudicated delinquent for violent offenses received probation.

Table 12. Most serious type of sentence received by convicted juvenile defendants in criminal court, by most serious conviction offense, 1990, 1992, and 1994

| Most serious conviction offense | Percent of convicted juvenile defendants in the Nation's 75 largest counties sentenced to-- | | | | | | |
| | | Incarceration | | | Nonincarceration | | |
	Total	Total	Prison	Jail	Total	Probation	Fine
All offenses	100%	68%	49%	19%	32%	31%	1%
All felonies	100%	69%	52%	16%	31%	30%	1%
Violent offenses	100%	79%	68%	11%	21%	21%	0%
Murder	100	100	100	0	0	0	0
Rape	100	100	25	75	0	0	0
Robbery	100	75	69	6	25	25	0
Assault	100	73	61	12	27	27	0
Property offenses	100%	57%	32%	25%	43%	40%	3%
Burglary	100	24	24	0	76	76	0
Theft	100	74	38	36	26	26	0
Drug offenses	100%	50%	34%	16%	50%	46%	3%
Public-order offenses	100%	60%	27%	33%	40%	40%	0%
Misdemeanor	100%	62%	5%	57%	38%	32%	6%

Note: 1,638 juvenile defendants were prosecuted as adults in the Nation's 75 largest counties during May 1990, 1992, and 1994. Data on type of sentence were available for 93% of cases involving juvenile defendants who had been convicted. Eight percent of prison sentences and 14% of jail sentences included a probation term. Fourteen percent of prison sentences, 19% of jail sentences, and 13% of probation sentences included a fine. Fines may have included restitution or community service. Total for all felonies includes cases that could not be classified into 1 of the 4 major offense categories. Detail may not add to subtotal because of rounding. General offense categories include offenses not shown. Zero indicates no cases in the sample.

Methodology

State Court Processing Statistics (SCPS)

The sample of juvenile defendants in criminal courts were selected from combined SCPS surveys from 1990, 1992, and 1994. Juvenile status was determined based on State statutes for maximum juvenile court jurisdiction. Age of defendant was age at arrest. In 1994 the maximum age for juvenile court jurisdiction was 17 or

Table 13. Disposition received by juveniles age 15 or older adjudicated delinquent, by most serious adjudicated offense, 1990, 1992, and 1994

Most serious adjudicated offense	Total	Placement	Probation	Other[a]
All offenses	100%	40%	50%	10%
Violent offenses	100%	44%	47%	9%
Murder[b]	100	77	21	2
Rape[c]	100	41	49	10
Robbery	100	57	37	6
Assault	100	38	51	11
Property offenses	100%	35%	54%	11%
Burglary	100	40	53	7
Theft	100	34	53	13
Drug offenses	100%	41%	48%	11%
Public-order offenses	100%	46%	45%	9%

Note: 370,424 defendants were formally processed in juvenile courts of the Nation's 75 largest counties in 1990, 1992, and 1994. These defendants were not transferred to criminal court for prosecution. Data on disposition available for 97% of all eligible cases. Detail may not add to subtotal because of rounding. The juvenile court sample represents counties from the National Juvenile Court Data Archive that were included in the Nation's largest 75 counties. General offense categories include offenses other than those displayed.
[a]Other outcomes includes such things as fines, restitution, and community service.
[b]Murder includes manslaughter.
[c]Rape includes other violent sex offenses.

Mechanisms by which juveniles can reach criminal court

All States allow juveniles to be proceeded against as adults in criminal court under certain circumstances. The following description of mechanisms that States use is summarized from State Responses to Serious and Violent Juvenile Crime by Patricia Torbet and others.

In all States except New Mexico, Nebraska, New York, and Connecticut, juvenile court judges may waive jurisdiction over the case and transfer it to criminal court. The waiver and transfer may be based on their own judgment, in response to the State prosecutor's request, or in some States at the request of juveniles or their parents.

In a related provision—called a presumptive waiver—juvenile offenders must be waived to criminal court unless they can prove that they are amenable to juvenile rehabilitation.

This type of provision shifts the burden of proof from the prosecutor to the juvenile. As of 1995, 12 States and the District of Columbia had enacted presumptive provisions.

Concurrent jurisdiction statutes, also called prosecutorial discretion or direct-file, give prosecutors the authority to file certain juvenile cases in either juvenile or criminal court. Ten States and the District of Columbia had concurrent jurisdiction statutes as of 1995.

Statutory exclusion of certain serious offenses from juvenile court jurisdiction is another mechanism in many States. This would also include mandatory waiver provisions. Thirty-six States and the District of Columbia exclude selected offenses from juvenile court jurisdiction. The most common offenses excluded are capital murder, murder of other types, and serious crimes against persons.

Several States exclude juveniles charged with felonies if they have prior adjudications or convictions.

Reverse waiver provisions have been enacted in 22 States that allow the criminal court, usually on a motion from the prosecutor, to transfer excluded or direct-file cases back to the juvenile court for adjudication and/or disposition.

"Once an adult, always an adult" provisions, enacted in 17 States and the District of Columbia, require that once the juvenile court jurisdiction is waived or the juvenile is sentenced in criminal court as a result of direct filing or exclusion, all subsequent cases involving the juvenile offender will be under criminal court jurisdiction. (For information about specific provisions of the various mechanisms listed above, see Juvenile Offenders and Victims: A National Report, 1995, pp. 85–89.)

---

younger in 39 States and the District of Columbia (Alabama, Alaska, Arizona, Arkansas, California, Colorado, Delaware, District of Columbia, Florida, Hawaii, Idaho, Indiana, Iowa, Kansas, Kentucky, Maine, Maryland, Minnesota, Mississippi, Montana, Nebraska, Nevada, New Hampshire, New Jersey, New Mexico, North Dakota, Ohio, Oklahoma, Oregon, Pennsylvania, Rhode Island, South Dakota, Tennessee, Utah, Vermont, Virginia, Washington, West Virginia, and Wisconsin).

In eight States the maximum age for juvenile court jurisdiction was 16 (Georgia, Illinois, Louisiana, Massachusetts, Michigan, Missouri, South Carolina, and Texas). In an additional three states, the maximum age for juvenile court jurisdiction was 15 (Connecticut, New York, and North Carolina), For example, in New York all felony defendants 15 and younger in State court were considered to be juveniles by definition and

Juvenile murder defendants and arrestees

In the 75 largest counties —

Juvenile murder defendant characteristic	In criminal court	In juvenile court
Sex		
Male	96%	94%
Female	4	6
Race		
White	25%	59%
Black	69	36
Other	6	5
Judicial processing		
Detained pretrial	87%	78%
Convicted/adjudicated delinquent	58%	58%
Sentence for murder convictions		
Prison/secured detainment	100%	77%
Probation	0	21
Maximum prison sentence for murder convictions		
Less than 2 years	8 %	--
2 to 10 years	16	--
10 or more years	76	--

Note: 174 juvenile defendants were prosecuted as adults for murder in the Nation's 75 largest counties during May 1990, 1992, and 1994. 1,343 murder defendants were formally processed in juvenile courts in the 75 largest counties during calendar years 1990, 1992, and 1994. Detail may not add to subtotal because of rounding. Zero indicates no cases in the sample.
--No data were available for length of detainment in juvenile facilities.

In the United States —

• 1,860 persons under age 18 were arrested for murder in 1980.

• The number of persons under 18 arrested for murder peaked in 1993 with 3,790 arrests.

• From 1993 to 1996 the number of murder arrests of those under 18 dropped nearly 25%.

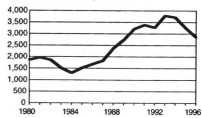

Murder arrests of juveniles

Note: Arrest estimates are based on data reported in the series Crime in the United States using an assumption that the annual proportion of juvenile arrests in the reporting sample is the same as in the U.S. population.

Source for Juvenile arrest data: Snyder, H. (1998). Juvenile Murder Arrests: 1980-96. Pittsburgh: National Center for Juvenile Justice.

Appendix A. Judicial processing of felony defendants under 25, by State juvenile age definition, 1990, 1992, and 1994

The table shown compares the judicial processing of juvenile felony defendants in criminal courts with that of other young felony defendants. Data on persons younger than 25 years prosecuted in State courts are presented in three categories. The first column includes those defendants between ages 18 and 24 at the time of arrest. The second includes felony defendants under age 18 who, by definition, were considered adults by State age statute. For example, in New York all 16- and 17-year-old defendants were considered adults under 18. Finally, defendants defined by State age statutes as under the original jurisdiction of the juvenile courts were considered juveniles in criminal courts.

An estimated 57,129 felony cases were filed against defendants age 18 to 24 in the State courts of the Nation's 75 largest counties during May 1990, 1992, and 1994. By comparison, 7,110 felony defendants under age 18 were prosecuted in the State courts during a similar time frame. Of these defendants under age 18, 23% or 1,638 cases were defined as juveniles by State statutes and the remaining 77% (5,472 cases) were defined as adults under 18.

Juvenile defendants compared to adults 18 to 24

Defendants defined as juveniles in criminal courts were more than twice as likely to be charged with a violent offense than defendants 18 to 24. Among violent felony defendants, juveniles in criminal court were more likely than defendants 18 to 24 to be—
- detained pretrial prior to case disposition
- convicted of a felony offense
- sentenced to State prison.

Juvenile defendants compared to adults under 18

The average prison sentence for juveniles convicted of violent offenses in criminal courts was about 10½ years (a mean of

	Percent of felony defendants age 18 to 24	Percent of felony defendants under 18 defined as – Adult	Juvenile
Most serious arrest charge			
Violent offenses	26%	36%	66%
Property offenses	35	36	17
Drug offenses	31	22	14
Public-order offenses	8	6	3
Pretrial release for violent felony charge	55%	71%	44%
Adjudication outcome for violent felony defendants			
Convicted			
Felony	45%	39%	56%
Misdemeanor	11	10	4
Not convicted	45	51	41
Most serious sentence for violent convictions			
Prison	57%	41%	68%
Jail	25	7	11
Probation	18	52	21
Mean prison sentence for violent convictions in months	98 mo	97 mo	127 mo

Note: Data for the specific arrest charge were available for 99% of the cases. Detail may not add to subtotal because of rounding.

127 months and a median of 78 months). For adult defendants under 18 the average prison sentence for violent offenses was about 8 years (a mean of 97 months and a median of 72).

Of juveniles sentenced to prison for violent offenses—
- 7% were sentenced to 2 years or less
- 43% from 2+ years to 6 years
- 26% from 6+ years to 10 years
- 22% to over 10 years, and 2% to life imprisonment.

reached criminal court by way of one or more juvenile transfer mechanisms. The mechanism by which these defendants reached criminal courts is unknown. Since 1994 New Hampshire and Wisconsin have lowered their juvenile age status from 17 to 16.

The SCPS sample was designed and selected by the U.S. Bureau of Census under BJS supervision. It is a 2-stage stratified sample, with 40 (or 39 in 1994) of the 75 most populous counties selected at the first stage and a systematic sample of State court felony filings (defendants) within each county selected at the second stage. The 40 (39 in 1994) counties were divided into 4 first-stage strata based on

court filing information obtained through a telephone survey. In 1990 and 1992, 14 counties were included in the sample with certainty because of their large number of court filings. The remaining 26 counties were allocated to the 3 non-certainty strata based on the variance of felony court dispositions. In 1994, 12 counties were included in the sample with certainty because of their large number of court filings. The remaining counties were allocated to the three non-certainty strata based on the variance of felony court dispositions.

The second-stage sampling (filings) were designed to represent all defendants who had felony cases filed with

the court during the month of May in 1990, 1992, and 1994. The participating jurisdictions provided data for every felony case filed on selected days during that month. In 1990, each jurisdiction provided data for the 5, 10, 15, or 31 days in May from which to sample all felony defendants who had felony charges filed. In 1992 and 1994, each jurisdiction provided data for 1, 2, or 4 weeks' filings in May. Data from jurisdictions that were not required to provide a full month of filings were weighted to represent the full month.

In 1990, data on 13,597 sample felony cases were collected from the 40 sampled jurisdictions, representing

Appendix B. Estimating the number of juveniles handled in adult courts

Sources for statistics on juveniles in adult courts

• The **National Judicial Reporting Program (NJRP)** is a biennial survey that compiles information on the sentences that felons receive in State courts nationwide and on characteristics of the felons. The 1994 survey estimated that 21,000 felons were younger than 18 at arrest, conviction, or sentencing in State courts nationwide. Of these felons, an estimated 12,000 were juveniles convicted of a felony in State courts.

• The **National Survey of State Prosecutors (NSP)** is a nationally representative sample drawn from a list of all prosecutors' offices that handle felony cases in State courts. The 1996 NSP estimated that 27,000 juveniles were proceeded against in criminal court by prosecutors' offices.

• The **National Juvenile Court Data Archive** which is supported by OJJDP grant number 95-JN-FX-0008, at the National Center for Juvenile Justice (NCJJ), contains the most detailed information available on youth involved in the juvenile justice system and on activities of U.S. juvenile courts. In 1990, 1992, and 1994, over 377,000 defendants age 15 or older were formally processed in juvenile courts in a selected number of the Nation's 75 largest counties. Of these defendants, approximately 1.9% were transferred to criminal court by way of *judicial waiver.*

• The **State Court Processing Statistics (SCPS)** program is a biennial data collection on the processing of felony defendants in the State courts of the Nation's 75 largest counties. During May of 1990, 1992, and 1994 an estimated 7,110 defendants under age 18 faced charges in criminal court—about a fourth of whom, based on age, would be considered juveniles by State law.

Difficulties in developing National estimates for the number of juveniles in adult courts:

• Lack of uniform reporting methods by States regarding juvenile transfer statistics, including the mechanisms by which juveniles reach adult courts

• Variation in the definition of *juvenile offenders* across States

• Frequent changes in State statutes defining juvenile court jurisdiction.

Appendix C. Juveniles adjudicated as adults in the Federal system

Juveniles may be adjudicated as adults in the Federal system if the offense charged was a violent felony or drug trafficking or importation and if the offense was committed after the juvenile's 15th birthday. Or, if the juvenile possessed a firearm during a violent offense, the juvenile may be adjudicated as an adult if the offense was committed after the juvenile's 13th birthday.

Before proceeding against a juvenile in Federal court, the U.S. attorney must certify to the court a substantial Federal interest in the case and at least one of the following:

• The State does not have jurisdiction.

• The State refuses to assume jurisdiction.

• The State with jurisdiction does not have adequate programs or services for juvenile offenders.

• The offense charged is a violent felony, a drug trafficking or importation offense, or a firearm offense (18 U.S.C. Section 5032).

While the U.S. Department of Justice does not systematically collect information on juvenile transfers to Federal courts, it is estimated that during the 12 months ending September 30, 1994, 65 juveniles were referred to the Attorney General for transfer to adult status.

Source: Juvenile Delinquents in the Federal Criminal Justice System, 1995, BJS Bulletin, NCJ-163066, 1997, pp. 1–2.

512 weighted juvenile cases in criminal courts during the month of May in the 75 most populous counties. In 1992 data on 13,206 sample felony cases were collected from the 40 sampled jurisdictions, representing 480 weighted juvenile cases in criminal courts during May in the 75 most populous counties. In 1994, 14,691 sample felony cases were collected from the 39 sampled jurisdictions, representing 646 weighted juvenile cases in criminal courts during May in the 75 most populous counties. Cases that could not be classified into one of the four major crime categories (violent, property, drug, or public-order) because of incomplete information were omitted from the analysis. Data collection was supervised by the Pretrial Services Resource Center of Washington, D.C.

For counties found in the SCPS and NJCDA samples see Appendix D. Because the data came from a sample, a sampling error (standard error) is associated with each reported number. In general, if the difference between two SCPS-generated numbers is greater than twice the standard error for that difference, we can say that we are 95% confident of a real difference and that the apparent difference is not simply the result of using a sample rather than the entire population. All differences discussed in this report were statistically significant at or above the 95-percent confidence level.

National Juvenile Court Data Archive (NJCDA)

Data for juvenile defendants processed in the juvenile courts of the 75 largest counties in 1990, 1992, and 1994 were provided by Howard Snyder of the National Center for Juve-

Appendix D. Jurisdictions in the Nation's 75 largest counties used in the State Court Processing Statistics and National Juvenile Court Data Archive samples

State/county	Adult courts 1990	1992	1994	Juvenile courts 1990	1992	1994
Alabama						
Jefferson			■	■	■	■
Arizona						
Maricopa	■	■	■	■	■	■
Pima			■			
California						
Alameda			■	■	■	■
Contra Costa				■		
Fresno						
Los Angeles	■	■	■	■	■	■
Orange	■			■	■	■
Riverside				■		
Sacramento	■	■	■	■		
San Bernardino	■	■	■	■	■	
San Diego	■	■	■	■	■	■
San Francisco		■		■	■	■
San Mateo				■		
Santa Clara	■		■	■	■	■
Ventura			■	■	■	■
Connecticut						
Fairfield				■	■	■
Hartford				■	■	■
New Haven				■	■	■
Dist. of Columbia						
Washington	■	■				
Florida						
Broward	■	■	■			
Dade	■	■	■	■	■	■
Duval	■	■	■	■	■	■
Hillsborough	■	■				■
Orange						■
Palm Beach	■	■		■	■	■
Pinellas	■	■		■	■	■
Georgia						
Fulton	■	■				
Hawaii						
Honolulu	■		■	■		
Illinois						
Cook	■	■	■	■	■	■
Du Page			■			
Kentucky						
Jefferson			■			
Maryland						
Baltimore				■	■	■
Baltimore City			■	■	■	■
Montgomery		■		■	■	■
Pr. George's				■	■	■
Massachusetts						
Essex	■	■				
Middlesex			■			
Suffolk	■	■				

State/county	Adult courts 1990	1992	1994	Juvenile courts 1990	1992	1994
Michigan						
Wayne	■	■	■			
Minnesota						
Hennepin				■	■	■
Missouri						
Jackson		■		■	■	■
St. Louis	■	■		■	■	■
New Jersey						
Bergen					■	■
Essex	■	■	■			■
Middlesex						■
New York						
Bronx	■	■	■	■	■	■
Erie	■	■	■	■	■	■
Kings	■	■	■	■	■	■
Monroe	■	■	■	■	■	■
Nassau						
New York	■	■	■	■	■	■
Queens	■	■	■	■	■	■
Suffolk		■		■	■	■
Westchester				■	■	■
Ohio						
Cuyahoga				■	■	■
Franklin				■	■	■
Hamilton	■					
Oklahoma						
Oklahoma	■	■				
Pennsylvania						
Allegheny	■	■	■	■	■	■
Montgomery	■	■	■	■	■	■
Philadelphia	■	■	■	■	■	■
Tennessee						
Shelby	■	■				■
Texas						
Dallas	■	■	■			
Harris	■	■	■			
Tarrant	■	■				
Utah						
Salt Lake	■	■	■	■	■	■
Virginia						
Fairfax	■	■				
Washington						
King	■	■	■	■	■	■
Wisconsin						
Milwaukee		■	■			

nile Justice (NCJJ). The data were provided for counties matching those in the SCPS program for the respective years. The juvenile court sample includes only those youths age 15 or older in formally processed delinquency cases not transferred to criminal court. Defendants processed informally in the juvenile justice system were not included in this analysis. Due to the nature of the sample, standard errors cannot be calculated because the probability of selection was unknown.

In Florida, 67 counties are administered in 11 juvenile justice districts. These districts contain one or more counties, and each county is in only one district. In the juvenile court data, cases from different counties could not be distinguished within a specific district. As a result, this analysis includes data from any Florida district that contains at least one sampled county. The Florida districts included are the following: District 4 (Baker, Clay, Duval, Flagler, Nassau, St. Johns, and Volusia); District 5 (Pasco and Pinellas); District 6 (Hardee, Highlands, Hillsborough, Manatee, and Polk); District 7 (Brevard, Orange, Osceola, and Seminole); District 9 (Indian River, Martin, Okeechobee, Palm Beach, and St. Lucie); District 10 (Broward); and District 11 (Dade and Monroe).

This and other BJS reports as well as State Court Processing Statistics are available from our Internet site: *http://www.ojp.usdoj.gov/bjs/*

Data used in this report are available from the National Archive of Criminal Justice Data at the University of Michigan, 1-800-999-0960. The BJS data sets are archived as ICPSR 6855, 2344, 6508, 6634, 6882, and 2038.

The Bureau of Justice Statistics is the statistical agency of the U.S. Department of Justice. Jan M. Chaiken, Ph.D., is director.

Shay Bilchik is administrator of the Office of Juvenile Justice and Delinquency Prevention, which is the primary Federal agency responsible for addressing the issue of juvenile crime and delinquency and the problem of missing and exploited children.

The National Juvenile Court Data Archive at the National Center for Juvenile Justice (NCJJ) is supported by OJJDP Grant 95-JN-FX-0008.

Kevin J. Strom and Steven K. Smith, Ph.D., of BJS and Howard N. Snyder, Ph.D., of NOJJ wrote this report. Melissa Sickmund, Ph.D., of NCJJ provided assistance and helpful comments. At BJS, Greg Steadman, Tim Hart, and Devon Adams provided statistical review. Tom Hester and Yvonne Boston edited the report, which was produced by Ms. Boston. Marilyn Marbrook supervised final publication and dissemination.

September 1998, NCJ 165815

Juvenile Delinquents in the Federal Criminal Justice System

John Scalia
BJS Statistician

During 1995, U.S. attorneys filed cases against 240 persons for alleged acts of juvenile delinquency. Of these, 122 cases were adjudicated in Federal court, representing 0.2% of the 56,243 cases (both adult and juvenile) adjudicated during 1995. Almost half of juvenile delinquency cases involved a violent offense (32%) or a drug offense (15%). Federal prosecutors declined further action against 228 other juveniles referred to them.

Many of the juveniles adjudicated in the Federal system are Native Americans. When Native American tribal jurisdictions lack resources or jurisdiction or when there is a substantial Federal interest, a U.S. attorney may initiate juvenile delinquency proceedings. Further, the Federal Government has jurisdiction over certain offenses committed in Indian country (18 U.S.C. § 1152 and 1153).

In Federal courts, juveniles adjudicated delinquent were about half as likely as convicted adults to receive a sentence of confinement (*Federal Criminal Case Processing*, 1982–93, NCJ-160088, May 1996). The average length of confinement ordered was 34 months. During 1995 the majority (59%) of juveniles adjudicated delinquent were placed on probation.

Highlights

- During 1995, 468 juveniles were referred to Federal prosecutors for investigation—49% of these cases were declined for further action.
- During 1995, 122 juveniles were adjudicated as delinquent in the Federal courts—47% for either a violent or drug offense.
- During the 12 months ending September 1994, an additional 65 persons who allegedly committed acts of delinquency were referred for prosecution as an adult by a U.S. attorney.
- 37% of juveniles adjudicated delinquent were committed to a correctional facility. The average length of commitment was 34 months.
- 61% of juvenile delinquents confined by the Federal Bureau of Prisons were Native Americans.

Federal Juvenile Delinquency Act

An act of *juvenile delinquency* is a violation of Federal law committed by a person prior to age 18 which would have been a crime if committed by an adult (18 U.S.C. § 5031). Under Federal law, a person accused of an act of *juvenile delinquency* may be processed as a *juvenile* provided the person has not attained age 21.

Federal juvenile delinquency proceedings

Adjudication of juveniles in the Federal system is limited. Federal law requires that prosecutors restrict proceedings against juveniles to those cases in which they certify to the court that there is a substantial Federal interest in the case and—

- the State does not have jurisdiction or refuses to assume jurisdiction;
- the State with jurisdiction does not have adequate programs or services for juvenile offenders; or
- the offense charged is a violent felony, a drug trafficking or importation offense, or a firearms offense (18 U.S.C. § 5032).

Unlike State-level criminal justice systems, the Federal system does not have a separate juvenile justice component. Juveniles are adjudicated by a U.S. district court judge or magistrate in a closed hearing without a jury. After a juvenile has been adjudicated delinquent, a hearing concerning the disposition of the juvenile is held.

From *Bureau of Justice Statistics Special Report,* February 1997, pp. 1-4. Reprinted by permission of the National Institute of Justice, National Criminal Justice Reference Service.

During the disposition hearing, a juvenile may be ordered to pay restitution, be placed on probation, or be committed to a correctional facility.

Juveniles under age 18 may be placed on probation or committed until they reach age 21. Juveniles between ages 18 and 21 may be placed on probation for up to 3 years or confined for up to 5 years, depending on the severity of the offense.

Transfer to adult status

A person who committed an offense prior to age 18 may be adjudicated as an adult if—

• the offense charged was a violent felony or drug trafficking or importation offense *and* if the offense was committed *after* the person's 15th birthday.

• the person possessed a firearm during a violent offense and the offense was committed *after* the person's 13th birthday.

• the person had been previously adjudicated delinquent of a violent felony or drug offense (18 U.S.C. § 5032).

While the Department of Justice does not systematically collect infor-

mation describing Federal juvenile transfers, it estimates that during the 12 months ending September 30, 1994, 65 persons accused of delinquency were referred to the Attorney

General for transfer to adult status. It is not known how many were charged directly as adults based on their prior criminal records.

Juveniles investigated by U.S. attorneys

During 1995, 468 juveniles were referred to Federal prosecutors for

investigation and prosecution. The U.S. attorneys declined to proceed against 49% of those juveniles referred to them—two-thirds of that

Table 1. Juveniles in delinquency proceedings terminated in U.S. district courts, 1989–95

Most serious offense	Number of Federal delinquency proceedings terminated						
	1989	1990	1991	1992	1993	1994	1996
Total*	206	217	194	144	124	134	122
Violent offenses	49	66	62	43	41	56	34
Property offenses	65	40	37	53	30	18	27
Fraudulent	11	4	4	2	3	3	4
Other	54	36	33	51	27	15	23
Drug offenses	66	52	44	31	28	38	16
Public-order offenses	26	52	49	17	25	17	28
Regulatory	1	3	21	4	7	2	10
Other	25	49	28	13	18	15	18

*Total includes cases for which an offense category could not be determined.

Data source: Administrative Office of the U.S. Courts, criminal docket data file, annual.

Juveniles in the State courts

In contrast to the Federal system, the State systems frequently charge juveniles with delinquency. During 1994 there were more than 1.5 million delinquency cases in courts with juvenile jurisdiction. Of these, almost 855,000 were formally processed in the juvenile justice system. Nearly half (49%) of those juveniles formally processed at the State level were charged with property offenses (table). Few (9%) were charged with drug offenses.

Approximately 58% of those juveniles formally charged at the State level were adjudicated delinquent (not shown in a table). Similar to those in the Federal system, approximately 29% of those juveniles adjudicated delinquent were committed to a correctional or other residential facility and 56% were placed on probation. Almost a third

(31%) of those charged with a violent offense were committed.

During 1994 less than 2% of all juveniles charged with offenses in the State courts were waived to adult status. Similar to the Federal system, approximately 44% of juveniles transferred were charged with a violent offense. Drug offenders represented few (11%) of the transfers.

While 12,300 juveniles were judicially waived to adult status during 1994, others were statutorily excluded from juvenile court jurisdiction based on their age and offense or concurrent jurisdiction provisions. In 13 States the upper age of juvenile court jurisdiction is 15 or 16 years. Many States also exclude certain serious offenses—such as murder and other violent offenses—from juvenile court jurisdiction.

Delinquency cases in State courts, 1994

Most serious offense	Number	Adult transfers
Total	855,200	12,300
Personal offenses	196,900	5,400
Property offenses	415,800	4,600
Drug offenses	73,400	1,300
Public-order offenses	169,100	1,000

Source: Jeffrey A. Butts, Howard N. Snyder, Terrence A. Finnegan *et al.*, *Juvenile Court Statistics 1994*, Office of Juvenile Justice and Delinquency Prevention (1996).

number immediately and the remainder subsequently.

Juveniles adjudicated in U.S. district courts

Few cases involving juvenile delinquents are processed in U.S. district courts because of statutory restrictions. Between 1989 and 1994, the number of juveniles adjudicated for acts of delinquency in U.S. district courts ranged from 217 during 1990 to 122 during 1995 (table 1). The District of South Dakota (12.3%), the District of Arizona (10.7%), the District of Montana (10.7%), and the Eastern District of North Carolina (9.8%) accounted for approximately 44% of the total Federal juvenile caseload during 1995 (not shown in a table).

Offense committed

Consistent with the statutory directive, juveniles charged with acts of juvenile delinquency in U.S. district courts were most frequently charged with more serious offenses such as drug (15%) or violent (32%) offenses.

Adjudication

Of the 122 juveniles charged with delinquency whose cases were terminated in the U.S. district courts during 1995, approximately 81% were adjudicated delinquent. Of adjudicated delinquents 87% admitted to the facts alleged in the indictment (or information) and 13% were adjudicated delinquent after a hearing (not shown in a table). Of juveniles who were not adjudicated delinquent, 90% had the charges dismissed and 10% were found not delinquent.

Disposition/sanction imposed

Of those juveniles adjudicated delinquent during 1995, 37% were committed to a correctional facility, 59% were placed on probation, and 4% received a sentence that did not include supervision or confinement (table 2).

Table 2. Disposition of juveniles adjudicated delinquent in U.S. district courts, 1995

Type of disposition	Number	Percent
Total	99	100.0%
Confinement only	32	32.3
Confinement and probation	5	5.1
Probation only	58	58.6
No probation	4	4.0

Data source: Administrative Office of the U.S. Courts, criminal docket data file, annual.

Approximately 35% of those juveniles committed to a correctional facility were adjudicated delinquent of a violent offense. Of those 37 juveniles committed during 1995, the average length of commitment required was 34 months (not shown in a table).

Juvenile delinquents confined by the Federal Bureau of Prisons

As of September 30, 1994, 124 juvenile delinquents were confined in a State juvenile correctional facility under contract to the Federal Bureau of

Table 3. Juvenile delinquents confined by the Federal Bureau of Prisons, 1994

Most serious offense	Number	Percent
Total*	124	100.0%
Violent offenses	77	64.7
Property offenses	16	13.4
Drug offenses	17	14.3
Public-order offenses	9	7.6

*Includes cases for which an offense category could not be determined.

Data source: U.S. Department of Justice, Bureau of Prisons, SENTRY system data file, fiscal year ending September 30, 1994.

Prisons (table 3). (The Federal Bureau of Prisons does not have its own facilities for juvenile delinquents.) Most (64%) were adjudicated delinquent of a violent offense.

Sixty-one percent of the confined juvenile delinquents were Native Americans (table 4). The majority (81%) of the Native Americans confined were adjudicated delinquent of a violent offense—sex offenses (32%), assault (28%), negligent manslaughter (20%), and robbery (1%). The remainder were adjudicated delinquent of a property offense.

Almost all (88%) of the juveniles confined were U.S. citizens; 4% were Mexican citizens, and 3% were Chinese citizens.

During 1994, 102 juvenile delinquents were released by the Federal Bureau of Prisons from a juvenile correctional facility. The average time served was—

- 14 months for all those released
- 21 months for drug offenders
- 17 months for violent offenders.

Table 4. Demographic characteristics of juvenile delinquents confined by the Federal Bureau of Prisons, 1994

Characteristic	Number	Percent
Total	124	100.0%
Race/ethnicity		
White	9	7.3
Black	15	12.1
Hispanic	19	15.3
Native American	75	60.5
Asian	6	4.8
Citizenship		
United States	109	87.9
Mexico	5	4.0
China	4	3.2
Other	6	4.9

Data source: U.S. Department of Justice, Bureau of Prisons, SENTRY system data file, fiscal year ending September 30, 1994.

Coordinating Council on Juvenile Justice and Delinquency Prevention

The Coordinating Council on Juvenile Justice and Delinquency Prevention, a council within the executive branch of Government, was established by the Juvenile Justice and Delinquency Prevention Act of 1974 (42 U.S.C. § 5616). The Coordinating Council encourages cooperation among the Federal agencies with juvenile delinquency programs.

Under the Act, the Coordinating Council is required to—
- review the programs and practices of Federal agencies concerning juveniles in their custody
- review the reasons why Federal agencies take juveniles into custody
- recommend how to improve Federal practices and facilities for holding juveniles in custody
- report on the degree to which Federal funds are used to deinstitutionalize status offenders, separate incarcerated juveniles from adults,

and remove juveniles from adult jails and lockups.

In 1995 the Coordinating Council established the Policy Committee on Youth in Federal Custody. The Policy Committee was charged with developing policies and procedures for apprehending and maintaining custody of juveniles, providing assistance to agencies addressing unique youth custody issues, and reporting annually on the number of juveniles taken into Federal custody.

As part of its study, the Policy Committee has surveyed Federal agencies on their policies and practices on taking juveniles into custody and on placing those juveniles into secure custody. In addition, the Policy Committee asked BJS to describe juveniles adjudicated in the Federal criminal justice system. The Policy Committee will issue a report and recommendations to the Coordinating Council.

The Bureau of Justice Statistics is the statistical agency of the U.S. Department of Justice. Jan M. Chaiken, Ph.D., is director.

BJS Special Reports address a special topic in depth from one or more datasets that cover many topics.

John Scalia of the Bureau of Justice Statistics wrote this report. William J. Sabol of the Urban Institute provided statistical review. Gina Wood of the Office of Juvenile Justice and Delinquency Prevention and Steve Shandy of the Criminal Division, Department of Justice, provided assistance in the preparation of this report. Tom Hester and Tina Dorsey edited the report. Marilyn Marbrook, assisted by Yvonne Boston, administered production.

February 1997, NCJ-163066

Data presented in this report may be obtained from the National Archive of Criminal Justice Data at the University of Michigan, 1-800-999-0960. The report and data are also available on the Internet: http://www.ojp.usdoj.gov/bjs/

Methodology

The primary source of data presented in this report is the BJS Federal Justice Statistics Program (FJSP) database. The FJSP database is presently constructed from the source files provided by the U.S. attorneys, the Federal courts, the U.S. Sentencing Commission, and the Federal Bureau of Prisons. Data tabulations, except where otherwise indicated, were prepared from BJS staff analysis of source agency datasets.

Juvenile delinquency proceedings were identified using a delinquency proceeding code included in the courts' database, the statute(s) charged (18 U.S.C. § 5031 et seq.), and a descriptive label in the name field—juvenile records in the database typically do not include identifying information such as names. Juveniles under jurisdiction of the Bureau of Prisons are housed in facilities specifically for juveniles.

With Juvenile Courts in Chaos, Critics Propose Their Demise

JUSTICE BESIEGED

By FOX BUTTERFIELD

CHICAGO—The nation's juvenile courts, long a troubled backwater of the criminal justice system, have been so overwhelmed by the increase in violent teen-age crime and the breakdown of the family that judges and politicians are debating a solution that was once unthinkable: abolishing the system and trying most minors as adults.

The crisis began building a decade ago, when prosecutors responded to the growth in high-profile youth crime by pushing for the trials of greater numbers of children, dramatically raising caseloads.

But the courts have become so choked that by all accounts they are even less effective than before, with more juveniles prosecuted but fewer convicted and no evidence of a drop in rearrest rates for those who go to prison.

The resulting situation angers people across the political spectrum, from those who believe the juvenile court is too lenient, to those who feel it fails to prevent troubled children from becoming ensnared in a life of crime.

In interviews around the country, judges, probation officers, prosecutors and defense lawyers described a juvenile court system in perhaps the worst chaos of its history.

In Chicago, where the first juvenile court was created in 1899, judges today preside over assembly-line justice, hearing an average of 60 cases a day, about six minutes per case. In New Orleans, public defenders have to represent their poor clients with no office, no telephone, no court records and little chance to discuss the case before trial. In New York, where the recent case of Malcolm Shabazz—who admitted setting the fire that killed his grandmother, Malcolm X's widow—focused new attention on Family Court, some officials say it is time to junk the system.

Almost everywhere, with juvenile courts starved for money, record-keeping is so primitive that often the judge, the prosecutor and the defense attorney have different records on the same defendant, making an accurate assessment of the case impossible. And because the courts cannot afford their own warrant squads, young defendants sometimes fail to show up for trial or simply skip out of the courtroom with virtual impunity.

Despite calls for tougher justice, the overcrowding and lack of resources mean that only a small percentage of the young people who move through the juvenile justice system are imprisoned, although there are other forms of punishment, the most common of which is probation.

Of the 1,555,200 delinquency cases referred by the police to prosecutors nationwide in 1994, 855,200, or just over half, resulted in what in adult criminal courts would be called indictments, said Jeffrey Butts, at the National Center for Juvenile Justice. Of these, Mr. Butts said, 495,000 defendants were found guilty.

In turn, 141,300 of these cases resulted in a juvenile's being incarcerated. That is 9 percent of those originally sent to prosecutors by the police.

By contrast, in adult criminal court, which is explicitly intended to be punitive, 90 percent to 95 percent of defendants who have been indicted plead guilty in a plea bargain, often as a way to win a lighter punishment. The philosophy of juvenile court traditionally was to rehabilitate rather than punish young offenders, a premise that has come under attack in recent years.

Congress is poised to pass legislation, backed by President Clinton, that would provide Federal grants to states that sharply increase the number of young people they try in adult court. The legislation, already passed by the House and likely to be adopted soon by the Senate, would further undermine the authority of the juvenile court at a time when many specialists predict there will be a new wave of youth crime, as the number of teen-agers increases by 15 percent in the next decade.

"The Family Court is bankrupt," said Peter Reinharz, chief of New York City's juvenile prosecution unit. "It's time to sell everything off and start over."

Mr. Reinharz is a longtime critic of the juvenile court, but even its staunchest defenders are now troubled by what they see.

"It is no longer just the chronic problems that have long plagued the court, like overcrowding and making do with less," said Bart Lubow, a senior associate of the Annie E. Casey Foundation who has studied juvenile courts around the nation. "Now there's a crisis of confidence, since the very notion that has been its cornerstone, that children are different from adults and therefore need to be treated differently, is in question."

Among the issues swirling in the nation's 3,000 juvenile courts are the following:

• As pressure to get tough on young criminals has increased, the number of juveniles arrested who are prosecuted in court has climbed to 55 percent in 1994 from 45 percent in 1985. But the percentage of young people convicted has not kept pace, rising to 33 percent in 1994 from 31 percent a decade earlier.

In Chicago, the figures show an even more dramatic effect of overloading the system. The Cook County State's Attorney has increased the number of juveniles he prosecutes to 85 percent of all those sent to him by the police, but about 70 percent of these cases are dismissed for lack of evidence or the failure of witnesses to appear, according to a new study by the Children and Family Justice Center of

the Northwestern University School of Law.

"This is the dirty little secret of Cook County," said David Reed, the lead author of the report. "You have lots more cases but almost the same number of judges and prosecutors, and they can only do so much work and prove a certain number guilty. So all these kids are brought in on criminal charges and then most are let go. It fosters cynicism about the court, makes the public and crime victims mad and teaches young people that justice is a joke."

• With an angry public demanding harsher punishments, it is becoming increasingly difficult for judges to differentiate between defendants who may have committed a youthful indiscretion and those who are on their way to a lifetime of crime. The distinction is critical. Almost 60 percent of those teenagers sent to juvenile court for the first time never return. But every time a young person is sent back to court, his likelihood of being arrested again increases until recidivism rates reach 75 percent by a fifth appearance, said Howard Snyder, of the National Center for Juvenile Justice.

• Despite a rush by legislators in all 50 states over the past decade to pass laws trying young people in adult court, there is no evidence that being convicted in adult court or sentenced to adult prison is more effective in reducing youth crime than the juvenile justice route. A new study of 5,476 juvenile criminals in Florida, which followed them from their arrest in 1987 through 1994, concluded that those tried as adults committed new crimes sooner after their release from prison, and perpetrated more serious and violent crimes, than those tried as juveniles.

Charles Frazier, a sociology professor at the University of Florida and a co-author of the report, said that keeping young people in the juvenile justice system works better because juvenile institutions provide more education and psychological treatment for inmates, helping offenders rehabilitate themselves. By

contrast, adult prisons now are more punitive and have largely abandoned trying to change criminals' behavior.

"Ultimately, you are going to release all these people back into the community, and the juvenile justice system does a better job of reclaiming them," Professor Frazier said.

19th-Century Origin
Firmly but Gently Disciplining Youths

The criticism of the juvenile court misses a fundamental point, some specialists believe. With the breakdown of the family, can any court system, juvenile or adult, do the job society once did: instill discipline and values in children, punish them if they are bad and then help redeem them?

"The juvenile court was set up 100 years ago, in a very different America, to help cure kids of immigrant families with manageable problems, like truancy, petty thefts and fighting," said Jeffrey Fagan, the director of the Center for Violence Research and Prevention at Columbia University.

As envisioned by the pioneering social worker, Jane Addams, the juvenile court was to be a surrogate parent and the judge a kindly doctor, seeking to understand the social conditions that had led the child astray, the way a doctor would study a disease. This paternalism was reflected in the informality of the courtroom, with the judge sitting at an ordinary table, not behind a bench, and wearing only street clothes, not a robe.

The court's guiding principle was to do what was "in the best interest of the child," not to protect the community or insure the child's constitutional rights. So punishments were kept light, since children were thought to still be in the process of forming their personalities, and thus more amenable to reform than adults. And all proceedings and records were kept confidential.

An antiseptic nomenclature was even invented to avoid stigmatizing children. A boy was "taken into custody," not arrested. He had a "petition of delinquency" drawn against him, rather than being charged. And there were no convictions, only "adjudications," and no sentences, only "placements."

But today, poverty, joblessness and violent teen-age crime seem far worse than they were in the 1890's, often making the court's customs appear a quaint anachronism.

Also, as a result, Professor Fagan said, "The juvenile court can no longer do what it was set up to do. It certainly can't do what the public expects it to do, control juvenile crime."

Statistics only hint at the magnitude of the troubles the court is asked to resolve.

Since 1960, the number of delinquency cases handled by juvenile courts nationwide has risen almost four times, to 1.55 million in 1994. During the same period, the number of cases involving abused or neglected children, which are also handled by juvenile courts, has increased five times faster than even the delinquency cases, said Mr. Butts of the National Center for Juvenile Justice. And these abused and neglected children are often the very ones who become delinquents.

Among delinquency cases, violent crimes are rising the fastest. From 1985 to 1994, juvenile crimes involving weapons soared 156 percent, murders jumped 144 percent and aggravated assaults were up 134 percent. Property crimes were up 25 percent.

A Case in Point

In a Chicago Court, Beating the System

Perhaps the most revealing place to see the troubles is in Chicago, home to the nation's oldest and largest juvenile court. The Chicago court is not the best; that may be in Louisville, San Jose or Oakland, where the judges command wide respect. Nor is it the most beleaguered; that distinction may belong to Baltimore or New Orleans. Cook County is just a good example of what goes on in a high-volume juvenile court.

A tiny 13-year-old defendant, so short he could barely see Judge William Hibbler seated behind the bench, was on trial for murder.

The defendant—who will remain unidentified in accordance with the court's rules of confidentiality—was wearing an Atlanta Braves baseball jacket, and he looked more like a team mascot than a hardened criminal. But the teen-ager was charged with first-degree murder for shooting a man who was trying to buy crack cocaine.

At an even younger age, he was arrested for armed robbery and burglary, though without being sent to prison. This time, after his arrest for murder, he had been allowed to return home because the court had failed to give him a hearing within the 36-hour limit specified for juveniles.

While free awaiting trial for murder, he had stolen a car.

Neither his mother nor father was in court. His father had died of alcohol poisoning; his mother, a crack addict, was in a boot camp on a drug charge.

Judge Hibbler, the presiding judge of the delinquency division of the Cook County Juvenile Court, wore a black robe, a small sign of how the court has shifted from its original

The Juvenile Caseload: A Closer Look

THE DELINQUENCY CASELOAD HAS SURGED . . .
Estimated number of delinquency cases handled in juvenile courts around the country. A youth may be involved in more than one case.

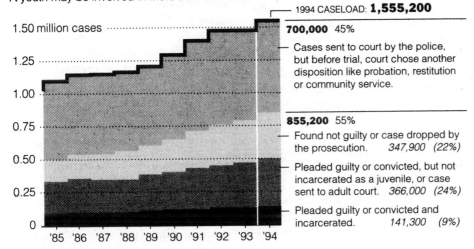

— 1994 CASELOAD: **1,555,200**

700,000 45%
— Cases sent to court by the police, but before trial, court chose another disposition like probation, restitution or community service.

855,200 55%
— Found not guilty or case dropped by the prosecution. *347,900 (22%)*
— Pleaded guilty or convicted, but not incarcerated as a juvenile, or case sent to adult court. *366,000 (24%)*
— Pleaded guilty or convicted and incarcerated. *141,300 (9%)*

. . . ESPECIALLY FOR SERIOUS CRIMES . . .
Change in cases for selected crimes.

VIOLENT CRIME*	CASES IN 1994	CHANGE SINCE '85
Murder	3,000	+144%
Aggravated assault	85,300	134
Robbery	37,000	53
Forcible rape	5,400	25
OTHER SERIOUS CRIME		
Weapons offenses	48,800	+156%
Simple assault	177,700	91

*The four crimes in the F.B.I.'s violent crime index.

. . . REFLECTING MORE ARRESTS
Arrests per 100,000 for violent crimes.*

Ages 10 to 17

All ages

Sources: National Center for Juvenile Justice; Office of Juvenile Justice and Delinquency Prevention; F.B.I.

The New York Times

informality and evolved, in the judge's phrase, into more of a "mini criminal court."

The courtroom is inside the Cook County Juvenile Center, a modern structure a block long and eight stories high that from the outside looks more like an office building than a courthouse with a juvenile jail attached. The building was recently reconstructed as part of an effort to reverse the turmoil overtaking juvenile court.

Inside, however, the waiting rooms are still painted a dingy brown and are jammed with largely black and Hispanic families, many of them holding crying babies. In the men's rooms the toilets are broken and the metal mirrors are scrawled with graffiti.

These dilapidated conditions, said Mr. Lubow of the Casey Foundation, "basically say to the families and kids who come to juvenile court that we don't take them seriously, that we value them less as people."

Now, after talking with his lawyer, the youth begrudgingly confessed to murder as part of a plea bargain. Judge Hibbler then solemnly ordered that he "be committed to the Illinois Department of Corrections, Juvenile Division, till 21 years of age."

The boy smirked. He knew he had beaten the system again. He could be free in as little as five years. Without the plea bargain, he could have been transferred to adult court and faced a minimum sentence of 20 years.

It was the kind of case that infuriates conservatives and others, suggesting that juvenile court is little more than a revolving door.

But it was also the kind of case that makes children's rights advocates argue that juvenile court is failing to help young people from troubled families by intervening early enough to prevent them from becoming ensnared in a life of crime.

Even many judges themselves, who are often the only defenders of the juvenile court, concur that the court is foundering. But the judges

tend to blame the politicians who have passed laws to try more teenagers in adult courts.

"There is a crisis," Judge Hibbler acknowledged. But, he contended, "Children don't stop being children just because they commit a crime, and calling for an end of the juvenile court is the same as saying we should do away with grammar schools and junior high schools and just put everyone in college."

Clogging the Courts
Convictions Flat As Caseload Soars

In the traditional juvenile court, probation officers played a key role.

They presided at what is still widely called "intake," or arraignment in adult terms. After the police decided which juveniles to send to court—usually about half were dismissed with the equivalent of a parking ticket—the probation officers would screen out children whose crimes were petty or who had no record. Nationwide, they filtered out about half the cases referred by the police.

But in Chicago in the late 1980's, in response to the epidemic of crack cocaine and the rise of teen-age gun violence, Richard M. Daley, then the Cook County State's Attorney, wrestled this power away from the court probation department. To appear tough on crime, he began prosecuting 97 percent of the cases forwarded to him by the police, according to an analysis by The Chicago Sun-Times.

Mr. Daley is now mayor of Chicago, and that figure is down to 85 percent, the State's Attorney's office says.

But Bernardine Dohrn, the director of the Children and Family Justice Center at Northwestern University, said that prosecuting such a high proportion of cases has overwhelmed the court, resulting in about 70 percent of the cases filed by the State's Attorney being dropped before trial.

A new study by Ms. Dohrn's center has found that while the number of delinquency cases heard each month has more than tripled in the last decade, the number of convictions has remained almost flat.

"They are clogging the system," Ms. Dohrn said, "and when you do this wholesale, you drive kids into the system who don't belong there and you don't find the kids who aren't in school and are getting into serious trouble. They are able to pass through for a long time without being stopped. So it's a double whammy, and dangerous."

Probation officers are also supposed to enforce the most commonly used punishment in juvenile court, probation—a court order requiring a young person to go to school or find a job and obey a home curfew the rest of the day.

But no one likes probation: not judges, who want more innovative alternatives; not the offenders, who chafe at the loss of freedom, and not the police or prosecutors, who regard probation as a farce. Worst of all, probation further undercuts the credibility of the court.

For judges, probation is part of a terrible dilemma. "I really have only two major choices," said Glenda Hatchett, the presiding judge of the Fulton County Juvenile Court in Atlanta.

"I can place these kids in incarceration, where they will learn to become better criminals, or I can send them home on probation, back to where they got in trouble in the first place," Judge Hatchett said.

Because governments have always regarded the juvenile court as a "poor stepchild" of the criminal justice system, Judge Hatchett said, there isn't money for the kinds of programs she believes would help, by reaching at-risk children and their parents when the children are 4, 5 or 6 years old, before it is too late.

Shifting Roles

Probation Officers Become Enforcers

Laura Donnelly is a Chicago probation officer with a master's degree in social work.

That makes her part of a vanishing breed, because today more and more probation officers have degrees in criminal justice. The change reflects the transition of the juvenile court from its origins in social welfare, treating the best interests of the child, to a criminal justice agency.

Ms. Donnelly has a caseload of 45 youths whom she visits a few times a month at home, school or work to make sure they are where they are supposed to be. Three of her clients have disappeared completely. She is confident she could find them, if she had enough time, which she does not.

She could also get a court-ordered arrest warrant, but the juvenile court cannot afford its own warrant squad, and police officers she knows are reluctant to spend time looking for children on warrants, unless the person is arrested on a new charge.

"A lot of officers don't want to waste their time on kiddie court when the judge is going to release the kid anyway," she said.

Ms. Donnelly stopped by a house on Chicago's South Side where one of her clients lived with his grandmother and 13 cousins, since his mother was a crack addict who couldn't be found. A husky 16-year-old, the boy was on probation for selling crack and was confined to his home 24 hours a day unless accompanied by his grandmother.

A charge of auto theft had been dropped when he repeatedly failed to appear for trial and the witnesses in the case tired of going to court without any result. That is a common way for young defendants to win.

Ms. Donnelly reminded the boy that he had another court date in two days, relating to a charge of theft and battery incurred while he was supposed to have been confined to home. He had forgotten about the appearance.

It was another day's work for Ms. Donnelly. "These kids have had nothing but chaos in their lives," she said. "That's what we have to overcome, to give them as much structure and consistency as we can."

"But how," she asked, "do you replace the absence of the family?" Sometimes she thinks the only answer is to move in herself. But she knows that would not work either.

A Move for Change

Young Suspects In Adult Courts

All these troubles have sparked a growing movement to drastically restructure and perhaps abolish the juvenile court.

Leading the charge are conservative politicians who have passed laws in all 50 states allowing juveniles to be tried in adult court and sent to adult prison.

In Illinois a person under 17 may be tried in adult court for crimes including murder, carjacking and armed robbery as well as possession of drugs or weapons within 1,000 feet of a school or housing project, a provision that disproportionately affects minorities. Illinois also has a version for juveniles of the "three strikes and you're out" law.

Congress is poised to pass the most Draconian law yet, with provisions for $1.5 billion in Federal grants to states that try larger number[s] of young people in adult court and making 14-year-olds subject to trial in Federal court if they commit certain felonies.

"It's the end of the juvenile court," said Ira Schwartz, dean of the School of Social Work at the University of Pennsylvania. "All you would have left is a court for larceny." Such a truncated court would not be financially viable and would probably be scrapped, he suggested.

At the same time, some left-wing legal scholars have also called for abolishing the juvenile court, though for very different reasons. Barry Feld, a professor of law at the University of Minnesota, believes that young people often fail to get adequate legal representation in juvenile court and would fare better in adult court, where they would be more likely to be assigned decent lawyers.

Under his plan, as a further protective measure, juveniles in adult court would be given a "youth discount," or lighter sentences, depending on their age.

Some children's advocates who in the past championed the juvenile court have begun urging still another solution—that the court scale back its judicial role and transfer its functions to community groups or social service agencies that would provide better treatment for young people in trouble.

In the rush to try juveniles in adult courts, some critical questions go unasked. For example, are 13- and 14-year olds really competent to stand trial like adults?

Often such young defendants cannot tell a coherent story to help defend themselves, said Thomas Grisso, a psychiatry professor at the University of Massachusetts Medical Center. What then should the court do? Wait till they are more mature?

As a result of all this ferment, Mr. Schwartz said, "What we have right now in the juvenile court is chaos, with every state moving piecemeal on its own." A century after the creation of the juvenile court, he said, "Unless we take it more seriously, what we are headed for is its abolition by default."

CHILDREN ON TRIAL

At Juvenile Court, an ongoing struggle to mend broken lives

By Louise Kiernan

The mother wore a dirty white T-shirt. She had one hand stuffed inside it, scratching her back as she stood in front of the judge.

While the lawyers around her talked, she rocked on her feet and looked around the courtroom.

Her 5-month-old son lay at her feet, asleep in a car seat. Her 15-month-old daughter played in someone else's arms.

The hearing took less than 10 minutes. The social workers and lawyers agreed that the mother could not care for her children. So did the judge.

With a few comments, the shuffling of some papers and no visible reaction from the mother, these two young children passed into the custody of their great-aunt and the hands of Cook County Juvenile Court.

It was one of 20 or so decisions Judge Lynne Kawamoto would make before lunchtime this Monday, and, as decisions at Juvenile Court go, it was a fairly easy one.

The mother had abandoned the baby with a relative and was found with the elder child in a friend's trash-littered apartment. Nothing distinguished this case from the morning's numbing litany but one fact.

This mother was 14 years old, the daughter of a drug addict. Just three months before, in this courtroom, she had been taken from her mother's custody, just as her children were now taken from hers.

Afterwards, the young mother, her aunt and the two children waited outside the courtroom for their paperwork.

The 14-year-old and her daughter sat at a child-sized table in the waiting area and played with donated toys.

The teenager, a short and heavy girl with unkempt hair, shrugged about losing her children.

"When my mom gets out of rehab, she'll be able to take care of me," she said. "When she come back, everything will be OK."

Then, as the toddler reached for her mother's game, the teenager slapped her arm.

"You're making me mad, girl," she said.

The child let go, and mother and daughter continued to play side-by-side, two children in the arms of a court system that will, for better or worse, help determine the course of their lives.

•

The Cook County Juvenile Center sits at the corner of Roosevelt Road and Ogden Avenue on Chicago's Near West Side.

At 10 stories high, it dominates the neighborhood of iron-faced storefronts and rundown three-flats, a skylight-crowned sugar cube of white steel and glass some of its 2,000 employees call the White Castle.

The nickname reflects both the building's incongruous grandeur and its bustling business. On any given day, the court handles well over 1,000 cases involving children accused of breaking the law or in need of its protection.

It is a place of contrasts as sharp as light and dark. Sunshine floods the halls of the new structure, the so-called west side, which houses the 15 courtrooms dealing with abused and neglected children. Colorful banners of animals hang from the ceilings, and play areas adjoin each waiting room.

The east side, the former court building now converted to hearing only delinquency cases, remains grim, with dark brick walls and high-backed benches where one or two teenagers usually sprawl out sleeping while they wait for their names to be called.

It is a place where people are so jaded that they talk matter-of-factly about the vaginal injuries of girls prostituted by their junkie parents and so soft-hearted that they pass out lollipops in court.

It is a place where mostly white, middle-class lawyers and judges make decisions about the lives of families and children who are mostly black, Hispanic and poor.

For all its contradictions, though, the court is an oddly self-contained community.

The gangbangers are there for selling drugs to the mothers who are there for leaving their children to get high. A sheriff's deputy who searches bags in the mornings waits to be searched herself on Wednesday nights, when she visits a child in the Cook County Juvenile Temporary Detention Center, the facility above the east side courtrooms where young people accused of crimes are housed while they await trial.

Not only do about 700 of the court's charges live in the building, but some of them virtually grow up here.

They start out on one side, as victims, and eventually move to the other, as perpetrators, before they graduate to the adult criminal court system or return as parents accused of hurting their own offspring.

Most days, people begin trickling through the revolving doors by about 9 a.m., a straggling parade of babies swaddled in social workers' arms, neatly braided and beaded little girls with fading electric-cord scars, sullen teenagers in gang colors, sweet-faced 5th graders accused of carrying stolen guns, crackhead mothers who'll slip back out for a fix as soon as they can and crackhead mothers who have fought their way back from addiction for a second chance at parenthood.

Snippets of conversations float above the noise of the hallways and waiting areas:

"I just got out of penitentiary yesterday. I been locked up nine years. And they told me this morning they picked up my son."

"Nah, I'm not active anymore. I got shot in the leg by a Gangster and I used it as an excuse to get out."

"They're saying Ronald sexually abused the kids. If anybody did it, my mother did. I am so tired of this bullshit."

Each story in this building is assigned its own chain of digits and, together, they function like some never-ending catalog of the wrongs done to children and the wrongs done by them.

The list dates back to 1899, when Cook County established the first juvenile court in the United States, and began its work with the case of an 11-year-old boy named Henry Campbell who had stolen from his mother.

The court was created under the ideal of parens patriae, or the state as parent, the philosophy being that it should help children and their families while protecting the public.

Never immune to criticism, the court had become so overburdened and inefficient by 1994 that one report dismissed the system as a "huge, unworkable failure." Another declared a "state of crisis."

Now, as the Juvenile Court of Cook County approaches its 100th anniversary, it is struggling to redefine itself and its mission amid unprecedented societal and political pressures.

Despite opening the new $95 million building in 1994, which doubled the number of courtrooms hearing child protection cases, and making a series of administrative changes, the court still bears a crushing burden.

Some 58,000 abused and neglected children came under its care last year. Another 28,000 are involved with the law. They all live in Chicago; children who live outside the city are sent to one of five suburban court districts.

So the seemingly intractable problems of urban poverty—drug and alcohol abuse, chronic unemployment, poor education, teenage pregnancy and gang violence—bear their most bitter and abundant fruit in the lives of the children who come here.

In the court's first year, the most common offense committed by a young man sent there was truancy. Today, it is possession of crack cocaine.

The concept of parens patriae has largely disappeared from the political and public agenda. The delinquency courtrooms now work more like the criminal system that juvenile court was designed to counter.

Indeed, an increasing number of juveniles end up in the criminal courts, tried as adults.

Government has chipped away at other tenets of the original juvenile justice system, including the confidentiality of hearings and records.

To some extent, then, the court faces a future that looks like a return to the days before it existed.

Yet there are also signs of renewal. Small gestures, like sponsoring musicians to play for children in the waiting areas. And large ones, like the recent launch of a drug treatment program for 300 young people on the city's West Side.

All the threads of the court's work, from the probation officers who check up on delinquents to the researchers who track down absent fathers, extend from the first-floor courtrooms.

What happens in those courtrooms during the course of a week spent there offers a snapshot of the court's struggles and hopes, of how it shapes the future of its children and itself.

Within the span of one hour Tuesday afternoon, five young men appeared before Judge William J. Hibbler.

All of them had been to juvenile court before, and they each kept their wrists crossed behind their backs as if they were wearing handcuffs.

Many children stand this way in the courtroom although the deputies remove their handcuffs before they enter. It is one of the noticeable tics of Juvenile Court. So is the absence of fathers.

Only one young man had his father with him, and the situation of the rest seemed summed up by the mother of the last boy.

The assistant state's attorney, reading from a form, asked her who her son's father was and whether he could be reached. "He's never been in his life," she answered. "I don't want him in his life now."

Hibbler, who is the presiding judge of the juvenile justice division, was conducting detention hearings.

These hearings are the first time many children accused of breaking the law see a judge.

The detention hearing determines if there is probable cause to believe the law was broken, and, if so, whether the child accused of breaking it should be kept in custody until his trial.

That hour's procession included two 16-year-olds accused of carrying guns; a 12-year-old who threw a Molotov cocktail at his school but wasn't there because he was on trial down the hall for another unspecified case; a 16-year-old arrested with crack cocaine; and a 16-year-old facing nine counts of aggravated battery for shooting at a group of people on a front porch. The last young man was identified by one victim who saw him in the court building the day before.

Then, in walked a 12-year-old, shaking, so unfamiliar with the process that he and his mother stood awkwardly in the doorway until the deputy told them to move up to the bench.

He wore a light-blue jacket, bare of the sports logo and college insignias that commonly adorn the clothes of even the tiniest babies in Juvenile Court.

While a police officer talked about him, the boy cried silently. His mother, a heavyset, older woman, wiped his cheek. The officer said he found the boy running down an alley with an unloaded automatic pistol.

"There's probably an easy way to remedy this situation," Hibbler said, not unkindly. "By not being in the alley but at home studying."

He sent the boy back home with his mother until his trial.

To see a child cry was almost a relief, a respite from the march of indifference. It faded with the next case.

The boy was 11, but he had already been placed on probation for aggravated assault with a handgun.

According to court records, he had waved a loaded gun at a 65-year-old man and said, "I've got this gun for you, mother———."

On Tuesday, he was in court for threatening his mother with a brick.

His ears barely reached the bench, and he wore an oversized Nike jacket with khaki pants so big they bunched like an accordion around his ankles. No family was with him.

He stood with his head cocked and his hands behind his back, and when the assistant state's attorney read out the injuries he had allegedly inflicted upon his mother, he interrupted her.

"I didn't push or bite her," he said scornfully.

The judge placed him in the detention center. A deputy led him from the room to a hall behind the courtroom. In the hall, he was handcuffed.

The two boys summarized as well as any the challenges facing the court's juvenile justice division, which Hibbler, when he is not in a courtroom, runs from an eighth-floor office within sight of the West Side neighborhood where he grew up.

"I can yell at one 10-year-old and tell it has an impact on him," Hibbler said. "I'm yelling at another 10-year-old and I can tell he's thinking, 'Does this old guy think I'm impressed by this?'

"What we need to do is create many different approaches. We need to understand that kids rely upon their family structure and create a more comprehensive approach to dealing with the families."

Since he took over the post created for him in 1995, Hibbler has orchestrated several efforts aimed at doing that, including a mandatory after-school program designed to keep children out of trouble during those hours when they might be without adult supervision.

"There are some I would agree we're not able to salvage," he said. "But the number of kids who fit that description is so small, we'll make a mistake if we gear our whole system toward them."

That idea runs somewhat counter to the prevailing public mood to get tough with juvenile crime. The visible expression of that sentiment occurs in the same half-sized courtroom that handles detention hearings in the afternoons.

In the mornings, Judge John W. Rogers Sr., a 19-year veteran of Juvenile Court and onetime Tuskegee airman, presides over what are known in legal parlance as transfer hearings.

He determines if a case will be tried in juvenile court or sent to the criminal courts.

Although many states have long had laws allowing juveniles to be tried as adults, they weren't used much until the mid-1980s, when violent juvenile crime and public fear of it began to grow.

Since then, Illinois has substantially broadened the types of crimes eligible for transfer to the adult court, largely fueled by a few sensational cases involving preteen killers, such as the two boys who dropped 5-year-old Eric Morse to his death from a high-rise building.

The case before Judge Rogers on Tuesday involved the newest category of transfer hearing, known as a presumptive, or 3.3 transfer.

Basically, the presumptive transfer places the burden on the minor to demonstrate that his case should remain in juvenile court.

This particular minor was known as "Macho" among the Traveling Vice Lords, according to the police officer who testified against him.

The 16-year-old was arrested after police officers found 445 plastic packets of crack cocaine under his mattress while searching his family's apartment for weapons. They suspected he had been involved in a shooting earlier that evening.

After they found the drugs, police said the teenager told them he was the "money man" for a drug operation run by a fellow gang member.

The amount of crack made the case eligible for transfer. In juvenile court, he would serve a maximum of four years, until his 21st birthday. As an adult, his sentence would range from six to 30 years. The hearing hinged on whether the teenager could be rehabilitated.

It didn't look promising. He had been in and out of Juvenile Court since he was 9. He was convicted of burglary at 10, of stealing a car at 13.

When he was arrested on the drug offense, he was awaiting trial on another case. He and a group of friends had poked out someone's eye.

Even his public defender, Tom Maroney, had to admit the boy had "an awful, awful record."

During a court break, the deputy allowed the 16-year-old to sit next to his mother. He put his arm around her and kissed her on the cheek.

The decision, when it came, was inevitable from the moment Judge Rogers, in reviewing the criteria for keeping the teenager in juvenile court, said, "Not a single thing is positive."

The teenager's mother, a worn, thin woman marked her 39th birthday that morning.

She blamed her son's friend for the arrest, saying she thought he planted the drugs in his bed. She said she didn't know he was in a gang. She couldn't explain the course of her son's life.

"I couldn't see the outside of him," she said. "I only saw the inside of him. Once he got out there, he figured he could get away with it. He didn't realize he was hurting me."

She had lost her job as an assistant in a day-care center, she said, because she had come so often to court—16 times on this case alone.

Now, she would begin making the trek to the Cook County Criminal Courts Building at 26th Street and California Avenue, where adults are tried.

"I brought the child here and I'm going to be here for him," she said. "My family, they get tired and just want me to go on to the next child. But if I give up, they'll give up, and I don't want that to happen."

O nce you get accustomed to the noise and the children scooting across the floor on toy firetrucks and the lawyers and social workers conducting last-minute interviews with their clients in hallways and the heroin-addicted mother crying on a crowded bench because she just lost custody of her fourth child, the most striking feature of Juvenile Court's child protection division is the amount of paper contained there.

Stand outside and look up, and the building almost seems lined in paper because so many files are propped against the office windows.

More files are heaped on the desks, the tables and, sometimes, the floors of the lawyers' offices.

Every morning, the three sets of lawyers for each courtroom—lawyers for the state, the parents and the children—load 50 or more files on metal carts and wheel them into court.

There, they and the judges rifle, shuffle and consult their files to such an extent that the rustling sometimes obscures what they're saying.

The topic of discussion, of course, is children, the children whose names appear across the top of each file folder in bold, black letters. Their court history appears below, in a series of scrawls that often covers the face of the folder.

That history generally begins with a temporary custody hearing, when the court decides if the child should be removed from the parent accused of abusing or neglecting him. The hearing takes place within 48 hours after the Department of Children and Family Services makes the initial decision to take the child following an investigation of the reported abuse.

The case may continue for five or six years, sometimes longer, before the child is returned home, adopted or otherwise leaves the system.

Kim King, supervisor of the juvenile division of the Cook County Public Guardian's Office, which represents the children, still has a handful of cases that date back to the year she started working there: 1987.

That children often spend significant chunks of their lives in legal limbo remains one of the Juvenile Court's worst problems, although the court has made some recent inroads into its backlog.

Three courtrooms are now devoted to terminating parents' rights, a step that frees children for adoption. Hearing officers, who handle certain courtroom procedures, have relieved some of the burden. Since April, the child protection division has closed more cases each month than it opened.

The decision made during a temporary custody hearing is crucial because it can mark the beginning of a long, painful odyssey.

For the first of what may be many times, the judge must predict whether a child will be safe.

"I was terrified when I came here," says Nancy Sidote Salyers, the judge who presides over the division. "I was terrified I would make a mistake because I knew the heady price a child would pay if I did," she said.

That knowledge hangs over the head of almost everyone who works at Juvenile Court. If a child gets hurt or killed after being returned home, like 3-year-old Joseph

Wallace, who was hanged to death by his mother in 1993, blame falls upon the people who put him there.

People deal with the pressure in various ways. Judge Kawamoto avoids the evening news. Assistant public defender Stephen Dore is a passionate collector of sports cards.

In one monthly training session for judges, Salyers arranged for an expert to talk about stress management. The expert polled them about what they did at night, and much to their surprise, they all gave the same answer.

"We go home totally drained, and watch television," said Salyers, "and we weren't in the habit of doing that before."

Minutes after the 14-year-old mother lost her children that Monday, another "TC"—court lingo for temporary custody hearing—began in a different courtroom.

These parents were white and middle-class and they had hired a private attorney to represent them, all of which made their case unusual.

Their infant had been admitted to a hospital with head injuries that doctors attributed to someone's shaking her. The hospital reported the suspected abuse, and DCFS took the baby.

The hearing lasted 4½ hours. A radiologist testified that the child had been abused. A psychiatrist and the parents testified that she had not.

By 6 p.m., when Associate Judge Timothy Szwed made his ruling, no one remained in the hallway but the couple's family and two janitors mopping the floor.

He decided the child should remain in a foster home. Because of the judge's caseload and scheduling conflicts among the lawyers, it would be another three months before the trial could take place.

The parents' attorney, clearly frustrated, said, "If you keep this itty-bitty baby who just came into the world from her parents much longer, that may be more damaging than the head trauma."

When the couple walked out, the mother collapsed, crying, into her family's arms.

From the parking garage across the street, you could see a handful of boys, in silhouette, at the windows of the detention center. They had turned their beds end-up against the high windows in their rooms and clambered on top to see out into the early evening darkness. From the crowd gathered below, a few faces strained up, searching.

One woman held a young boy in front of her and pointed to a window. "There he is," she said. "There he is."

On Wednesday nights, parents and grandparents can visit the children in the detention center. The line usually starts forming about 6 p.m. in front of the revolving doors, and by the time people are allowed into the building at 7, it has swelled to 200 or 300 people.

A peculiar kind of camaraderie arises among them as they wait outside Wednesdays, Saturdays and Sundays, in all kinds of weather.

"He don't have a good mother," the 70-year-old grandmother said to the woman next to her. "He don't have a good father—and that's my son. They've been beating him since he was little. He deserves a break, and I know it."

The woman nodded in sympathy. She was there for her nephew, she said. His mother had died, and she was his only family.

They both carried plastic grocery bags.

"Underwear," the aunt said. "My nephew keeps calling me and saying he needs underwear. I never bought so much underwear in my life."

Upstairs, the bags were searched for contraband. No food. No games. Only five pairs of underwear or socks at a time. No spray-on deodorant. Only unwrapped bars of soap. No towels, only a face cloth.

Then, the parents were allowed to go to the units where their children live.

Shirley Lewis had not seen the Audy Home before Wednesday night. She sat across from her son at a crayon-bright plastic table in the common area of one of the two intake units, where children stay until their detention hearings.

Behind a glass panel, the boys without visitors watched television. Lewis kept sneaking glances at the row of rooms to her left as she peppered the 13-year-old with questions.

"You seen the doctor already?" she asked. "You told them you got asthma? You told them you got sickle-cell trait?"

She paused. "You don't get no cover, no pillow to sleep with? They don't put nothing on top of that plastic?"

Her son shook his head.

There are 30 residential units in the detention center, which most people still call by its old name, the Audy Home, after a long-dead superintendent, Arthur Audy.

When the facility was built in 1973, it was designed to hold, at most, 498 children, but typically it houses as many as 200 more. The extras sleep on cots in the common areas.

Most of the detention center residents—they aren't called inmates—are awaiting trial in juvenile or criminal court. Judges can also place juveniles in the detention center as part of their sentences or for violating probation.

They range in age from 10 to 17. About 93 percent of the residents are male.

The average stay is four to six months, but those being tried as adults generally spend much more time there. One teenager lived in the detention center for four years.

The residents attend classes 5½ hours a day, 12 months a year, at the Nancy B. Jefferson Alternative School, a Chicago Board of Education facility on the second floor. Truancy is not a problem.

The detention center, which occupies the three floors above the school, has its own 4-H club, Girl Scout troop, theater group and a talent show every Sunday night. But it resembles a prison more than a boarding school.

The residents must walk down the center of the hall, on a striped yellow-and-black line, eyes down and hands in their pockets to stop them from making gang signs at each other.

There are fights. At least one boy has been gang raped. Occasionally, residents flood the floors below by stopping up the toilets.

"I wish it was a 24-hour-a-day school because it's hard upstairs," said one 16-year-old boy who has lived in the detention center for 18 months.

On a Tuesday afternoon, he and half a dozen other residents gathered in a room that serves as a combination chapel and auditorium. They had been allowed to come downstairs to record the songs they had written and performed for a play.

Loose-limbed and restless, they wrestled with each other and danced and told jokes. One boy turned backflips.

They seemed like children, not criminals. Not predators. The way people view them does not escape their notice.

"Everybody here is not bad," said the 16-year-old, ignoring the horseplay, and speaking in a voice so deep it sounded like it belonged to a middle-aged man.

"It's not how they say it is, that everybody here deserves to get 40, 50 years. It's not like that."

Later, Meade Palidofsky, artistic director for the Music Theatre Workshop, an outside group that works with the residents, tried to set another date to continue the recording session.

"How's Thursday for everybody?" she asked.

A sardonic chorus answered.

"I can't. I have to take a walk down the street that day."

"What about that game of one-on-one basketball in the park?"

"Me neither. I have to get me one of them Arch Deluxes."

The language of juvenile court retains the tatters of its idealism. Juveniles are not charged with crimes. They are referred to the court. The lawyers don't call them defendants. They call them minor respondents. Minor respondents are not convicted of crimes. They are found delinquent, no matter how serious the offense.

"She's delinquent of first-degree murder," Judge Christopher J. Donnelly said Friday morning of the teenage girl who sat before him, motionless except for her right foot, which had tapped ceaselessly throughout the conclusion of her trial.

Just 14 years old and barely 5 feet tall, she had stabbed another teenage girl to death in July after an argument over a pair of gym shoes.

The 14-year-old and her friend began fighting with a neighbor, Latoya Ford, and her younger sister in an apartment-building hallway. The friend had made fun of Latoya, who was 16, for wearing K-Swiss shoes.

Adults broke up the melee, but when Latoya walked past the 14-year-old's apartment on the way to the stairwell leading to her family's apartment four floors above, the girl reached through the open door and stabbed her in the neck.

Latoya bled to death as she crawled up the stairs.

When he announced his verdict, Donnelly said, "Sometimes you really have to wonder where we're going in society because this all grew out of an argument over gym shoes. Not only that, but name brands of gym shoes."

Although 90 percent of the cases Donnelly deals with are felonies, this was only the second murder case he has presided over in almost two years at Juvenile Court. Most murders get transferred to the criminal court system.

The remark, though, was in keeping with the 40-year-old judge's courtroom character, as was the way he delivered it—standing behind the bench.

Donnelly often stands in court out of restlessness and an admitted desire to "make a point." Not without some pride, he says he is known among the gangbangers as "DOC Vader" because he sends so many delinquents to the Department of Corrections.

He can be harsh with young men and women who appear before him. One probation officer called it "his Scared Straight approach," but added, "a lot of his kids don't come back."

When one young man walked into the courtroom wearing a Georgetown Hoyas jacket, Donnelly asked, "You have nicer clothes than what you're wearing now, don't you? Well, what are you saving them for? This is the exact occasion for wearing your nice clothes."

To another he committed to the Department of Corrections after three drug possession cases, he said: "I want you to realize two things—*look at me*—your past has now caught up with you. You better realize now that drug dealing won't be tolerated. You have to find another way to live."

In his chambers, behind a desk whose contents include a popsicle-stick pen holder and a book entitled "Why Courts Don't Work," Donnelly's demeanor turned thoughtful.

He talked about the roots of crime, how hard it would be to grow up where the children in his courtroom do, how silly he feels yelling at his own children now about their messy rooms.

He talked about traveling between two worlds, the one where he lives, and the other, where he works, and he marveled that only 10 miles separated them.

What divides them, he said, is this: "They have no hope. They expect to die young. They expect they won't have any success. These kids have lost touch with the American dream."

There are happy endings at Juvenile Court. Everyone says so.

"About once a month," estimated assistant state's attorney John McNamara.

"We had one or two last week," said Jim Hedges, who works for the Department of Children and Family Services as a courtroom facilitator.

"There are happy endings sometimes," said Janet Alexander, an assistant public guardian. "You just don't always see them happen."

On Wednesday afternoon, a happy ending happened in a hallway.

A 14-year-old named Randy waited with his mother and uncle for his case to be called. Two men stood with them.

Randy had stolen Bill Nelson's car. He had robbed the store where Harvey Floyd works as a security guard.

But the men had come to court to help the 14-year-old. Nelson decided to drop charges in exchange for his personal version of community service.

"Three weeks of car washing," he said. "And I have 13 cars."

He collects them. Floyd also showed up to vouch for the boy and was surprised to run into Nelson. The two had grown up together.

"It was bad in our neighborhood, but when we did something wrong, people got on us," Floyd recalled. "The younger brothers don't have anybody on them to keep them straight."

As boys, they had gotten into their share of trouble, the men said. Nelson, who is 30, acknowledged he had seen the inside of Juvenile Court before. That's why they decided to help.

"He's a good kid," Nelson said of Randy. "He just needs some guidance."

A onetime honor student, Randy had fallen in with "the wrong crowd," according to his mother, Meishelle Vaughn.

"He's been in court before," she said. "Quite a few times. But now, he's got somebody to work with him."

Randy didn't say much. "It's better than going upstairs," he offered, referring to the detention center.

Another happy ending almost happened Thursday in Salyers' courtroom. Twice a week, Salyers trades her administrative duties for a black robe and hears cases on the private guardianship calendar. She created the calendar after she became presiding judge two years ago to deal with a grab bag of cases that had languished in the system for years.

Among them were some 20,000 cases that were essentially lost. For many years, if a child's situation was considered stable, the case was transferred out of its assigned courtroom to the private guardianship calendar. But the calendar essentially didn't exist, and so the cases went into limbo.

Much of the work of Calendar 49, as it's known, consists of closing cases that should have been closed long ago.

The children have grown up or been in the care of private guardians for years and no longer need the court's supervision.

Sometimes, the parents come back into their children's lives.

In the waiting area, a man read a book about dinosaurs with his 10-year-old stepson. His wife sat behind him with their daughter. Two other boys, her sons by a previous relationship, and their guardian, an aunt, sat with them.

After nine years, the mother, a one-time drug addict, wanted her sons back. The boy's aunt agreed. "I think she deserves a second chance," she told Salyers. "I really do."

The mother said she had finished two parenting classes and found a job. Her daughter had been returned to her custody almost a year ago, and she was ready for her sons.

"I have no problems with having my boys and my daughter at the same time," she said. "There's enough love in my heart to give all my kids."

Salyers, concerned about the boys switching schools mid-semester and the lack of lengthy visits between them and their mother, postponed the case for three months with the instruction that the family spend as many weekends together as possible.

Afterwards, one son sat alone on a bench, his face turned away. The mother wrapped her arm around the youngest, who is 9. "It just takes time, OK?" she said. "It will happen. It's OK."

By 4 p.m. Friday, the hallways had emptied out. Behind smoked-glass doors, a few courtrooms finished up the afternoon's business, but most lawyers and judges had retreated to their offices to prepare for the whirlwind that would resume Monday morning.

Four children played outside Courtroom C, while their mother's case, the last one of the day, was heard inside.

They had been waiting since early that morning, and they were restless and bored. One child pushed a play chair up and down the floor. Another repeatedly slammed the doors of a miniature stove.

Each waiting area contains an assortment of toys and books provided by the Citizens Committee on the Juvenile Court. The toys were selected for their indestructibility, but the children play so hard and so anxiously that the committee already has a room full of broken playthings.

A sheriff's deputy watched over the four children. She held the youngest, who was no more than a year old, against her shoulder. She swayed back and forth, trying to get the baby to nap.

The deputy, Andrea Gerber, had worked at Juvenile Court for just two months, and she was new enough to be surprised by what she saw.

"When you read about the cases here, they're so awful you wonder who could do that," she said. "Then, you see the families, and you know. It's because they have no money, they're so young. They're so lost."

She spoke softly. "But you feel you can make a little difference here," she said, "even if it's just giving a little kid a hug."

In her arms, the baby slept.

A NEW ORDER IN THE COURT

States let juvenile offenders answer to their peers instead of adults in special courts.

BY TRACY M. GODWIN

Will everyone please rise. Hear ye, hear ye ... LaPorte Teen Court Program is now in session. The Honorable Steven King presiding." These are familiar words that can be heard in many courtrooms across the country. In this courtroom, however, the defendant, defense attorney, prosecuting attorney, bailiff, court clerk and jurors are all under 19. No, this is not a mock trial; the cases are real—this is teen court, also known as youth court or peer court.

In a growing number of communities across the country, teen court programs represent an alternative approach to juvenile justice. Young offenders are held accountable through a sentence imposed by their peers. Youths who volunteer to assist in the teen courts also learn about the legal system and get an opportunity to develop and practice new skills. Through serving justice and providing education, teen courts have an impact on a wide segment of a community's young people. This impact sets teen court apart from many other approaches to juvenile justice.

Most teen court programs target first-time, misdemeanor, nonviolent offenders between the ages of 11 and 18. Teen courts are typically established as diversion programs and require juveniles to admit guilt prior to participating. The primary function of the program is determining an appropriate sentence for the young person. A few teen courts will determine the guilt or innocence of a defendant who pleads "not guilty." Participation on the part of the juvenile offender is strictly voluntary, and parental consent and participation are mandatory.

Teen court services emphasize concepts such as accountability, positive peer influence, competency development, and youth empowerment and involvement. As part of their sentencing, most programs require defendants to complete a certain number of community service hours and serve at least once as a teen court juror. Other common sentences imposed by peer juries include oral and written apologies to victims, essays on a subject related to the offense, and attendance and participation in educational workshops.

The interest in teen court programs has skyrocketed over the last few years. More than 280 teen court programs are operating in 31 states and the District of Columbia as of November 1996, the American Probation and Parole Association reports.

One of the best attributes of teen courts is their flexibility, making them easily adaptable to the local needs and concerns of individual communities. The courts are administered by juvenile courts, juvenile probation departments, law enforcement agencies, private nonprofit organizations and schools. A court's location within communities often depends on the position of the person who first became interested in the concept or on available resources.

Recognizing teen courts' powerful and positive effect on local communities, Minnesota, North Carolina and West Virginia are among states encouraging and supporting teen court programs on a statewide basis.

Leading the way

Minnesota is launching a statewide teen court campaign. Minnesota Planning, the state's strategic and long-range planning office, is evaluating the most effective way to introduce the community-based youth courts to the state. The program is supported by Gov. Arne H. Carlson, who earmarked $3 million for Min-

From *State Government News*, January/February 1997, pp. 14-16. © 1997 by The Council of State Governments. Reprinted with permission.

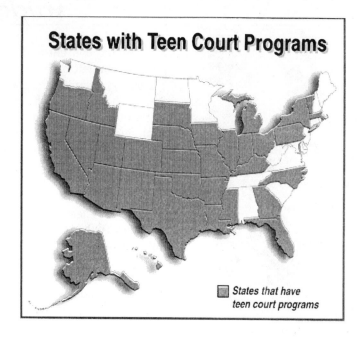

States with Teen Court Programs

■ States that have
teen court programs

nesota teen courts in the 1997–1998 biennial budget. Carlson plans to support a bill to establish the courts in this year's session.

"Teen courts provide a unique way to hold youth offenders accountable," Carlson said. "The program gives youth and communities more ownership over how to handle their problems."

Minnesota Planning last year conducted a statewide survey of more than 3,100 youths and representatives from courts, law enforcement, schools and other community groups. Survey responses demonstrated an enthusiasm for teen courts: 71 percent of adults and 86 percent of youths who responded indicated that teen courts are a good idea and would be effective in their communities. Those surveyed were equally enthusiastic about taking an active role in teen courts: 77 percent of the adults and 79 percent of the youths indicated they would be willing to volunteer for teen court activities.

In addition to gauging interest, the survey gathered suggestions for teen court operations, including opinions about target populations, appropriate sentences and available community resources to implement these programs. Survey responses helped Minnesota Planning design a framework for Minnesota communi-

ties to establish teen courts. Mankato and the Roseville area will be among the first to launch programs in early 1997, pending funding approval.

More on board

Teen courts also are getting a start in West Virginia, where legislation established pilot projects in three of the state's 55 counties. The pilot programs will be in Monongolia, Raleigh and Mineral counties. The legislation calls for the Governor's Committee on Crime and Delinquency to administer teen courts, with most day-to-day operations delegated to the county juvenile probation departments.

Delegate Brian Gallagher initiated and pushed through the legislation. "Often we tend to go too far in the direction of not using innovative approaches to solving juvenile problems," Gallagher said. "Rather than focusing all our efforts on sending juvenile offenders to Criminal University (prison), we need to examine our resources and channel them toward more creative and acceptable options, such as teen court."

West Virginia plans to evaluate the effectiveness of the three pilot projects until July 1998. If the program proves to be effective, the goal

is to expand the program on a state-wide basis.

North Carolina is expanding its support for teen court programs in the state. The General Assembly appropriated $30,000 to develop teen court programs in 1993 and increased that amount over the following two years, growing to $100,000 for fiscal 1997. The Administrative Office of the Courts monitors and disburses the monies. Four counties are slated to receive funds—Cumberland, Rockingham, Buncombe and Durham.

An initial evaluation of the state's first teen court in Cumberland County yielded little information on the program's impact on juvenile crime. Bob Atkinson, administrator of the Community Penalties Division of the AOC, attributes the lack of information to the short time the program had been in operation at the time of the study. He hopes the AOC will be given funds to conduct further evaluations.

Atkinson reports that he doesn't know "a better laboratory for teenagers on how courts operate." The educational value for young people is high and communities with teen courts report they are doing something to help young offenders. Atkinson sees the interest in teen courts gaining momentum and would like to see it expand.

Many states are wrestling with ways to respond to the small percentage of serious and violent juvenile offenders. Teen court presents an efficacious prevention strategy at the front end of the juvenile-justice system. The programs demand a high level of youth participation. They let communities address the problem of juvenile crime locally. Furthermore, youths who participate in teen court gain a personal stake in the future and well-being of their communities. When youths see the value of living and behaving as responsible and productive citizens, it can go a long way toward enhancing public safety.

Rolling the Dice in Juvenile Court

By Steve Mills
Tribune Staff Writer

At the age of 13, Sergio Wray already needed a second chance.

Charged with first-degree murder and attempted murder for shooting two teenagers at a birthday party in March 1993, Wray faced a minimum 20-year prison sentence if tried as an adult. In Juvenile Court, he could have been released on probation.

The decision to transfer his case to criminal court or to keep it in Juvenile Court belonged to Arthur Rosenblum, a white-haired jurist who relied on gut feeling when the law failed him—a rather common occurrence, he had come to believe, especially in the most complicated cases.

And though he might sound more than a little arrogant when he says it was his job to "determine if these kids could be saved or not," it is not altogether inaccurate.

In the drab, narrow courtroom where he presided, Rosenblum decided who deserved the protection and second chances the Juvenile Court offered and who would be sent to the rough-and-tumble of criminal court.

It was, in many ways, a task worthy of Solomon: searching the defiant young faces for traces of remorse, looking for a glimmer of hope in stacks of reports, weighing the merits of the lawyers' arguments.

Still, more often than not it came down to sizing up the young person who stood before him and then predicting whether he could be redeemed. That Rosenblum was wrong as much as he was right was a measure of the impossible job before him.

Wray's case offered no easy answers. But in Juvenile Court, where the problems of the most troubled youths are sorted out in a justice system that relies more on instinct than on the cold letter of the law, none of these cases was simple.

His lawyer portrayed him as a bright child who had made a youthful mistake, one he immediately regretted. After the shooting, Wray had banged his head over and over against a washing machine, hollering that he was sorry.

What's more, Wray's family—his mother, grandmother and even his godmother—cared about him. In Juvenile Court, such support is critical.

Prosecutors said Wray did not deserve another chance. They said he was a violent street-gang member who had previous weapons arrests, and who would not hesitate to use a gun in another crime.

Rosenblum considered the case. Then he stared into Wray's brown eyes.

The judge decided that the slim young boy who sat before him in his best clothes was worth gambling on. The case would remain in Juvenile Court.

"If you make a decision that's wrong, and you send them to adult court, you know they're going away for a long time," said Rosenblum, who now is retired. "But if I keep them, then maybe—just maybe—they'll see the light.

"Ninety percent of the time, it won't work out. You can't make a flower from a bad seed, from bad dirt," he added. "But sometimes you have to have some humanity."

In 1993, when 65 children were slain in the Chicago area—murders chronicled in the series "Killing our children"—18 of them were the victims of killers who were little more than children themselves.

One of those killers was Sergio Wray. The third child of a Baptist minister and a nurse's aide, he was a member of the Vice Lords street gang by the time he was 13. His errant shot killed one of his best friends and wounded another.

Another killer was a 10-year-old boy, a rail-thin kid who, when left to baby-sit four of his younger brothers and three other kids while his mother helped cook Christmas Eve dinner at a friend's, kicked a toddler to death. He was the youngest of the killers.

And then there was Odis Matthews, who at 14 shot and killed Craig Rogers as the boy pedaled across a playground, and Chris Jackson, who allowed 9-year-old Terry Holloway Jr. to look down the barrel of his semi-automatic handgun, then pulled the trigger, killing him.

Now, these children are on the precipice of adulthood. Some of them have children themselves. One, a girl who strangled a child with a telephone cord, received probation for her crime and later had her two children taken away by the Illinois Department of Children and Family Services.

Their futures were decided in the oldest Juvenile Court in the nation, their journeys shaped by people—judges, attorneys, probation officers, parents—who are not often seen, in a system that is not often examined.

Cook County's Juvenile Court is an institution that, at its founding a century ago, was viewed as forward-thinking but that, by 1993, was struggling.

It was widely seen as a dumping ground for inexperienced and underqualified judges and lawyers, a court that was more of a stepping-stone than a destination and one that would abide poor performance. Tragedies were just waiting to happen. Sadly, they often did.

As ever, the juvenile justice system is charged with twin goals: rehabilitating the youngest of criminals and holding them accountable for their crimes—the latter demand stoked with greater frequency nowadays.

The lives of these children, though, reflect a more scattershot approach, with the hope Juvenile Court holds sometimes administered arbitrarily.

Some of these children, because their cases remained in Juvenile Court, received little more punishment than probation. Others were sentenced to one of the state's youth prisons, even though their crimes were strikingly similar to those that received probation. Still others, because of their age, were tried as adults and sent to adult prisons.

'I know it all'

The Juvenile Court system invested almost everything it had in Sergio Wray. That he later failed to deliver on its good faith reflects how difficult it can be to turn around the most violent teens.

The shooting at the birthday party was really over nothing. Boys were slapping each other in the head, engaging in good-natured horseplay, when Wray announced that he would kill the next boy who slapped him.

When it happened, he grabbed a .45-caliber pistol and opened fire, his wild shots killing 14-year-old Charles Coleman and wounding Raymond Sims, 16. As it turned out, Coleman had not even slapped Wray.

Wray was found guilty of first-degree murder in Juvenile Court. At first, it looked as if he would go to prison. But a probation officer had a change of heart about him, and he decided that his initial evaluation—that Wray should be locked up—was shortsighted.

Wray, the probation officer said, had become a role model for other youths while being held in the Cook County Temporary Juvenile Detention Center, the holding facility commonly known as the Audy Home. He had done well in school. And he showed potential.

He was just the kind of kid who would benefit from probation.

So instead of sending Wray to prison, Judge John W. Rogers gave him 60 days of home confinement plus 5-years' probation for the murder.

Wray's family was so happy, they celebrated on the way home from court by stopping at a restaurant for supper. His grandmother bought him new gym shoes.

"I had told him that being in Juvenile Court was his chance. I had told him not to blow it this time," said Wray's mother, Electra.

The probation officer enrolled Wray in a community leadership program and arranged for him to get psychological counseling. His attorney, Assistant Cook County Public Defender Darron Bowden, got involved with Wray's life, visiting him at home, bringing him to his church, even offering to share a stage with Wray at the motivational talks he gave.

"Sergio was probably one of the brightest kids I ever met in here," Bowden said. "Everybody saw the potential he had. Everybody."

But less than three months after his home confinement was over, before he had even put a dent in his probation, Sergio Wray was arrested for a carjacking. According to police, he stole a car at gunpoint, forced the motorist to strip naked, then kicked him out of his vehicle.

The promise was gone. Bowden cannot explain it. Wray provides little insight beyond cliches such as "I got off on the wrong track."

But this time he was tried as an adult. He pleaded guilty to carjacking and was sentenced to 10 years in prison.

Because of his age, he started his sentence in a youth prison. But by 17, when officials were considering transferring him to an adult facility, he already had been disciplined more than a dozen times—for assault, fighting and issuing threats. Prison officials wrote that Wray, in a few years, had become a "sophisticated" criminal.

"He identifies with the criminal lifestyle," an official wrote.

Indeed, the official said, Wray wanted to be moved to an adult prison.

Today, Wray is in solitary confinement at the maximum-security Pontiac Correctional Center, his past five years a travelogue of sorts through the state's prison system, both the youth and adult divisions: St. Charles, Joliet, Stateville, Sheridan, Pontiac.

The juvenile system is through with him.

"I know it all when it comes to prison," he said, sitting on a wooden stool in an interview at Pontiac, his tattooed arms shackled to its metal pole.

Not too young to kill

In 1993, he was the youngest killer.

He was just 10, and in the aftermath of the slaying there were only questions: What would make a 10-year-old kick a toddler to death? And what do you do with a 10-year-old killer?

Tom Schneider had been a juvenile probation officer for two decades when he was assigned to investigate the boy's background and write the report to help Judge Stuart Lubin decide the boy's sentence.

He might have been just the person for this case. When he was a kid of 14, Schneider had been caught riding in a stolen car and was sentenced to 6-months' probation. In college, he studied criminal justice.

It seemed natural when he graduated to head for Juvenile Court.

Schneider approached the case with some trepidation. He had worked with some juvenile killers in the past, but never with one so young.

"When I first got the case, I thought, 'Where are we going to place this kid?' " he said. "I mean, you look at it and say, 'Boy, there must be something wrong with him.' But the more I learned, things didn't seem so easy."

Schneider started by taking the boy to McDonald's, forging a bond over cheeseburgers. When the boy ordered a Happy Meal so he could get the toy, Schneider noted how the boy still was very much a child.

Then they would drive somewhere in Schneider's Toyota station wagon and talk, at first about nothing in particular. As the boy grew comfortable with him, Schneider edged closer to what happened on Christmas Eve.

"I basically told him, 'It's not going to be easy but we're going to talk about this until I understand what happened,' " said Schneider.

Then one day the details began to tumble out. The boy resented that he had to baby-sit his four brothers and the three other children his mother was supposed to be watching that night. Baby-sitting forced him to be the grown-up—to dress the children, to play with them, even to discipline them.

When one of the children, 23-month-old Lauren O'Neal, began to cry, he feared that she would wake the other kids. He kicked her and threw a shoe at her. He even threw a basketball at her.

It was an impulsive act, and he knew he had hurt her. He told Schneider he wished he could bring her back.

Schneider never doubted the remorse was genuine. For the first year or so following the slaying, the boy had trouble sleeping. He had nightmares. He complained of a loss of appetite—not uncommon reactions.

Lubin had few choices. Because of the boy's age, he could either put him on probation or send him to a residential treatment facility, the kind of place that specializes in dealing with the most violent children.

The boy's background was critical to making the decision. At the end of 1993, when Lauren was killed, the family of seven was struggling. They lived in a small two-bedroom apartment on West Jonquil Terrace, in one of the roughest parts of Rogers Park. They did not have a working stove.

The mother baby-sat to supplement her public-assistance money. She had six children by five different men, none of whom lived in the home.

The boy was a good kid, though. He was quiet, likable and well-mannered. He had not been in trouble and did well at Gale Community Academy. One teacher gushed that she would like to "have a whole class like him." And, in spite of the singular lapse in judgment, the mother was otherwise a responsible parent who was devoted to her children. Teachers said she pushed them to do well in school.

On the bench for close to three years when he had to decide the boy's future, Lubin began to announce his ruling.

"Well, I just want you to know that I don't think you're a bad person," Lubin told the boy, his voice shaking. "I think you . . ." He stopped, then stood up from the bench and abruptly announced a recess.

A public defender for 17 years before he became a judge in 1991, Lubin had handled tough cases, even in Juvenile Court. But the sight of the boy in front of him, so small next to the attorneys, shook his emotions.

"What do you say to someone like that? I was trying to make him feel that this wasn't the end of his life," Lubin recalled recently. "I just felt so bad for everybody—for (the boy) and the baby that was killed."

"I had to get off the bench. I came into my chambers and cried."

When he returned, Lubin said he believed the boy had been put in an impossible situation, one "that was beyond your means to deal with." He sentenced him to 5-years' probation and mandatory psychotherapy.

"It was the best thing for (the boy)," said Richard Hutt, the assistant public defender who was the boy's lawyer. "We thought this would give him a chance."

The prosecutor had agreed.

For adults, probation is a matter of keeping their nose clean and checking in. But for juveniles, the probation officer does all the work.

Juvenile probation officers work at their limit. With some 8,000 children on probation in Cook County, each officer watches over close to 40 children, a caseload they say is manageable only if they are "work-smart."

Their days are a mix of home and school visits, court appearances and endless hours in the office, writing reports that, in the bureaucratic language of the justice system, try to quantify remorse and rehabilitation.

Meeting Schneider once a week was only part of the probation. The boy also got psychological counseling once a week at the Adler School of Professional Psychology downtown, sometimes using games to deal with the killing and his feelings about it, other times simply talking about it.

Schneider, meantime, checked up on the boy at his uncle's home, where he had been placed when his mother lost custody of him because of her neglect. He made unannounced visits, and often dropped by his school.

He became a central part of the boy's life.

"I'm not part of the family, but in a way I am. I got involved in that family, maybe more than others," he said. "I knew them almost as well as my own."

Today, the boy—who declined to be interviewed and is not named because he is still a juvenile—is a high school sophomore. If he was a typical 10-year-old back in 1993, these days he is a typical 15-year-old. He enjoys basketball and video games. His favorite subject is social studies, and his grades are good enough that with just a little improvement he can give some thought to college.

Few people, including some of the boy's best friends, know of his past, giving him the chance to fulfill the aim and the promise of Juvenile Court—to build a new life without the stigma of being a killer.

"He's your boy next door. The good kid," said Schneider. "Take away this one terrible night and he'd be the kid you'd point to, saying, 'Why can't you be like him?' "

But that one night remains a riddle of sorts. As much as the boy has talked about what happened, he has never been able to explain why it happened, a fact that Schneider and Hutt find troubling. Whether he ever will is unclear.

His psychotherapy ended after three years, according to Schneider and Hutt, because the therapist decided he could help the boy no more. They were getting no closer to finding the answer to the night Lauren was killed, and might never.

Still, said Hutt, the boy's progress is something to be cheered, especially in Juvenile Court.

"It is," he said, "as close to a success story as we come."

A winner, a loser

Odis Matthews and Chris Jackson could not be any more alike, or any more different. Killers both at the age of 14, they were raised brimming with anger over absentee fathers and neglectful mothers. They skipped school, belonged to gangs, sold drugs.

But today, five years after those slayings, Matthews and Jackson stand on either side of a thin line between hope and despair, between rehabilitation and recidivism.

At 19, Matthews has his first real job, a fianceé, a family of infant twins and a 1-year-old son, and a shot, albeit a slim one, at redemption.

Jackson, despite his many desperate promises to stay out of trouble, was behind bars awaiting trial this summer for the third time since his August 1996 release from youth prison. In July, he pleaded guilty to possession of crack cocaine, and was sentenced to 2-years' probation.

Their situations are so tenuous, though, they could easily switch places.

But how they each reached this point in life says as much about the weaknesses of the juvenile prisons as about their strengths. It speaks, too, to the fact that, in some cases, the system can do nothing; it is all up to the kid.

Matthews grew up on the South Side and Jackson on the West Side, but their murder convictions in Juvenile Court sent them to the same place: the Illinois Youth Prison at St. Charles, in the far western suburbs.

Set on 125 acres of gently rolling hills, just beyond a cornfield, St. Charles has the look of a small college campus, with a handful of once-elegant red-brick buildings that date to the turn of century amid newer, plainer structures.

But St. Charles, one of the state's seven youth facilities, is ringed by two tall fences, both of them topped with razor wire. Inmates are locked behind heavy, blood-red doors. When they walk the grounds, which they do only to get from one place to another, it is in two straight lines.

If there is any confusion at St. Charles, it is over purpose. The more than 300 workers there try to follow the justice system's mandate to rehabilitate young criminals, while also meeting the public's growing demand to punish them.

At St. Charles, that outcry is translated into numbers. Designed to hold 318 prisoners, its inmate population has been over 550 during most of the summer. At one point, it reach[ed] 603, said Superintendent Jerry Butler. Cells designed for one prisoner hold two; cells made for two hold four.

Critics say the overcrowding makes the prisons little more than warehouses for delinquent children. And most of those children are being locked up for more violent offenses than ever before. More are involved in gangs, and more use or sell drugs.

Consequently, services are stretched thin. More than half of school-age prisoners attend classes for only half a day, rather than a full day. So when Jackson left the prison at St. Charles, his reading and math skills were little improved from when he arrived three years earlier.

"All the benefits of the juvenile division that you don't get in the adult division—better conditions, more supervision, a better counselor ratio—those benefits are being seriously compromised," said Steven Drizin, a lawyer at the Children and Family Justice Center at Northwestern University's law school.

Even if they do make progress, many kids leave prison to return to the same neighborhood where they had committed their crime, to the same broken family that provided little or no support, to the same street gang, with ties maintained or strengthened from their time behind bars.

Still, the rate of recidivism among juveniles is lower than among adults. A Department of Corrections study of prisoners leaving both adult and juvenile prisons from 1993 to 1996 found nearly 40 percent of adults were locked up again.

Of the juveniles, 35 percent were returned to custody, though the majority of them were for technical parole violations, such as missing curfew.

In Cook County Juvenile Court, Matthews and Jackson had been found guilty of murder, which sent them on their way to St. Charles.

Matthews, faced with a transfer hearing that could have landed him in Criminal Court, pleaded guilty to killing Craig Rogers, a 13-year-old who was gunned down as he rode his bike across a playground on the South Side. He agreed to plead guilty to avoid being transferred to criminal court.

Like so many of the killings of children in 1993, the reasons behind Rogers' killing were trivial: There had been fighting between Matthews' gang, the Gangster Disciples, and Rogers' Mickey Cobras.

Prosecutors did not try to transfer Jackson's case, though the reasons are unclear. He was found guilty of murder for shooting Terry Holloway Jr. in the face and was sent to St. Charles.

Matthews and Jackson both were greeted at St. Charles by members of their gangs bearing shampoo and deodorant, the traditional offerings for a new inmate. By continuing their gang affiliation behind bars, Matthews and Jackson got protection from rivals and instant community.

Indeed, St. Charles was suffering from many of the same ills plaguing the adult prisons. Still, it was not as dangerous as the adult prisons. Compared with Stateville or Menard, where many murderers serve their sentences, the youth prison offered a measure of hope to inmates willing to change.

Matthews and Jackson were not willing, however.

Although Matthews feared St. Charles when he arrived, he soon fell into its slow rhythm. He rose early and marched in formation to the dining hall, where other youths served him from steam-heated trays. Then he went to the commissary, where he worked stocking shelves.

Afternoons were for school. He also got psychological counseling, sitting with other youngsters and talking about his crime and his anger. Never, though, did he take the work or school seriously. He was simply marking time.

Indeed, he remembers the days passing as if they would never end, sitting in his cell watching daytime talk shows, the boredom broken by fights. Once, he said, he met Rogers' brother there, but he did not let on who he was.

If he knew anything, it was that he would return to selling dope upon his release. "What else was I going to do?" he said. "I didn't have nothing."

Jackson, whose tough attitude belies his likable manner, thought the time at St. Charles would be as easy as taking a deep breath. And it was. He hooked up with fellow gang members, lifted weights and started fights, determined to make a name for himself.

"He would get into a fight at the drop of a hat," said Butler.

When he got out, he picked up right where he left off. Though Jackson says he learned to control his fierce anger through counseling, he kept getting into trouble. He was arrested last year for shooting at a police officer and was sent to the adult prison at Vandalia. Out again this summer, he pleaded guilty to possession of crack cocaine and was put on probation.

And he remains angry. Calling from the county jail one morning, he spoke with a fatalism, saying he feared spending his life behind prison walls.

"Everything is going downstream for me," he said. "I always tell myself that I ain't going back to jail. But I can't seem to beat it. I can't stay out of jail. I just keep going back to the same thing."

Like Jackson, Matthews rejoined his gang when he left St. Charles. He was arrested on a weapons charge and sent to the state prison at Vandalia. When he got out, he said he returned to the streets and sold drugs.

But then one day, he said, he just decided he had had enough. Sometimes, he explained, people just change. It was partly that the streets had lost their dangerous allure.

"Maybe I just growed out of it," he said of his drug-dealing days. "I don't hang around those types of people anymore. I don't do that stuff. I don't need it."

If Matthews made anything of his time at St. Charles, it is only in hindsight.

Even Butler, the superintendent, admits that dramatic turnarounds are rare in his line of work. If a kid makes the discovery Matthews finally made, it is all the better. But he would be happy with even the smallest change.

"If that kid leaves with his hair combed, his pants pulled up, smelling good," he said, "then that's something society couldn't give him and something that we did."

[**Editor's note:** This is Part 3 of a 4-part series.]

Unit 6

Unit Selections

Key Points to Consider

❖ How tough should juvenile corrections be? Should it be equally tough for all juveniles in the system? Why or why not?

❖ What are the available viable alternatives to juvenile incarceration and probation?

❖ What scientific data is there about the effectiveness of juvenile corrections and the various types of programs you have identified? Where can this data be found?

❖ Who should set the agenda for juvenile corrections? What should their qualifications be?

 **Links**   **www.dushkin.com/online/**

These sites are annotated on pages 4 and 5.

Today more than ever, we face a dual set of problems when discussing juvenile corrections: (a) the problems of all corrections—overcrowding, violence, and apathy; and (b) the perpetual problems of growing up. There is a danger that we will do with our youth what we are doing with adults—spending ourselves into the poorhouse without getting any bang for our correctional policy bucks.

In regard to overcrowding, there is no question that our juvenile correctional facilities are being overwhelmed by vast numbers of young, violent offenders. Whether this is a policy problem or a young people problem is a separate issue. The corrections community has a number of good ideas and observations to make here, but, unfortunately, the knowledge that the correctional community has is rarely translated into realistic public policy. The other players—the legislators, police, courts, and media—have more public voice and thus more power to influence the fate of those juveniles who are swamping correctional institutions. But, as has been the case for years, there persists general apathy about the corrections component of the justice system—until something goes wrong or one of the state's adult or juvenile charges "acts out." Then, all these other voices are heard and they usually result in some politically popular legislation that drives corrections further into the hole. Apparently, the critics have forgotten that corrections gets its juvenile clients after all the other social institutions—from family through school and church and the community—have failed the youths.

The strongest element of stability and cohesion that corrections has, the most organized voice, is the American Correctional Association. A lot of good thinking has come out of the ACA historically and more lately as it has networked, embraced, and incorporated a wider variety of concerned professionals.

We agree with the ACA that managing programs and services for juvenile delinquents and aggressive adolescents is complex and demanding (Glick, 1998). Indeed, this is due both to the nature of the client, the turbulent juvenile, and to the inherent complexity of the juvenile justice system itself. This system continues to evolve and modify as times change—much more than does the adult system. And it continues to grow as more clients are sent out of mainstream society. It has become a multibillion dollar industry.

The Office of Juvenile Justice and Delinquency Prevention's (OJJDP) *Comprehensive Strategy for Serious, Violent and Chronic Juvenile Offenders,* (Wilson and Howell, 1993) has been often cited in ACA publications. It suggests for juvenile corrections that: Costs of juvenile corrections must be reduced; conditions of confinement improved; detention and training school populations decreased; risk assessments used more extensively; identification of treatment needs improved; and detention visualized as a treatment opportunity. Isn't this the purpose in

the first place—and have we moved this far away? We need a continuum of programs in which our use of alternatives could increase. Inequality needs to be eliminated, due process enhanced, the community involved, effective rehabilitation programs developed, prevention deemed a top priority, and aftercare brought into the mainstream.

The challenge is to create or develop a system of juvenile corrections that balances the safety of the public with the safety of the juvenile, that ensures the progress of society while ensuring the growth of the juvenile. All the while, these seemingly contradictory missions have to be carried out in a facility that meets the constitutional requirements of decency and humanity under the protection of the right against cruel and unusual punishment.

In addition, corrections skills are needed in the community in both prevention and remedial programs, for instance, as in probation for juveniles.

As the articles in this unit point out, good theory leads to good policy. Our students need to develop interpersonal skills to be good change agents. And we all need patience for correctional programs to work—patience that apparently was not available from family, school, or other community organizations. Our students need exposure to the critical and constructive role that corrections must play in our plans for juvenile justice.

The right of the State, as parens patriae, *to deny to the child procedural rights available to his elders was elaborated by the assertions that a child, unlike an adult, has a right not to liberty but to custody. He can be made to attorn to his parents, go to school, etc. If his parents default in effectively performing their custodial functions—that is, if the child is "delinquent"—the state may intervene. In doing so, it does not deprive the child of any rights, because he has none.*

—In re Gault
Supreme Court of the United States, 1967

The Bastard Stepchild of *Parens Patriae*: The American Juvenile Incarceration Structure

by KENNETH WOODEN

The practice of incarcerating children and the conditions existing therein have legal roots dating back to England during the late fourteenth and early fifteenth centuries. There, under the doctrine of *parens patriae,* the King's Court of Chancery held power of guardianship over children who were abandoned or willfully neglected by their parents.

In 1636, *parens patriae* was introduced in America when young Benjamen Eaton of Plymouth Colony, indentured by the state, was given to Bridget Fuller, a widow, and ordered by the governor "to kelp him at schoole two years and to imploy him after in shuch service as she saw good and that he should be fit for; but not to turne him over to any other, without ye gov'n consente."

Still another legal concept that derived from the Common Law of England was that of *mens rea*—guilty mind. A child of seven or younger could not be found guilty of a crime because he had not reached the age of reason. From age eight on, however, the law forced the child to stand trial and endure the severity of full criminal prosecution. For example, in the early 1800's a child of eight who was accused of "malice revenge and cunning" for setting fire to some barns was convicted and hanged. In 1828 a New Jersey boy of thirteen was hanged for a crime he committed when he was twelve.

In 1727 the city of New Orleans built the first institution in America for neglected or homeless children. Up to that time and well into the nineteenth century, neglected and delinquent youths were placed in jails, prisons and almshouses with adults. Even today the same practice persists in many areas of the United States: the laws of forty-six states still approve placing juveniles in county jails, and thirty-four of these states don't even require a special court order.

It wasn't until 1825 that New York City set up the House of Refuge, the first separate institution whose sole purpose was to aid juvenile offenders. Within a few years other cities—Philadelphia and Boston, for example—followed suit and established similar accommodations. Although these facilities were set up to deal with juvenile offenders, unfortunately they were eventually obliged to admit neglected children because there was no place else for them to go once they became wards of the state. This practice is still common in all but three states.

These "houses of refuge" proved to be a historical milestone in the American family culture. For the first time family-centered discipline was replaced by institutional discipline administered by city, county or state governments. Parents, grandparents, older sisters and brothers were replaced by guards and superintendents.

Progressive in its philosophy, the New York House of Refuge early initiated the practice of "binding out" or placing delinquent children in foster homes. In his daily journal the superintendent of the Manhattan House of Refuge recorded the following entry on May 10, 1828:

We saw the eight boys for Ohio start in good spirits.... It excited considerable warm good feeling to see so many little fellows bound for such a good and suitable place from the House of Refuge, among the passengers on board the steamboat.

Sixty-five years later, in 1893, foster home advocate Homer Folks vigorously promoted the practice of binding out delinquent children. Folks believed that of all the children incarcerated within institutions, "only a very small number show lack of moral sense and are dangerous to the community." The genuine human concern of this nineteenth-century progressive has been echoed by each new generation of reformers for the last eight decades. As children's justice becomes an increasingly popular issue in the 1970's, more and more groups are quoting the National Council for Crime and Delinquency, which has said that only 10 percent of all juvenile offenders require incarceration.

However, the rhetoric of reformers and progressive organizations did little to prevent the powerful growth of the state-supported and state-operated training school complex. Massachusetts created the first such penal facility for children in 1847. Called the Lyman School for Boys, it became one of the worst institutions in America and one of the first training schools to be closed down in 1972 for massive failure and child brutality. By 1960 there were two hundred training schools in fifty states, the District of Columbia, Puerto Rico and the Virgin Islands. The daily population numbered 40,000, with close to 100,000 children a year being processed through their gates. By 1974 the national network of these schools had a combined operating budget of close to $300 million and a recidivism* rate of eight out of ten children.

The early juvenile penal facilities were located on the outskirts of urban areas, but as the cities grew in size and encompassed the old "reform schools" and "houses of refuge," there was a movement to relocate on large acreages in rural areas. Thus began what is known in youth corrections as "the colony system." Whole institutions became self-sufficient entities. The economics of the small towns where they located have become tightly interwoven with the institutions because a majority of the local townspeople have become dependent on them for their livelihood.

World War I imposed its military mentality on the youth correctional system, when, according to one historian, "Living units became barracks; cottage groups, companies; housefathers, captains; superintendents, majors or more often colonels; and the kids wore uniforms." That influence is still alive in Texas and Arizona State training schools; I personally witnessed boys in the atmosphere of a military stockade, forced to march and take orders in a military fashion from guards in military-style uniforms.

One of the most distressing social phenomena in juvenile justice is that earlier liberal reforms designed to help children ended up hurting them. In 1890 the first juvenile courts were organized and they quickly spread throughout the country after the turn of the century. Compulsory educational laws were also passed, making it mandatory for children to attend school. Yet another reform was the progressive Social Security Act of 1935, a section of which permitted governmental agencies, using tax monies, to provide for the neglected child. What has happened, though, is that the well-meaning intent of reform has turned into the tyranny of reform: the state now has gained greater social control over the dependent youngster. Children who fail to attend school for any of an assortment of reasons are hauled into juvenile court and incarcerated in state training schools for years. State welfare agencies, with vast sums of money, arbitrarily take children from blood relatives and ship them to institutions in and out of state.

In 1967 the United States Supreme Court concluded that "the Latin phrase (*parens patriae*) proved to be great help to those who sought to rationalize the exclusion of juveniles from the constitutional scheme; but its meaning is murky and its historical credentials are of dubious relevance." Regardless of such legal rhetoric, America's youth are still being incarcerated in every state of the union. Because of old legal procedures and laws, because of our national tradition of juvenile institutionalization and because numerous "social reforms," neglected and delinquent juveniles find themselves caught in the destructive net of incarceration behind locked doors in one of four different institutions: juvenile detention center, county or municipal jail, state training school or private facility approved by the presiding juvenile system.

First offenders are usually sent to one of the 300 detention centers, where approximately 13,000 kids* sit for an average of twelve days with nothing to do, awaiting the court's decision on their fate. Because the police and most juvenile workers fear they'll run away, they are detained behind locked doors. Most detention centers I have visited throughout the country are situated in or near the same building that houses the juvenile court. To the casual observer or group on tour given by the personnel, these facilities look rather harmless and almost like college dorms. But behind the public relations veneer, a penitentiary atmosphere prevails; guards, heavy iron doors, countless keys and closed circuit TV give paramount security and control. Solitary confinement is readily employed for the slightest infraction.

According to the National Council on Crime and Delinquency, 50 percent of the youngsters in detention centers have committed no crime and 40 percent will be released from custody after court appearance. Still in increasing numbers, children are filling up our detention centers, and the politicians are calling for new multimillion-dollar facilities that will be operated by county governments. The politics of jobs are very real.

Where no juvenile detention center exists, the child is held in a county or municipal jail until he appears before a juvenile judge. United States Senator Birch Bayh, chairman of the Senate Subcommittee on Delinquency, commented during hearings on the subject in September of 1973: "On any given day, there are close to 8,000 juveniles held in jails in the United States. It is esti-

---

* Recidivism rate is really a failure rate; it refers to the number of children who return to the institution.

* A shocking report entitled "Hidden Closets" by George Saleebey, former Deputy Director of the California Youth Authority, reveals that in January, 1975, California was locking away noncriminal youngsters at such a rate that, based on national figures, the Golden State would account for one third of all children so incarcerated throughout the country. Prior to this controversial report, California was listed as having a moderate amount of children in detention. If the report is accurate, the ramifications are ominous as to how little we really know concerning the actual numbers of children locked away.

mated that more than 100,000 youths spend one or more days each year in adult jails or police lockups."

These local penal accommodations, the oldest facilities in the United States for both youthful and adult offenders, are, in the words of Daniel P. Starnes, a leading expert in the field of corrections, "notorious as a constant source of verified filth, perversion, sadism and corruption." More than a million town drunks and men and women of violence, most with criminal records, enjoy the company of nearly 100,000 youngsters annually, 75 percent of whom are locked in the same rooms with adults. In 1970, 66.1 percent of these were later released, free of any charges.

In 1970, a statewide breakdown of a national survey by the University of Chicago showed that in Illinois ten thousand children made up 6 percent of the total city-, county-jail population for that year. Out of 160 jails in the state, 142 detained juveniles and only 9 of them segregated the children from adults. A mere 15 percent of the 142 jails had supervisory personnel to keep the children from the harm of molestation and rape.

Training schools, which operate in every state except Massachusetts, represent the nadir in a class filter system for juvenile malefactors who are picked up by police, arrested, detained in a juvenile hall and eventually sentenced by a judge for rehabilitation. Almost all are state-operated and -controlled. The laws that govern their legal functions specify that training schools are to provide custody and to rehabilitate the child so that his confinement will build toward a more useful life for himself and his community.

I found basically two types of training schools. The first is a miniature penitentiary with high walls surrounding the grounds. All the buildings and cell block wings therein are interlocked by long corridors. Not only are individual cell doors secured, but each

wing is also locked at all times. There is almost always a self-sufficient industrial complex on the grounds—laundry, hospital, maintenance shop and any other facility needed to keep strangers out and the children in. Dubious educational and religious services are available to the children, along with the standbys of solitary confinement and of bloodhounds to locate any who run away.

The second and more common type of training school is the cottage system. Its concept was introduced in 1856 to give children the closest thing to some form of home life. Those in charge are "house parents" rather than "guards." The outside area is usually quiet and pleasant and bears little semblance to a penal facility. The cottages are usually small, esthetically pleasing, dormlike structures. Unfortunately, those I have seen have no back or side doors, or if they do, the doors are always chained and locked. The windows are also secured with heavy wire and in the event of emergencies such as fire, escape would be impossible except through the front door.

Such a situation occurred in Arizona sometime during the 1960's, according to several state employees I interviewed. After a fire the charred remains of seventeen youngsters were found piled in front of a chained exit door, but the full circumstances of their needless deaths have been kept from the general public to this day.

The cottage system always reserves one building for secure treatment, solitary confinement. Any child who acts up in a solitary cottage is further isolated in a special single room for indefinite periods of time.

Still another facility for the incarceration of wayward youths is the private institution. Few people know much about these private institutions and very little has been written about them. Generally these facilities are for children of well-to-do parents or parents who have special benefits because of their

job or station in life. They are usually located in isolated, wooded, rural areas. Their geographic setting and private nature adds greatly to the public's lack of information about their performance. These private "hospitals," "ranches," "homes," etc., run the gamut—from exceedingly good to exceedingly poor; from state-approved and licensed to unsupervised and unevaluated. Some have established excellent reputations; others have recently sprung up in response to newly available state and federal monies. Some, like the Menninger Foundation in Topeka, Kansas, have the noble purpose of truly helping to relieve and direct the troubled; others are designed to help themselves by warehousing and administratively exploiting both disturbed and normal children while the owners amass sizable fortunes.

In many cases the only difference between the private institution and public state training schools is the cost. The control philosophy is the same. The children are usually there by court order. They are locked in the buildings during the day and in their rooms at night. The view from the windows is obscured by steel and thick wire mesh. Solitary confinement is used consistently as punishment for breaking minor rules. Most frightening of all is the unsupervised environment that allows for a new agent of control—chemical restraints—to be used with little thought to their ultimate effects on the child's body or mind. And all the while the American taxpayer is paying, directly or indirectly, financially and socially.

What we have today, then, is a juvenile justice system that originated as a small community concern, by people of good will but whose reform programs and laws created a national industry. Without public awareness a system that was designed to help children in trouble has become a tyrannical monster, destroying the very children it was mandated to save.

WHEN SHOULD KIDS GO TO JAIL?

BY DAVID C. ANDERSON

While America's latest crime wave appears to be subsiding, the legitimate fears it aroused in urban America leave a powerful political legacy. Along with new police strategies and more prisons, legislators continue to call for harsher treatment of juvenile offenders long granted special status because of a historic belief in the diminished culpability of children and adolescents. Nearly all states now permit the "waiver" of youngsters charged with serious crimes to adult courts; in more than half, legislatures have specifically excluded those charged with certain crimes from juvenile court jurisdiction. In some cases the exclusions apply to children as young as 13. Legislation moving forward in the current Congress would expand adult federal court jurisdiction over offenders as young as 14 and give prosecutors, rather than judges, the power to transfer a juvenile case to adult court.

Therein lies an important debate. The nation approaches the one hundredth anniversary of the first juvenile court, established in Chicago by Progressive Era reformers in 1899. It formally recognized that childhood should exist in the eyes of the criminal law. Youth, Progressives believed, can partly excuse even violent misbehavior and always permits hope for rehabilitation. Is that historic commitment really obsolete?

The question remains germane even as juvenile crime trend lines turn down, because demographics suggest a possible new crime wave. Scholars like James Alan Fox of Northeastern University have predicted a "baby-boomerang" 20 percent increase in the juvenile population and juvenile crime by 2005. The Justice Department predicts a doubling of juvenile arrests for violent crime by 2010.

The Senate Judiciary Committee report on the new juvenile crime bill relies heavily on such predictions to justify treating more juvenile offenders as adults. Defenders of special treatment find themselves hampered by the history of the juvenile court, whose usefulness has fallen into real question as it has succumbed to an advanced identity crisis.

THE WHOLE CHILD

The Illinois Juvenile Court Act of 1899, which established the Chicago court, was based on the British idea of *parens patriae*. It granted the state the power to intervene on behalf of children when their natural parents failed to provide care or supervision. "Jane Addams and the dauntless women of Hull House," who established the new court, "strove to develop a safe haven, a space to protect, to rehabilitate and to heal children, a site of nurturance and guidance, understanding and compassion," writes William Ayers in a new book about the Chicago court. Judges serving in the court were to receive social-science and child development training so that they could craft sentences in the best interest of the "whole child."

The idea spread rapidly. Thirty-two states had set up juvenile courts or probation services by 1910; by 1925, they existed in all but two states. The belief that a court should take over the nurture and discipline of troubled youth informed both philosophy and procedures. Sanford J. Fox, writing in an issue of *The Future of Children* devoted to articles about the juvenile court, recalls Judge Ben B. Lindsey, who served in Denver from 1901 to 1927. "Children who came to the Denver court were 'his boys' and were seen by him as fundamentally good human beings whose going astray was largely attributable to their social and psychological environment," Fox writes. "According to Lindsey, the role of the juvenile court judge was to strengthen the child's belief in himself and make available to him all of the support and encouragement from outside the court that the judge could harness on his behalf."

Today's juvenile courts continue the practice of dealing with cases of child abuse and neglect, along with "status offenses"—truancy, running away from home, unmanageability—as well as juvenile delinquency. A 1994 survey counted 1.9 million juvenile court filings (an increase of 59 percent since 1984); about two-thirds were for juvenile delinquency.

In the 1960s, pressures from both the left and the right began to move treatment of juveniles away from the original vision. In the early juvenile courts, *parens patriae* meant substituting the benevolence of an individual judge for the adult court's adversarial process, fact-finding by juries of peers, guaranteed rights to counsel and cross examination, and protection against self-incrimination. It also meant indeterminate sentences—locking up youngsters in treatment until the adults in charge agreed that they were rehabilitated, rather than for fixed periods of time. That was all well and good so long as juvenile court judges and treatment administrators were fairminded, insightful, and caring. Where they weren't, juvenile offenders were routinely exposed to gross miscarriages of justice.

The Supreme Court recognized the problem in the 1967 case of 15-year-old Gerald Gault, who was charged with making an obscene phone call. A juvenile court judge ordered him to training school for six years; in adult court, the same case was worth a $50 fine or two months in jail.

In its ruling, the court rejected the whole idea of *parens patriae* and concluded that traditional juvenile justice violated the 14th Amendment's guarantee of due process. "Juvenile court history has again demonstrated that unbridled discretion, however benevolently motivated, is frequently a poor substitute for principle and procedure," the court wrote.

The *Gault* decision upheld a juvenile defendant's right to protection against self-incrimination, to notice and counsel, and to question witnesses. The result was to bring lawyers into juvenile court for both the prosecution and defense and to force greater objectivity on the proceedings. While this curbed some of the abuse, it also curbed the capacity of judges to deal with the offender's broader problems. "*Gault's* insistence on procedural safeguards in juvenile courts formalized the connection between a youth's crime and the subsequent sanctions, and ironically may have legitimated more punitive dispositions for young offenders," writes Barry Feld, Centennial Professor of Law at the University of Minnesota.

Through the 1970s and early 1980s, responding to pressure from a crime-weary public, legislatures began pushing for punishment rather than treatment, especially of youngsters who looked like "hard-core" juvenile career criminals. They required juvenile courts to impose determinate or mandatory minimum sentences based on the severity of the crime rather than the needs of the offender. Some juvenile courts adopted the more punitive approach without any prodding from a legislature.

Juveniles sentenced to confinement, meanwhile, all too often wound up in training schools or detention centers that mocked the historic commitment to therapy, education, and rehabilitation. Inquiries and lawsuits during the 1970s and 1980s found juvenile inmates regularly subjected to systematic humiliation, solitary confinement in squalid cells, beatings, and homosexual assaults.

All this occurred in the face of evidence that more constructive approaches could work. In the early 1970s, the Massachusetts Department of Youth Services, led by Jerome Miller, closed most of its training schools, reserving only a few institutions for the worst offenders. The rest went to residential community-based programs or home to their families while the state contracted with private agencies for appropriate social services. An evaluation 15 years after the training school

> # Is our historic commitment to rehabilitating juvenile delinquents really obsolete?

closings found that half of 875 youngsters released from DYS programs were rearrested within three years; during that time, 24 percent wound up recommitted to DYS or incarcerated in adult prisons. That compared favorably with other states. In California, for example, 70 percent of youngsters released from reform schools were rearrested within only one year, and 60 percent were reincarcerated three years after release.

To this day, Massachusetts remains the leading example of how reform might help. A 1992 meta-analysis of 443 juvenile delinquency program evaluations lent support to the Miller approach. The author, Mark Lipsey, found that programs

reduced the delinquency of their clients by 5 percent overall, from 50 percent to 45 percent, compared with control groups. But he found higher effects for programs that emphasized community-based rather than institutional treatments. Even so, use of secure training schools and detention centers continued to increase nationwide. The rate of confinement for juveniles rose from 241 per 100,000 to 353 per 100,000 between 1975 and 1987, according to one national study. Another found that while the number of juveniles in the population declined by 11 percent between 1979 and 1989, the number locked up in institutions rose by 30 percent.

States also encouraged the shift of more juvenile cases to adult courts by either lowering the age of adult court jurisdiction for crimes or giving judges or prosecutors discretion to order waivers. The trend continued despite research demonstrating that such measures were having less than the desired effect. Adult courts are typically far more lenient with property offenders than are juvenile courts. And in states where judges supervised transfer of juvenile cases to adult courts, they tended to send up many more burglary and larceny cases than robberies, rapes, and murders. The property offenders therefore benefited from the "punishment gap," getting off with a year or two of lightly supervised probation, the routine in adult court, when the juvenile judge might have ordered them into a youth prison.

ADD CRACK COCAINE AND STIR

The juvenile court's identity crisis was therefore well advanced by the mid-1980s, when crime rates spiked as crack dealers and gun dealers began aggressive distribution of their products to willing markets of young people. Juvenile delinquency cases not only increased; they involved more violence. Howard Snyder, a researcher for the National Center for Juvenile Justice, found that delinquency caseloads rose 23 percent between 1989 and 1993, nearly three times the percentage increase in the juvenile population. Juvenile offenses against the person (homicide, rape, robbery, assault) rose 52 percent, compared with a 15 percent increase for drug and property crimes. Weapons-law cases increased by 87 percent.

The statistics underlay a lurid popular perception. The news and entertainment media discovered the drug issue in general and crack in particular during the late 1980s, giving broad play to the teenage drug dealer turned outlaw millionaire, an image of adolescent fantasy come horribly true. This only deepened questions about the credibility of juvenile courts. Young thugs were driving luxury cars, flaunting designer warm-ups and gold chains, arming themselves with assault weapons and paying their mother's rent. Did they suffer from deprivation and a poor self-image? Were they really going to be helped by fatherly judges and caring social workers? Wouldn't they, not to mention the rest of us, be better served by a heavy dose of grown-up punishment?

The idea could drive even sober academics to feverish prose. James Q. Wilson, an influential political scientist at the University of California at Los Angeles, wrote of "innocent people being gunned down at random, without warning and almost without motive, by youngsters who afterwards show us the blank, unremorseful face of a seemingly feral, presocial being." William Bennett, with John DiIulio and John Walters, describes " 'superpredators'—radically impulsive, brutally remorseless youngsters . . . who murder, assault, rape, rob, burglarize, deal deadly drugs, join gun-toting gangs, and create serious communal disorders. . . .[N]ot even mothers or grandmothers are sacred to them."

While such rhetoric rings powerful chimes with the public, should it drive public policy? However legitimate, fear and loathing inspired by excesses of some juvenile criminals at the height of the crack plague can inhibit careful thinking about a problem whose practical and moral complexities demand more than a turn to harsher punishments.

The majority of young people who break the law are not feral, presocial predators. Though juvenile violence increased at a shocking rate during the late 1980s, the more than 2,000 homicides reported each year remain a tiny percentage of all juvenile crime. Of the 1.4 million arrests referred to juvenile courts in 1992, 57 percent involved property offenses as the most serious charge, while 21 percent involved crimes against the person. There is real danger that legislative nets cast to capture the "superpredators" will sweep in thousands of lesser fry as well, at appalling social and financial cost.

Furthermore, whatever goals the move against special treatment might accomplish, greater public safety does not appear to be one of them. A Florida study published in 1996 matched 2,738 juvenile delinquents transferred to adult courts with a control group that remained in the juvenile system. "By every measure of recidivism employed, reoffending was greater among transfers than among the matched controls," the researchers stated. A 1991 study compared juveniles tried in New York adult courts with New Jersey youngsters whose cases remained in juvenile court. It,

too, found higher recidivism rates and prompter new arrests for the New York youngsters.

An ethically sensible and potentially effective policy on juvenile crime should include three elements: broader crime control, social work outside the criminal courts, and a reconception of juvenile justice.

Crime control. By now the accumulating evidence documents overwhelmingly that the burst

> Recent studies suggest preventative social work should remain a part of juvenile crime strategy.

of youth crime in the late 1980s was caused by the rapid spread of drugs and guns. What to do about drugs remains uncertain. The crack epidemic appears to be expiring more as a result of natural causes than of smart policy, with saturated markets, aging addicts, and a skeptical new generation of street kids. But guns, in this context, are worth discussing.

Franklin Zimring of the Earl Warren Legal Institute, Alfred Blumstein of Carnegie Mellon University, and others have pointed out that guns account for the entire recent increase in youth homicide. In a striking article published in the *Valparaiso University Law Review* last spring, Zimring, a law professor at the University of California at Berkeley, noted that the number of reported killings committed with guns by youngsters between the ages of 10 and 17 increased sharply after 1984, from about 500 to more than 1,000. The number of non-gun homicides remained stable through those years, at slightly fewer than 500.

"If there were a large group of 'new, more violent juvenile offenders,' that was the proximate cause of explosive increases in homicide," Zimring writes, "one would expect the increase in killing to be spread broadly across different weapon categories." Instead, it appears that "a change in hardware rather than a change in software was the principal cause of higher youth homicide." In that light, the most effective response looks like aggressive gun control focused on juveniles, backed up by the sort of innovative policing now credited with reducing juvenile gun use and homicides in Kansas City, Boston, and New York.

Social work. Beyond programs designed to deal with youngsters after arrest, students of juvenile crime remain fascinated with the idea of intervening in the lives of children and teenagers "at risk" of delinquency in hopes of averting criminal behavior before it starts. Research documents some success. The most famous study was of the Perry Preschool, in Ypsilanti, Michigan, which provided two years of enriched schooling and weekly home visits to small children from poor minority families. By the time the kids had turned 27, half as many had been arrested as a control group that did not benefit from the enriched classes.

Other programs replicate the effect. A Syracuse University effort enrolled 108 low-income families, mostly headed by young single mothers, for five years of day care for their children along with parenting training beginning during pregnancy. Ten years after the families completed the program, only 6 percent of the children had been referred to probation, compared with 22 percent of a matched control group. Another New York study found that providing nurses for regular visits to young mothers at home with their infants greatly reduced instances of child abuse and neglect. A Houston program that enrolled families with small children from Mexican-American barrios found that a combination of home visits and day care reduced the children's aggressive behavior.

In 1996, a team of researchers from RAND led by Peter Greenwood reviewed seven such studies and calculated that day care/home-visit programs could reduce by 24 percent the number of crimes the client children could be expected to commit. The group also reviewed programs that give parents special training to deal with children who have begun to behave disruptively in school and at home; the training was found to reduce the youngsters' eventual juvenile criminality by 29 percent.

The RAND group also examined the Ford Foundation's Quantum Opportunity Program, which will provide an "at-risk" youngster with cash and scholarship incentives averaging $3,130 per year to stay in high school and graduate. That simple approach might reduce the criminality of its clients by an astonishing 56 percent.

The RAND researchers attempted to estimate the cost-effectiveness of such approaches in comparison with increased incarceration resulting from California's new Three Strikes Law. They found that if fully applied across the state, two of the social work approaches, parent training and graduation incentives, were more cost-effective; taken together, they could reduce crime by 22 percent at a cost of about $900 million per year. Greenwood and others had previously calculated that the Three Strikes Law might achieve a similarly defined crime reduction of 21 percent at a cost of $5.5 billion per year.

These results should be regarded with caution. The RAND study is a self-consciously artificial exercise designed to provoke pointed comparison rather than nail down a policy choice. It is based on necessarily speculative assumptions about how the effectiveness of well-resourced and well-managed pilot programs will "decay" as they are massively expanded. It also attempts to estimate the number of crimes children might commit over the course of their lives if they don't benefit from the programs, an imponderable calculation. Yet however speculative, the results remain tantalizing; they certainly warrant close attention to preventative social work as part of a juvenile crime strategy.

Juvenile justice. Even as get-tough rhetoric encourages politicians to press for diminishing jurisdiction of the juvenile court or abolishing it entirely, other issues encourage some thoughtful academics in the same direction. Barry Feld, in a forthcoming paper, reviews legal decisions that imposed adult due process on juvenile courts, new laws that force more juvenile cases into adult courts, and the shift in attitudes away from treatment toward punishment.

> Legislative, judicial and administrative changes within the past few decades have transformed the juvenile court from a nominally rehabilitative social welfare agency into a scaled down, second-class criminal court for young people that provides neither therapy nor justice. . . . No compelling reasons remain to maintain a punitive juvenile court separate from an adult criminal court.

He calls for integration of juvenile and adult courts while "formally recogniz[ing] youthfulness as a mitigating factor in sentencing." Pointing out that the law has long recognized diminished responsibility of young people who break the law, he proposes a fractional "youth discount." "A 14-year-old offender might receive, for example, 25 percent of the adult penalty, a 16-year-old defendant, 50 percent, and an 18-year-old adult the full penalty, as is presently the case."

The appealing simplicity of such an idea, however, may be deceptive. Feld himself acknowledges that implementing it sensibly would require many states to get rid of mandatory minimum sentences to which legislators point with pride, and to increase judges' discretion that legislators have fought for years to curb. For youth discounts to work, Feld writes:

> the adult sentencing scheme itself must be defensible in terms of equality, equity, desert, and proportionality. A sentencing scheme which simply attempts to apply idiosyncratically "youth discounts" to the flawed indeterminate sentencing structures . . . runs the risk simply of reproducing all of the existing inequalities and inconsistencies.

Other scholars continue to believe in the need for a separate court that recognizes the possibility of rehabilitation for youthful offenders. They have been encouraged by recent research suggesting, contrary to decades of pessimistic findings, that rehabilitative programs can make a difference to the lives of delinquent youth.

They point to a 1990 mega-analysis that weighed 80 evaluations of rehabilitation programs, distinguishing between those that took care to match services with the needs and learning styles of the offenders and those that did not. The "appropriate" programs were found to reduce recidivism by as much as 50 percent. And Lipsey's 1992 meta-analysis, which found positive effects for community-based, rather than institutional, programs, also affirmed the value of those that took behavioral, skill-oriented, or multi-modal approaches.

Such studies provide practical hope to shore up the moral case: so long as rehabilitative programs do not expose the public to more crime than prison does, they are worth pursuing. They create positive experiences for youngsters coming out of chaotic social environments (at lower financial cost than prison), and they send a broad message about a society's willingness to help young people in trouble. It's a valid argument, and it looks all the better with reason to believe continued experimentation with such programs might still produce real cuts in recidivism.

WHAT KIND OF COURT?

But if there should be a juvenile court, how should it look? To some the best answer is: about the way it looks now, but with more resources, better people, and uniform standards nationwide. "Although there have been significant changes in the mission and function of the juvenile court since 1899, [the] basic differences between children and adults remain and continue to support the need for a specialized court," concludes a group assembled by the Center for the Future of Children.

The group made a dozen recommendations that included elevation of all juvenile courts to the highest level of general jurisdiction, improved training for juvenile court judges, a requirement that judges serve at least two to three years, and greater use of alternative dispute resolution. The group also called for guaranteed legal representation, transfer of juveniles to adult court only on the basis of a judicial hearing, and a greater variety of sanctions.

Mark Moore, a professor of criminal justice policy and management at Harvard's Kennedy School of Government, offers a more innovative and sophisticated idea. He recognizes the need for the transfer of some juvenile cases to adult courts if they show "unusual maturity, acted alone, or persisted in committing crimes."

For the rest, he proposes a court whose goal would be "to help organize the increasingly complex task of child rearing by intervening in situations where breakdowns in child-rearing capacities have occurred." It would do this in the manner of a bankruptcy court faced with a failing business:

> It can decide to "liquidate" the existing arrangements and transfer the child to the care and custody of someone other than the current caretakers. Or, the court can seek to "restructure" the enterprise, keeping the family together but insisting that caretakers live up to their duties and overseeing the provision of publicly available services that would allow them to do so.

What would this mean for the youngster picked up for a first-offense burglary who turns out to have dropped out of school, is running with a street gang, and has developed a taste for drugs? Under the current system, transfer of such a case to adult court would result in a mild penalty—a year or so of sporadic supervision by an overworked probation officer. The current juvenile court might supplement that with an order to attend Narcotics Anonymous meetings and go back to school, which might or might not happen.

Moore's court would call in members of the offender's immediate family or others prepared to provide supervision and order them to make sure the youngster goes to school and a drug treatment program, stays away from his gang friends, and otherwise stays out of trouble. A social worker or probation officer would serve as a "special master" responsible for making sure the judge's orders are followed. Should the caretakers fail to meet their obligation, the judge might sanction them, remove the child to a residential program, or both. With further offenses, the delinquent might finally be ordered to juvenile jail or prison.

Moore points out that such a court could deal more logically than current juvenile courts with the status offenses like truancy and running away from home that may be precursors to criminal behavior. It would also keep jurisdiction over child abuse and neglect cases, as well it should, given research documenting the propensity of their victims to act out violently later on.

All this would, of course, require more resources for juvenile justice and a sense of unity on the value of such an approach. Both are problematic in the ongoing political climate. But Moore's basic goal is hard to gainsay: he would hold "children, and those who care for children, accountable for their actions in their joint efforts to move children from the status of defenseless barbarians to resourceful citizens."

Is that really possible without threatening public safety? "One can err by allowing a child sufficient freedom and engagement with the community to put himself or herself and others at risk," Moore says. But it's also an error to keep a delinquent so locked up and isolated "that he or she never has the opportunity to learn how to become integrated into the community." The existing setup, he says, penalizes public officials "for the first kind of error and tolerate[s] the second kind of error. Yet it is the second kind of error that is arguably the most expensive."

That aptly summarizes the whole discussion. It is still possible to imagine ways juvenile delinquents might be sanctioned and supervised effectively as juveniles, not adults, without removing them from the community. The drift away from historical juvenile justice remains premature.

Quick Fix

Pushing a medical cure for youth violence

By Annette Fuentes

Several prestigious New York City medical centers have been experimenting on 6- to 11-year-old boys in an effort to prove that violence, aggression and even criminal behavior are caused by biological factors. One of these studies, first launched in 1992, was still underway in April when patient advocacy groups charged the researchers with violating federal ethics rules, unleashing a torrent of media scrutiny and outrage.

Critics are asking why peer review panels at the New York State Psychiatric Institute (NYSPI), Mount Sinai Medical Center and the National Institute of Mental Health (NIMH), approved the experiments. Serious ethical considerations are raised by the age of the boys, the fact that many were poor minorities, and that the experiments were not designed to provide treatment for an existing illness. Investigators are looking at the researchers' use of fenfluramine, a drug banned last fall by the Food and Drug Administration (FDA) when the agency discovered that it had caused heart damage as part of the popular diet drug fen-phen. And legal advocates are examining the role of New York City's chief juvenile justice prosecutor in helping one team of researchers gather young subjects. Responding to the outcry, Congress held hearings in April on the FDA's role in approving the drug for experiments on children.

But the studies also raise larger questions about the social and political implications of research into the roots of violence that focuses on disenfranchised, inner-city communities. NIMH, the federal agency that funded much of the research, has granted millions of dollars to studies investigating serotonin, the chemical that transmits signals between cells in the brain, and how it is connected to violent behavior. If they discover biological factors that lead to violence in minority boys, the research could inaugurate wholesale drug intervention for youngsters identified as "at-risk" for anti-social behavior.

In an era when the government trades its previous commitment to battling poverty for a strategy of battling the impoverished, research that seeks the causes of violence in individuals and their body chemistry has an obvious appeal. If biology, not sociology, can be the predictor of crime, then that could justify clamping down on suspect populations.

The New York City experiments involved one team of psychiatric researchers at NYSPI, part of Columbia University, and another team doing similar research at Queens College and Mount Sinai Medical Center in Manhattan. Several of the researchers had been laboring since 1990 to find a link between behavior and genetics in their sample of urban youth. "The proliferation of violence by youth in our society is reaching epidemic proportions," the NYSPI researchers told reporters in a prepared statement. "Each day we see instances of children committing violent acts against other children and adults, most recently [the schoolyard murders in] Jonesboro, [Ark.]. . . . The correlation between serotonin and aggression in children needs to be studied in order to identify children at highest risk for impulsive, aggressive behavior."

The NYSPI researchers, led by Daniel Pine and Gail Wasserman, were trying to prove that their subjects—young brothers of jailed delinquents—were predisposed to criminal behavior because of familial histories of aggressive behavior. In an article published last September in the *Archives of General Psychiatry,* Pine and Wasserman conclude: "In young boys, aggressive behavior and social circumstances that are conducive to the development of aggressive behavior are positively correlated with a marker of central serotonergic activity." In other words, kids who grow up around aggression are likely to be aggressive *and* have low levels of serotonin.

The Queens College/Mount Sinai team was led by Jeffrey Halperin, whose findings were published last October in the *Journal of the American Academy of Child Adolescent Psychiatry*. Halperin's study also sought to correlate behaviors with serotonin levels in children. Based on a study of boys with aggressive pasts and Attention Deficit Hyperactivity Disorder (ADHD), he points to a correlation in his data between aggressive behavior in parents and lower serotonin levels in aggressive boys with ADHD, a psychiatric diagnosis that some researchers believe is a predictor of aggressive behavior in adults. But Halperin says he couldn't determine "the extent to which this association is environmentally and/or genetically transmitted."

In both studies, researchers gave boys one-time doses of fenfluramine to help measure the amount of serotonin in their brains. All the boys had restricted diets for a month and were required to fast for 12 hours prior to the test. They were attached to IVs for up to six hours as blood samples were taken and only allowed to drink water. Halperin's group consisted of 41 boys with ADHD. Twelve of Halperin's subjects on medication for ADHD were required to stop taking it for a month before the test—a procedure known as "a wash-out." Pine and Wasserman followed virtually the same protocols in their two studies, which involved 34 boys in one and 100 in the other.

Many aspects of these experiments raise red flags for those who monitor the ethical implications of medical research on human subjects, but it was the use of fenfluramine that captured media attention. Though one dose of fenfluramine is unlikely to cause permanent heart damage, there is no research on the drug's effects in children. One study on adults showed that 90 percent of healthy subjects who were given doses of the drug experienced fatigue, headaches, lightheadedness and lack of concentration.

The FDA's director, Dr. Michael Friedman, acknowledges that his agency approved researchers' continued use of fenfluramine on the boys even after the drug had been pulled from the market because it caused heart valve damage in some dieters. But he defended that decision at hearings before the House Committee on Government Reform and Oversight in April, saying that in February NYSPI revised the parental consent form to provide warnings about possible harmful side effects. But that was five months after fenfluramine was pulled from the market, and the FDA allowed NYSPI to enroll two more youths in the study before publicity halted it in April.

Researchers at NYSPI also received cooperation from other governmental agencies. Wasserman began assembling subjects in 1991, at first using the New York City Department of Probation to find 6- to 10-year-old boys whose older brothers were incarcerated delinquents. After one month, probation officials balked, deciding that families of the youth might feel coerced into participating.

Wasserman and her colleagues ultimately were aided by Peter Reinharz, head of the family court unit of the city's law department. Reinharz reportedly gave the researchers access to family court records, which are supposed to be confidential. His actions are being investigated by the Legal Aid Society. "We've filed a Freedom of Information request to find out which youth were identified," says Jane Spinak, the head of Legal Aid's juvenile rights division. "We think many of them were our clients. We believe their civil rights may have been violated."

Attorneys at Disability Advocates and New York Lawyers in the Public Interest get credit for exposing the experiments. They came across the two studies while doing their own research for an ongoing case against the state Office of Mental Health. That suit challenges the state's practice of permitting research on incapacitated patients—children and adults—at psychiatric facilities, arguing that it violates the patient's right to informed consent. "There are so many angles that are problematic," says Ruth Lowenkron of New York Lawyers in the Public Interest. "To see this kind of non-therapeutic research raises questions about what was told to the parents. How was consent obtained? In the Mount Sinai experiments, kids were taken off their medication. What happened to them?"

When the lawyers found out about the violence research studies in December, they filed a complaint with the Office of Protection from Research Risks (OPRR) at the Department of Health and Human Services. OPRR is the government agency charged with monitoring all medical research involving human and animal subjects to insure that it conforms with federal guidelines on informed consent and safety. Gary Ellis, OPRR head, says his office is investigating four complaints related to the studies, the most recent of which was filed in April. The complaints question whether the children in the studies and their families were adequately informed of the risks of the experiments and were therefore able to give real informed consent to participate. Ellis says his office will also investigate whether the studies violated government rules against exposing healthy children to potential harm in experiments that offer no therapeutic benefit. For its part, NYSPI asserts that the children in one group were at risk for suicide, so the experiments did offer some promise of helping them. Ellis says his investigation will take up to six months to complete.

A racial component of the research also raises disturbing questions. In one of Pine and Wasserman's experiments, 60 percent of the 34 boys who participated were black, and the other 40 percent Latino. NYSPI insists that the racial/ethnic mix of the boys Pine and Wasserman studied simply reflects the population living around the institute. But for Ronald Walters, a political scientist at the University of Maryland, the New York studies are just a continuation of what started at NIMH in the early

'90s. Walters served on a panel appointed by then Health and Human Services secretary Louis Sullivan in 1992 that reviewed government-funded research into violence for potential race bias. Then, as now, Walters and other critics believed such research reflects a widespread view among many whites that black and Latino people are predisposed by biology to commit crimes and violent acts. "Why haven't members of the Black and Hispanic Congressional Caucuses been more concerned with this?" asks Walters. "Black and brown children will be the obvious target in the inner city. This research is a shortcut way to deal with violence."

The experiments in New York were conducted in the shadow of a long-running controversy over the very nature of the research: looking for biological causes for violence in individuals instead of examining social and economic factors. Six years ago, the federal National Institutes of Health was embroiled in a debate over the legitimacy of a five-year plan to study the causes of violence that including looking at genetic and biological factors. Dubbed "the violence initiative," the plan was scuttled after Dr. Frederick Goodwin, then head of the Alcohol, Drug Abuse and Mental Health Administration of NIMH, gave a speech in 1992 in which he compared inner-city males to Rhesus monkeys. A coalition of psychologists and sociologist from predominantly African-American organizations attacked Goodwin's pronouncements and his research agenda. Plans for a national conference on genetics and crime were jettisoned, discussions of the violence initiative became muted and Goodwin was forced to resign his post.

Although Goodwin no longer heads the NIMH agency, research into the genetic and biological roots of aggression has continued. According to a 1993 article in *Science* magazine, NIMH was then funding close to 300 research projects into aggression and violence, many with multiyear grants. Since 1990, Pine, Wasserman and their colleagues have received three grants from NIMH totaling more than $7 million. Wasserman launched her initial work with a $1.25 million grant from the private Leon Lowenstein Foundation. Halperin has received nearly $1 million from NIMH since 1990 for his research. None of the researchers responded to interview requests, but senior researchers at NYSPI defended the studies in an interview published in the April 23 issue of *Nature*. Pine told *Nature* that his studies obeyed all federal ethics rules. He called violence "a major public health problem" and criticized his critics for opposing any study of "the relationship between aggression and biology."

The search for a link between ethnicity and violence is not new. The phrenology movement of the late 1800s claimed criminal behavior could be predicted by examining the contours of the human head. Early criminolo-gists and psychologists studied the skulls of juvenile delinquents—mostly Irish immigrant youth back then—in their search for the causes of aggression and anti-social behaviors.

So how real is the link between serotonin levels in the brain and aggressive or violent behavior? In the past decade, psychiatric researchers have developed a fascination with serotonin. Serotonin deficits have been linked to depression and alcoholism, and drugs such as Prozac are designed to raise serotonin levels to inhibit depression. Today, some researchers believe that low levels of serotonin also are responsible for impulsive, even violent behavior. But there is no proof that genetics determine serotonin levels or even that serotonin levels alone are the cause of anything.

Neurobiologist Evan Balaban of the Neurosciences Institute in San Diego is critical of serotonin research like that conducted in New York. He and two colleagues published an article in the October 1996 *Journal of Neurogenetics* that reviewed the findings in 100 studies claiming violent people have very low serotonin levels. They found the studies methodologically suspect and the results inconclusive. While they concurred that biology is important, it is not the sole causative factor. They concluded: "Geneticists and other biologists who are interested in understanding aggressive behavior should take a second look at whether the human and animal literature justifies linking the words 'serotonin' and 'aggression' with the words 'specific relationship.' "

Dr. David Shore, director for clinical research at NIMH, says research into the biological causes of violence and aggression represents a small slice of the work funded by his agency. But Shore says that this kind of research is legitimate. "I don't think data linking violence and serotonin are strange," he says. "There have been studies that have shown all sorts of behavioral problems." Shore defends NIMH's funding of both studies: The researchers not only had to pass the peer review process at their own institutions but survive scrutiny of a panel of NIMH experts. He noted that the panel met in May and that the controversial New York studies were part of its agenda. Halperin's grant, now in its seventh year, is up for renewal, but Shore would not comment on whether the council voted to continue his funding.

Sadly, it has become easier and easier to convince a frightened public that the goal of combating youth crime justifies any means. It has come to the point where NYSPI can boldly declare that the Jonesboro shootings in Arkansas are a justification for violating the integrity of six-year-old boys from Harlem and the Bronx.

Annette Fuentes *is a 1997–98 Prudential Fellow at Columbia Graduate School of Journalism, researching issues on children and the news.*

HARD TIME
A special report.

Profits at a Juvenile Prison Come With a Chilling Cost

By FOX BUTTERFIELD

TALLULAH, La.—Here in the middle of the impoverished Mississippi Delta is a juvenile prison so rife with brutality, cronyism and neglect that many legal experts say it is the worst in the nation.

The prison, the Tallulah Correctional Center for Youth, opened just four years ago where a sawmill and cotton fields once stood. Behind rows of razor wire, it houses 620 boys and young men, age 11 to 20, in stifling corrugated-iron barracks jammed with bunks.

From the run-down homes and bars on the road that runs by it, Tallulah appears unexceptional, one new cookie-cutter prison among scores built in the United States this decade. But inside, inmates of the privately run prison regularly appear at the infirmary with black eyes, broken noses or jaws or perforated eardrums from beatings by the poorly paid, poorly trained guards or from fights with other boys.

Meals are so meager that many boys lose weight. Clothing is so scarce that boys fight over shirts and shoes. Almost all the teachers are uncertified, instruction amounts to as little as an hour a day, and until recently there were no books.

Up to a fourth of the inmates are mentally ill or retarded, but a psy-chiatrist visits only one day a week. There is no therapy. Emotionally disturbed boys who cannot follow guards' orders are locked in isolation cells for weeks at a time or have their sentences arbitrarily extended.

These conditions, which are described in public documents and were recounted by inmates and prison officials during a reporter's visit to Tallulah, are extreme, a testament to Louisiana's well-documented violent history and notoriously brutal prison system.

But what has happened at Tallulah is more than just the story of one bad prison. Corrections officials say the forces that converged to create Tallulah—the incarceration of more and more mentally ill adolescents, a rush by politicians to build new prisons while neglecting education and psychiatric services, and states' handing responsibility for juvenile offenders to private companies—have caused the deterioration of juvenile prisons across the country.

Earl Dunlap, president of the National Juvenile Detention Association, which represents the heads of the nation's juvenile jails, said, "The issues of violence against offenders, lack of adequate education and mental health, of crowding and of poorly paid and poorly trained staff are the norm rather than the exception."

Recognizing the problem, the United States Justice Department has begun a series of investigations into state juvenile systems, including not only Louisiana's but also those of Kentucky, Puerto Rico and Georgia. At the same time, private juvenile prisons in Colorado, Texas and South Carolina have been successfully sued by individuals and groups or forced to give up their licenses.

On Thursday, the Juvenile Justice Project of Louisiana, an offshoot of the Southern Poverty Law Center, filed a Federal lawsuit against Tallulah to stop the brutality and neglect.

In the investigations by the Justice Department, some of the harshest criticism has been leveled at Georgia. The department threatened to take over the state's juvenile system, charging a "pattern of egregious conditions violating the Federal rights of youth," including the use of pepper spray to restrain mentally ill youths, a lack of textbooks, and guards who routinely stripped young inmates and locked them in their cells for days.

A surge in the inmate population forced Georgia's juvenile prison budget up to $220 million from $80 million in just four years, but the money went to building new prisons, with little left for education and psychiatric care. "As we went through a period of rapid increase in juvenile crime and record numbers of juvenile offenders," said Sherman Day, chairman of the Georgia Department of Juvenile Justice, it was "much easier to get new facilities from the Legislature than to get more programs."

After reacting defensively at first, Gov. Zell Miller moved quickly to avert a takeover by agreeing to spend $10 million more this year to hire teachers and medical workers and to increase guard salaries.

Louisiana, whose juvenile system is made up of Tallulah and three prisons operated by the state, is the Justice Department's latest target. In hundreds of pages of reports to a Federal judge who oversees the state's entire prison system under a 1971 consent decree, Justice Department experts have depicted guards who routinely resort to beatings or pepper spray as their only way to discipline inmates, and who pit inmates against one another for sport.

In June, two years after the Justice Department began its investigation and a year after it warned in its first public findings that Tallulah was "an institution out of control," consultants for the department filed new reports with the Federal judge, Frank J. Polozola of Federal District Court in Baton Rouge, warning that despite some improvements, conditions had deteriorated to "a particularly dangerous level."

Even a former warden at Louisiana's maximum-security prison, acting as a consultant to Judge Polozola, found conditions at Tallulah so serious that he urged the judge to reject its request to add inmates.

"I do not make these recommendations because of any sympathy for these offenders," wrote the former warden, John Whitley. "It shocks me to think" that "these offenders and their problems are simply getting worse, and these problems will be unleashed on the public when they are discharged from the system."

The Private Prison
When the Profits Are the Priority

Some of the worst conditions in juvenile prisons can be found among the growing number of privately operated prisons, whether those built specifically for one state, like Tallulah, or ones that take juveniles from across the country, like boot camps that have come under criticism in Colorado and Arizona.

Only 5 percent of the nation's juvenile prisons are operated by private, for-profit companies, Mr. Dunlap of the National Juvenile Detention Association estimates. But as their numbers grow along with privately operated prisons for adults, their regulation is becoming one of the most significant issues in corrections. State corrections departments find themselves having to police contractors who perform functions once the province of government, from psychiatric care to discipline.

In April, Colorado officials shut down a juvenile prison operated by the Rebound Corporation after a mentally ill 13-year-old's suicide led to an investigation that uncovered repeated instances of physical and sexual abuse. The for-profit prison housed offenders from six states.

Both Arizona and California authorities are investigating a privately operated boot camp in Arizona that California paid to take hundreds of offenders. A 16-year-old boy died there, and authorities suspect the cause was abuse by guards and poor medical care. California announced last Wednesday that it was removing its juveniles from the camp.

And recently Arkansas canceled the contract of Associated Marine Institutes, a company based in Florida, to run one juvenile institution, following questions of financial control and accusations of abuse.

A series of United States Supreme Court decisions and state laws have long mandated a higher standard for juvenile prisons than for adult prisons. There is supposed to be more schooling, medical care and security

because the young inmates have been adjudged delinquent, rather than convicted of crimes as adults are, and so are held for rehabilitation instead of punishment.

But what has made problems worse here is that Tallulah, to earn a profit, has scrimped on money for education and mental health treatment in a state that already spends

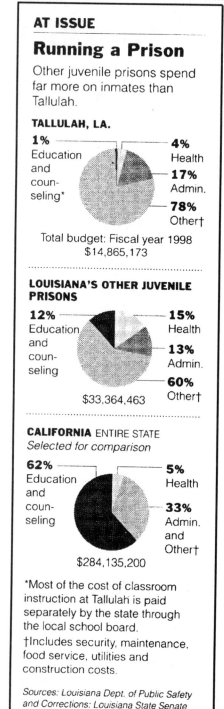

AT ISSUE

Running a Prison

Other juvenile prisons spend far more on inmates than Tallulah.

TALLULAH, LA.

1% Education and counseling*
4% Health
17% Admin.
78% Other†

Total budget: Fiscal year 1998
$14,865,173

LOUISIANA'S OTHER JUVENILE PRISONS

12% Education and counseling
15% Health
13% Admin.
60% Other†

$33,364,463

CALIFORNIA ENTIRE STATE
Selected for comparison

62% Education and counseling
5% Health
33% Admin. and Other†

$284,135,200

*Most of the cost of classroom instruction at Tallulah is paid separately by the state through the local school board.
†Includes security, maintenance, food service, utilities and construction costs.

Sources: Louisiana Dept. of Public Safety and Corrections; Louisiana State Senate Judiciary Comm.; California Youth Auth.

The New York Times

very little in those areas.

"It's incredibly perverse," said David Utter, director of the Juvenile Justice Project of Louisiana. "They have this place that creates all these injuries and they have all these kids with mental disorders, and then they save money by not treating them."

Bill Roberts, the lawyer for Tallulah's owner, Trans-American Development Associates, said that some of the Justice Department's demands, like hiring more psychiatrists, are "unrealistic." The state is to blame for the problems, he said, because "our place was not designed to take that kind of inmate."

Still, Mr. Roberts said, "There has been a drastic improvement" in reducing brutality by guards. As for fights between the inmates, he said, "Juveniles are a little bit different from adults. You are never going to stop all fights between boys."

In papers filed with Judge Polozola on July 7 responding to the Justice experts and Mr. Whitley, the State Attorney General's office disputed accusations of brutality and of high numbers of retarded and mentally ill inmates at Tallulah.

In a recent interview, Cheney Joseph, executive counsel to Gov. Mike Foster, warned there were limits to what Louisiana was willing to do. "There are certain situations the Department of Justice would like us to take care of," he said, "that may not be financially feasible and may not be required by Federal law."

The Entrepreneurs
A Idea Born Of Patronage

The idea for a prison here was put forward in 1992 by James R. Brown, a Tallulah businessman whose father was an influential state senator.

One of the poorest areas in a poor state, Tallulah wanted jobs, and like other struggling cities across the country it saw the nation's prison-building spree as its best hope.

Louisiana needed a new juvenile prison because the number of youths being incarcerated was rising

steeply; within a few years it more than doubled. Adding to that, mental health experts say, were hundreds of juveniles who had no place else to go because of cuts in psychiatric services outside of jail. Mental health authorities estimate that 20 percent of juveniles incarcerated nationally have serious mental illnesses.

To help win a no-bid contract to operate a prison, the company Mr. Brown formed included two close friends of Gov. Edwin W. Edwards—George Fischer and Verdi Adam—said a businessman involved in the venture's early stages, who spoke on the condition of anonymity.

None of the men had any particular qualification to run a prison. Mr. Verdi was a former chief engineer of the state highway department. Mr. Fischer had been the Governor's campaign manager, Cabinet officer and occasional business partner.

Tallulah opened in 1994, and the town of 10,000 got what it hoped for. The prison became its largest employer and taxpayer.

From the beginning, the company formed by Mr. Brown, Trans-American, pursued a strategy of maximizing its profit from the fixed amount it received from the state for each inmate (in 1997, $24,448). The plan was to keep wages and services at a minimum while taking in as many inmates as possible, said the businessman involved in the early stages.

For-profit prisons often try to economize. But the best-run companies have come to recognize that operating with too small or poorly trained a staff can spell trouble, and experts say state officials must pay close attention to the level of services being provided.

"Ultimately, the responsibility belongs to the state," said Charles Thomas, director of the Private Corrections Project at the University of Florida.

Louisiana officials say they monitored conditions at Tallulah and first reported many of the problems there. But in fiscal year 1996–97, according to the State Department of Public Safety and Corrections, Tallu-

lah still listed no money for recreation, treatment or planning inmates' return to society. Twenty-nine percent of the budget went to construction loans.

By comparison, 45 percent of the $32,200 a year that California spends on each juvenile goes to programs and caseworkers, and none to construction. Nationally, construction costs average 7 percent of juvenile prison budgets, Mr. Dunlap said.

"That means either that Tallulah's construction costs are terribly inflated, or the services they are providing are extraordinarily low," he said.

The Inside
Hot, Crowded, Spartan, Neglectful

Part of Tallulah is a boot camp, with boys crammed so tightly in barracks that there is room only for double bunks, a television set and a few steel tables. Showers and urinals are open to the room, allowing boys who have been incarcerated for sexual assault to attack other inmates, according to a report in June by a Justice Department consultant, Dr. Bernard Hudson.

The only space for the few books that have recently been imported to try to improve education is a makeshift self on top of the urinals. Among the aging volumes that a reporter saw were "Inside the Third Reich," "The Short Stories of Henry James" and "Heidi."

From their wakeup call at 5:30 A.M., the inmates, in white T-shirts and loose green pants, spend almost all their time confined to the barracks. They leave the barracks only for marching drills, one to three hours a day of class and an occasional game of basketball. There is little ventilation, and temperatures in Louisiana's long summers hover permanently in the 90's.

The result, several boys told a visitor, is that some of them deliberately start trouble in order to be disciplined and sent to the other section of Tallulah, maximum-security cells that are air-conditioned.

Guards put inmates in solitary confinement so commonly that in one week in May more than a quarter of all the boys spent at least a day in "lockdown," said Nancy Ray, another Justice Department expert. The average stay in solitary is five to six weeks; some boys are kept indefinitely. While in the tiny cells, the boys are stripped of all possessions and lie on worn, thin mattresses resting on concrete blocks.

The crowding, heat and isolation are hardest on the 25 percent of the boys who are mentally ill or retarded, said Dr. Hudson, a psychiatrist, tending to increase their depression or psychosis.

Although Tallulah has made some improvements in its treatment of the emotionally disturbed over the last year, Dr. Hudson said, it remains "grossly inadequate."

The prison still does not properly screen new arrivals for mental illness or retardation, he reported. The part-time doctor and psychiatrist are there so infrequently that they have never met, Dr. Hudson said. Powerful anti-psychotic medications are not monitored. Medical charts often cannot be found.

And the infirmary is often closed because of a shortage of guards, whose pay is so low—$5.77 an hour— that there has been 100 percent turnover in the staff in the last year, the Justice Department experts said.

Other juvenile prisons that have come under investigation have also been criticized for poor psychiatric treatment. But at Tallulah this neglect has been compounded by everyday violence.

All these troubles are illustrated in the case of one former inmate, Travis M., a slight 16-year-old who is mentally retarded and has been treated with drugs for hallucinations.

Sometimes, Travis said in an interview after his release, guards hit him because his medication made him sleepy and he did not stand to attention when ordered. Sometimes

they "snuck" him at night as he slept in his bunk, knocking him to the cement floor. Sometimes they kicked him while he was naked in the shower telling him simply, "You owe me some licks."

Travis was originally sentenced by a judge to 90 days for shoplifting and stealing a bicycle. But every time he failed to stand for a guard or even called his grandmother to complain, officials at Tallulah put him in solitary and added to his sentence.

After 15 months, a judge finally ordered him released so he could get medical treatment. His eardrum had been perforated in a beating by a guard, he had large scars on his arms, legs and face, and his nose had been so badly broken that he speaks in a wheeze. A lawyer is scheduled to file suit against Tallulah on behalf of Travis this week.

One reason these abuses have continued, Mr. Utter said, is that juveniles in Louisiana, as in a number of states, often get poor legal representation. One mentally ill boy from Eunice was sentenced without a lawyer, or even a trial. Poorly paid public defenders seldom visit their clients after sentencing, Mr. Utter said, and so are unaware of conditions at places like Tallulah.

Another reason is that almost all Tallulah's inmates are from poor families and 82 percent are black, Mr. Utter noted, an imbalance that afflicts prisons nationwide to one degree or another. "They are disenfranchised and no one cares about them," he said.

The New Guard
A Retreat From Brutality

In September, Tallulah hired as its new warden David Bonnette, a 25-year veteran of Angola State Penitentiary who started there as a guard and rose to assistant superintendent. A muscular, tobacco-chewing man with his initials tattooed on a forearm, Mr. Bonnette brought several Angola colleagues with him to impose better discipline.

"When I got here, there were a lot of perforated eardrums," he said. "Actually, it seemed like everybody had a perforated eardrum, or a broken nose." When boys wrote complaints, he said guards put the forms in a box and pulled out ones to investigate at random. Some were labeled, "Never to be investigated."

But allegations of abuse by guards dropped to 52 a month this spring, from more than 100 a month last summer, Mr. Bonnette said, as he has tried to carry out a new state policy of zero tolerance for brutality. Fights between boys have declined to 33 a month, from 129, he said.

In June, however, Ms. Ray, the Justice Department consultant, reported that there had been a recent increase in "youth defiance and disobedience," with the boys angry about Tallulah's "exceptionally high" use of isolation cells.

Many guards have also become restive, the Justice Department experts found, a result of poor pay and new restrictions on the use of force.

One guard who said he had quit for those reasons said in an interview: "The inmates are running the asylum now. You're not supposed to touch the kids, but how are we supposed to control them without force?" He has relatives working at Tallulah and so insisted on not being identified.

The frustration boiled over on July 1, during a tour by Senator Paul Wellstone, the Minnesota Democrat who is drafting legislation that would require psychiatric care for all incarcerated juveniles who need it. Despite intense security, a group of inmates climbed on a roof and shouted their complaints at Senator Wellstone, who was accompanied by Richard Stalder, the secretary of Louisiana's Department of Public Safety and Corrections.

Mr. Stalder said he planned to create a special unit for mentally ill juvenile offenders. One likely candidate to run it, he said, is Trans-American, the company that operates Tallulah.

JUVENILE BOOT CAMPS:
Lessons Learned

by Eric Peterson

In response to a significant increase in juvenile arrests and repeat offenses over the past decade, several States and many localities have established juvenile boot camps. The first juvenile boot camp programs, modeled after boot camps for adult offenders, emphasized military-style discipline and physical conditioning. OJJDP has supported the development of three juvenile boot camp demonstration sites. This Fact Sheet describes those demonstration projects, their evaluations, and lessons learned that will benefit future boot camp programs.

PILOT PROGRAMS

In 1992 OJJDP funded three juvenile boot camps designed to address the special needs and circumstances of adolescent offenders. The programs were conducted in Cleveland, Ohio; Denver, Colorado; and Mobile, Alabama.

Focusing on a target population of adjudicated, nonviolent offenders under the age of 18, the boot camp programs were designed as highly structured, 3-month residential programs followed by 6 to 9 months of community-based aftercare. During the aftercare period, youth were to pursue academic and vocational training or employment while under intensive, but progressively diminishing, supervision.

EVALUATIONS

OJJDP undertook impact evaluations for all three sites that compared the recidivism rates for juveniles who participated in the pilot programs with those of control groups. The evaluations also compared the cost-effectiveness of juvenile boot camps with other dispositional alternatives.

Reports of the three impact evaluations are available. The evaluations of the Mobile and Cleveland programs are interim reports that present data from the earliest cohorts. As neither program had stabilized when the data were collected, OJJDP is considering expanding the evaluation to include the remaining cohorts. The Denver program is no longer active.

FINDINGS

Most juvenile boot camp participants completed the residential program and graduated to aftercare. Program completion rates were 96 percent in Cleveland, 87 percent in Mobile, and 76 percent in Denver.

At the two sites where educational gains were measured, substantial improvements in academic skills were noted. In Mobile approximately three-quarters of the participants improved their performance in reading, spelling, language, and math by one grade level or more. In Cleveland the average juvenile boot camp participant improved reading, spelling, and math skills by approximately one grade level.

In addition, where employment records were available, a significant number of participants found jobs while in aftercare.

The pilot programs, however, did not demonstrate a reduction in recidivism. In Denver and Mobile, no statistically significant difference could be found between the recidivism rates of juvenile boot camp participants and those of the control groups (youth confined in State or county institutions, or released on probation). In Cleveland pilot program participants evidenced a higher recidivism rate than juvenile offenders confined in traditional juvenile correctional facilities. It should be noted that none of the sites fully implemented OJJDP's model juvenile boot camp guide-

From *Office of Juvenile Justice and Delinquency Prevention Fact Sheet No. 36*, June 1996. Reprinted by permission of the National Institute of Justice, National Criminal Justice Reference Service.

lines, and that some critical aftercare support services were not provided.

LESSONS LEARNED

Several significant lessons have emerged from the pilot programs:

The appropriate population should be targeted. Boot camps should be designed as an intermediate intervention. At one site, youth who had been previously confined were significantly more likely to recidivate, while youth with the least serious offenses were also more likely to recidivate.

Facility location is important. Cost issues and community resistance were major obstacles to securing residential and aftercare facilities. To increase attendance and reduce problems, aftercare facilities should be located in gang-neutral areas accessible by public transportation.

Staff selection and training needs are critical. To reduce staff turnover, fill gaps in critical services, and ensure consistent programming, the screening, selection, and training of juvenile boot camp and aftercare staff must be sensitive to the programmatic and operational features of a juvenile boot camp. This is particularly important with regard to youth development issues. Moreover, continuous treatment between the residential and aftercare phases should be integrated philosophically and programmatically, particularly through staffing.

Aftercare programs are challenging to implement. Successful aftercare programs require attention at the outset to develop a comprehensive model with the flexibility to respond to local needs and concerns. Aftercare programs are unlikely to succeed if their participants fail to receive the full range of services prescribed for them. Aftercare programs must be broad-based and flexible enough to meet the particular educational, employment, counseling, and support needs of each participant. The aftercare component should form dynamic linkages with other community services, especially youth service agencies, schools, and employers.

Coordination among agencies must be maintained. All three sites experienced difficulties in maintaining coordination among the participating agencies. Considerable attention should be paid to building and maintaining a consensus among participating organizations concerning the program's philosophy and procedures.

Effective evaluation begins with planning. To assess the program's successes and failures, quantifiable data should be collected about participation in treatment by juveniles in the boot camp and in the control group. Measures of program success should include a broad spectrum of outcomes. Recidivism measures should capture all subsequent delinquent activity, not simply the first new adjudication, and data on new offenses should include information on the origin and circumstances of the complaint to determine whether there is a monitoring effect, in which the intensity of the supervision causes an increase in recorded offending.

When boot camps are used as an alternative to confinement, savings can be achieved. Communities often implement juvenile boot camps, in part, to reduce costs. The experience of the pilot sites indicates that when boot camps are used as an alternative to traditional confinement, costs can be reduced considerably because of the significantly shorter residential stay. However, if boot camps are used as an alternative to probation, savings will not be realized.

CONCLUSION

Juvenile boot camps embrace a variety of objectives: reducing recidivism, improving academic performance, cutting the cost of treating juvenile offenders, and inculcating the values of self-discipline and hard work. In attempting to reach these objectives, OJJDP is collaborating with the Office of Justice Programs (OJP) to enhance program models, policies, and practices of juvenile boot camps. As a result, many of the lessons learned from OJJDP's three demonstration sites have been incorporated in the OJP Boot Camp Corrections Program.

FOR FURTHER INFORMATION

Jurisdictions considering or operating a juvenile boot camp may receive technical assistance from the National Institute of Corrections. This assistance is available without regard to whether the jurisdiction is receiving, or contemplating applying for, Federal funding.

To order any or all of the three pilot program evaluation reports, or a copy of a Program Summary on juvenile boot camps that OJJDP will release in summer 1996, please call the Juvenile Justice Clearinghouse, toll free, at 800–638–8736.

Eric Peterson is a Program Specialist in OJJDP's Research and Program Development Division.

A WAYWARD BOYS' 'SHOCK INCARCERATION' CAMP

■ MOBILE, ALA.—At last, the drill instructors have quit yelling, and the 10 young members of B Company are seated rigidly at their desks in a classroom trailer. The boys rose this morning to a 5 o'clock bugle call, made their beds, showered, marched to breakfast, ran 3 miles and mopped their barracks. Now, they watch intently as Jerry Pogue, a tall man in a gray, pinstriped suit, paces in front of the blackboard and a list of scribbled words. "Discipline," he says as he underlines it.

"D-I-S-C-I-P-L-I-N-E." He asks the boys—all in their third week of detention in one of America's three federally funded juvenile boot camps—to describe the role discipline has played in their lives. The "recruits" seem tongue-tied, so he mentions the merits of a hard regimen. Hands shoot up. "Sir," says recruit Phillip, a 15-year-old convicted of criminal mischief. "All this waking up at 5 in the morning, marching and push-ups—that can't change our environment when we get back out, Sir." A consensus emerges: The boys just don't understand the link between the Environ-mental Youth Corps' daily rigors and their hoped-for transformation into law-abiding teenagers.

Philip's concerns mirror those raised by grown-up skeptics, many of whom question the lasting value of 90 days of verbal abuse and calisthenics for miscreants from troubled neighborhoods. Yet with juvenile arrests up 12 percent in five years and prisons overcrowded, many politicians tout juvenile boot camps as cheap alternatives to detention homes for young, nonviolent offenders. The concept also has caught on in Washington, where the Clinton administration is proposing $172 million for boot camps for 13-to-17-year-olds and other programs to combat juvenile crime.

Outside record. Large numbers of adults who go through boot camps wind up breaking laws again, but backers of juvenile camps argue that "shock incarceration" works well with teens. A University of South Alabama study of Mobile's EYC camp found that its graduates are arrested for 30 percent fewer felonies and 70 percent fewer misdemeanors than boys released from other correctional facilities. "The touchy-feely approach people used with juveniles in the '60s and '70s just doesn't work with 1994 delinquents," explains Michael Lucci, the ex-marine who runs the camp.

With its juvenile crime rate soaring 250 percent in the past 10 years, Mobile County plans to open a second and bigger EYC camp in December. "A boot camp may not be right for every city, but it's right for Mobile," says Circuit Judge John F. Butler. "I'd rather see a kid spend 90 days here—improving his self-esteem and physical strength and learning the negative benefits of crime—than put him in some correctional warehouse for nine months to a year." Indeed, Mobile can count more than a few EYC successes. A 15-year-old named Daryl, for instance, is now back in high school, showing up every day and getting better grades than ever. He walks a fine line, however, as schoolmates try to temp him back into his former life of $300-a-day drug sales. "But I show them my books, and I keep walking," Daryl says. "I learned that at boot camp, and I'll keep it with me." BY JOHN SIMONS

Unit Selections

Key Points to Consider

❖ Will policy responses to school shooting incidents be based on good theory or will they be knee-jerk responses? Explain your answer.

❖ Where and how does the community fit into the creation of juvenile justice policy and practice?

❖ It has been proposed that we need to simultaneously sanitize the community and appropriately socialize its newest members if we hope to have a better future. What do you think?

❖ In addition to the national initiatives in *Safe Start* and *Safe Schools,* what else needs to be done to improve the quality of life for children as they grow into the delinquency-prone years?

❖ Should what you would want for your own children and teens in the future be provided for every child and teen? If so, how should it be done?

 **Links** | **www.dushkin.com/online/**

These sites are annotated on pages 4 and 5.

As much as I enjoy looking forward, my experiences in diagnosing behavior and dealing with people and organizations is that one of the best predictors of the future is the past. For example, in the past, the series of decisions made around *in re Gault,* 387 U.S. 1 (1967) transformed a rehabilitation-oriented juvenile court system into an adversarial adult court. Moreover, the process essentially moved the system from informal/traditional to formal/bureaucratic. More recently, the justice model has demanded both revenge and time served. This has been followed by a trend toward mediation and restorative justice that may swing the pendulum back. The nature of society and of the juvenile environment and culture in the United States has changed radically, fueled by technology and an ability to share in the culture that has never before existed in our history.

When we consider technology and cultural exposure as trends of the future, we must begin to consider seriously writers who have discussed these phenomena deeply and then we must try to apply these trends to the future of juveniles and the juvenile justice system. In *The Third Wave,* Alvin Toffler predicts that we will live and function in a freeflowing style of organization as opposed to traditional hierarchies. In the future we will have to be even more adaptable than we are today. Trends will deemphasize representative democracy and promote participatory democracy. Our society and organizations will rapidly synthesize vast amounts of information and expand opportunities for human intelligence, intuition, and imagination to make a more significant contribution to culture and society. At a very surface level this future would encourage values that would better incorporate juveniles into society and push the juvenile justice system more toward emerging concepts of restorative justice.

While Toffler is fascinating, I prefer the work of John Naisbitt for understanding what is coming for adult and juvenile criminal justice. In his nationwide

best seller, *Megatrends,* and its successor books, Naisbitt has discussed "ten new directions transforming our lives." These 10 trends show us moving into a very different version of human and organizational life than we enjoy today. We will move from an industrial society to an information-based society, from short-term thinking to long-term perception, from centralization to decentralization, from institutional help to self-help hierarchies, from networking and either/or thinking to multiple-option thinking.

Among these, the trends that will most affect juveniles and juvenile justice are the change from (1) institutional help to self-help; (2) an industrial to an information-based society; (3) centralization to decentralization; (4) hierarchies to networking, and (5) getting out of the either/or mentality. While it is problematic, given the past behavior of some of our policymakers, we must hope that we change from short-term thinking to long-term thinking. All of Naisbitt's predictions assume a technology that continues to become more complex, to become more sophisticated, more available, more expensive and, despite its problems, more essential for full functioning in the current world. This scenario will be played out in a population that has continuing fluctuations in the size of the at-risk populations.

If Naisbitt is accurate, these futures will enable a world in which the community will have a stake in the life of each juvenile. This was precisely the thinking that created the concept of delinquency and the mechanism of the juvenile court 100 years ago. It is already agreed, although scorned by cynics when it was restated, that it takes a community to raise a child. The articles in this section certainly seem to augur that future.

References
Naisbitt, John, *Megatrends,* New York: Warner, 1982.
Toffler, Alvin, *The Third Wave,* New York: Bantam Books, 1980.

Tribune file photo by Ovie Carter

Friends and family visit the grave of Arthur Williams in 1993. Williams was murdered at age 14.

What can we do?

There are no formulas, no magic words, to end the kind of violence against children that occurs every year in the Chicago area.

If experts agree on anything when they talk about dealing with violence, it's that you can't start too early, and you can't start too late.

Early is better, of course. That's when a child can be set on a course of success. But lives that have gone the wrong direction can be changed too. That task is more difficult,

though it's not impossible. Even a child who has spent time in juvenile prison for murder can turn around.

Declaring that a society could be judged by how it treats its children, the Tribune began to explore the issues surrounding violence against children with a 1993 series called "Killing our children." In 1994, possible solutions were examined in "Saving our children." Last month, with the publication of "Killing our children: The search for justice," the

newspaper reported on the aftermath of the 65 killings in 1993.

After reading one of this year's articles, a reader called to say, "This series is absolutely incredible. I'm moved, and I'm hoping that . . . you reach some conclusion—I fear you won't—and that there are some things that we out here in the world can do to try and make this situation better."

A fair request. Today, the Tribune turns to people we have met along the way—families, teachers, court workers, even a killer—who see the problem first-hand and have a sense of how to fix it.

They're not all what we traditionally consider experts, and they don't always agree. But no one is closer to the violence. Here are their thoughts.

TOM SCHNEIDER has been a juvenile probation officer in Cook County for 25 years. His present caseload includes 44 young offenders who have been convicted of crimes from vandalism to murder.

If there is anything I've learned as a juvenile probation officer, it's that violence—and especially violence to children—does not occur, nor is it nurtured, in a vacuum.

The causes are numerous, and the solutions are equally numerous. The trick of it, though, is that solutions are different in each case.

When I first started at Cook County Juvenile Court in 1973, there were two courtrooms devoted to abuse and neglect cases. Now there are 16. Then, guns were much more difficult for kids to get. Since the mid-1980s, when crack began to take hold, children in far greater numbers have started to carry guns—and use them.

I've seen kids who were victims of terrible physical and emotional abuse turn around and become victimizers themselves. I've worked with nine children who later have been murdered in gun-related gang violence.

To change this, help has to come early. The probation department and the state's attorney's office now have an early offenders program that seeks to identify young offenders when they are first charged and divert them to specialized programs.

We even have a group for young sex offenders made up of kids as young as 10. Though it's appalling, it's all too real. This is the time to identify those kids and intervene.

The task of reversing violent behavior is daunting, not to mention time-consuming. No cookie-cutter approach works for every child. You have to consider their unique problems, from abusive parents to drug use, from learning disabilities to poverty. Rarely does a case boil down to just one issue.

You learn to savor the smallest victories. There's nothing like running into a former probationer years later and seeing that they have turned their lives around.

To achieve that kind of success, though, you have to use whatever resources are available, although sometimes you can't find just what these kids need. More frequently, it's in short supply. Parenting training, even for teenage fathers, and violence prevention groups are helpful but sometimes hard to get children into.

I have been involved in the anger management groups for male offenders; they provide an invaluable outlet for at-risk juveniles, both to learn other non-violent responses and to confront their fears, especially for their own safety.

Because violence is often tied to drug and alcohol abuse, programs are needed to deal with those problems. We need more slots in outpatient programs and more beds in residential facilities. We need more intensive outpatient programs, where youths spend several hours a day in treatment while living at home.

I have seen these programs work, and I know that violence cannot be effectively addressed until substance abuse is brought under control.

The juvenile probation department has a drug program that works with police to identify drug users and place them in programs. It has been successful.

But perhaps most important is we have to give children a sense they

have a stake in society. Without basic skills and job training, many teenagers see little choice for themselves but to join with gangs.

Because most children involved in crime are underachievers in the classroom and see school as a humiliating experience, we need basic learning and vocational training.

Mentoring also is invaluable. Finding a father in the home of a juvenile delinquent is rare. Without a model for responsible behavior, there's almost no reason to expect a child to learn it. I met with seven young men recently in a violence prevention group session, and they all raged at their inattentive or absent fathers.

Mentoring is a tough job, though, and almost every youth will test their mentor. These kids are used to rejection; in fact, they almost expect to be rejected. It's their way of protecting themselves against disappointment. They need consistency in their lives, and the worst thing you can do is make a promise you can't deliver.

But it's difficult to recruit volunteers for work that rarely pays quick dividends. It takes a strong, resilient mentor to overcome this.

When it works, and it does, the results are gratifying.

These days, the trend is to toughen the approach toward criminals, including violent juveniles. I understand the need to protect society, and I agree that the needs of victims must be kept in mind when dealing with violent criminals. They need to understand and appreciate the harm and pain they have caused.

Still, there is no denying that the approaches we take in juvenile court work. To take each juvenile offender as an individual, trying to understand his background, his family situation, his possible history as a victim himself, his special treatment needs, then using a combination of approaches, is invaluable. It will serve the young offender, and it will serve us all.

The solutions to these problems are not easy, and the answers are not simple, especially in a popular culture where movies and music glorify violence and romanticize gang life. But just because we try to understand violent behavior, especially in children, does not mean we excuse it.

But we can't solve the problem if we don't understand it.

'WE CAN'T ACCEPT THIS'

ALICE THOMAS-NORRIS of Hillside, a certified nurse assistant and home health aide, is the mother of Rolanda Marshall, who was shot and killed in 1993, at age 14. Marshall's slaying remains unsolved.

The main thing is that America has been in denial for so many years. We need to repent and restore the faith in mankind. Mankind has strayed so far off the path that we accept anything as being normal.

That these things happen—that someone was in the wrong place at the wrong time and got shot—we accept this and we simply can't anymore.

These are human beings. We have become desensitized to the killings, to the robberies, to the rapes. We accept this as being normal, like it goes with the territory of living in the big city. But we have to start admitting that this isn't normal. We've been lying to ourselves. Kids being killed isn't normal. The blood is crying out from the ground for justice.

We can't accept all the garbage, the acts of violence, that come on TV. We need limits on what's on.

We have to realize that everything that happens to me affects you, and everything that happens to you affects me. And I don't think we all understand that. Because if my child could be killed, so could yours.

And guns. We have to do something about guns. Guns are being manufactured 24 hours a day. Why

are there so many guns when we're supposed to be a peace-loving nation?

'YOU HAVE TO MAKE THE CHANGES YOURSELF'

TOMMIE TURNER was 15 and a member of the Black Gangster Disciples street gang in 1993, when he and three friends were arrested for the murder of Randolph Scott, a 14-year-old from their South Side neighborhood. Turner is serving a 20-year term at Shawnee Correctional Center in Downstate Vienna.

I wish there were some kind of golden answer that would solve violence. But it's a lot of things—education, family structure, spirituality and maybe just growing out of it. You get older and then some of this hard-core violence just doesn't make any sense anymore to you.

Sometimes I think if people could see what prison is like, or if they could see their friends in the grave, then maybe they'd figure things out. But I saw friends go to prison and I saw friends get killed. You think that happens only to somebody else.

But mostly it's an individual thing. Nobody's going to do it for you. You have to make the changes yourself that are going to keep you out of prison or keep you from selling drugs.

You've got to choose the right kinds of friends. If you want to stay straight, you've got to find people who are going to stay straight with you, people who are going to encourage you and not get you in trouble.

But sometimes the change happens when you get tired. I've known guys who say, "Man, I'm tired. I want to be a family man. I don't want to be in this violence or drug dealing no more." Sometimes that's

just your head. You've got to know what you want to do.

'BY THE TIME THEY GET TO ME, IT'S TOO LATE'

JERRY BUTLER is superintendent of the Illinois Youth Center at St. Charles, one of the state's seven youth prisons. Several juvenile killers from 1993 spent time at St. Charles.

In corrections, we're kind of downstream. The problem is upstream. The problem is in the neighborhoods and in the schools and the families. By the time somebody gets here, it's almost too late, really.

We need neighborhoods where people care and take an interest in what their neighbors do. We can talk about drugs and guns, but we need to do something about them. We need to fix the fabric of our culture—a lot of the fabric that made up the good old days has been lost.

Maybe then we'll get back some of the concepts from the good old days: respect, kids being responsible for their behavior—the guidelines for behavior.

Most of our kids here aren't here just because of the criminal act they've committed. It's not just one thing. They've got substance problems, family problems, neighborhood problems. And the entities in society that were supposed to help them have failed.

Where was the church? Where was the family? Where was the school? Those places used to be more involved. They need to get involved again. PTA meetings should be packed, standing room only. And those parents should be involved in everything else in their community: church, school, clubs, the whole thing.

Because by the time they get here to me, it's too late. We're expected to redo all that society was supposed to do in those first 13 or 14 years, and we can't do that. We can't give these kids completely new lives.

'AS LONG AN IMPRISONMENT AS POSSIBLE'

GLEN WEBER, assistant Winnebago County state's attorney, has been a prosecutor for 11 years and tried Mardell Traylor for abusing 23-month-old Cardell Redmond after Traylor was acquitted of the murder of 15-month-old Jasmine Bolden.

First and foremost is the need for strict and harsh punishment—as long an imprisonment as possible. But to achieve that you need diligent prosecution and judges who understand the need for long-term imprisonment and punishment.

People who hit children are just so fundamentally rotten to the core that you're really not going to get very far with any kind of education or training. I've seen it first-hand, where people are in these parenting classes—and it's all good-intentioned stuff—but it doesn't work. These people still hit kids. They get out of class and they hit their child. It's such a simple concept—you don't hit kids. But they don't get it.

I subscribe to the same theory on a broader scale too. The only education for these gangbangers is to see that their fellow gang members are no longer out on the street. That's all they understand, really.

Maybe in a perfect world, if we had all the money and all the resources, training and education would work. Well, I don't know, I'd probably still want to spend more money on imprisonment. These criminals don't rehabilitate.

'A HELPING HAND FROM OUTSIDE'

IRA COWARD is a former teacher at DuSable High School, which is across the street from the Robert Taylor Homes public housing complex on the South Side. This fall he began as a teacher at the school for juvenile detainees at the Cook County Juvenile Detention Center. Coward, an ordained minister in the Pentecostal Church of God, often takes youths to church and on outings, lecturing them about the importance of school and moral conduct.

This generation of youths is not lost but in need of the investment of resources and concerned people in order to change their lives and to save our society. I am convinced that they have great potential, which has not been realized. We cannot afford to ignore their plight because our destinies are connected.

We must somehow lift them above a feeling of helplessness. They feel like they're stuck and there's nothing to be done. It's like a person in quicksand—the more they struggle to get out, the more they go down. They need some help. These kids need a helping hand from outside.

It's hard to rise when you don't know there's anything else to be exposed to. A lot of them haven't been downtown. They've never been any farther than the store or the school. They think that's the world.

In the 'hood, they're deprived of their childhood. I take them to the beach. I take them out of their element, where they don't have to be tough. I had a van before it got stolen. We'd just pack it up and go to the Indiana Dunes or to church.

But churches generally are more interested in building glass cathedrals and empires than in investing in what they should be investing in.

Churches should be providing after-school activities. You tell them don't do this, or don't do that but you give them nothing else to do. Give them activities, recreational outings, mentoring, tutoring, field trips. after these kids see enough, they realize there is something else.

Money—that's not going to work. You have to have people who are willing to give of themselves, give their time.

'I'M MY OWN WOMAN'

CAROLYN HUGHES is a single mother of five living in the Englewood neighborhood. She used to reside in Robert Taylor Homes, but moved out in 1993 after Arthur Williams Jr., a boy nicknamed A.J., was killed by a gang sniper. Hughes' son, Larry Oliver, was good friends with A.J. Hughes' own life turned around after she ended an abusive relationship with a man.

My message for all women is to watch their step. I'm a loner now. I just stay to myself. I have the twins' father come by but he's like my best friend. Men want to boss you. When you get with them they just change up, and they change so quick. It wouldn't hardly matter until you get abused so much.

I do what I want to do and I feel good about it. Because I'm my own woman and I'm not being programmed to do what they want me to do.

I think they need more police who will come when you call them. They were shooting the other night again. They got this things they call CAPS (Community Alternative Policing Strategy). I don't see CAPS doing too much of nothing. The dope dealers are still outside there, and it's so bad on the kids. They can't help but see what's going on.

The main thing I would say for the mayor of Chicago: He needs more patrol officers. The police, they're not doing their job.

'GIVE A PERSON A CHANCE'

LARRY OLIVER, 19, was a close friend of Arthur Williams Jr., a 13-year-old killed in 1993. For a while

ONTHERECORD

By Steve Mills
TRIBUNE STAFF WRITER

Patrick Tolan
Psychologist, UIC Institute for Juvenile Research

Patrick Tolan researches the causes of urban violence and how that violence can be prevented. As director of the Institute for Juvenile Research at the University of Illinois at Chicago, he studies the mental health needs of urban children and their families. He trains psychologists and social workers to help families cope with violence.

Q: In 1993, 65 children were murdered in the Chicago area, the majority from abuse at the hands of a parent or guardian or from handgun violence. It's enough to make you think things are hopeless.

A: There's reason to hope. We know much more than we did even five years ago. People are starting to realize this isn't just a matter of "There's something the matter with kids today," and it's something we can fix easily. People see it will take time and regular attention.

Q: Is there any way to predict who will be violent?

A: To a degree, yes. The most important predictors of violence are a history of abuse, being raised in families where discipline is unpredictable and where kids are on their own too much. Kids having difficulty with self-control also may be violent.

Q: Are there programs that have shown promise?

A: Many have. Family intervention programs, in particular, have shown reductions in arrest rates of almost 50 percent in children who have repeated arrests, which we consider among the most serious groups.

Q: Is that true for all kinds of violence?

A: We have more information about how to intervene with youth violence, particularly the kind we think of as criminal. We have less information about how to intervene with child abuse.

Q: Why is that?

A: It's a matter of focus. It took longer for it to become legitimate to intervene with families who are abusing children. There is a history of parental rights that looks at children as property, and there's a competing value of a parent's right to raise their children as

they see fit. But there's never been a competing interest in attacking somebody on the street.

Q: Let's talk about gang violence first.

A: There has been success in recruiting younger kids out of gangs. And we know that when kids leave gangs, their violence level goes down. We do that by keeping kids busy and supervised, involved in organized structured activities when they're not in school. If they don't make use of those resources, including therapy, you go to tougher sanctions to get them to use them.

Q: But how do you persuade kids to leave gangs?

A: With some kids, all you need to do is offer them attention and positive social activities. A lot of kids want to be involved in things other than gangs, but the gangs are all they have. Some kids need a way to get out that assures their safety. Some kids just need their gang tattoos removed so they can get a job.

Q: You make it sound relatively easy.

A: It requires focus and intensity. But there are methods for doing it. It's just a matter of having well-trained people focused and giving them time and resources.

Q: Child abuse seems to be a thornier issue. What do we do?

A: The first thing is anything that makes the child safe. But the other thing is to offer the parent, if it is a parent, ways to change their behavior. Parenting classes, drug and alcohol treatment. It can be as simple as a visiting nurse or social worker involvement. Then you also do increased monitoring, so if it's becoming stressful in the home, someone is there to intervene. It's how the child welfare system is supposed to work.

The major issue for child abuse is not that the models for intervention don't work. It's that they are understaffed and the resources and training aren't there.

Because of the idea of family privacy and because people sometimes confuse abuse with discipline—that you shouldn't tell people how to raise their kids—ideas have developed slowly.

On the other hand, it's such an offensive idea that someone would beat on a child that the idea of helping a person like that is offensive. It's understandable that you'd just want to lock them up. But if you want to prevent that person from abusing another child, you have to take a long-term view.

Q: Can a tendency to be violent be changed?

A: Not everybody can be changed. There are people who, for whatever reason—chemistry or because so much violence has been done to them—are not going to change. It's just like alcoholism or obesity. It's hard to change human behavior.

But we know how to help people eat right. It's a matter of getting them to the programs. It's the same with abuse. We know how to change those behaviors. But a lot of those families don't think it makes sense to get family therapy.

Q: Prosecutors and legislators have a different take on all this.

A: There are people who are going to be beyond the reach of our programs. I've worked with families that have tested my belief in these programs. So I'm not suggesting if everybody got treatment we wouldn't have problems. But we can help a majority of them.

As a front-line clinician, I've had days where I've said, "Get this father away from me. I can't stand what he's done." But we can make a difference in the future if we pursue a course of treatment instead of just locking people up.

Q: But are some people just bad?

A: As a psychologist, I always can find a reason for people's behavior. But as a person, can my rationality be pushed to where I say that some person is just evil? Yes. Maybe another way to look at it is to ask whether we shouldn't take a chance on some people. Yes. But they're much, much rarer than people think.

Q: What's the thinking on how early to get to kids?

A: The thinking is that the earliest is best, but it's never too late.

Q: What's cutting edge now?

A: Three things: One is community coordination—a coordinated effort among police, schools and mental health to work with high-risk families. Sort of combining community policing and block watches with probation tracking high-risk kids, both to get them resources to change and intervening right away.

Second is the idea of early intervention with kids who are high-risk with what we call wraparound services. There, the intervention is working with how the family deals with its own problems, but also how they deal with the schools, jobs, everything.

The third innovation is the extent to which people are realizing that if these policies aren't guided by sound research, we're just throwing our money away.

An edited transcript

Oliver ran with a gang and was involved in drug dealing, but now he works in the mail room of a firm at the Chicago Board of Trade and has hopes of a better life.

All fast money ain't good money. You're out there, the money's coming easy. It's coming real quick. But you gotta think of the consequences. You got the police down there who's gonna whup ya. You're gonna go to jail. You got other people who are gonna hate you. It's no good like that.

I know a lot of guys that need jobs. Give a person a chance. Let 'em try to do something. Me and my cousin we'd go fill out applications and it's just a stereotype: just because you're young and black they think you're mugging people. A lot

of white people aren't going to hire you like that. They're not going to hire you just because you fill out an application.

Just give 'em a chance. Let 'em try to do something. Let 'em work.

I speak in ebonics. People in my job notice that. They look at me a certain way but I can still hold a conversation with 'em. But it's the way I be sayin' things. It's street slang, ebonics. They speak way more proper than me. But I understand the things they're sayin' and they can understand me. See beyond that. We're from two different types of cultures.

'REALLY GET INVOLVE WITH THE KID'

STUART LUBIN, Juvenile Court judge, was a public defender for 17 years before he became a judge in 1991. He handled the case against a 10-year-old boy who was accused of kicking a toddler to death in 1993.

You just have to find somebody to really get involved with a kid, to really care about him. If a person has a sense of his own worth, then he's less likely to inflict harm on someone else.

How do you do that? By having a mentor, for example. By ensuring that someone gets an education. By counseling somebody. By instilling some kind of faith or moral values in a person. By having somebody volunteer or do community service to show kids they can make a differ-

Whom to call

➤ **ABUSE PREVENTION AND PARENTAL COUNSELING**
- The 24-hour National Abuse Hotline 1-800-4ACHILD
- The DCFS Hotline, Illinois 1-800-25-ABUSE
- South Suburban Family Shelter Inc. hotline 708-335-3028
- Family Shelter Service hotline, Glen Ellyn 630-469-5650
- Jane Addams Hull House, Chicago 312-906-8600
- Casa Central, Chicago 773-645-2300
- Children's Advocacy Center of Northwest Cook County, Hoffman Estates 847-885-0100
- Family Service of South Lake County, Highland Park 847-432-4981
- Illinois Action for Children, Chicago 312-986-9591
- Juvenile Protective Association, Chicago 312-440-1203
- A Safe Place/Lake County Crisis Center for the Prevention and Treatment of Domestic Violence, Waukegan 847-249-4450
- Metropolitan Family Services, Chicago 312-986-4000
- On Our Own Inc., Chicago 312-435-1007
- The Paternal Involvement Project, Chicago 773-651-9262
- Rainbow House, Chicago 312-935-3430
- Teen Living Programs, Chicago 773-883-0025

➤ **YOUTH ACTIVITIES, VOLUNTEER PROGRAMS**
- Boys and Girls Clubs of Chicago 312-627-2700
- Boy Scouts of America, Chicago Area Council 312-421-8800
- Center for Volunteerism, United Way/Crusade of Mercy, Chicago 312-906-2425
- Chicago Youth Centers 312-648-1550
- Girls Scouts of Chicago 312-416-2500
- Volunteers of America, Chicago 312-707-8707
- YMCA of Metropolitan Chicago 312-932-1200
- YMCA of Metropolitan Chicago 312-372-6600

➤ **TEEN PREGNANCY**
- Aunt Martha's Youth Service Center, Matteson 708-747-2701
- Illinois Caucus for Adolescent Health, Chicago 312-427-4460
- Jewish Children's Bureau of Chicago 312-444-2090
- Ounce of Prevention Fund, Chicago 312-922-3863

ence. To give them some hope for the future and show how valuable life is. To have them try to put themselves in the place of their victim, to help instill a sense of empathy.

And to teach kids not to just react to situations but to analyze them and to respond to them in a more appropriate manner. The hardest thing, I think, is to teach kids to think about the consequences of their actions. To think, to wait a second and say, "If I do this, what's going to happen to me?" If somebody looks at you the wrong way, does that mean you should shoot them? A lot of kids come into court and say, "He gave me a hard look." But so what. Why should kids get so angry that they risk their futures?

The really violent kids make up a small minority of the cases in Juvenile Court—maybe 5 percent. And for them it's really tough to find something that works. But sometimes even with them there are programs that work.

Sometimes, of course, the only thing is the Department of Corrections. Sometimes it's just that they have the strength within themselves. You can call it an epiphany. Maybe it's just the maturation process, a function of getting older and more mature.

You just don't know what's going to work for a certain kid. You just try something and if it doesn't work you try something else. And if nothing works you go to the Department of Corrections.

'SEEK EDUCATION LIKE NOURISHMENT'

RUTH MITCHELL is an English teacher at DuSable High School; she is divorced and is raising an 8-year-old boy. Some of her students were profiled in Tribune stories looking at the aftermath of the slaying of a 13-year-old boy.

Education is a great equalizer. It will provide access to careers, not jobs. Education will provide the means to make decisions, not deal with directives given out with food stamps and a monthly welfare check. Education must be looked upon with respect and sought after like nourishment.

My mother always made my sister and me her top priorities. As a parent, I make my son my first priority. His health, education, welfare and happiness are the concerns that I handle on a daily basis. I decided to become a parent; he did not decide to come into this world. As his mother I am his guide, caregiver, teacher, role model, coach, disciplinarian, confidant and a host of other titles. In my family we believe in our children. We have no fear of them and we are right there at every moment—watching, correcting, sharing and protecting them. When parents show the proper amount of care and concern for their children, those children succeed in all areas of life.

The National Juvenile Justice Action Plan: A Comprehensive Response to a Critical Challenge

by Sarah Ingersoll

"More and more of our Nation's children are killing and dying. The only way we can break the cycle of violence is through a truly national effort implemented one community at a time. Everyone has a role—businesses, schools, universities, and especially parents. Every community and every citizen can find practical steps in the Action Plan *to do something now about youth violence."*

Attorney General Janet Reno

O n the heels of the crack epidemic, the Nation has witnessed the drive-by murder of a 3-year-old girl playing in the wrong place at the wrong time, a 12-year-old boy caught in a deadly feud over drug turf, and a homeless man set on fire in the subway by boys who should have been in school. Lurid headlines have captured the public's attention as youth violence takes center stage in the domestic debate.

Responses to these events have been as swift as they have been varied, but often they are

Sarah Ingersoll is a Special Assistant to the Administrator of the Office of Juvenile Justice and Delinquency Prevention.

reactions to a crisis rather than solutions based on analysis.

A Comprehensive Plan

In 1994, Attorney General Janet Reno convened the first meeting of the restructured Coordinating Council on Juvenile Justice and Delinquency Prevention, which comprises nine juvenile justice practitioners and representatives from the U.S. Departments of Justice (DOJ), Health and Human Services (HHS), Housing and Urban Development, Labor, Treasury, and Education (ED); the Office of National Drug Control Policy; and the Corporation for Na-

From *Journal of the Office of Juvenile Justice and Delinquency Prevention*, September 1997. Reprinted by permission of the National Institute of Justice, National Criminal Justice Reference Service.

The Action Plan *encourages helping youth throughout their development.*

tional Service. The Attorney General charged the Council to create an agenda to reduce youth violence. *Combating Violence and Delinquency: The National Juvenile Justice Action Plan* (Coordinating Council on Juvenile Justice and Delinquency Prevention, 1996) is the Council's call to action. Drawing on decades of research, previously summarized in the Office of Juvenile Justice and Delinquency Prevention's (OJJDP's) *Comprehensive Strategy for Serious, Violent, and Chronic Juvenile Offenders* (Wilson and Howell, 1993), the *Action Plan* encourages helping youth throughout their development while responding to juvenile crime in a way that ensures public safety. The Coordinating Council calls on citizens to work together to advance the *Action Plan*'s eight key objectives to combat youth violence:

◆ Provide immediate intervention and appropriate sanctions and treatment for delinquent juveniles.

◆ Prosecute certain serious, violent, and chronic juvenile offenders in criminal court.

◆ Reduce youth involvement with guns, drugs, and gangs.

◆ Provide opportunities for children and youth.

◆ Break the cycle of violence by addressing youth victimization, abuse, and neglect.

◆ Strengthen and mobilize communities.

◆ Support the development of innovative approaches to research and evaluation.

◆ Implement an aggressive public outreach campaign on effective strategies to combat juvenile violence.

OJJDP is working to implement the *Action Plan* through a coordinated initiative of demonstration grants, training and technical assistance, research and evaluation programs, and information dissemination activities. The following examples demonstrate the scope of these initiatives.

Strengthening the Juvenile Justice System

Attaining the first objective of the *Action Plan* requires strengthening the Nation's juvenile justice system. Through Formula Grants, Title V Community Prevention Grants, and State Challenge Grants, OJJDP provides States with funds to plan and implement comprehensive State and local programs to prevent and control delinquency and enhance the effective operation of the juvenile justice system.

In five program sites, OJJDP is demonstrating the graduated sanctions approach that is part of the Comprehensive Strategy for Serious, Violent, and Chronic Juvenile Offenders. OJJDP is also supporting development of a stronger juvenile justice system through the SafeFutures Program; developing, testing, and expanding model juvenile community assessment centers; and promoting statewide adoption of the Comprehensive Strategy through intensive technical assistance and training in Florida, Iowa, Maryland, Rhode Island, and Texas.

In addition, OJJDP is training juvenile justice system personnel to implement the balanced and restorative justice model. Restorative justice holds the offender responsible for making restitution to the victim and restoring the state of well-being that existed in the community before the offense. The balanced approach also suggests that the juvenile justice system improve the ability of offenders to pursue legitimate endeavors after their release. Training and technical assistance are also being provided to probation officers and juvenile justice practitioners to enable them to estab-

lish restitution and community service programs. States interested in juvenile code reforms that reflect the balanced and restorative justice model are also receiving training and technical assistance. By the end of 1995, at least 24 States had adopted, or were examining, codes or procedures incorporating the concepts of balanced and restorative justice.

Prosecuting Serious, Violent, and Chronic Offenders

The second objective of the *Action Plan* addresses how to deal with juvenile offenders whose offenses, or offense history and failure to respond to treatment, merit criminal prosecution. In recent years, no other juvenile justice policy has received more legislative attention or yielded such a multitude of different approaches for dealing with serious, violent, and chronic juvenile offenders.

OJJDP has published a research summary of legislative changes taking place across the country between 1992 and 1995. *State Responses to Serious and Violent Juvenile Crime* (Torbet et al., 1996) covers such topics as juvenile court jurisdictional authority, including waiver and transfer mechanisms; sentencing options, including blended sentencing practices; corrections options for juveniles; confidentiality and information sharing; victim rights in the juvenile justice system; and comprehensive State system reforms to respond to serious, violent, and chronic delinquency. In addition, OJJDP is funding the National Conference of State Legislatures to help improve State juvenile justice systems by providing State legislators and staff with the latest research, effective State policies, and model responses to youth violence through both publications and intensive training.

With each new legislative debate regarding new provisions, State legislators and criminal justice officials are faced with a lack of reliable current information on the effectiveness of newly adopted laws and policies. To address this information gap, OJJDP is currently funding three studies in

OJJDP is funding studies to determine the impact of waiver and transfer provisions on juvenile offenders.

Arizona, Florida, New Jersey, New York, Pennsylvania, South Carolina, and Utah to determine the outcome and impact of waiver and transfer provisions on juvenile offenders under varying legal and administrative configurations. The research will control for the presenting offense, offense history, and offender's age and will include the kind of case attribute information that is often missing from studies in this subject area.

The studies are being done collaboratively. Universities and research organizations are teaming up with key State and local criminal justice agencies to answer critical questions about the process, impact, and comparative effectiveness of new strategies. Two of the current studies involve replication and expansion of prior research and will provide information on differences in processing and outcome in the strategies of the 1980's compared with those of the 1990's; another looks at long-term trends.

All of the studies have gone beyond the limited data routinely available in automated record systems to study in greater detail critical aspects related to offenses, such as the offender's role in the commission of the crime, harm to the victim, and involvement of drugs or guns in the offense. It is hoped that more indepth characterization of cases will reveal patterns in the determinations made by prosecutors and judges to transfer a juvenile to criminal court for prosecution.

One of the goals of the research program is to explore the possibility of developing a system to collect routine information from a broader range of sources on the processing, outcomes, and impacts of criminal prosecution nationally. Researchers from all sites will collaborate to produce a cross-jurisdictional comparison of critical dimensions of the process.

In addition to these studies, OJJDP and the Bureau of Justice Statistics will be funding State-initiated studies of juvenile transfers through the State Justice Statistics Program for Statistical Analysis Centers in fiscal year 1997.

Targeting Guns, Drugs, and Gangs

Objective three of the *Action Plan* also identifies programmatic and strategic prevention, intervention, and suppression activities that target three critical areas affecting juvenile violence—guns, drugs, and gangs.

Guns. From 1985 to 1992, the number of homicides committed by juveniles with firearms more than doubled. Under Partnerships To Reduce Juvenile Gun Violence, OJJDP is funding four initiatives—one in California, two in Louisiana, and one in New York—that are linking community mobilization efforts with law enforcement to address this problem. An evaluation of the Partnerships effort is also being sponsored by OJJDP. In addition, OJJDP has held

a national satellite teleconference on programs designed to reduce youth gun violence. The teleconference, which is available on videotape from OJJDP's Juvenile Justice Clearinghouse, was viewed by approximately 8,130 people at 271 downlink sites.

Drugs. In response to an increase in drug use by young people, OJJDP is administering the $1 million Youth Substance Use Prevention Grant Program of the President's Crime Prevention Council, which will support 10 community-based, youth-led prevention initiatives. OJJDP is also funding an evaluation of the program that will build local program grantees' capacity for designing, implementing, and interpreting evaluations; determine whether youth-led delinquency and substance use prevention activities have a greater impact on youth than adult-led prevention activities; and define the elements critical to implementing a successful youth-led prevention activity. OJJDP is also continuing to fund the Community Anti-Drug Abuse Technical Assistance Voucher project and the Congress of National Black Churches' National Anti-Drug/Violence Campaign—programs that help grassroots organizations and churches address juvenile drug abuse. The Race Against Drugs Program is a unique drug awareness, education, and prevention campaign implemented with the help and assistance of 23 motor sports organizations, the Federal Bureau of Investigation, Drug Enforcement Administration, U.S. Navy, and others. OJJDP is also working with the American Probation and Parole Association to train and help juvenile justice practitioners identify and treat drug-involved youth. OJJDP held a national satellite teleconference on preventing drug abuse among youth

The Youth Substance Use Prevention Grant Program will support 10 community-based, youth-led prevention initiatives.

that was viewed by approximately 10,000 people at 300 downlink sites.

Gangs. OJJDP is implementing and testing a research-driven, community-based approach to suppressing, intervening in, and preventing gang violence through its Comprehensive Response to America's Youth Gang Problem Initiative. Five jurisdictions experiencing an emerging or chronic gang problem (Mesa and Tucson, Arizona; Riverside, California; Bloomington, Illinois; and San Antonio, Texas) have been funded under this initiative to implement the comprehensive model for 3 years. OJJDP has established the National Youth Gang Center to promote effective and innovative strategies, collect and analyze statistical data on gangs, analyze gang legislation, and review gang literature. OJJDP also funded Boys & Girls Clubs of America gang-prevention programs that have reached 6,000 youth at risk for gang involvement. OJJDP has also established the interagency, public/private Gang Consortium as part of the Comprehensive Response initiative. The Consortium seeks to facilitate and expand ongoing coordination activities and enhance youth gang prevention, intervention, and suppression policies and activities, including information exchange and technical assistance services provided by the many Federal agencies with program emphasis on youth gangs and related problems. OJJDP's national satellite teleconference on strategies to prevent, intervene in, and suppress juvenile gang violence was viewed by approximately 17,000 people at 635 downlink sites.

Enhancing Opportunities for Youth

Objective four of the *Action Plan* calls for the Nation to provide positive opportunities for youth. Research demonstrates that mentoring, afterschool activities, conflict resolution programs, remedial education, and vocational training can prevent young people from becoming delinquents. OJJDP is actively disseminating a va-

OJJDP is testing a research-driven, community-based response to youth gangs.

riety of research-based documents. *Delinquency Prevention Works* (Office of Juvenile Justice and Delinquency Prevention, 1995a) and the *Guide for Implementing the Comprehensive Strategy for Serious, Violent, and Chronic Juvenile Offenders* (Howell, 1995) both offer many examples of effective prevention and intervention programs. Other helpful publications are the OJJDP Bulletins in the Youth Development Series, which OJJDP created this year to present findings from the Program of Research on the Causes and Correlates of Delinquency, a lon-

gitudinal research program studying 4,000 young people in Denver, Colorado; Pittsburgh, Pennsylvania; and Rochester, New York. Series titles developed thus far are *Epidemiology of Serious Violence* (Kelley et al., 1997), *Gang Members and Delinquent Behavior* (Thornberry and Burch, 1997), and *In the Wake of Childhood Maltreatment* (Kelley et al., 1997). In addition, OJJDP has published a number of individual Bulletins on specific promising programs, including *Allegheny County, PA: Mobilizing To Reduce Juvenile Crime* (Hsia, 1997),

Conflict resolution education reduces juvenile violence and improves school attendance.

Treating Serious Anti-Social Behavior in Youth: The MST Approach (Henggeler, 1997), and *Mentoring—A Proven Delinquency Prevention Strategy* (Grossman and Garry, 1997).

DOJ is also funding expanded opportunities for youth and training for youth service professionals. Boys & Girls Clubs have provided afterschool activities that have increased school attendance, improved academic performance, and reduced the juvenile crime rate in high-risk neighborhoods. In addition to funding the Law-Related Education Program and the Teens, Crime, and the Community Initiative, which involves young people in community safety efforts, OJJDP has provided professional development training for youth workers and programmatic support to 93 mentoring programs funded under the Juvenile Mentoring Program (JUMP). A recent national evaluation of the Big Brothers Big Sisters of America mentoring program found that the young people involved in this program were 46 percent less likely

to start using drugs, 33 percent less likely to exhibit aggressive behavior, and 27 percent less likely to start using alcohol than their peers. Mentoring is a component of OJJDP's SafeFutures initiative, which assists communities in combating delinquency by developing a full range of coordinated services. In addition to JUMP and SafeFutures, OJJDP supports more than 90 mentoring efforts in individual States through its Formula Grants Program (Grossman and Garry, 1997). OJJDP recently held a national satellite teleconference on mentoring.

Addressing conflict resolution programming in schools, the community, and juvenile justice settings, a 1995 OJJDP satellite teleconference provided more than 10,000 participants with information on conflict resolution programs that have reduced the number of violent juvenile acts, decreased the number of chronic school absences, reduced the number of disciplinary referrals and suspensions, and expanded classroom instruction. These conflict resolution programs

and approaches are described in *Conflict Resolution Education: A Guide to Implementing Programs in Schools, Youth-Serving Organizations, and Community and Juvenile Justice Settings* (Crawford and Bodine, 1996), published by OJJDP and ED's Safe and Drug-Free Schools Program. OJJDP has funded a training and technical assistance program that supports the implementation of conflict resolution efforts at the local level.

Supported by OJJDP in collaboration with the U.S. Departments of Health and Human Services, Commerce, and Defense, the Communities In Schools dropout-prevention program has reached more than 97,000 youth and their families, increased students' likelihood of attending and staying in school, and improved their academic performance. OJJDP and ED have also funded the National School Safety Center to focus attention on the problems of youth who do not attend school regularly because they are truants or dropouts, are afraid to attend school, have been suspended or expelled, or are in need of help to be reintegrated into mainstream schools after spending time in juvenile detention and correctional settings. Four forums on Youth Out of the Education Mainstream were held in summer 1996 to highlight effective and promising programs. Intensive training and technical assistance are being delivered to 10 sites to implement comprehensive approaches to this problem.

Breaking the Cycle of Violence

In 1995, child protective service agencies investigated an estimated 2 million reports alleging the mistreatment of almost 3 million children (National Center on Child Abuse and Neglect, 1997). Studies show that childhood abuse and neglect increase a child's odds of future delinquency and adult criminality. Data from the Rochester Youth Development Study (RYDS) show that self-reports of youth violence increased with exposure to more types of family violence. RYDS is one of three coordinated, longitu-

The CD–CP program serves as a national model for police-mental health partnerships.

their criminal and juvenile justice systems to child abuse and neglect, and to enhance system coordination with child and family service agencies. Five communities (Huntsville, Alabama; the Sault Sainte Marie Tribe of Chippewa Indians in Michigan; Kansas City, Missouri; Toledo, Ohio; and Chittenden County, Vermont) have been selected for funding under the Safe Kids/Safe Streets Program. The funding agencies are also sponsoring an evaluation of the program.

In addition, OJJDP is working with the Executive Office for Weed and Seed and HHS to implement the David Olds Nurse Home Visitation Program in six sites. Six hundred low-income, first-time mothers (some of whom are drug addicts) and their babies will be served through this prenatal and early childhood home-visitation program. Through home visits in the first 2 years of a child's life, program nurses work intensively with new mothers to improve key aspects of health and early child development and strengthen the mother's parenting and vocational skills.

In October 1995, OJJDP entered into a 3-year cooperative agreement for a project called Training and Technical

Assistance for Family Strengthening, which is being implemented by the University of Utah, Department of Health Education, in Salt Lake City. This project allows the university to continue work it has been conducting since 1990 to identify the most effective family programs for the prevention of delinquency. This project is designed to help close the gap between the state of research and the state of practice in family-focused prevention. The university will synthesize and disseminate information about model family strengthening programs through training and technical assistance and the development of written materials.

OJJDP is also funding the Yale/New Haven Child Development–Community Policing (CD–CP) Program to engage community police and mental health professionals in addressing the psychological burdens of increasing levels of community violence on children, families, and communities. The CD–CP Program, a collaborative effort of the New Haven (Connecticut) Department of Police Services and the Child Study Center at the Yale University School of Medicine, serves as a national model for police-mental health partnerships (Marans and Berkman, 1997).

In addition, OJJDP is sponsoring four regional children's advocacy centers to coordinate the response of judicial and social service systems to child abuse. The regional centers act as clearinghouses, distributing resource materials and other tools, providing training and technical assistance, and facilitating information sharing. OJJDP supports the National Network of Children's Advocacy Centers, which provides funding, training, and technical support to local children's advocacy centers.

dinal research projects of OJJDP's Causes and Correlates Program, the largest shared-measurement approach ever achieved in delinquency research.

The fifth objective of the *Action Plan*, therefore, challenges us to eliminate the disturbing cycle of domestic violence, child abuse and neglect, and youth violence. OJJDP is collaborating with other bureaus in the Office of Justice Programs to support Safe Kids/Safe Streets: Community Approaches to Reducing Abuse and Neglect and Preventing Delinquency. This initiative is designed to help youth at risk for abuse and neglect and their families, to encourage communities to strengthen the response of

Studies show that childhood abuse and neglect increase a child's odds of future delinquency.

Deterring delinquency requires a substantial investment of financial and human resources.

Thanks to such efforts, nearly 300 communities now have children's advocacy centers. Moreover, through OJJDP's support of the National Court Appointed Special Advocates Association, some 700 communities have established court appointed special advocate (CASA) programs providing volunteers to serve as advocates in court proceedings for victims of child abuse (Office of Juvenile Justice and Delinquency Prevention, 1997).

Putting the *Plan* Into Action

The remaining objectives of the *Action Plan* focus on mobilizing communities, engaging a variety of disciplines to ensure that research serves as the foundation of program activities, and conducting an outreach campaign on effective strategies to combat juvenile violence.

OJJDP is helping communities mobilize to prevent juvenile delinquency and transferring the research base on the causes and correlates of delinquency through the Title V Community Prevention Grants. These grants have been distributed to 49 States, 5 territories, and the District of Columbia. Nearly 4,000 participants have been trained in risk- and protective-factor-focused delinquency prevention, and 3-year Community Prevention Grants have been awarded to approximately 400 communities. OJJDP's *Title V Delinquency Prevention Program Community Self-Evaluation Workbook* (Office of Juvenile Justice and Delinquency Prevention, 1995b) is helping communities evaluate their progress and results under this program.

In partnership with the Bureau of Justice Assistance, OJJDP will be pro-

viding additional information on strategies that work through a public information campaign. Using the Comprehensive Strategy and *Action Plan* as guides, community leaders and other concerned citizens will have access to information on effective delinquency prevention; gang, gun, and drug violence reduction; and juvenile justice reform strategies and programs.

Through its Juvenile Justice Clearinghouse, OJJDP annually distributes more than 2 million copies of Reports, Summaries, Bulletins, Fact Sheets, and other publications providing research findings and program information. OJJDP publications are available through a toll-free telephone line, and by mail, fax, and the Internet. OJJDP also continues to present national satellite teleconferences on key juvenile justice issues and is currently completing production of an interactive CD-ROM on effective prevention and intervention programs. Information about these services and activities can be obtained by calling the Juvenile Justice Clearinghouse, toll free, at 800-638-8736.

Conclusion

Deterring delinquency and reducing youth violence require a substantial, sustained investment of financial and human resources by both the public and private sectors. If this Nation truly intends to ensure public safety and reduce youth violence and victimization, it must make a greater commitment to a juvenile justice system that holds juvenile offenders immediately accountable (before they become hardened criminals) and responds appropriately to the issues that bring young people to the courtroom

in the first place. All young people should be guaranteed the opportunity to be healthy, safe, and able to learn in school and to engage in positive, productive activities. This requires the targeted and coordinated use of new and existing resources. The research-based goals and objectives of the *Action Plan* and the model established by OJJDP's Comprehensive Strategy can be successfully implemented, but only if a long-term commitment is made to work together to achieve them.

References

Coordinating Council on Juvenile Justice and Delinquency Prevention. 1996 (March). *Combating Violence and Delinquency: The National Juvenile Justice Action Plan.* Report. Washington, DC: U.S. Department of Justice, Office of Justice Programs, Office of Juvenile Justice and Delinquency Prevention.

Crawford, D., and R. Bodine. 1996 (October). *Conflict Resolution Education: A Guide to Implementing Programs in Schools, Youth-Serving Organizations, and Community and Juvenile Justice Settings.* Washington, DC: U.S. Department of Justice, Office of Justice Programs, Office of Juvenile Justice and Delinquency Prevention, and U.S. Department of Education, Safe and Drug-Free Schools Program.

Grossman, J.B., and E.M. Garry. 1997 (April). *Mentoring—A Proven Delinquency Prevention Strategy.* Bulletin. Washington, DC: U.S. Department of Justice, Office of Justice Programs, Office of Juvenile Justice and Delinquency Prevention.

Henggeler, S.W. 1997 (May). *Treating Serious Anti-Social Behavior in Youth: The MST Approach.* Bulletin. Washington, DC: U.S. Department of Justice, Office of Justice Programs, Office of Juvenile Justice and Delinquency Prevention.

Howell, J.C., ed. 1995 (June). *Guide for Implementing the Comprehensive Strategy for Serious, Violent, and Chronic Juvenile Offenders.* Washington, DC: U.S. Department of Justice, Office of Justice Programs, Office of Juvenile Justice and Delinquency Prevention.

Hsia, H.M. 1997 (June). *Allegheny County, PA: Mobilizing To Reduce Juvenile Crime.* Bulletin. Washington, DC: U.S. Department of Justice, Office of Justice Programs, Office of Juvenile Justice and Delinquency Prevention.

Kelley, B.T., D. Huizinga, T.P. Thornberry, and R. Loeber. 1997 (June). *Epidemiology of Se-*

rious Violence. Bulletin. Washington, DC: U.S. Department of Justice, Office of Justice Programs, Office of Juvenile Justice and Delinquency Prevention.

Kelley, B.T., T.P. Thornberry, and C.A. Smith. 1997 (August). *In the Wake of Childhood Maltreatment*. Bulletin. Washington, DC: U.S. Department of Justice, Office of Justice Programs, Office of Juvenile Justice and Delinquency Prevention.

Marans, S., and M. Berkman. 1997 (March). *Child Development–Community Policing: Partnership in a Climate of Violence*. Bulletin. Washington, DC: U.S. Department of Justice, Office of Justice Programs, Office of Juvenile Justice and Delinquency Prevention.

National Center on Child Abuse and Neglect. 1997. *Child Maltreatment 1995: Reports From the States to the National Child Abuse and Neglect Data System*. Washington, DC: U.S. Department of Health and Human Services, National Center on Child Abuse and Neglect.

Office of Juvenile Justice and Delinquency Prevention. 1995a (June). *Delinquency Prevention Works*. Program Summary. Washington, DC: U.S. Department of Justice, Office of Justice Programs, Office of Juvenile Justice and Delinquency Prevention.

Office of Juvenile Justice and Delinquency Prevention. 1995b. *Title V Delinquency Prevention Program Community Self-Evaluation Workbook*. Washington, DC: U.S. Department of Justice, Office of Justice Programs, Office of Juvenile Justice and Delinquency Prevention.

Office of Juvenile Justice and Delinquency Prevention, 1997 (March), *Court Appointed Special Advocates: A Voice for Abused and Neglected Children in Court*, Bulletin. Washington, DC: U.S. Department of Justice, Office of Justice Programs, Office of Juvenile Justice and Delinquency Prevention.

Thornberry, T.P., and J.H. Burch II. 1997 (June). *Gang Members and Delinquent Behavior*. Bulletin. Washington, DC: U.S. Department of Justice, Office of Justice Programs, Office of Juvenile Justice and Delinquency Prevention.

Torbet, P., R. Gable, H. Hurst IV, I. Montgomery, L. Syzmanski, and D. Thomas. 1996 (July). *State Responses to Serious and Violent Crime*. Washington, DC: U.S. Department of Justice, Office of Justice Programs, Office of Juvenile Justice and Delinquency Prevention,

Wilson, J.J., and J.C. Howell. 1993 (December). *Comprehensive Strategy for Serious, Violent, and Chronic Juvenile Offenders*. Program Summary. Washington, DC: U.S. Department of Justice, Office of Justice Programs, Office of Juvenile Justice and Delinquency Prevention.

Saving the Nation's Most Precious Resources:

OUR CHILDREN

The role of parents is critical since studies have shown that youngsters' basic intellectual capacity and their emotional and character formation are established by the age of three.

By Gene Stephens

TOO MANY of America's children have been neglected, abused, and ignored. Without change, the dark spectre of generational warfare predicted by some could become all too real. If that deadly conflict occurs, it will be because no one pays attention to the all-too-evident trends and there is failure to pursue diligently new directions that can lead to a safe, sane, productive 21st-century society.

The concept of youth at risk has been defined in many ways and under many names (*e.g.,* children at risk, children in trouble, at-risk teens, even at-risk families). A decade ago, the Domestic Policy Association in Dayton, Ohio, teamed with the Kettering Foundation in Washington, D.C., to work with communities across the U.S. to identify and save the nation's "at-risk" youth. In its literature,

Dr. Stephens, Associate Law and Justice Editor of USA Today, *is professor of criminal justice, University of South Carolina, Columbia.*

the movement suggested that up to 15% of the 16- to 19-year-old population was "at risk for never reaching their potential, at risk of being lost in society." Others would add children of any age if they are at risk of failing to become self-supporting adults; if indicators are that they are headed for a life in institutions (for delinquency, crime, mental illness, addiction); might become dependent on taxpayer or charity support programs; and may face life on the streets, homeless and unemployed. Expanding the category well beyond 15% of the population are those who add teens and preteens who take on child-rearing themselves and/or drop out of elementary or secondary school—most of whom, according to statistical probability, will face a life of underemployment, diminished expectations and opportunities, and failure to become productive, contributing citizens.

The task of "saving" these youngsters has become even more formidable, made more difficult by the expanding gap between rich and poor; the larger

number of single-parent households and homes where both parents work; the growing gun culture with increasingly higher-tech weapons reaching the street level; and the increasing negativity about children manifested by curfews, treating younger and younger youths as adult criminals, and declaring kids "undesirable" in gated communities. Possibly most alarming is that only one of three American households today includes a child under 18. Increasing numbers of lower- and middle-income children are growing up with little or no adult supervision, often without adequate resources for nurturing (and sometimes insufficient necessities for survival), and with a clear message from society that they are not wanted.

Without hope for the future and a stake in society, they often turn to peers for attention and guidance; to easily obtainable guns for protection, security, and status; and to sex and drugs for comfort, relief of boredom, and sometimes for subsistence. The gang often becomes their "family"—the only place

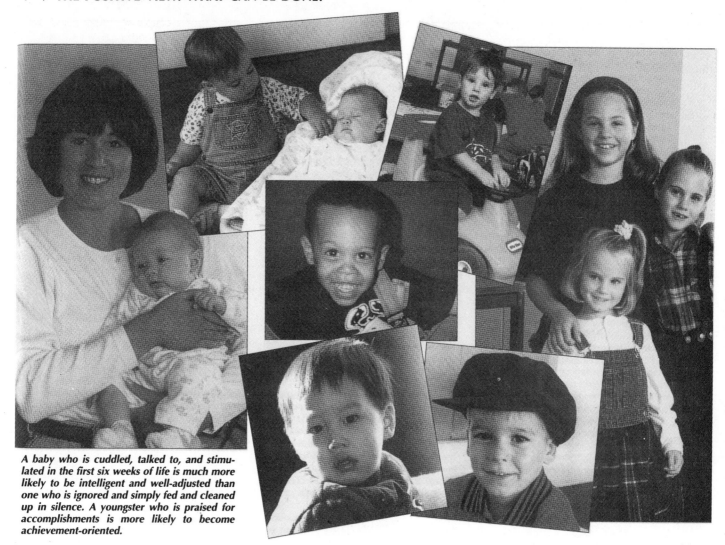

A baby who is cuddled, talked to, and stimulated in the first six weeks of life is much more likely to be intelligent and well-adjusted than one who is ignored and simply fed and cleaned up in silence. A youngster who is praised for accomplishments is more likely to become achievement-oriented.

they get attention and approval—and anti-social values fill the void left by family and society.

Their lack of faith in a future leaves them present-oriented and oblivious to society's laws. Living for today makes sense to them, especially when every day they are bombarded by media messages of enormous material wealth on the one hand and ever-prevalent violence and death on the other. Is it any wonder many of these youth seemingly without emotion steal and even attack others to obtain what they need and/or desire or just for momentary thrills or release of anger?

Criminologist James Fox of Northeastern University has extrapolated from social/demographic trends that a juvenile crime wave such as the U.S. never has seen will occur over the next decade. Citing statistics indicating 30% of children grow up in single-parent homes, most without fathers, with 20% raised

in poverty, Fox predicts the 4,000 murders by teenagers in 1995 will skyrocket as the 39,000,000 kids under age 10 grow and increase by 20% the portion of the population in the teen years in the first decade of the 21st century.

Of course, having youth at risk is not a problem unique to the U.S. Wars, social upheaval, rapidly changing economic systems, political instability, and cultural animosity have placed millions of youngsters at risk across the planet. Thousands die of starvation, while others wander aimlessly in search of home and family. Many atrophy in sweatshops; others are sold into prostitution to support their families. Even more horrifying are those who are sacrificed for their body parts to satisfy a graying world population and those who are killed simply because they were born the wrong sex to satisfy their parent(s).

Nevertheless, catastrophe is *not* inevitable. There are some signs of hope—a

slightly decreased birth rate among American teenagers in the mid 1990s; a bipartisan concern raised in Washington for "saving the children"; many community-based experiments to try to meet the needs of youth; and a movement to consider insufficient prenatal care, poor parenting skills, child abuse, and child neglect as public health as well as social problems.

Beyond this, whereas data is sketchy, a striking change in the rearing of children in many families is taking place. Countering the trend to ignore or even abuse children is a movement to cherish and nurture youngsters by thousands of parents who are taking turns working while the other stays at home and makes childcare almost a full-time vocation. Whatever is lost in job advancement and professional development seems to have been gained tenfold in the joy and satisfaction they find in watching their offspring blossom. These parents express the belief they have not given up anything valuable compared to what they have received. There is an unrecognized renaissance in parenting that is progressing quietly in neighborhoods across the nation.

Psychoanalyst Sigmund Freud postulated decades ago that an adult's behavior best could be explained by examining the significant events of the first six years of his or her life. These childhood experiences were seen by Freud as the subconscious motivator of actions taken later in life. Recent scientific advances have indicated he was on the right track, but might have given too much latitude to the time period. Now, it appears that basic intellectual capacity and emotional and character formation are established by the age of three, and, increasingly, evidence points to the prenatal period and first year of life as most important.

The implication of these findings is enormous. Focus must be changed from reactive, remedial attention when the problems begin to show up in misbehavior or delinquency in the teen or preteen years to a proactive, preventive approach in the formative period—prebirth to one year old. Prenatal care-unavailable to many unwed and/or poor mothers to be—becomes a critical element in reducing youth at risk, as does effective nurturing in the days and weeks immediately following birth.

Children crave attention more than anything else, especially positive attention. Researchers find a baby who is cuddled, talked to, and stimulated in the first six weeks of life is much more likely to be intelligent and well-adjusted than one who is ignored and simply fed and cleaned up in silence. Later, the youngster who is rewarded with praise for accomplishments is much more likely than others to become optimistic and achievement-oriented.

Since studies indicate any attention is a reward, as any attention is better than none, even spankings or harsh words in effect serve as rewards, thus reinforcing rather than extinguishing the behavior given attention. Many scholars feel this helps explain why kids who are abused grow up to be child abusers themselves. At-risk children, often starved for attention, are particularly susceptible to accept abuse as a reinforcer. Beyond this, the only time they get attention seems to be for anti-social behavior, including by the juvenile and criminal justice systems. The first time they get positive re-inforcement often is from a gang or from the inmate subculture in a juvenile institution or prison.

How does one extinguish unacceptable behavior? One way is by ignoring it, usually accomplished by a "time-out"—removing the child from the "playing field" and eliminating his or her ability to seek and gain attention. This can be done in a number of ways, ranging from having youngsters sit in a corner for a few minutes to placing them in a closed room alone for a few minutes. Later, they can be praised for learning to become toilet-trained, walk, talk, master new words, read, excel in classes, play with friends without hitting, do things for others, accomplish new tasks, etc.

To be successful in shaping socially acceptable, law-abiding behavior, positive reinforcement must become a way of life for parents, teachers, and others. It is a philosophy of rearing children—your own and others as well—that must be taught and reinforced by parents and all members of the community to be most effective. Pats on the back, awards, and ceremonies to celebrate accomplishments are particularly effective in fostering pro-social behavior and giving the at-risk youth a stake in society, thus helping overcome lack of hope and lack of faith in the future.

EFFECTIVE PROGRAMS

Parent education. Teaching positive reinforcement and other skills to prospective parents has proven effective in reducing the at-risk population. In *Licensing Parents,* author Jack C. Westman wonders why it is "you need a license to drive a car or own a dog, but not to raise a child." Clearly, there are many concepts and skills that are necessary to nurture a child successfully from total dependence to independent living. Short of requiring a license, parent education can provide information and skills to evaluate clearly whether to have a child and, if so, how to learn and use good child-rearing practices. Such classes are offered in many school districts and, in some cases, through community centers and churches.

To be effective in reducing teenage parenting, these classes must reach children early—sixth grade or shortly thereafter. Many teenagers enrolled in programs that force them to carry a computerized crying and wetting doll around for a couple of weeks decide to postpone parenthood.

Healthy Start. Both the U.S. Department of Health and Human Services (DHHS) and the U.S. Department of Justice (DOJ) have Healthy Start programs. The DHHS's was designed to strengthen the maternal and infant care systems at the community level, while the DOJ's is part of the National Institute of Justice's research focus on family violence through investigation of interdisciplinary approaches involving children, their families, and their communities. Caseworkers in these programs aid families before the child's birth, striving to reduce stress and improve family functioning, foster parenting skills, enhance child health and development, and, ultimately, prevent abuse and neglect. A similar initiative, Healthy Families America, was launched in 1992 by the National Committee to Prevent Child Abuse to help establish home visitation programs, service networks, and funding opportunities so all new parents can receive necessary education and support.

Mentoring. A large majority of at-risk children have no stable male role model, as they are being raised by their mothers and/or other female relatives. Some have no available family and are bounced around among foster homes and institutions. The stable father figure is important both to male and female children, but particularly to young boys. Because of the macho culture where respect is gained by toughness and fearlessness, young males without family and material resources are particularly at risk of being "disrespected" by peers. Without guidance from mature males they respect, their response often is to adopt violent reaction to disrespectful and/or challenging rhetoric or actions by peers and others.

Positive male role models have proven to be possibly the most effective remedy to this at-risk situation. So convinced are the leaders in Kansas City, Mo., that they are on a quest to recruit, train, and assign 30,000 mentors—one for every at-risk child in the city. Other communities greatly have expanded existing mentoring programs, such as Big Brothers and Big Sisters.

Mentoring appears to be one of the few remedial programs that work and thus is a cornerstone in any at-risk project. To be successful, it takes thorough understanding and commitment from mentors, who must be willing to spend considerable time with youngsters and become involved—at least to the level of listening to and advising them concerning all aspects of life; encouraging and assisting them in social, moral, and intellectual development; and attending and applauding significant events in their lives. In return, patient mentors see the youth blossom, cast off pessimism, and flourish.

A word of warning: A disinterested or uncommitted mentor can do much harm to an at-risk young male, since inattention and/or broken promises can reaffirm his negative image of himself and the world, deepen his despair and hopelessness, and add to his frustration and anger.

Nonviolent conflict resolution. Handling disrespect or physical attack without violent retaliation has proven to be a difficult task for at-risk youth. Already burdened by anxiety and feelings of inferiority, the conditioning often is to react violently to "prove" his manhood (or her self-worth). Few at-risk youth have been exposed to views/skills to cope with adversity via rational dialogue and problem-solving behavior. Now, though, programs are appearing in schools and community centers in many locales to provide attitudes and skills necessary to resolve conflict nonviolently.

Models have been developed by the American Bar Association, the U.S. Department of Justice, and the Public Broadcasting System, as well as by educators. One of the best involves training school staff (from teachers to administrators, from custodians to bus drivers and cafeteria workers) in creative nonviolent conflict resolution methods. Older students are taught the methods in required classes, and they then teach younger students, taking advantage of peer pressure. For the very youngest—kindergarten and the lowest primary grade students—the nonviolent approach is integrated into all activities in all classes. For example, preschool and kindergarten children are taught, and the approach is followed, that there is to be "no hitting, no spanking, no slapping, no pushing" by children or adults. Seeing adults spank or shake children reinforces the legitimacy of violence to resolve conflict.

Community schools programs. Not all communities use their schools effectively in breaking the cycle of violence and frustration among at-risk youth. A Federal initiative—the Community Schools Program—has been effective in rallying the community around the school. Other examples of successful partnerships include:

• In Missouri, 6,000 volunteers keep 675 schools open for extra hours.
• Boys & Girls Clubs offer mentoring in New Jersey schools.
• In New York City, Safe Haven programs provide secure environments and positive after-school tutoring and enrichment programs.
• Year-round schools in many communities facilitate better learning—since students no longer have the entire summer to forget—and foster more opportunities for extracurricular programs, from tutoring and mentoring to family activities and counseling.

Character education in schools generally revolves around universally accepted values (e.g., love, truthfulness, fairness, tolerance, responsibility) that find little opposition based on differing political, social, and religious beliefs. Schools with large numbers of at-risk youth have reported pregnancy and dropout rates cut in half, along with reduced fights and suspensions, after character education took hold.

Youth service. Surveys by the Gallup Poll, Wirthlin Group, and others consistently find that 95% of teenagers believe it is important for adults and teens to get involved in local civic, charitable, cultural, environmental, and political activities. More than 75% of teens say they already are participating in some volunteer programs, such as working at soup kitchens for the poor, nursing homes for the elderly, or shelters for the homeless.

Programs such as Americorps, Job Corps, and Peace Corps provide young people with a chance to learn the joy of giving to others. At the same time, it gives them a stake in society by developing skills, discipline, and grants and loans to go to trade school or college. Many communities and even some states (Georgia, for instance) are developing youth-oriented community service programs of their own.

Community policing. Law enforcement programs increasingly are working in partnership with the community to identify crime-breeding problems and implement solutions. Many of the at-risk youths' difficulties thus become community issues and lend themselves to community solutions. Homelessness, poverty, lack of positive adult role models, and poor health care may lead to safe shelters, community assistance, mentors, and in-school or community clinics.

One of the best examples of this approach took place in Milton Keynes, England, which faced a rash of shoplifting, burglary, and store robberies. Rather than seek out, arrest, and prosecute the young offenders, Police Commander Caroline Nicholl instituted a series of conferences wherein police, merchants, and neighbors met with offenders and suspects to identify reasons for the youth crimes. As a result, Nicholl says, "We learned about child abuse, bullying, alcoholism, and many other problems, and the community set to work on these."

Restorative justice. Most at-risk youth encounter the justice system early in life. Where juvenile justice once focused on their *needs,* it now focuses on their *deeds* and a belief that someone—adult or child—has to pay for the offense.

Countering this trend is a restorative justice movement, which holds that the purpose of justice is to bring peace and harmony back to the community by restoring victim, community, and the offender to a symbiotic relationship. Often, restoring includes restitution, service, and reclamation. In the case of juvenile offenders, the youth usually makes restitution to the victim either by his or her own earnings or through closely monitored personal service (cutting the lawn, raking leaves, chopping wood, or making home repairs); several hours of service to the community; an apology to the victim; counseling; and preparing essays and/or school talks on the harm the offense does to society. Once the restitution is completed, the child's record is purged.

There are literally hundreds of these programs being tried in small and large communities across the nation and, indeed, worldwide.

A COMPREHENSIVE PLAN

The following plan represents a consensus from groups to whom I have given the same assignment over the past decade: "Develop a program to turn your community's youth into productive, happy, law-abiding adults." These groups have included students from high school to graduate school, practitioners from police to social service workers, and community leaders, all participating in brainstorming and planning sessions to alleviate the youth-at-risk problem. Here is a comprehensive 10-point plan based on my years of experience with these exercises:

1. Commit to positive reinforcement through community- and school-based parenting classes (mandatory in schools), ongoing media campaigns, and positive attention and recognition in all schools (preschool through high school) and community-based programs.

2. Promote nonviolent conflict resolution among peers through mandatory educational programs for students, parents, teachers, counselors, and administrators, as well as through media and community campaigns.

3. Encourage mentoring for all children. Civic, business, and community campaigns should recruit and train mentors, matching them by needs and temperament. Programs such as Big Brothers and Big Sisters should be expanded.

4. Establish community-school partnerships to offer before- and after-school tutoring. Enlist youths to perform services to the community to enhance their stake in society. Year-round programs are particularly important to provide children with safe havens and enrichment and remedial initiatives before and after school, as well as during vacation periods.

5. Develop community-oriented proactive policing programs that begin with a philosophy of prevention. Examples include midnight basketball leagues, police-youth athletic leagues, neighborhood housing project substations, and foot patrols. These all involve partnerships of police, parents, church, business, civic, and community organizations.

6. Initiate ethical and cultural awareness programs that build on partnerships among family, church, school, media, civic, business, and other community groups. These should emphasize finding common ground on basic values, such as respect, responsibility, and restraint.

7. Design youth opportunity programs to provide all youngsters with the chance to reach their potential, regardless of circumstances. They could be run through school, business, and community partnerships that provide in-school jobs and child care, career counseling and training, opportunity scholarships, and recognition for achievement.

8. Set up peer counseling hotlines to help youths to aid each other through the trying times of adolescence.

9. End child neglect and abuse via guaranteed health and child care through parent/school/church/business/government/community partnerships to provide an array of services—*e.g.*, community and school health clinics for all; a home for every child; capable parent(s), whether biological or adoptive, for all kids; nurturing child care; and mandatory parenting classes for all parents-to-be.

10. Establish proactive focus throughout the community, with all public and private organizations joining parents and neighbors in seeking to prevent social problems via early identification, appraisal, and remedy. When delinquency or crime does occur, youthful offenders should be handled under a restorative approach, recognizing that the offense touched victim, offender, families of each, and the community. Harm is to be ameliorated and restoration of the community is to be achieved via mediation-arbitration, restitution, service to victim and community, reclamation, and/or reconciliation.

Every community, state, and nation can develop programs guided by this model. The more comprehensive the program and the more dedicated the participants, the more likely it significantly will reduce or even eliminate the youth-at-risk problem in the community (at whatever level). All plans, though, have to adopt certain guiding principles that must permeate the approach to have any real expectations of success.

First, remember all children want attention above everything. Thus, attention is a reinforcer of behavior and no attention is an extinguisher of it. Praising reinforces good behavior, and punishing bad behavior often reinforces it.

Second, instill optimism and faith in the future in all children, as that is a key to success. Pessimism and hopelessness not only will lead to more at-risk youth, but eventually to inability to sustain society itself.

Third, try to remember your own adolescence. The very nature of this traumatic period of every person's life is to challenge authority (including legal authority). Most youngsters drift through this troubled period and become basically law-abiding, mature adults *unless* they become labeled as delinquents/criminals/losers/incapable/etc. and then seek solace and acceptance with other social outcasts. No child successfully negotiates adolescence without firm, but tender, loving care and concern from attentive adults. Even then, many carry scars well into adulthood.

Fourth, consider how much harder this whole process of developing intellectually, socially, and morally and obtaining the adult mentoring and self-esteem necessary to move from childhood to adulthood is for the at-risk child. We must reach out and lend a hand to help this bundle of possibilities to have an opportunity to meet all the promise that lies in the world's most precious resource—its children.

Breaking the cycle of juvenile violence

By Roger Przybylski

Juvenile crime continues to be the focus of much attention in Illinois and across the country. At the national level, Congress has introduced legislation to extend federal jurisdiction to selected crimes committed by juveniles, and several states are currently debating juvenile justice system reforms. In Illinois, the Juvenile Justice Reform Act, which would significantly change the way juvenile offenders are handled, will likely be reintroduced in the legislative session in November.

The mounting concern about juvenile crime and the need for juvenile justice reform are due, at least in part, to the surge in juvenile violence that began nearly a decade ago. This surge stands in sharp contrast to the falling violent crime rates that most of the country has experienced in recent years.

Contradictory trends

Professor James Alan Fox of Northeastern University suggests that the nation is experiencing two crime trends—one for the young and one for the mature—that are moving in opposite directions. From 1990 to 1994, the overall rate of murder in America declined about 4 percent. For this

Roger Przybylski was director of the Authority's Research and Analysis Unit from 1994 through September 1997.

same period, the rate of killing at the hands of adults aged 25 and older declined 18 percent, and that for young adults, aged 18 to 24, rose only 2 percent. However, the rate of murders committed by teenagers aged 14 to 17 jumped 22 percent.

The escalation in youth crime during the past 10 years actually occurred while the population of teenagers was on the decline. But this

"Demographics do not have to be our destiny."

—*Attorney General Janet Reno*

demographic trend is about to change. By the year 2005, the number of teens between the ages of 14 and 17 will increase by 20 percent nationwide. (In Illinois, the teenage population is expected to grow more modestly, rising by 20 percent by the year 2010.) As a result, Fox argues, we will likely face a future wave of youth violence that will be even worse than that of the past decade.

Although these demographic projections are cause for concern, the future is far from predetermined. As Attor-

ney General Janet Reno recently stated, "Demographics do not have to be our destiny." More young people will not mean more violence if the rate of offending can be reduced.

Precursors of violence

Several studies on juvenile crime and victimization provide valuable new knowledge about the precursors of violence and the steps that must be taken to interrupt the trajectory toward a criminal career. These studies offer new insights about the pathways to delinquency and the cycle of violence that often begins in the home. Taken together, they offer compelling evidence that the best way to influence the rate of offending and reduce juvenile violence is through a multidisciplinary approach that incorporates both prevention and early intervention.

The National Youth Survey, conducted by the University of Colorado, Center for Violence Prevention, has been studying a nationally representative sample of about 1,700 youths since 1976. The most recent wave of interviews occurred in 1993, when many of the youths were already in their thirties. One of the major findings from the survey is that there is a considerable time lag between the peak age of offending and the peak age for arrest, suggesting that the justice system is intervening too late. The peak age of serious vio-

Suffering abuse and neglect as a child increases the likelihood of engaging in violent crime by 38 percent.

—Researcher Cathy Spatz Widom

lent offending in the NYS sample was 17, while the age of onset was even younger. In contrast, arrests peaked around the ages of 18 and 19, and arrest rates remained high until age 25.

Risk factors

The National Research Program on the Causes and Correlates of Delinquency, sponsored by the U.S. Department of Justice, Office of Juvenile Justice and Delinquency Prevention, has studied large samples of high-risk, inner-city youth in Denver, Pittsburgh, and Rochester, N.Y. The OJJDP-sponsored research found that chronic violent offenders exhibited co-occurring problem behaviors and multiple risk factors, such as dropping out of school and gang membership.

Dropping out of school can have a profound impact on a young person's life. While high-school dropouts experience lower earnings and more unemployment during their work careers, they also are more likely to end up on welfare or in prison than students who complete high school or college.

Another important finding from the OJJDP research was that children who were neglected or abused, or who witnessed violence in the home, were more likely to commit violent acts themselves later in life.

This cycle of violence also has been documented in a series of studies sponsored by the National Institute of Justice, the National Institute of Alcohol Abuse and Alcoholism, and the National Institute of Mental Health. The research is examining the lives of 1,575 child victims identified in court cases of abuse and neglect dating from 1967 to 1971. By 1994, almost one-half of the victims—most of whom were then in their late twen-

ties and early thirties—had been arrested for some type of offense. Eighteen percent had been arrested for a violent crime.

Cathy Spatz Widom, a researcher from the State University of New York at Albany who has studied extensively the impact of abuse and neglect, has reported that suffering abuse and neglect as a child increases the likelihood of engaging in violent crime by 38 percent. And while the likelihood of later violence is greater for children who experience violence firsthand, neglected children also display an elevated level of violence later in life.

Prevention and early intervention

It is apparent from each of these studies that reducing juvenile violence requires a multidisciplinary prevention and early intervention effort involving a variety of institutions. Risk-focused approaches to prevention have been successfully used to reduce cardiovascular disease and traffic fatalities, and they hold considerable promise for reducing juvenile violence. Risk factors can be found not only in the family, but in school, the community, and the individual and his or her peers. Protective factors that can mediate the impact of risk factors have also been identified. The interaction of risk factors and protective factors explain why some youth succumb to delinquency and others do not. As risk factors are decreased and protective factors enhanced, the likelihood of delinquency and violent offending can be reduced.

Recent research by the Rand Corporation provides compelling evidence that prevention and early intervention efforts not only work, they also can

be cost-effective. In its recent study, "Diverting Children from a Life of Crime, Measuring Costs and Benefits," Rand assessed the cost-effectiveness of several prevention strategies, and found that they compared favorably with a high-profile incarceration alternative (California's three strikes law guaranteeing extended sentences for repeat offenders) in terms of serious crime averted per dollar expended. While the estimated crime reductions that were achievable through the additional incarceration of the three strikes law were considerable—about 20 percent—the monetary cost of implementing "three strikes" was approximately $5.5 billion per year. For less than $1 billion more per year, Rand reports, parent training and graduation incentives could roughly double the amount of crime reduction.

In light of what we know about the precursors of violent offending, prevention and early intervention programs are critical. The juvenile justice system cannot solve the complex problem of juvenile violence unilaterally; it cannot make up for the failures of families and the shortcomings of other institutions.

Breaking the cycle

In Illinois, more than 1.3 million cases of child abuse or neglect were reported to the Department of Children and Family Services between fiscal years 1983 and 1995; the number of cases reported annually has skyrocketed. And although we know that three out of every four state prison inmates did not complete high school, an intolerably high number of children—more than 35,000—drop out of school in Illinois each year. If we are to have an appreciable impact on violent juvenile offending, the number of children exposed to these risk factors must be reduced. Until we break the cycle of violence that starts in the home, and find ways to keep young people in school, there will always be a pool of individuals predisposed to delinquent behavior.

Reducing juvenile violence requires the coordinated efforts of social service agencies, juvenile justice agencies, schools, and other institutions in both the public and private sectors. Improving public safety requires breaking the cycle of violence and preventing juvenile violence before it occurs.

More states seeing benefits of early intervention and prevention programs

SUBSTANTIAL RESEARCH INDICATES that the best programs and policies to prevent juvenile crime are based on a continuum of care that starts early in the child's life and continues through the teens. Studies show that quality early education and care in preschool and beyond help children get better grades and reduce dropout rates. Better education provides access to more employment opportunities, which in turn helps reduce crime.

Prevention in early childhood

State legislatures are increasingly seeing the advantages of supporting strong early childhood programs. As of 1995, 27 states funded preschools, 14 states supported Head Start programs, and eight states supported both.

For the last several years, **Colorado** has heavily funded early childhood education and care. In 1996, the General Assembly increased funding for at-risk preschools by $4.2 million to accommodate 1,850 more preschoolers. Increased legislative support means that Colorado serves 8,500 at-risk children across the state. In addition, the legislature allocated $7 million for violence prevention programs and approved third-year funding for a pilot program for family centers in at-risk communities.

Child abuse and neglect prevention

Because much research connects child abuse and neglect with juvenile crime, lawmakers are increasingly funding programs aimed at reducing abuse and neglect. The Healthy Start Program, started in **Hawaii** in 1985, focuses on families at risk of child abuse and neglect. Social workers visit new parents at home and provide child care education, as well as health-related services for infants. Evaluations show substantial decreases in abuse and neglect; only 0.5 percent of program participants reported child abuse or neglect, compared with confirmed abuse and neglect in 2.7 percent of nonparticipating families. Due to Healthy Start's success, the National Committee to Prevent Child Abuse launched a national initiative called Healthy Families America to help all states and the District of Columbia develop similar programs.

In 1994, **Tennessee** created a Healthy Start program along with an initiative to provide early child care and education for at-risk 3- and 4-year-olds, and double the number of school-related family centers, among other resources.

Family preservation programs

At least 21 other states have started comprehensive family preservation programs, including **Michigan**. Its Families First program, started in 1988, provides at-home counseling to families in danger of losing their child to foster care due to abuse and neglect. The program provides four to six weeks of counseling and communication education. Michigan's program reportedly has saved $55 million in its first three years, and the program costs $6,000 to $8,000 less per family than the cost of a year in foster care.

Sharing information

While youth who commit first-time, less serious offenses have contact with social services and schools, research shows that few of these resources are equipped to handle troubled children and their families. The Hennepin County Attorney's Office in **Minnesota** conducted a study on the extent of communication between child welfare agencies and the juvenile justice system. The study found that most delinquent children younger than age 10 who were referred to social services did not get the help they needed. In addition, most of these children had contact with other public agencies—91 percent of the children's families had received Aid to Families with Dependent Children, and 81 percent had a history of child abuse or neglect. Therefore, the researchers decided that the child welfare system could best identify and help these youth, and in 1995, the Minnesota legislature initiated an early intervention program for delinquents younger than 10. The program combines the services of the County Attorney's Office and Children and Family Services, among others.

Experts agree that effective prevention and intervention require that agencies outside the juvenile justice system get involved, and information sharing is a key component. In more than 30 states, laws allow the release of juvenile offenders' names under certain circumstances. For example, **Connecticut, Maryland, Texas, and Virginia** require law enforcement to notify school officials of students' delinquency.

—*Kristi Turnbaugh*

(Source: National Conference of State Legislatures (1996), "A legislator's guide to comprehensive juvenile justice.")

Understanding the Roots of Crime: The Project on Human Development in Chicago Neighborhoods

by Christy A. Visher

Why do some communities and not others become the settings for high rates of delinquency, crime, substance abuse, and drug marketing? Why do some people and not others become habituated to a life of criminal behavior? What is the relationship among community structure, family functioning, and a person's own individual development as factors in influencing criminal behavior? If answers to these questions could be found, they would contribute greatly to our understanding of criminal behavior and could serve as the basis for prevention strategies. In a major National Institute of Justice (NIJ)-sponsored study now under way, researchers are seeking these answers, and others, in an attempt to achieve that understanding.

The cornerstone of NIJ's health and justice initiative, the Project on Human Development in Chicago Neighborhoods, is an unprecedented, long-range program of research designed to study a broad range of factors at the level of the community, the family, and the individual believed to be important in explaining early aggression and delinquency, substance abuse, and criminal behavior, including violence.

The Project is directed by Felton Earls of the Harvard School of Public Health and Albert J. Reiss Jr., of Yale University. A group of distinguished scientists (see exhibit 1) has been in-volved in the planning and design of the study from its inception.

The project's rationale

A critical premise of the Project is that an individual's behavioral development is deeply rooted in multiple contexts. Moreover, the complex interactions among them—the relationships of individual traits, community characteristics, the school and family setting, and peer group relations (friends and acquaintances)—also affect that development.

The program of research is also based on the theory that patterns of criminal behavior have a long gestation period. Because they develop over time, knowledge about what evokes, sustains, or alters this long-term development can be put to good use in devising means of prevention and intervention.

It is difficult to know how much influence to assign to any one of these factors in contrast to the others; that is, to find out the extent to which someone is the product of neighborhood influences and the extent to which her or his behavior results from individual development. Previous research has been unable to disentangle these factors to help distinguish the effects of one from the others. The Project on Human Develop-ment in Chicago Neighborhoods will attempt to do this and will give equal attention to influences at the individual level and the community level that may affect development throughout the course of a person's life.

Focus on prevention

Because the Project was conceptualized with an eye to interventions that may deter criminal behavior, preventable conditions will receive particular emphasis. Thus, special attention will be given to conditions that develop before birth (during the mother's pregnancy), as well as in infancy and early childhood. The objective is to ascertain which elements of a child's development influence the pathways from behavioral problems in the early years to aggression and crime—particularly violent crime—later in life.

If interventions are to be used to the best effect in preventing criminal behavior, it is essential to know at what points in a person's development they should be applied. Accordingly, the program of research will identify opportunities during childhood and adolescence when interventions are most likely to produce the greatest benefit. Testing various strategies that promise effective intervention will also be part of the Project. Such knowledge can promote the develop-

From the *National Institute of Justice Journal*, November 1994, pp. 9-12. Reprinted by permission of the National Institute of Justice, National Criminal Justice Reference Service.

Exhibit 1. Scientific Directors and Advisory Group

Robert Cairns, Ph.D.
Professor of Psychology
University of North Carolina

Felton Earls, M.D.
Professor of Human Behavior
and Development
Harvard School of Public Health

David Huizinga, Ph.D.
Research Associate
University of Colorado

Terrie Moffitt, Ph.D.
Associate Professor of
Clinical Psychology
University of Wisconsin

Stephen Raudenbush, Ed.D.
Associate Professor of Education
Michigan State University

Albert J. Reiss, Jr., Ph.D.
Professor of Sociology
Yale University

Robert Sampson, Ph.D.
Professor of Sociology
University of Chicago

Elizabeth Susman, Ph.D.
Professor of Behavioral Health
Pennsylvania State University

ment of informed public policies and programs geared to prevention.

How the study was designed

Taken together, the elements of the study design constitute a unique approach:

◆ Investigation of behavioral problems, by age, including early aggression, delinquency, substance abuse, and criminal behavior among both males and females.

◆ Examination of how influences generated in the neighborhood, school, and family contexts interact with the strengths and vulnerabilities of individuals to affect the onset of antisocial behavior and its patterns from preadolescence to adulthood.

◆ Comparison of these contexts and individual differences by group (African-Americans, Hispanics, and Caucasians) and further distinguishing the groups by social class and gender.

◆ Use of an accelerated longitudinal approach, involving nine age cohorts spaced from birth to age 32, permits information-gathering in a relatively brief period of time that would otherwise take several decades.

The startup phase

Over the past 5 years, NIJ, in conjunction with the John D. and Catherine T. MacArthur Foundation, has supported the planning and design of the study. It is a major component of NIJ's research program and addresses NIJ's statutory mandate to study "the causes and correlates of crime and juvenile delinquency." NIJ and its funding partner, the MacArthur Foundation, have jointly invested $10 million in the development and design phase. More than 100 scientists with numerous theoretical perspectives, who represent several disciplines—among them pediatrics, biology, psychology, sociology, and criminology—have been involved thus far.

Laying the groundwork. The early phases, under way since 1989, included exploring particular study topics and finding out which study methods would work best. Pilot studies were carried out to answer specific questions, and two volumes on the method used to conduct a study with an accelerated longitudinal design were produced. A series of reports presented in outlines the design of a comprehensive study of the roots of crime. These reports included exhaustive reviews of previous studies in relevant topic areas: early child-

hood development and conduct disorder, adolescent development and juvenile delinquency, the influence of family and community factors on crime and criminal behavior, and the development of criminal careers.

The pilot studies, whose findings are summarized in a box (*Findings of the Pilot Studies*) explored several specific issues, some of which will be studied in greater depth over the course of the project, including:

◆ The amount of interaction fathers have with their infants and preschool children and the impact of that interaction.

◆ The effect of endocrine influences on aggression (for example, the accuracy of measures of the hormone testosterone in saliva in aggressive and nonaggressive boys).

◆ The influence of peer groups (friends and acquaintances) on delinquency.

◆ The use of social services such as counseling by adolescents and their parents.

The researchers also conducted pilots to find measurement tools that would be useful for the study. Thus, they developed and tested various psychological measures appropriate to the different age groups in the study. For example, they wanted to find out how best to measure stress and family interaction. They also wanted to make certain the measures they chose were appropriate to the various cultural groups being studied.

How the information will be gathered

Information will be collected over a period of 8 years on 11,000 people, male and female, and at three points during the project on approximately 40,000 additional individuals who live in the same community areas. An innovative study design, which essentially accelerates the pace of a long-term study, permits tracing in just 8 years how criminal behavior develops from birth to age 32. The acceleration occurs through the study of the nine groups of people (cohorts) whose ages overlap.

Findings of the Pilot Studies

Studying the development of the individual in the social context

Before the study began, the research design, measurement strategies, and method of data analysis were examined and then refined. Sample sizes were set for the age cohorts and the neighborhoods. The researchers showed that continuity and change over time in behavior—aggression, delinquency, and criminal activity—could be revealed by linking the information, even when information from different age cohorts was used. They also developed a detailed analytic plan to study how the social context (family, school, or neighborhood) can affect individuals' behavior.

Does testosterone affect aggression in children?

The link between the male hormone testosterone and aggression has been demonstrated in animal studies and in some studies of adult men. Other research has shown that aggressive children continue to display this type of behavior into adulthood. But the results of the pilot study conducted for this project cast strong doubts on the possibility that testosterone levels explain aggression in young children or can be used as a marker for later aggression in adolescence or adulthood. In a study of a small group of highly aggressive prepubertal boys, no significant difference was found between their testosterone levels and those of nonaggressive children.

The father's role in child/adolescent development

The involvement of fathers in their children's development was found to have positive effects, according to the findings of another pilot study. This study of fathers' interaction with high-risk infants revealed that three-fourths played with their children on a daily basis (although for one-third of these children the paternal figure changed during the 3-year period covered by the study).

Another study involved interviews with fathers (both those who live with their children and those who do not). Researchers found that fathers furnished unique information about family processes, including child behavior.

Effects of neighborhood characteristics on drug use and sales

A large city in the Northeast was studied to examine the extent of neighboring, local personal ties, income level, participation in community organizations, and extent of deviant-criminal subculture. Researchers wanted to find out if the type of neighborhood affects the amount of criminal behavior that takes place in it.

They found that differences by neighborhood in these community characteristics could account for the differences among certain neighborhoods in the amount of substance abuse and explained differences in substance abuse by individuals within a given neighborhood. This study is being expanded in Chicago.

Peer social networks

Conventional wisdom and previous research hold that friends and acquaintances exert strong influences on young people's behavior. The primary focus of pilot studies was the availability of reliable information about peer social networks. Researchers found that the peer associates of highly deviant adolescents could be interviewed, that information about gang activity can be obtained through studies of peer social networks, and that large numbers of students in a classroom can be sources of information about social status and social networks of their friends and acquaintances.

Is delinquency related to child caretaking arrangements?

Children in high-risk neighborhoods were found to have different caretaking provided for them than the caretaking arrangements for children in the overall sample: there were more single mothers and single fathers in the high-risk sample. However, the arrangements did *not* affect delinquency among high-risk children. By contrast, in the general, citywide sample, child caretaking arrangements were related to delinquency. For example, children in the larger, citywide sample who lived with single mothers were much more delinquent than those living with two parents. In the high-risk sample, children with single mothers were no more delinquent than those in two-parent families. This illustrates complex interactions between family structure, neighborhood characteristics, and behavior.

Juvenile Justice Comes of Age

As younger and younger kids commit worse crimes, legislators are overcoming political and institutional obstacles in order to update juvenile justice systems.

By Donna Lyons

Youngsters under 18 who rob, rape and murder have forced an examination of outdated juvenile justice systems designed for another time. Violent juvenile crime rates have soared 67 percent in the last 10 years. And although the percentage of youth doing these things is low (one out of 200), juveniles are still disproportionally represented among violent criminals.

Today's young offenders turn as easily toward crime and violence as young men of past generations took up smoking in the boys' room, says New York Senator Steve Saland, who has become the Senate's expert on juvenile crime and delinquency. He says that many aspects of family courts and the juvenile justice system have become archaic. "We need to face the fact that the existing system is incapable of dealing with the most serious, violent kids out there."

Fixing the system isn't easy. Optimistic congressional leaders have placed juvenile justice among their top 10 priorities this year, but state experience shows that the politics of the problem are messy, and that planning for reform is a tedious and long-term undertaking. Advocacy groups and the public tend to think that changing the system to take care of serious juvenile crime should be easy enough. Researchers point out that we know more today than ever about "what works" and what does not to control juvenile crime. Make punishment for offenders swift and sure. Provide services that prevent young lives from spiraling into crime and violence. But legislators find numerous political and institutional hurdles to a quick fix.

Donna Lyons is NCSL's criminal justice expert.

LEGISLATIVE STRUGGLES

An agreement to reform New York's juvenile justice system was announced in February by Senate Republican leaders and Republican Governor George Pataki. The proposal includes longer sentences for violent juveniles and lockdown and limited privileges for the most serious offenders. It would significantly alter family courts to promote juvenile accountability and parental involvement, and would allow those courts to issue search and arrest warrants and to hear from victims in sentencing young offenders.

"This has been a long, laborious process—but one that is certainly well worth the fight," says Saland, who is Republican chairman of the Senate Committee on Children and Families. Indeed, the Senate's pact with the governor follows three years' work on juvenile justice reform, which still must earn the approval of the Democratic Assembly. Public fear of juvenile crime has been particularly acute in New York where rates of juvenile violence, especially homicides, have been well above the national average.

Lawmakers elsewhere wrestle with the same issues of how to update systems, created primarily for young thieves and vandals, to deal as effectively with juvenile rapists and armed robbers. Consensus for change can be difficult to come by when the policy issues involved are so ideologically divisive. Members split on issues like whether you should spend money to prevent crime or to punish young offenders. And it is an arduous task for legislatures to get a handle on juvenile justice, which reaches into courts, corrections, education and children's services. Trying to make comprehensive changes is complicated by the differing perspectives of all the commit-

From *State Legislatures*, May 1997, pp. 12-18. © 1997 by the National Conference of State Legislatures. Reprinted by permission.

"LAST CHANCE" PROGRAMS DIVERT SOME YOUNG OFFENDERS

States are transforming juvenile justice, and among their innovations are "third systems" that lie between traditional juvenile justice and adult corrections. To date, at least a dozen states have created systems that blend juvenile and adult system jurisdiction when juveniles commit serious crimes. Designed to rehabilitate criminal youths, third systems often apply strict discipline, education and behavior modification.

"We can't just write off 14-year-olds," says Regis Groff, director of the Colorado Youthful Offender System, which was created by the General Assembly in 1993. "Kids who are convicted of certain felonies and sentenced to adult prisons can be better served in special programs that might be harsh, but are designed for them," says Groff, a former state senator.

Designed primarily for gun- and gang-related offenders and operated in the adult corrections department, the YOS program is a precondition for a suspended sentence for some juveniles 14 to 18 years old who are sent, under state law, directly to district court. These youths are then committed to YOS for up to six years. The military-type program couples positive peer culture with education. Its focus on self-control and physical activity helps break down a violent mentality so youths begin to develop positive self-concepts and learn the value of service to others, according to Groff.

What sets YOS apart from the adult system is the opportunity for youths who successfully complete the program to phase into supervised community release for six to 12 months. But YOS is a one-time shot—if they offend again

they will go into the adult system. So far, Groff said, of 18 kids who have gone through the program only two have committed new offenses.

Other states are following Colorado's lead with "last chance" systems for tough, young offenders. North Carolina created a labor intensive community service program for 16- to 25-year-olds sentenced as adults. As in Colorado, discipline is combined with education and rehabilitation. Connecticut, Minnesota, Missouri and Wisconsin have created third, or dual jurisdiction, systems for serious offenders. In 1996 alone, six states applied the concept of blended juvenile and adult system jurisdiction. Kansas, Utah and Virginia included third systems in major reform acts, while Massachusetts, Michigan and New Mexico incorporated similar sentencing options for some serious offenders.

While the popularity of intermediate systems is on the rise, some experts contend that early intervention, not middle-tier programs like YOS, is key to keeping young people out of juvenile and criminal justice systems.

"It's just another rearrangement of boxes and kids, but not a solution," says former House Majority Leader Bill Purcell, who now directs the Child and Family Policy Center at Vanderbilt Institute for Public Policy Studies in Nashville, Tenn. Purcell said that while states may benefit from changing procedures to allow dual sentencing, they first must develop thoughtful, broad policy on how they are going to deal with all aspects of juvenile crime and justice.

—*Julie Featherstone, NCSL*

tees. To manage the issue, many states have formed task forces, interim study committees or other special work groups to deliberate and make recommendations on juvenile justice reform.

Recent crime statistics show downturns in overall rates of violent crime. This might have eased political pressure on legislatures to act, but now Congress and the Clinton administration want to have a say. Federal measures could change guiding philosophies on detention of juveniles and put new "get tough" requirements on states. Proposals include things like graduated sanctions for young offenders and other programs that various states have done already—and often done well. More than a dozen states have significantly reformed their juvenile systems in recent years. And in a manner that might be instructive to Capitol Hill, state legislatures are substantially changing juvenile justice despite what sometimes are partisan differences, and often as a result of spade work that has developed consensus among the "stakeholders" in state and local criminal justice and child welfare systems.

IT CAN BE DONE

"It's doable politically if you are willing and patient enough to take it one bite at a time," says Representative

Jeanne Adkins, chair of the House Judiciary Committee in Colorado, where both chambers are controlled by Republicans. Perseverance has paid off in Colorado, where reforms started four years ago when Adkins got together with a like-minded Republican attorney general to deal with gangs and other juveniles who commit crimes with guns. Several high-profile crimes had fueled public alarm about juvenile violence, including news of two youngsters in Adkins' suburban Denver district accused in the shooting death of a sheriff's deputy. A bill Adkins carried in 1993 to impose tougher sanctions for juveniles who commit gun crimes made it out of the House, but was killed in the Senate. Later that year, popular Democratic Governor Roy Romer stole some thunder when he called a special legislative session in which lawmakers approved juvenile gun restrictions and sentencing measures. Included in the package was legislation creating the Youthful Offender System, an intermediate system for juveniles who otherwise would have been sentenced as adults. At least a dozen states have since emulated Colorado's "third system."

The special session may have been the most climactic point in juvenile justice reform in Colorado, but it did not divert the legislature's attention from the issues. An Interim Committee on Youth Violence, a task force on the recodification of the children's code and the Legisla-

"We all say we want what is best for kids and the public, but these things can fall apart once you get into fighting over money."

—Representative Michael Lawlor, Connecticut

tive Oversight Committee followed with more than three years of work to retool many aspects of the system.

"The push and pull of prevention versus punishment was always there," says Adkins, who was instrumental in the study efforts along with chairing the Legislative Oversight Committee, "but we ended up with a cohesive, bipartisan effort." Her 1996 legislation approved by the General Assembly addresses detention, transfer to adult court and parental responsibility, and places limits on a juvenile's right to a jury trial. Other legislation last year ensures that no less than 20 percent of crime prevention grants focus on early childhood.

Recent Colorado law also established performance-based audits of certain programs so that future policy and funding can be based on more than just anecdotal evidence. This helps reduce interagency politics, which can be as difficult as the partisan issues, according to Adkins. She compliments the governor for involving key department heads in the work of the legislature. "People who could truly make changes were at the table suggesting them," she says.

AVERTING AGENCY POLITICS

Lawmakers often must coordinate the many arms of state and local government involved in juvenile justice, since agency responsibilities may overlap in some areas and leave cracks elsewhere. In Connecticut, legislation in 1995 to transform juvenile justice policy incorporated a second stage of planning for the agency reorganization necessary to successfully carry out the law.

"We all say we want what is best for kids and the public, but these things can fall apart once you get into fighting over money," says Connecticut Representative Michael Lawlor, who co-chairs the Joint Judiciary Committee for House Democrats. He also worked to build consensus for the reform package in the Senate. "The policy decisions that changed laws ultimately would affect budgets and missions of a number of agencies," he says. The General Assembly dealt with this by requiring that the agencies meet and make recommendations on bureaucratic and budget changes necessary under the new law. A plan presented to the Legislature last year

resulted in reallocation of about $62 million and authorization of another $16 million to expand existing programs. A contract study reviewed and documented what dispositions were being given juveniles in various courts and created an offender profile for the state. This information provided a factual basis for the reorganization plan and helped to extinguish turf battles.

Lawlor says the reform act represented a fusion of punitive measures for tough kids and shifting of resources to allow for early intervention and alternative sanctions for others. A number of factors aided bipartisan agreement. A joint committee structure in Connecticut, in which the chambers and parties are used to working together, proved practical. Further, new rules implemented in 1994 by House Speaker Thomas Ritter were intended to get bills out of committees quicker and avoid bogging down policy in partisan politics. And observers say that on issues like youth policy, the culture of the legislature traditionally has been one of rolling up its sleeves and finding workable solutions. Connecticut also has a fairly centralized justice system and a recent, decent track record in adult sentencing. The reform legislation charged the judiciary's Office of Alternative Sanctions with creating a range of options to deal with juvenile offenders, akin to a successful overhaul of its adult system.

Lawlor says that a key to lasting, bipartisan satisfaction with the reforms has been the reported average savings of $125,000 per year for each youth diverted from juvenile corrections facilities to alternative programs or the adult system. Also a selling point: Expansion of pretrial alternatives for lower risk offenders helped the state address litigation it faced over crowding of detention facilities.

Although the judiciary in Connecticut was given a freer hand in creating a range of sanctions for young offenders, lawmakers invested much discretion with prosecutors for transferring kids to adult court. "All kids selling drugs are not alike," Lawlor says. "Many can be handled in the juvenile system, but a few are up-and-coming Al Capones. The prosecutors know who the really bad kids are."

PARTISAN STRIPES

Significant juvenile justice reform has in recent years happened more often in states where the same political party controls both chambers of the legislature, with little difference as to which party happens to have leadership. In 1994, Democratic-controlled legislatures in Arkansas, Florida, Minnesota and Oklahoma made substantial changes to youth policy, as did Missouri and Texas in 1995, and Kentucky and Virginia in 1996. In addition to Republican-led Colorado reforms that began in 1993, GOP-controlled legislatures in Oregon, Pennsylvania and Wisconsin in 1995, and Kansas and Utah in 1996 passed important reforms. Some of these legislatures had the possible advantage of working with a governor of the same political stripe, but six states significantly revised juvenile justice policy with a governor of a different party from one or both chambers in the statehouse.

The ease with which lawmakers in Connecticut and elsewhere have prevailed over partisanship may be harder to come by elsewhere. Although New York may be primed for juvenile justice reform in 1997, it also has a history of partisan gridlock over criminal justice issues. But despite what often have been troubled relations between Republican Governor Pataki and the Legislature, especially the Assembly, major adult sentencing reforms were achieved in 1995. Some lawmakers are optimistic that the same bipartisan agreement can be forged on juvenile justice.

At press time, Assembly Democrats said they were still working on a set of juvenile crime initiatives but had not yet unveiled legislation. Speaker Sheldon Silver has said his interests include longer sentences for violent juveniles, arrest powers for family courts, sanctions like restitution and community service, and parental responsibility—proposals similar to those agreed to by Saland and the governor. Observers say the pact between the Senate and the governor puts political pressure on Assembly leaders to act, and speculate that the Democrats are developing proposals to balance tougher sentencing with certain preventive approaches and service components absent from the Republicans' package. Last year under Saland's leadership, the Senate passed a sweeping Juvenile Justice Reform and Delinquency Prevention Act that failed to get Assembly attention.

PREVENTION IN CALIFORNIA

This will be a cutting-teeth year for committee leadership in California. In part because of term limits, brand new legislators chair the committees that must deal with recommendations issued last fall by a task force on juvenile crime. Created by the Legislature, the task force was composed of an Assembly Republican and a Senate Democrat, along with district attorneys, corrections and social service officials, judges, and other representatives of law enforcement and child welfare systems. Concern was raised early on that the group, heavy with gubernatorial appointments, might serve as a rubber stamp for Republican Governor Pete Wilson's policies. This resulted in an understanding that 14 of the 17 members had to agree on each of the final recommendations. Ultimately, it meant that the task force was silent on lightning-rod issues like transfer of juveniles to adult courts.

The task force recommended that prevention of juvenile crime should be a priority—policy already embraced by the Legislature. Earlier in 1996, California lawmakers created two programs for prevention and early intervention grants when Senate President Pro Tem Bill Lockyer wangled $50 million for the prevention efforts during final budget negotiations. The legislation already is getting good reviews for bringing together local agencies and service providers that previously had not worked to-

FEDERAL PLANS FOR JUVENILE JUSTICE

The 105th Congress opened with no shortage of proposals to modify the federal approach to juvenile justice. Two separate bills (S 3 and S 10) are offered by the Senate majority, along with a minority measure (S 15). The House, similarly, has a majority bill (HR 3) and a minority proposal (HR 278). What these bills have in common are provisions to prosecute juveniles as adults in federal courts, to allow preconviction detention, to open juvenile records and to provide more money to reduce juvenile gun crime. While part of these plans would place conditions on states to receive grants, others are actions aimed at federal prosecution of certain juvenile offenders.

In late February, the president offered his strategy for dealing with gangs and youth violence. The administration's proposal (HR 810, S 362) contains provisions similar to the others. But the bill also proposes funds to be used by prosecutors, courts, probation, parole, public defenders, victims' offices, and others in state and local criminal justice systems to develop better ways to respond to violent, serious juvenile crime. Other funds are earmarked for initiatives that will help children who are most likely to be led into crime, including antitruancy and other school and community-based programs.

The administration's juvenile crime bill continues mandates on states that receive federal money for juvenile justice. Most of these mandates have been in place since the Juvenile Justice and Delinquency Prevention Act of 1974. Those include keeping juvenile offenders separate from adults, removing young status offenders (youth arrested for offenses such as truancy that wouldn't be crimes if they were adults) from adult lock-ups and taking measures to correct disproportionate minority confinement. At the same time, the bill would give greater authority to the federal agency to waive requirements where states can justify a need for flexibility. Today, Congress is more interested in guaranteeing punishment for youthful offenders. S 10 would eliminate the stringent mandates of the 1974 act and replace them with a requirement that juveniles who are detained are not in institutions where they would have "regular sustained physical contact" with adult prisoners.

While the federal approach to juvenile crime appears to have toughened since the 1974 act, the motivations seem surprisingly similar. In findings of the 1974 act, Congress noted that juveniles accounted for almost half of the serious crimes in the United States and concluded that state and local communities do not have sufficient expertise or resources to deal comprehensively with juvenile delinquency. The federal Office of Juvenile Justice and Delinquency Prevention (OJJDP) created at that time would now, under various proposals before Congress, evolve into a renamed "crime control" agency.

Last year's pre-election season renewed partisan sparring about Washington's appropriate role in juvenile crime. Passed during the waning days of the 104th Congress, the omnibus appropriations bill included an incentive grant pushing states toward graduated punishments for juveniles, beginning with sanctions for first-time nonviolent offenders. While that move may have whetted the appetite of members who are anxious to do more, the slow start of this Congress adds to uncertainty about what direction it will steer on juvenile justice.

—*Jon Felde, NCSL*

STATES ACTIVE IN JUVENILE JUSTICE REFORM

More than a dozen states in recent years have passed major juvenile justice system reforms. They include: Arkansas, Colorado, Connecticut, Florida, Kansas, Kentucky, Missouri, Oklahoma, Oregon, Pennsylvania, Texas, Utah, Virginia and Wisconsin. Some of the reform acts broadly address early intervention and prevention, graduated sanctions for juvenile offenders, parental responsibility, and treating serious offenders like adult criminals, including opening of certain juvenile records and proceedings.

Nearly all states have passed laws addressing various components of juvenile justice reform. Significant, selected state laws have included:

Authorizing photographs, fingerprints of certain young offenders: Alabama, Arizona, Hawaii, Idaho, New Hampshire, North Dakota, Ohio.

Opening certain juvenile records, proceedings: Georgia, Indiana, Louisiana, Pennsylvania, South Carolina, South Dakota.

Creating juvenile criminal history that can follow one to adult court: Georgia, Oklahoma, Virginia.

Providing mandatory adult handling of certain serious crimes, offenders: Alabama, Arizona, Delaware, Georgia, Indiana, Kansas, Massachusetts, Michigan, Minnesota, Mississippi, Nevada, North Dakota, Utah, South Carolina.

Lowering the age of allowable transfer to adult court of certain young offenders: Colorado, Idaho, Michigan, New Mexico, North Carolina, West Virginia, Wisconsin, Wyoming.

Defining, setting penalties for gang-related crime: Arkansas, Arizona, California, Florida, Georgia, Kansas, Illinois, Indiana, Michigan, Nevada, North Dakota, Tennessee, Wisconsin.

Establishing, funding juvenile crime prevention: Arkansas, Arizona, California, Colorado, Connecticut, Florida, Georgia, Illinois, Oklahoma, Ohio, Oregon, Mississippi, Missouri, North Carolina, Tennessee, Texas, Utah, Virginia, Washington, Wisconsin, Wyoming.

Holding parents responsible: Alaska, Arizona, California, Colorado, Idaho, Illinois, Indiana, New Hampshire, Michigan, New Mexico, Oregon, Rhode Island, Vermont, Virginia, Washington.

gether. There remains sentiment in the Senate that local funding for juvenile crime prevention can have more impact than anything else the Legislature might do. Bills introduced by Senator Lockyer early this year would support the commitment to prevention by creating a Youth Violence Prevention Authority in state government, as well as renew grant programs and establish early intervention strategies in schools.

The governor has reportedly been shopping the Legislature for interest in proposals for direct, legislative transfer of certain serious juvenile offenders to adult court. California's current "fitness law" relies entirely on judicial discretion for waiver to adult court, while the governor, prosecutors and victims' groups have suggested giving district attorneys more transfer authority or providing statutory certainty that certain juvenile offenders will be treated as adult criminals.

Legislation introduced by Senator Adam Schiff, the new chair of the Senate's subcommittee on juvenile justice, could significantly change the state's approach to transfer of juveniles to criminal courts. One bill would procedurally combine the separate "fitness hearing" to send a juvenile case to adult court and the preliminary hearing that takes place in district court. Another would create blended juvenile and adult jurisdiction for some serious offenders [reviving the "third system" concept floated unsuccessfully last year], and for the first time under California law allow direct file in adult court cases of juveniles who commit murder or rape. Noticeably absent from the California task force recommendations was comment on the transfer issue, reportedly because the panel found this to be a touchy subject on which they could not agree.

VOTERS DECIDE

Perhaps the most difficult of all for legislatures is when frustrated citizens decide to take matters into their own hands. Ballot initiatives in two Western states gave voters the say in setting policy for trial and sentencing of violent juveniles.

In Oregon, voters approved a 1994 citizen initiated "get tough" juvenile crime measure that requires certain violent 15-, 16- and 17-year olds to be tried as adults and receive mandatory sentences. The measure prohibits judges from treating first-time young offenders differently from repeat offenders. Lawmakers, while sympathetic to judges' concerns, have limited options for amending voter-initiated policy.

In Arizona, the Legislature is working to implement juvenile justice reforms approved by 63 percent of the voters last fall as an amendment to the state's Constitution. The measure, championed by the governor, mandates transfer of certain juvenile offenders to adult court. It requires that juveniles 15 and older be tried as adults when accused of certain violent offenses or if they are chronic offenders. Less definitive than the Oregon initiative, Arizona's voter-approved reforms left it to the Legislature to define violent and chronic juvenile offenders. New judiciary chair Senator John Kaites is garnering support for the implementation legislation by rounding it out with prevention and early intervention.

THE CHILDREN'S CRUSADE

A '60s-style campaign aims to put kids first in this year's budget battles and the presidential race

By ELIZABETH GLEICK

FOR MARIAN WRIGHT EDELMAN, THE youngest daughter of a Baptist preacher, from adversity springs strength. From defeat comes inspiration. If her courage ever fails her, she is not about to say so. Life as she lives it day by day is a series of battles fought along starkly moral lines. That, is why Edelman—who helped register black voters in the segregated South, who stood on the steps of the Lincoln Memorial during Martin Luther King Jr.'s "I Have a Dream" speech and who gave Robert Kennedy a personal tour to see the malnourished children in the Mississippi Delta—is manning the barricades once more.

As the president of the Children's Defense Fund, she has for nearly 25 years been the single loudest voice on behalf of those too young to speak for themselves. But to hear her tell it, the test of her mettle is now. "I knew it would take 20 years, 25 years to seed a movement," she says. "You just have to keep planting and watering and fertilizing. And then, when it is time, you do what you have to do. But you have to stand up—win, lose or draw. And it's time."

Edelman has summoned Americans to a rally at the Lincoln Memorial this Saturday to Stand for Children. Like the Million Man March, the event is less about defining an agenda than it is about evoking a spirit—and filling what organizers see as a terrifying vacuum of leadership and resolve at a time when every premise about what this country owes its children is being challenged. "Children are never going to get what they need until there is a fundamental change in the ethos that says it is not acceptable to cut children first," says Edelman of the current budget battles in Washington. She hopes to use this period of fiscal conflict to mobilize the troops. "God really did put rainbows in the clouds," she says. "Without Newt Gingrich and the incredible threat to everything, we would never have been able to bring folks together in this way.

So, in many ways this is the thing that will launch the children's movement."

Unlike the civil rights movement, however—or for that matter the seatbelt, drunk-driving and environmental movements, all of which have changed the way Americans live—the children's movement is more like a series of spasms than a focused, well-coordinated effort. True, when a Polly Klaas or Megan Kanka is abducted and murdered, or when Elisa Izquierdo falls through the gaping holes in New York City's social-services system, outraged parents and community leaders can rear up, roar and carry the day for "three strikes" or Megan's Law. And in the endless wrangle over welfare reform, which hit the headlines again last week, children have proved to be a deal breaker. "I can win any argument by saying we need reform of welfare, but not at the cost of kids," says Senator Edward Kennedy, who derailed Bob Dole's welfare proposal by branding it the "home alone" bill because there was no money specifically targeted for child care.

Even so, despite activism by Edelman and her allies, most political leaders still don't do what she wants them to do: ask, every time they cast a vote or cut a dollar, "How will this affect kids?" And even if they did, they would not necessarily answer the question Edelman's way because of the growing

Do you favor or oppose spending more of your tax dollars on programs to help children?

73% Favor

22% Oppose

From a telephone poll of 1,011 adult Americans taken for TIME/CNN on May 8 and 9 by Yankelovich Partners Inc. Sampling error ±3.2%. Not sures omitted.

sense, embraced by both major presidential candidates, that government has its limitations. "Read between the lines of everything Marian Wright Edelman says, and what you get is this," says Robert Rector of the conservative Heritage Foundation. "The problem affecting kids is material poverty, so if we give the family more money for housing and food, things will turn out better for the kids. The reality is that despite 30 years of this effort, there is no evidence whatsoever that [this] has a positive effect on kids at all, except for cases of gross malnutrition."

In the broadest sense, Edelman's positions are extremely popular. Who, after all, would ever stand against children? In a recent TIME/CNN poll, 73% of those surveyed favor having more of their tax dollars go to programs that benefit the young. For the most part, that sentiment has proved beneficial. Since Edelman launched the Children's Defense Fund in 1973, American children are doing better in such areas as math and science proficiency, immunizations and infant survival rates, thanks in part to government action.

BUT AS AMERICA POLARIZES INTO A land of rich and poor, the number of children on the losing side is growing at an alarming rate. According to a report released last month by the Department of Health and Human Services, the percentage of children in "extreme poverty" (with a family income less than half the official poverty level) has doubled since 1975: it now stands at 10%, or 6.3 million children. The ranks of the merely poor include 1 in every 5 children in the U.S. In 1992 there were 850,000 substantiated cases of child abuse or neglect, while the homicide rate for teens more than doubled between 1970 and 1992.

Such numbers are not just a snapshot of how we live today. To experts who understand the trajectory of childhood development, the statistics predict a grim future for American society. As Douglas Nelson, executive director of the Annie E. Casey Foundation, puts it, "It may well be that the nation cannot survive—as a decent place to live, as a world-class power or even as a democracy—with such high rates of children growing into adulthood unprepared to parent, unprepared to be productively employed and unprepared to share in mainstream aspirations."

The Children's Defense Fund works to fix this disconnect between what Americans say they want for children and what they actually do for them. With offices just a few blocks from Capitol Hill, the Defense Fund stands out among youth advocacy groups for its Washington-based organization and strategic coalitions, its many alliances with state and local groups, and its many service-oriented programs. In the District of Columbia, the Defense Fund has established City Lights, which works with severely troubled adolescents. At what was once the Tennessee farm of *Roots* author Alex Haley, the Fund conducts leadership training sessions. And, often in partnership with Junior Leagues,

it runs public-education programs throughout the country, exposing business and community leaders to the problems of the young. In the mid-1980s, the Children's Defense Fund helped focus national attention on the problem of teen pregnancy. In the late '80s, it put together a coalition that was instrumental in the 1990 passage of a multibillion-dollar child-care bill for low-income working parents.

Edelman learned early that you have to play politics to change lives. When Head Start funds were made available to the states in 1965, for example, Mississippi did not sign up. But a group of public, private and church organizations, with Edelman on its board, applied for the money and saw Head Start become a powerful catalyst in the state's black community. When then Senator John Stennis tried to get Congress to cut off its funding, Edelman, at that point 25, went to Washington to fight back—and won. "This was my first big lesson about government," she says. "There was no one in Washington for these folks, like General Motors had. That was seed No. 1 for the Children's Defense Fund." In the 1970s, Edelman helped defeat a proposal to turn Head Start funding over to the states. Today, with devolution again the coin of the realm, Edelman, a child of the segregated South, remains deeply skeptical that all states will voluntarily care for their neediest citizens. "Where you can see a general need everywhere," she contends, you try to have a national solution."

As she travels around the country stirring up support for the march in Washington, Edelman talks about "the silence of good people about the injustice of it all." By this she means, in large part, her old friend the President. Marian and her husband, Peter Edelman, a lawyer whom she met when he was an adviser to Bobby Kennedy, have known the Clintons for many years. Mrs. Clinton worked as a lawyer for the Children's Defense Fund, resigning from the board when she became First Lady. In August 1995, the President almost nominated Peter, who currently works for the Department of Health and Human Services, to the federal district court in Washington, changing his mind at the last minute, fearing he was too liberal. Last fall, as Edelman watched the welfare battle take shape, she privately implored the President not to compromise federal standards. When Clinton nevertheless signaled his sup-

Should each of the following programs for children be among the highest priorities for government, an important priority or a low/no priority?

	Highest	Important	Low/No
Free immunization shots against disease	67%	26%	5%
Nutrition programs for children who need them	61%	32%	6%
Health insurance for all children	54%	29%	15%
Day-care programs for poor children so their parents can work	52%	33%	12%
Providing information and assistance to teens on preventing unwanted pregnancies	51%	30%	17%
Prenatal health-care programs for pregnant mothers who need them	49%	36%	13%
Preschool education programs	45%	34%	20%

port for a Senate bill that would transform federal welfare spending into a system of smaller, block grants to the states—thereby eliminating the safety net of protections that children have, regardless of which state they live in— Edelman spoke out.

In "An Open Letter to the President," which ran last Nov. 3 in the Washington *Post*, Edelman urged Clinton to oppose welfare and Medicaid block grants. She wrote, "Do you think the Old Testament prophets, Isaiah, Micah and Amos—or Jesus Christ—would support such policies?" If he were to let federal protections go, she warned, "we may not get them back in our lifetime or our children's." She concluded: "What a tragic irony it would be for this regressive attack on children and the poor to occur on your watch. For me, this is a defining moral litmus test for your presidency." In the end, Clinton withdrew his support for the bill, perhaps in part because he was shamed by his old friend, but also because it was good politics to do so. Senator Daniel Patrick Moynihan had forced the White House to disclose its estimate that more than 1 million additional children would be thrown into poverty by the Senate measure. (The Clintons and the Edelmans remained friends. Peter rode Air Force One to Yitzhak Rabin's funeral last fall and stayed up most of the night playing hearts with the President on the trip home.)

The word moral appears seven times in Edelman's letter, and the certitude with which she plunges ahead is both her greatest strength and her greatest flaw. What looks like "morality" to her is merely discredited 1960s liberalism to others. Her opponents believe that all of Edelman's big talk about children masks her true goal: to solve the problems of poverty—for people of all ages— through the expenditure of federal money. While most Americans agree children deserve extra help, when policymakers start talking about solutions they speak completely different languages. "As long as liberals talk about economics and government and conservatives talk about culture and values, there will never be a political debate that reaches a successful conclusion," says William Galston, a former domestic-policy adviser in the Clinton White House.

The unshakable conviction that they have God on their side may also help explain why advocates for children are

not more effective lobbyists. A 1995 report on how state legislative leaders view children's issues and the people who come to lobby on their behalf discovered a vast chasm of misunderstanding and miscommunication. Few of the 177 legislative leaders who were interviewed could identify by name the children's-advocacy organizations in their states. Many complained that those who ask them to act on behalf of children do not understand the legislative process and tend to arrive too late in the budget cycle. Says Michael Iskowitz, Senator Kennedy's aide on children's issues: "Just expecting people to do the right thing is often not enough. You have to give them a range of arguments about why it is in their interest."

Chief among those arguments are votes and money, yet the study found that children's advocates rarely work in political campaigns or contribute to candidates. Worse still, they have little organized, grass-roots support. "[The legislators] are not getting calls in their office asking, 'What are you doing for kids?' " says Margaret Blood, who ran the study. Even some of Edelman's supporters acknowledge this has been a problem with her work. "CDF has been enormously effective on a national level," says Eve Brooks, president of the National Association of Child Advocates. "It has been less effective in building a constituency that stays in place."

It is a truism that children can't vote, but Sylvia Ann Hewlett, author of *When the Bough Breaks: The Costs of Neglecting Our Children,* has discovered that their parents don't vote either. In the last national election, only 39% of adults with children at home cast a ballot, as compared with 61% of the elderly. During the 1950s, says Hewlett, who runs a non-

Should current government programs to help children be cut back, expanded, or are they about right?

10% Cut back
49% Expanded
37% About right

profit organization aimed at getting parents to the polls, 65% of parents voted.

In their interviews, the legislators indicated that if children's advocates are to be effective, they will need to organize themselves more like the National Rifle Association and the American Association for Retired Persons—with well-defined goals, politically active members, and lobbyists who work throughout the entire legislative session. (The Children's Defense Fund operates on an annual budget of $13 million, compared with $66 million for the N.R.A.; AARP has annual revenues of $300 million.)

The latter comparison is particularly apt since the elderly may have strengthened their own safety net at the expense of the young. "Is there a disproportionate amount of money being spent on people over the age of 65 versus under the age of three?" asks one legislative leader. "Yes, unquestionably. Is it in part a function of their lobbying efforts? Yes, unquestionably. Is it largely a function of their need? No, it is not." Yet as Ira Schwartz, dean of the School of Social Work at the University of Pennsylvania, notes, "Seniors and those in the work force don't understand that the survival of the Social Security system is really dependent on the future of our children." Or perhaps they do: AARP has endorsed the Stand, in part, says spokesman Peter Ashkenaz, because so many grandparents are rearing children.

In the end, the most pressing question for children's advocates is the one that Saturday's march intentionally sidesteps: setting a common agenda. It is a daunting task, not just because children's issues are so numerous and so fragmented, but because no one is certain what solutions, if any, will work. Even people committed to reducing teen pregnancy may disagree vehemently about the means to that end. Some feel that social trends like no-fault divorce pose the greatest threat to children.

"One of the biggest problems we have is that it's so hard to show results," says Frank Sanchez Jr., who runs delinquency-prevention programs for the Boys & Girls Clubs of America. The child who doesn't get into trouble is the dog that doesn't bark. "We don't have a lot of studies to build a broad, knowledgeable base," agrees Kristin Moore, executive director of the research firm Child Trends Inc., because most of the efforts to help kids are "too late, too shallow, too brief and too cheap."

Among some children's advocates, enthusiasm has faded for homegrown, experimental approaches. In 1988 Lisbeth Schorr and her husband, National Public Radio's Daniel Schorr, wrote *Within Our Reach: Breaking the Cycle of Disadvantage,* which enthusiastically described 24 new programs for children. Today half of them are gone, and Schorr has had a change of heart about what such initiatives can accomplish. "Foundations fund innovative programs for several years with the idea that when they work, public funds will pick up the cost and continue the program, she says. "But that hasn't happened for years. It's an illusion. Anything you want to do in an organized way, a big way, needs government funding." Adds Vivien Stewart of the Carnegie Foundation: "In this country we are very good at pilot programs, but we are very bad at scaling up to a point where we can actually turn some of these things around. It can't be done with the resources of small organizations."

Senator Dan Coats, an Indiana Republican, could not disagree more. Originator of the "charity tax credit" endorsed by Bob Dole last week, Coats believes "federal programs have almost become an excuse for people not to become personally involved." A tax credit that allows people to support local social initiatives, he contends, would keep both donor and recipient accountable. "If you want to know that your money is really going to make a difference," he asks, "would you rather give $1,000 to Habitat for Humanity or to HUD?" Yet one study that Catholic Charities cited in Senate testimony earlier this year estimates that private giving in the year 2000 would have to be 50 times greater than it has been to replace government support for social services.

The Coats thesis notwithstanding, many of the nonprofit groups that work with children have rallied to Edelman's call. Her Stand for Children has been endorsed by almost 3,000 organizations. Thousands of Girl Scouts are expected to attend, as well as thousands more teachers and members of the YWCA and the YMCA. The latter group, which serves 17 million children and families, and whose leadership is generally conservative, has gone out of its way to avoid the politics associated with the rally. "We hope not to be sidetracked by who is calling this event," says Y public-policy senior associate John Brooks. "Supporting kids shouldn't be a partisan issue."

Nor, in the final analysis, should it be limited to children in poverty or in crisis. "Any broad-based politics about family issues is going to have to engage parents as citizens and as actors, not simply as objects of attention," says Theda Skocpol, a professor of government and sociology at Harvard, who believes Edelman must inspire "the missing middle," the working parents stressed out by juggling work and family. One reason why children's issues are likely to become a prominent campaign issue is that both parties are working hard to attract blue-collar mothers. "Women are more likely to vote the family issues and want to be sure children get the right start," says Stanley Greenberg, pollster for the Democratic National Committee.

Politicians are not invited on Saturday, though. They would only obscure what Edelman, a veteran of many marches, sees as this event's main goal: to inspire the heady awareness—found in the civil rights campaigns and the antiwar movement—that individuals can change the world.—*Reported by Melissa Ludtke with Marian Wright Edelman, Ann Blackman and Ann M. Simmons/Washington, and Tammerlin Drummond/Miami*

Crime and Punishment, Juvenile Division

By PATRICK T. MURPHY

CHICAGO—After a tragedy like the one in Jonesboro, Ark., this week, Americans cry out for vengeance, for justice, for change! We want quick solutions, whether it is to a Mississippi flood, teen-age pregnancy, or children throwing children out of windows or blasting them with shotguns in schoolyards.

There is outrage that 11- and 13-year-olds cannot be tried as adults, cannot be sent to the penitentiary and may be released from a juvenile prison as early as their 18th birthdays. (In most states, a juvenile delinquent can be held until he is 21. That is apparently not the case in Arkansas.) Any child old enough to kill is old enough to be tried as an adult, the argument goes.

But before the mob descends on our legislatures demanding Draconian laws, it may be prudent to consider a few points. First, child murderers are exceedingly rare, in rural America and in inner-city America. And when these crimes occur and the children go off to juvenile institutions, other 11- and 13-year-olds do not repeat their crimes. In

Chicago a few years ago, a 10- and 11-year-old threw a 5-year-old to his death from a housing project window. It did not set off an epidemic of little boys killing each other.

Eleven- and 13-year-olds are not short adults. They are children. Their sense of time is a universe apart. Their judgment is skewed because they have no real point of reference or life experiences other than what their parents have given them or what they have seen on television. In my experience, even the toughest-talking among them are fragile and often terrified.

We can send children off to jail, as we did 100 years ago, or execute them, as we did 200 years ago. But we will be admitting defeat. A hundred years ago, Jane Addams and others created the first juvenile courts. The bold premise was that children should not be treated like adults. Because their characters are not formed, we have a chance to influence them, to divert them from becoming hardened criminals. In most cases, the system still works. We manage to get most children

through a rocky adolescence without resorting to harsh penalties.

But it is time to do some tinkering with the juvenile court premise. Older predator children should be treated more harshly and, in some cases, tried and punished as adults. Very young children convicted of particularly heinous crimes could be compelled to take part in mandatory reporting programs for an indeterminate part of their adulthood once they are released from a juvenile prison.

In addition, the entire juvenile court system, including court records, should be opened to the public through the press. Right now, for the most part, the public is in the dark about what motivates children to commit their crimes. We cannot begin to reform the system when the public does not know what goes on inside it.

There is another reason to get the records of these youngsters. We cannot pass judgment in the Jonesboro case in particular, but it has been my experience, having represented hundreds of children who have gotten in various degrees of trouble, that in virtually every case their parents shared at least some of the blame. Sometimes, parents are so involved in their own lives that they forget their responsibility to direct, discipline and nurture their children. Other times, the circumstances are more dire. I will never forget the parents of one of the boys who threw the 5-year-old out of the window here. The father, when he was out of prison, taught his son gang signs. The mother slept through most of her child's trial.

Senator Richard Durbin of Illinois has introduced Federal legislation that would impose criminal sanctions on parents who even uninten-

tionally make their weapons available to young children. A good idea. But much worse than making a gun available to a child is walking away from parental responsibilities. In extreme cases, like the one in Chicago, we must begin to analyze the responsibility of parents and to consider imposing criminal and civil liability if the evidence shows that their abuse or neglect has led to their children's heinous acts.

Children today are a lot less innocent than they were 30 years ago when I first began representing them. Why are they growing up so fast? The proliferation of guns did not cause it, and sending children to the penitentiary will not prevent

it. Turn on the television any night, and you and your children will be bombarded with violence and sex that would have been unthinkable even a decade ago.

But let's not turn the clock back to the harsh justice of the 19th century. Let's treat juveniles who commit crimes like the children they are. If we as a society are saying that it is already too late for an 11- and 13-year-old, we have a lot of soul-searching to do.

Patrick T. Murphy, the Public Guardian for Cook County, is the author of "Wasted: The Plight of America's Unwanted Children."

Project on Human Development in Chicago Neighborhoods, 211
property crime index, 105
prosecutors, 145, 148
prostitution, in Japan, 102
Purcell, Bill, 215

AE Article Review Form

We encourage you to photocopy and use this page as a tool to assess how the articles in **Annual Editions** expand on the information in your textbook. By reflecting on the articles you will gain enhanced text information. You can also access this useful form on a product's book support Web site at ***http://www.dushkin.com/ online/.***

NAME: DATE:

_____

TITLE AND NUMBER OF ARTICLE:

_____

BRIEFLY STATE THE MAIN IDEA OF THIS ARTICLE:

_____

LIST THREE IMPORTANT FACTS THAT THE AUTHOR USES TO SUPPORT THE MAIN IDEA:

_____

WHAT INFORMATION OR IDEAS DISCUSSED IN THIS ARTICLE ARE ALSO DISCUSSED IN YOUR TEXTBOOK OR OTHER READINGS THAT YOU HAVE DONE? LIST THE TEXTBOOK CHAPTERS AND PAGE NUMBERS:

_____

LIST ANY EXAMPLES OF BIAS OR FAULTY REASONING THAT YOU FOUND IN THE ARTICLE:

_____

LIST ANY NEW TERMS/CONCEPTS THAT WERE DISCUSSED IN THE ARTICLE, AND WRITE A SHORT DEFINITION:

_____

ANNUAL EDITIONS revisions depend on two major opinion sources: one is our Advisory Board, listed in the front of this volume, which works with us in scanning the thousands of articles published in the public press each year; the other is you—the person actually using the book. Please help us and the users of the next edition by completing the prepaid article rating form on this page and returning it to us. Thank you for your help!

ANNUAL EDITIONS: Juvenile Delinquency 00/01

ARTICLE RATING FORM

Here is an opportunity for you to have direct input into the next revision of this volume. We would like you to rate each of the 45 articles listed below, using the following scale:

1. **Excellent: should definitely be retained**
2. **Above average: should probably be retained**
3. **Below average: should probably be deleted**
4. **Poor: should definitely be deleted**

Your ratings will play a vital part in the next revision. So please mail this prepaid form to us just as soon as you complete it. Thanks for your help!

RATING

ARTICLE

1. Juvenile Population Characteristics
2. Juvenile Arrests 1996
3. The Coming Crime Wave Is Washed Up
4. The Crackdown on Kids: The New Mood of Meanness toward Children—To Be Young Is to Be Suspect
5. Part I: The Nature and Severity of Juvenile Crime and Part II: Juvenile Justice System History and Development
6. The Extent of Female Delinquency
7. Juvenile Offenders: Should They Be Tried in Adult Courts?
8. Frustrated Officials Find Standard Answers Don't Suffice
9. Why the Young Kill
10. Of Arms and the Boy
11. Early Violence Leaves Its Mark on the Brain
12. The Real Root Cause of Violent Crime: The Breakdown of the Family
13. When Our Children Commit Violence
14. From Adolescent Angst to Shooting Up Schools: Where Rampages Begin
15. The Culture of Youth
16. Preventing Crime, Saving Children: Sticking to the Basics
17. Great Idea for Ruining Kids
18. Boys Will Be Boys
19. Crimes by Girls Flying Off the Charts
20. Tokyo's Teen Tribes
21. Law Enforcement and Juvenile Crime
22. Fighting Crime, One Kid at a Time
23. Kids and Guns: From Playgrounds to Battlegrounds

RATING

ARTICLE

24. A Sad Fact of Life: Gangs and Their Activities are Spreading into Small-Town America
25. Criminal Behavior of Gang Members and At-Risk Youths
26. Juvenile Felony Defendants in Criminal Courts
27. Juvenile Delinquents in the Federal Criminal Justice System
28. With Juvenile Courts in Chaos, Critics Propose Their Demise
29. Children on Trial
30. A New Order in the Court
31. Rolling the Dice in Juvenile Court
32. The Bastard Stepchild of Parens Patriae: The American Juvenile Incarceration Structure
33. When Should Kids Go to Jail?
34. Quick Fix: Pushing a Medical Cure for Youth Violence
35. Profits at a Juvenile Prison Come with a Chilling Cost
36. Juvenile Boot Camps: Lessons Learned
37. A Wayward Boys' 'Shock Incarceration' Camp
38. What Can We Do?
39. The National Juvenile Justice Action Plan: A Comprehensive Response to a Critical Challenge
40. Saving the Nation's Most Precious Resources: Our Children
41. Breaking the Cycle of Juvenile Violence
42. Understanding the Roots of Crime: The Project on Human Development in Chicago Neighborhoods
43. Juvenile Justice Comes of Age
44. The Children's Crusade
45. Crime and Punishment, Juvenile Division

(Continued on next page)

We Want Your Advice

ANNUAL EDITIONS: JUVENILE DELINQUENCY 00/01

BUSINESS REPLY MAIL
FIRST-CLASS MAIL PERMIT NO. 84 GUILFORD CT

POSTAGE WILL BE PAID BY ADDRESSEE

Dushkin/McGraw-Hill
Sluice Dock
Guilford, CT 06437-9989

ABOUT YOU

Name _____ Date _____

Are you a teacher? ☐ A student? ☐
Your school's name

_____

Department

_____

Address _____ City _____ State ____ Zip ____

School telephone #

_____

YOUR COMMENTS ARE IMPORTANT TO US !

Please fill in the following information:
For which course did you use this book?

_____

Did you use a text with this *ANNUAL EDITION*? ☐ yes ☐ no
What was the title of the text?

_____

What are your general reactions to the *Annual Editions* concept?

_____

Have you read any particular articles recently that you think should be included in the next edition?

_____

Are there any articles you feel should be replaced in the next edition? Why?

_____

Are there any World Wide Web sites you feel should be included in the next edition? Please annotate.

_____

May we contact you for editorial input? ☐ yes ☐ no
May we quote your comments? ☐ yes ☐ no